Understanding Sentence Structure

Linguistics in the World

Linguistics in the World is a textbook series focusing on the study of language in the real world, enriching students' understanding of how language works through a balance of theoretical insights and empirical findings. Presupposing no or only minimal background knowledge, each of these titles is intended to lay the foundation for students' future work, whether in language science, applied linguistics, language teaching, or speech sciences.

What Is Sociolinguistics?, by Gerard van Herk
The Sounds of Language, by Elizabeth Zsiga
Introducing Second Language Acquisition: Perspectives and Practices, by Kirsten M. Hummel
An Introduction to Language, by Kirk Hazen
What Is Sociolinguistics? Second Edition, by Gerard van Herk
Understanding Sentence Structure: An Introduction to English Syntax, by Christina Tortora

Forthcoming
The Nature of Language, by Gary Libben
An Introduction to Bilingualism and Multilingualism: People and Language in Contact, by Martha Pennington

Understanding Sentence Structure

An Introduction to English Syntax

Christina Tortora

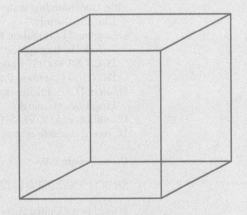

WILEY Blackwell

Registered Office
John Wiley & Sons, Inc., 111 River Street, Hoboken, NJ 07030, USA

Editorial Office
9600 Garsington Road, Oxford, OX4 2DQ, UK

For details of our global editorial offices, customer services, and more information about Wiley products visit us at www.wiley.com.

Wiley also publishes its books in a variety of electronic formats and by print-on-demand. Some content that appears in standard print versions of this book may not be available in other formats.

Library of Congress Cataloging-in-Publication Data

Names: Tortora, Christina, author.
Title: Understanding sentence structure: an introduction to English syntax / Christina Tortora.
Description: 1 | Hoboken, NJ : Wiley-Blackwell, 2018. | Series: Linguistics in the world | Includes bibliographical references and index. | Identifiers: LCCN 2017059534 (print) | LCCN 2018000441 (ebook) | ISBN 9781118659748 (pdf) | ISBN 9781118659595 (epub) | ISBN 9781118659489 (hardback) | ISBN 9781118659946 (paper)
Subjects: LCSH: English language–Syntax. | BISAC: LANGUAGE ARTS & DISCIPLINES / Linguistics / General.
Classification: LCC PE1365 (ebook) | LCC PE1365 .T67 2018 (print) | DDC 425–dc23
LC record available at https://lccn.loc.gov/2017059534

Cover Design: Wiley

Set in 11/13pt Minion by SPi Global, Pondicherry, India

Printed in the United States of America

V10004754_092118

For Honus

From *De sphaera mundi* (by Johannes de Sacrobosco), 1550 edition.

Brief Contents

Contents

Preface

welcome, students and teachers and DIYers!
I wrote this book for my beginning syntax students. But since I believe that my students are no different from any other English-speakers studying syntax for the first time, this book is for all those people out there who have no background in this area but who want to learn. The reader I have in mind has never thought about syntax and doesn't know anything about grammar. Maybe you've never been taught anything substantive about grammar in primary or secondary school, and maybe you just have a few preconceived notions about English grammar which amount to no more than deep-seated, culturally-based dogmas, like "*ain't* isn't a word," or "two negatives make a positive." You might not even be sure what it means to say that "two negatives make a positive," or if you are, perhaps you secretly wonder why the latter is patently not true for languages like Spanish and Italian (and so why would it be true for English?). You may be an undergraduate or MA student studying to be an English Language Arts teacher and feel insecure about your knowledge in this area and want to change that. Perhaps you've heard of "syntactic trees" but have never drawn one and wonder if you can learn to do it. You might have tried to read a more advanced book on the subject (and were intrigued) but thought you'd do better if you could start at a more basic level. Maybe you have no self-confidence with grammatical terms like object, verb, preposition, relative clause, pronoun, tense, intransitive, accusative, and the like, but you want to build your confidence up. Or you might be a budding computer scientist who wants a basic understanding of the structure of natural language. Whatever your personal goals, fears, desires, insecurities, or curiosities are as a beginning syntax student — and whether you're in a class, or you simply want to learn on your own — this book welcomes you with open arms.

what you already bring to this book
Like many linguists, I take sentence structure to be a product of the human mind. This book is therefore designed to bring into your consciousness knowledge which you already have. If you're reading this book, you know English, so you're already an authority on the subject. If you've been speaking English as one of your native languages since childhood, this book helps you use this native knowledge to your advantage, to learn about syntax. If English is not your only native language, your other languages will give you even more power to learn. Those of you who instead came to learn English as an older child (or as an early teen or adult) will also bring to the table tools you already have at your disposal from the different languages you speak.

this book and variation in English world-wide

Since there are so many different "Englishes" spoken in the world, I can't anticipate what variety of English (or, which *English dialect*) you're a personal authority on. So while I can push you to tap into your individual knowledge, the existing regional and sociolinguistic variation dictate that each reader will have a different understanding of what is possible and what is not possible in their own English.

To give just a few very simple examples: some English speakers use the reflexive pronoun *theirselves* while others use only *themselves*, for the "third plural." The form **their**selves is consistent with **my**self, **your**self, and **her**self (because *their*, *my*, *your*, and *her* are all possessive pronouns). The form **them**selves is consistent with **him**self and **her**self (because *him* and *her* are accusative pronouns). Thus, both uses are perfectly logical and rule-governed, and the variation exists precisely because of this. (You'll learn more about reflexives in Chapter 7.)

Similarly, for embedded questions, some speakers might use "subject–auxiliary inversion" (as in *Mary wondered what <u>would</u> <u>Sue</u> fix next*), where the word order is *would* > *Sue*, while other speakers might not, as in *Mary wondered what <u>Sue</u> <u>would</u> fix next* (where the word order is *Sue* > *would*). Again, the variation exists precisely because both uses are perfectly logical and rule-governed. (You'll learn more about embedded questions and why grammatical structure gives rise to these variant possibilities in Chapters 5 and 11.)

Likewise, for the verb *to run*, some people predominantly use the form *run* for the past tense (*Sue run to school this morning*), while others are more likely to use the form *ran* (*Sue ran to school this morning*). Use of the form *run* as the past tense of *to run* is consistent with use of the form *put* as the past tense of *to put* (*Sue already put her tools away*). On the other hand, use of the form *ran* as the past tense of *to run* is consistent with use of the form *dug* as the past tense of *to dig* (*Sue dug a hole to plant the azalea*). There are thus systematic reasons for either choice, and therefore this book has to take such syntactic variation into account. (You'll learn more about verb forms in Chapter 8.)

But since it's completely impossible to cover all the existing variation in one book, the reader should not expect comprehensive coverage in this regard. Nevertheless, the book includes enough analysis of variation across the United States and in the world to provide the reader with the necessary tools to analyze their own English, even if there's a particular regional or social variant that you realize you use which I haven't been able to cover. My main concern is for you to use whatever English(es) you know as a vehicle to learn about the complexities of sentence structure. This is one of the features of this book which makes it a fit for Wiley's series *Linguistics in the World*.

features of this book

Since the primary purpose of this book is to get the beginning student comfortable with syntactic analysis, it doesn't adopt the most current phrase structure theories. If you've never thought about grammar in your life, I don't believe that it helps you to use more advanced tools to introduce basic concepts. This is because there are features of more advanced tools whose motivation you can only genuinely understand once you've first had enough practice with the more fundamental principles of sentence structure. For example: one of the most basic skills to develop when learning syntax for the first time is the ability to properly analyze constituent structure. It's essential to automatize (= to make automatic) your ability to recognize the hierarchical relationships between major sentential constituents and to become comfortable talking about them using the language of syntax. This takes practice with basic tools. Such skills can't be developed overnight, and it isn't always productive to try to build up such basic skills with advanced phrase structure theories whose complexity relies on an already automatized facility with the basics. Perhaps you've seen structures in some introductory textbooks that utilize more current theories of phrase structure involving "bar-levels," like those I introduce in Section 11.4. In my own experience, if a student new to syntax is asked from the start to draw trees using bar-levels — when they haven't yet automatized the ability to pick out lexical categories or major sentential constituents — then their ability to manipulate bar-levels can become just an exercise in guesswork (at worst), or an exercise in manipulating a system without appreciating the motivation for it (at best). A student's well-meaning desire to "get the bar-levels right" (for example, to make their teacher happy) can result in focusing their energies on the wrong thing, such that development of the more foundational skills ends up getting neglected. So while the phrase structure rules I use in this book might seem outdated to syntactic theorists of today, I assure the reader that I use these tools for very specific pedagogical purposes. Once you work through this book, you'll be ready to really appreciate the elegance of more advanced theories of phrase structure, like that presented in Liliane Haegeman's *Introduction to Government and Binding Theory* or Andrew Carnie' *Syntax: A Generative Introduction*, which you will find referenced later.

As you work through this book, you will develop different kinds of skills simultaneously. You'll become an adept analyzer of more and more complex structures. This in turn means that you'll develop a greater and greater appreciation of the fact that sentence structure is a product of the human mind. You'll see that the "rules" we're using are not something out there in the world, created by some authority outside of your own brain: rather, they represent the grammatical rules that are part of your own (unconscious) structural instincts. This book will engage you in a discovery process in which you'll learn how to best create tools that accurately capture what we do as humans, and you'll thus develop a greater appreciation of linguistics as a cognitive science. As you proceed, you'll also come to appreciate syntax as an object of scientific inquiry and develop methodologies which are applicable to other STEM disciplines. In some English classes you've taken, you might have been told "there is no right or wrong answer." But when you approach human language as part of the natural world (like you would mammalian vision, for example), sometimes there simply is a right answer and a wrong answer, and these can be ascertained via scientific methods. You will learn how to form *hypotheses* that make *predictions*, and to develop the skill of testing to see whether the predictions of a particular hypothesis are borne out, which in turn tells you what the right and wrong answers are. It can be a thoroughly satisfying enterprise to develop the power to determine what the correct analysis is for a given structure, based on the simple idea that certain hypotheses make predictions which we can see are borne out with empirical evidence, while other hypotheses must be rejected, because they make incorrect predictions.

Note that, because of the pedagogical purpose of this book, I mix and match historical stages of phrase structure theory. The student should thus take this book as an amalgam of what I believe to be some of the "greatest hits" of syntax, suitable for a beginner's consumption. Relatedly, the reader should understand that most of the ideas presented in this book do not originate with me. While the selection, packaging, and presentation of the material are particular to this work, most of the concepts themselves come from decades of research in syntactic theory (in some cases), or even thousands of years of research in grammar (in other cases). The concepts I discuss (such as lexical categories like Noun and Verb) are so entrenched in our understanding of grammar and syntax that authors who write about these concepts present them as general knowledge, and rightly so. But this should not detract from the fact that all ideas have their origins somewhere, and the more recent the concept or analysis, the easier it can be to trace it back to a specific scientist or group of scientists. Where possible, I make reference to the relevant literature at the end of some of the chapters, to give a flavor of this, and also with an eye towards directing you to further reading.

How to use this book

This book is designed like a DIY manual. This means it can be used in many different ways: teachers can use it to learn how to teach others; teachers can use it in the classroom with students; or students can use it to teach themselves. In order for learning to be successful, though, the reader needs to take the design seriously.

Exercises: You'll notice that there are no exercises at the end of each chapter. This is because I don't believe you should be waiting until the end of the chapter to practice your skills. Rather, since each skill follows from the previously developed one, the reader will be most successful only if they do each exercise right at the point where I put it. If you see an exercise and think you don't need to do it in order to move on to the next paragraph, you do so at your own risk, and I can't guarantee you'll properly develop the skills and attain the knowledge that this book is designed to give you. Of course, stopping to do the exercises along the way means that it'll take longer to read each chapter. But this will be an investment worth making. So try to resist the temptation to take short-cuts!

Side notes and **term boxes:** In addition to the exercises, information is hierarchized through the use of two different kinds of text box: the *Side Note* and the *Term Box*. The side note is designed to help you make your way through a streamlined text, with elaborations, additions, opportunities, and notes visually presented as asides. You don't want to skip the side notes, but at the same time, you can wait until you're done with a particular section before going back to read them. The term box is a way to keep you on track with the new terms you're learning. In case you forget what a term means, or need elaboration that goes beyond what I said about a term bolded in the text, you can avail yourself of the term box. At the end of each chapter, I provide a list of terms/concepts that appeared in the text, the term boxes, the side notes, and the exercises to help keep you on track.

By the end of the book, if you did everything you were guided to do, you'll be able to converse intelligently with a syntactician about the basics of how humans unconsciously structure sentences. When finished with this book — or a course based on this book — you'll be prepared to take a more advanced course on syntactic theory. I've been using drafts of the chapters from this book in my classes for many years, to test run them on my own students, in order to see what works and what doesn't. If you're a teacher who's thinking of using this book in a class, my own experience suggests that you can use the book to run your class in the following way: For a single week (whether your class meets once a week for 3 or 4 hours, or twice a week for 1.5 to 2 hours), direct your students to read a chapter and do all the exercises, in preparation for the class meeting in which that particular chapter is to be discussed for the first time. Then, in class, invite your students to raise which questions in each exercise they'd like to go over. You may find that you can cover approximately a chapter a week in this way without any lecture preparation involved. Of course, this depends on the chapter in question, the teacher, the students, the time you have, and the purpose of the class. For example, it's possible to get though Chapters 1 and 2 in a single week, if you put aside Section 2.4. It's also possible to get through Chapter 5 in a week, if you put aside Section 5.4. Chapter 6 tends to take longer (often, it takes me two weeks to cover it), because relative clauses take a while for students to absorb, given their semantic complexity. Chapters 3, 4, and 7, on the other hand, each tend to fit comfortably within one week.

It is my belief, though, that the differences in pace that teachers in different contexts experience won't diminish the learning process for the students. If you're a student training to be a teacher in Adolescence Education and you use this book to learn grammar/syntax, you may very well find yourself able to bring the lessons contained herein to your own junior high or high school classes that you teach. Many of my own students have gone on to successful careers in teaching English Language Arts and have reported that eighth graders are capable of grasping the material. It seems that they get a kick out of tree-drawing, often treating it as a fun game.

However you choose to use this book, I wish you the very best in your journey of discovery, and I hope you come to embrace syntax as a thing of beauty in the natural world.

Acknowledgments

This book would not exist without my students at the College of Staten Island (CSI). Far more than anyone or anything else in my experience, it's been my CSI undergrads and MA students who've taught me that the only thing to worry about with "teaching" is the learning. And they taught me how beginners genuinely learn to do syntax, and why they should even want to do it, when it's not the goal of everyone in the classroom to become a syntactician or a linguist.

As all teachers know, it's not easy to reach a random collection of 30 different minds simultaneously. This is especially true with an unknown subject matter like syntax, which involves a "way of thinking" that the students are not accustomed to. Furthermore, each person has a different reason for being in the classroom, and in my case, my beginning syntax class at CSI has since 2003 often been scheduled very late at night, after my students put in a full day of work or childcare or classes, without having had a chance to get a bite to eat and with nothing but broken-down junk-food vending machines as the source of their nourishment during class break. Described in this way, it might seem like very few people would care about figuring out how to prove whether a string of words forms a constituent or not, or to tell whether A immediately dominates B. Yet, no matter how mixed the class is in terms of level of preparation, no matter the uniqueness of each person's goals, no matter what just happened on that particular day, or how tired or hungry they might be at that particular moment, or what my own frame of mind is, my students have consistently proven — with a force of energy that I rarely see in other contexts — that they're always up for growth and change. I'm grateful to work with people who want something so badly, that they're not going to be shy about teaching me the ways that I could help make things happen, including backing off to let them think on their own or help each other out without me intervening, and including just writing something down, just the way I said it when I was right there in front of them, so that they could read and contemplate it outside of the classroom, in their own time.

This became the idea behind this book: my students were interested in reading my notes if I wrote them in the way that I talked in the classroom, and structured them in the way I structured the class. Over the years students pushed me to turn these notes into a book. As I wrote this book, I always imagined myself together with my students in front of me, asking me to repeat something or to let them work on a problem before I moved on to the next point, and encouraging me to go off on relevant side discussions (but making sure that I made clear when the side comment was over, and when the main point started up again). I shared the chapters with my students in each class, in a place where the cultural norm thankfully is to be frank about what you think. I am indebted to every student for the candid feedback they gave me on this work, which began in earnest in 2013. Thank you to Aminah Abdel, Steven Arriaga, Olivia Ayala, Anisa Bekteshi, Rena Berkovits, Andrea Beyer, Alexandria Boachie Ansah, Rose Bonamo, Anthony Bongiorno, Saffire Borras, Tyler Cabell, Annmarie Cantasano, Bianca Cardaci, Tameeka Castillo, Armando Cataldi, Dana Cavaliere, Allison Cespedes, Nicolle Cillis, Martin Clifford, Lorenza Colonna, Samantha Conti, Krystal Cordero, Julia Correale, Ava Cozzo, Phil Criscuolo, Lizette Cruz, Jayde Cuesta, Alyssa Culotta, Jezel Cuomo, Iolanda Dagostino, Brittany Debrosse, Ashley Delacruz, Valeriana Dema, José Diaz, Stephanie Dimarco, Francesca Dimeglio, Tom Diriwachter, Shelley Disla, Nawal Doleh, Evelyn Dominguez, Shannon Doyle, Shelley Faygenbaum, Christina Friscia, Remonda Ghatas, Michelle Granville-Garvey, Elinora Gruber, Emily Hernandez, Yarlene Hernandez, Yashanti Holman, Nicole Ianni, Kelly Hughes, Kaitlyn Kane, Raven Kennedy, Medine Kovacevic, Jacquelyn Kratz, Melynda Kuppler, Tamara Laird, Matt Leavy, Marilyn Lombay, Samara Lugo, David Lyev, Angelica Mannino, Nino Marino, Aprile Martin, Danielle Masino, Samantha Matos, Radia Ouali Mehadji, Noelle Mejias, Chelsea Morales, Liana Morse, Tom Mottola, Connie Neary, Cassandra Nelson, Deanna Nobriga, Lauren O'Brien, Kelly Ortega, Lorenzo Pacheco, Samantha Paholek, Kristie Palladino, Lauren Pansini, Stephanie Parathyras, Corinne Paris, Jessica Patrizi, Kaitlyn Pellicano, Zachery Pierre, Gyancarlos Pinto, Jenny Pisani, Kenneth Price, Vanessa Reyes, Samantha Sblendido, Ashley Schoberl, Saundra Scott, Gaby Shlyakh, Shira Shvartsman, Moné Skratt Henry, Vicky So, Michelle Spano, Jessica Spensieri, Lea Steinwurzel, Jamie Sterner, Estie Szczupakiewicz, Adelina Taganovic, Rebecca Tapia, Jessica Taranto, Chauna Thomas, Joe Tilghman, Nicole Tozzi, Christine Vecchio, Celeste Velez, Alexsandra Villafane, Christian Winston, Ewa Wojciechowska, and Nadia Zaki.

I also thank all those CSI students I taught syntax to from 2003 to 2013, who although they didn't read chapters of this book, were responsible for the seeds of the idea: Greg Acanfora, Holly Acerra, Saima Akram, Javier Alvarez, Kimberly Amatrudo, Tiffany Amatrudo, Anna Amodio, Phil Anastasia, Linda Appu, Peter Barnes, Cathleen Boylan, Denise Burton, Cynthia Calvanico, Cathy Cannizzaro, Christine Cannizzaro, Michelle Choi, Chu-han Chuang, Christina Ciccarelli, Vincent Coca, Kimberly Corbisiero, Shirlene Cubas, Ghada Daoud, Agatha Demeo, Ann Desapio, Yevgeniy Deyko, Antoinette Dibenedetto, Chrissa Diprossimo, Jennifer Donadio, Patrick Fair, Giselle Fani, April Fedele, Michelle Fiorenza, Ashley Fotinatos, Pearl Friedman, Yasmin Garcia, Rosy George, Irene Giacalone, Jaclyn Grann, Kristen Gugliara, Katherine Han, Leanora Harper, Nicole Jonas, Michael Jones, Kevin Justesen, Mary Kay, Etab Khajo, Lafleur King, Karolina Konarzewska, Lori Krycun, Fikriye Kurtoglu, Georgia Laios, Lucie Lauria, Felicia Layne, Kathryn Lobasso, Ramona Lofton, Lori Lorenzo, Stephanie Lorenzo, Sara Losack, Aiko Maeukemori, John Magalong, Lauren Maligno, Cortney Mancuso, Jaime Manus, Glenda Marquez, Dominika Marscovetra, Aubrey Mcgoff, Patrick Misciagna, Fotini Mitilis, Michelle Morandi, Danielle Narwick, Danielle Nygaard, Patroba Omer, Robert Pollack, Garth Priebe, Lisa Quagliariello, Billy Quilty, Carla Radigan, Vinny Raimondo, Jessica Rella,

Thomas Riley, Erin Rios, Christine Russo, Matt Safford, Bill Safte, Erica Salzillo, Dilini Samarasinghe, Christine Sanders, Lauren Stabile, Barbara Stanul, Jaclyn Scimone-Avena, Jodi Szmerkowicz, Enrico Turchi, Rosalia Turriciano, Rocio Uchofen, Jillian Vitale, Erica Vitucci, Jillian Wagner, Paul Wiley, Johnny Ye, Pamela Zambrano, and Konstantina Zontanos.

I'd also like to thank friends and colleagues for reading, using, commenting on, and encouraging this work, especially John Bailyn (for trying out the book with his class at Stony Brook before it was published, and for his very helpful and crucial comments); Richard Larson (for sharing in the belief that teaching Linguistics in the most effective way and to the widest possible audience is the most important part of our profession, and for our many conversations about this); Lori Repetti (for her friendship and for sharing thoughts on teaching beginning students); and Bill Safte (my former student and current colleague, who taught this course brilliantly when I was on leave in Spring 2018, and who gave me very important feedback as he used the manuscript with his students). I especially want to thank Jason Bishop, for using bits of this book for his Intro to Ling class, but more importantly for his unparalleled empathy and camaraderie, and for being the best colleague anyone could ever hope to have. I also thank my former PhD students Frances Blanchette and Teresa O'Neill, for their excitement about the project, and I thank my parents George Tortora and Marina Duque-Valderrama, for always being okay when I have to put work before all else.

Finally, I thank my husband, advocate, cheerleader, and most important person in my life, John Shean. His ability to listen to me and take me seriously never, ever wanes, no matter how many hours and years, and no matter how miniscule anyone else in the world might think my particular concerns are. I thank him for this and for never ceasing to gracefully deal with all of the material problems associated with my sometimes long bouts of inattention to him or to our home or to our meals together, on account of my work. I thank him for making me survive the biggest losses in my life, and for making me carry on. As a small gift, I dedicate this book to him, in the summer of our 25th wedding anniversary.

1 Let's get Parsing!

expected outcomes for this chapter

- You'll acquire a basic sense of what linguists mean by "sentence structure."
- Regardless of your belief that you know very little about sentence structure, you'll see that you actually know quite a bit — and this will help you gain some confidence, for the chapters to come.
- You'll become familiar with the following terms (see words in bold and term boxes): *cognition, structure, parsing, ambiguity, constituent, modification, syntax, grammar, phrase structure rules, phrase structure trees, subject, noun phrase, verb phrase, hierarchical organization.*

1.1 some introductory words

The purpose of this chapter is to get us started immediately. I want you to see right away what sentence structure is, and how you already have the power to analyze — or **parse** — sentences. I want you to see that this power derives from your natural human disposition to automatically analyze strings of words as structured. Consider the immediately preceding sentence, for example. In fact, please read that whole sentence over again, starting with the words "*I want you to see that this power …*" Let's write the sentence down; you can do this on a separate sheet of paper, so that you have it in front of you, all by itself. We're going to analyze this sentence, and it'll be easier to do that if we can look at it in isolation. Let's give the sentence an example number, like "Example

Understanding Sentence Structure: An Introduction to English Syntax, First Edition.
Christina Tortora.
© 2018 John Wiley & Sons, Inc. Published 2018 by John Wiley & Sons, Inc.

(1)." It'll be useful to treat it like a specimen — like something we can dissect and examine. We'll be doing a lot of this kind of thing in this book: analyzing individual sentences in isolation as a way to learn about sentence structure.

Term Box 1

When we **parse** a string of words, we are mentally assigning structure to the string. We are thus analyzing the string as if it were a sentence in a language, with syntax. As humans, we naturally parse certain strings of symbols as linguistic structures without realizing we're doing this — that is, we do it unconsciously. As syntacticians, we parse such strings consciously, with an eye towards understanding how humans structure such strings. <u>Related words</u>: *parsing; parser*

Side Note 1: (Be proactive!)

You can learn a lot from this book, if you do what is suggested each step of the way. The more you do the mini-exercises as you read, the more surely you'll integrate everything into your knowledge and skill base.

Have you written the sentence down and considered it? If you did, I bet you understood *as structured* as having something to do with *strings of words*. I'll illustrate this in Example (1a), where I've indicated your mental grouping of these particular words <u>with underlining</u>):

What you did, mentally:

(1a)   I want you to see that this power you have derives from your natural human disposition to automatically analyze <u>strings of words as structured</u>.

So, I'm pretty sure you understood me to be saying that "strings of words" are "structured." On the other side of the same coin, I bet you didn't understand the words *as structured* to be associated with, say, the words *your natural human disposition*, as follows:

What you did NOT do, mentally:

(1b)   I want you to see that this power you have derives from <u>your natural human disposition</u> to automatically analyze strings of words <u>as structured</u>.

If I'm right, then it's pretty amazing that you mentally put together the underlined words in (1a) automatically, without consciously thinking about it; it's equally amazing that you didn't put together in your mind the underlined words in (1b); so it's not as though you thought that "structured" should have anything to do with "your natural predisposition." Furthermore, it's certain that you unconsciously put the words together in the way I think you did without anyone ever explicitly teaching you how to do it. In fact, it came so naturally to you that you might be thinking it's strange for me to point out that (1b) was NOT something you did.

Side Note 2: (Just in case you're doubtful)

You might be thinking here, "Well of course I put *as structured* together with *strings of words*, as in (1a); they're right next to each other! The words *your natural human disposition* are too far away from the words *as structured* for me to have thought that these two sets of words could belong together, as in (1b)!"

In case you are thinking this: Yes, there are in fact a lot of other words in between *your natural human disposition* and *as structured*, making these two sets of words distant from one another. However, as we'll see below, **distance** (i.e. how far away words are from each other) doesn't always dictate how you mentally structure words into sentences. Sometimes, you automatically mentally put together groups of words that look far away from one another. The examples in (2b)/(2c) below will illustrate this.

1.1.1 before we talk about sentence structure: the Necker Cube

As human beings, there are lots of things that we do mentally which come naturally to all of us, which are below the level of consciousness; that is, we don't consciously think about them. And although you may not realize this, structuring sentences is one of them. But before we look more carefully at what "structuring sentences" means and how it works, let's look at an example of another thing you do automatically — or, instinctively — without realizing you do it, without you even trying, and without anyone having taught you how to do it. I like this particular example because it helps understand what is meant by your cognitive instincts (or, your automatic mental processes).

Perhaps you've actually already seen an example of a Necker Cube, and maybe you've even doodled a million of them. In case you haven't, though, let's look at a Necker Cube in Exercise [1]:

EXERCISE [1]

Consider the Necker Cube here. What do you see?

If you spend some time looking at this picture, you'll notice something amazing: in particular, you'll realize that this two-dimensional line-drawing actually gives rise to your perception of two possible cubes — or, put differently — two possible **structures**. In one structure, you're interpreting the lower left corner of the drawing (from your perspective) as the lower left front of the cube, so that the front of the cube is pointing downwards towards the left. In the other structure, you're interpreting this same lower left corner as the lower left rear of the cube, so that the front of the cube is pointing upwards towards the right.

Term Box 2

When something can be mentally assigned more than one possible structure, like this Necker Cube, we say that it's **structurally ambiguous**. Related words: *structural ambiguity, structurally unambiguous*

Side Note 3: (Don't try this at home)

There are two other things you could try to see when staring at a Necker Cube, but I warn you, these exercises become irritating very quickly:

First, you could try to see both cubes at the same time, but I'm sure you'll find this to be impossible. No matter how you try, you either see one cube or the other, but not both simultaneously.

Second, you could try to see the picture in Exercise [1] as a two-dimensional line-drawing. As you'll see, though, it's actually extremely difficult to see this object as anything other than a pair of three-dimensional cubes.

These exercises can be frustrating, because they make you try (and fail) to go against your cognitive instincts.

It's important to note that there aren't really two cubes here on the page. The only thing that's on the page is a two-dimensional line-drawing. So there's nothing outside of your mind which forces you to see the two cubes. Your perception that there are two possible cubes in the drawing simply has to do with how your brain is "hardwired" to structure the image as two distinct cubes. And just as importantly, these are the ONLY two structures that you can see; your mind doesn't create any other logical possibilities. So if I tried to teach you through explicit instruction to see the drawing in Exercise [1] in other ways (as in Side Note 3), I would do so in vain.

The structures you see in the Necker Cube are thus a product of your mental processes. Our little study of the object in Exercise [1], then, is not about the object itself; rather, it's about your mind.

1.1.2 how is sentence structure like the Necker Cube?

When we study sentence structure, we're studying the same kind of thing. Like the Necker Cube, sentence structure is not something that's actually out there in the world. Rather, sentences are structured by your mind. Let me make this analogy more concrete by asking you to consider the string of words in Example (2) (just like I asked you to consider the Necker Cube in Exercise [1]):

(2) Sue poked the dog with the stick.

I'm absolutely certain that you understand this string of words. I'm also reasonably certain that, if you think about the string in (2) for long enough, you'll "see" two possible meanings (just as you saw two possible structures with the Necker Cube). Let me give you a moment to think about (2), and what you think it means.

Side Note 4: (a hint)

If you think you already see two meanings, you don't have to consider my hint here.

However, if you're having a little trouble getting at the two possible meanings, I'll help you along a little bit: *who do you think has the stick in sentence (2)?*

Ok, so now that you've thought about (2), I'm going to assume that you see the two different meanings that I do, which are as follows: In one meaning, *Sue poked the dog, which happened to have the stick*. In this meaning, I don't know what Sue used to poke the dog with (her finger maybe?), but it doesn't matter; the important thing is, I'm certain that the dog has the stick. In the second meaning, *Sue used the stick to poke the dog*.

You should take a moment to make sure you agree with my characterization of the possible meanings of the sentence in (2).

There are a few questions which arise now, but let's shoot to the most important one: how are you getting these two different meanings? That is, why do you interpret the sentence in these two different ways? It has to do with how you're grouping the string of words *with the stick* with the rest of the words in (2) (*Sue poked the dog*). It turns out that there are two strategies at your disposal, and you use these strategies instinctively, probably without you realizing it. In one strategy, you structure the words *with a stick* together with the words *the dog*. Let's use [square brackets] to represent this grouping, in (2a):

(2a) Sue poked [**the dog with the stick**].

When you mentally group *with a stick* and *the dog*, as in (2a), you're essentially thinking that the words [the dog with the stick] form a kind of meaningful unit, to be analyzed all together. That is, [the dog with the stick] refers to a particular dog, as opposed to some other dog (maybe one without a stick or one with a bone).

Term Box 3

In this case, we would say that the string *with the stick* modifies *the dog*. That is, *with the stick* is a modifier. Related words: *modification*.

Term Box 4

A string of words that you put together to form a meaningful unit is what we call a constituent. So, [the dog with the stick] in (2a) is a constituent. There are other constituents in this sentence (in fact, the whole sentence itself is also a constituent, making [the dog with the stick] a smaller constituent within a bigger constituent). We'll talk more about constituents throughout the rest of the book. Related words: *subconstituent*.

So this is one strategy you use for structuring the words in the sentence in (2). There is, however, another strategy at your disposal. In this second strategy, you do NOT group the string of words *with the stick* with the words *the dog*. This second structural strategy is represented in (2b), where [the dog] is grouped separately from the three words *with the stick*:

(2b)   Sue poked [**the dog**] with the stick.

When you mentally group *the dog* without the words *with a stick*, you're thinking that the words [the dog] form a kind of meaningful unit all by itself, at the exclusion of *with the stick*. In this case, then, *the dog with the stick* doesn't form a constituent (see Term Box 4). In terms of meaning, *the dog* doesn't have the stick, and in fact, we don't know what he has, if anything. So *with the stick* doesn't modify the constituent [*the dog*] (see Term Box 3).

In this particular strategy, you are instead mentally grouping the words *with the stick* with something else. If you think about it, you're actually grouping these words with the word *poked*; it's as if the constituent [the dog] were invisible, or somehow out of the way, as schematized in (2c). Here, the string *with the stick* modifies *poked* directly, so that we interpret "the poking" as having been done with the stick:

(2c)   Sue [**poked with the stick**].

Of course, [the dog] isn't literally invisible, and it isn't literally floating there in a cloud, on top of the sentence. In the single sentence in (2), these two words come right after the word *poked*, and right before the word *with*, both when these words are on the page, and when these words are coming out of your mouth. The schematization in (2c) is just meant to give you a rough picture of how you interpret the words *with the stick* as somehow being grouped with the word *poked*, despite the fact that they're separated from each other by other words (see Side Note 2)!

So to sum up, when you hear or read the string of words in (2), you interpret these words in one of two ways. This a direct result of the fact that you can mentally assign the string in (2) one of two different possible structures, just as you assigned two possible structures to the Necker Cube in Exercise [1]. The sentence is thus structurally ambiguous (see Term Box 2). I'll repeat the two structures that you assign to (2) here:

(3)   Sue poked the dog with the stick.

Structure 1: Sue poked [**the dog with the stick**].

Meaning: *Sue poked the dog which had the stick.*

Structure 2: Sue poked [**the dog**] with the stick.

Meaning: *Sue used the stick to poke the dog.*

In Chapter 3, I'll prove that this description of your instincts is correct, and that you indeed automatically assign two different structures to the string of words in (2).

Side Note 5:

Like sentences, a single word can have more than one meaning. Consider, for example, the word *bat*. This word can mean either "the stick used for baseball," or "the flying mammal." We can therefore say that the word *bat* is also ambiguous. Crucially, however, it isn't *structurally* ambiguous, like the sentence in (2)/(3): the two meanings of *bat* don't derive from two different structures.

EXERCISE [2]

The following sentences are like (2) in that they are structurally ambiguous. Just as I did in (3), provide the two different structures for each sentence, and for each distinct structure you provide, state which meaning it corresponds to. Note that the meaning you give must be an unambiguous paraphrase of the structure you provided (much as the meanings I gave in (3) were).

{1} Mary saw the man with the telescope.
{2} Steve shot the man with the gun.
{3} Sue attacked the piñata with the ax.
{4} Bill opened the door with the key.
{5} Lisa fixed the refrigerator in the kitchen.
{6} Bob ate the ice cream from the freezer.
{7} Jane painted the tile on the roof.

1.1.3 in sum: what does *sentence structure* mean?

This brings us to the main point, which is to clarify what linguists mean by sentence structure. If we just look at the words in example (1a), or in example (2), or if we look at any of the strings of words on these pages, we see that in the world, these are just strings of ink marks. But when you — as an English-speaking human — read these ink marks (or likewise, when you hear them spoken as words), you assign structure to them. Furthermore, that unconscious mechanism you have which adds structure to strings of words is one and the same mechanism which allows you to take words you know and create your own sentences — structures which can be written, or spoken, or just thought. Thus, like the structures in the Necker Cube in Exercise [1], sentence structure is a product of the human mind.

Let's think of this "mental mechanism" as a set of **rules**. And just as no one ever explicitly taught you how to see the two cubes in Exercise [1], no one ever explicitly taught you these sentence-structuring rules; you just naturally developed them as a child, in the process of language acquisition (as it's called in linguistics). These rules are what is often meant by **syntax**, or **grammar**. For our purposes, then, let's think of "syntax" as those rules that the human mind uses to create sentences out of words. As a human, you can use these rules both to create sentences on your own and also to assign structure to strings of words that you read, or that you hear someone else say. This book is thus about how we, as human beings, structure sentences.

So, as we analyze sentences in this book, we're really studying how you, as a human being, instinctively structure sentences. Of course, this book is in English, we'll be discussing how English speakers structure sentences using English words, and I'll be tapping into your knowledge as an English speaker to bring these tacit rules to your consciousness. But keep in mind that this structure is a product of the human mind, so what we're doing in this book could be done with any language.

Side Note 6:

In the remainder of the book, I may say things like "... the structure of this sentence is ..." or "... in that sentence, the noun is modified by an adjective ..." and so forth. In other words, I might talk about words and sentences as if they have a life of their own, independent of our minds. But please don't be fooled by this; we'll always be working with the underlying assumption that the structure we're talking about is mentally created. Sometimes it's just easier to talk about words and sentences as if they were objects out there in the world (even though we know they're not). In a similar way, it's easier to talk as if the drawings in Example (4) are cubes, even though we know they're not cubes; in the world, they're just line-drawings. It's just that sometimes for the purposes of discussion it's more efficient to pretend that the object under investigation is outside of the human mind.

1.1.4 an important clarification: not all objects give rise to ambiguity

Before we continue, I need to clarify something right now. Both the Necker Cube in Exercise [1] and the subsequent linguistic analogy drawn with Example (2)/(3) were meant to illustrate the fact that you, as a human being, mentally assign structure to objects in the world. In both cases, I used objects which happened to be structurally ambiguous to make my point. (More accurately: I used objects which have properties that allow us humans to assign more than one structure to them.) I did this because it's simply easier for students who are new to this kind of discussion to see how the mind assigns structure to an object if that object can give rise to two possible structures. However, it's very important to note that not every object (spatial or linguistic) is structurally ambiguous. For example, compare the structurally ambiguous line-drawing in (4a) (our Necker Cube) with the **unambiguous** line-drawing in (4b):

(4a) The Necker Cube: (4b)   An unambiguous cube:

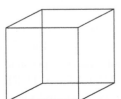 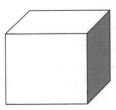

As we already saw, if you stare at (4a), you'll see two structures. In contrast, no matter how long you stare at the cube in (4b), you'll only ever see one structure, namely, a cube which points downward towards the left. The structure in (4b) is thus unambiguous. That doesn't mean, however, that you're not mentally assigning a structure to the line-drawing in (4b). Just as with the Necker Cube, the picture in (4b) is nothing more than a two-dimensional line-drawing on the page (with some shading on the rightmost piece of the drawing). Nevertheless, your mind does assign a structure to it — namely, that of a single, three-dimensional cube.

The point of this example is to clarify that not all objects give rise to our mental construction of multiple structures. That is, not all objects are structurally ambiguous; some objects cause us to assign only a single structure to them. And if we once again draw an analogy with sentences, we can see that in contrast with (3), not all sentences are structurally ambiguous. Some sentences, like the one in (5), only have one possible structure — and therefore, only one possible meaning. I've repeated our example (3) here, so that you can easily compare (5) with it:

(3) Sue poked the dog with the stick.

Structure 1: Sue poked [**the dog with the stick**].

Meaning: *Sue poked the dog which had the stick.*

Structure 2: Sue poked [**the dog**] with the stick.

Meaning: *Sue used the stick to poke the dog.*

(5) Sue knows the dog with the stick.

Structure 1: Sue knows [**the dog with the stick**].

Meaning: *Sue knows the dog which had the stick.*

In contrast with the string of words in (3), the string of words in (5) doesn't have more than one meaning. This is because your mind will only assign one structure to this string of words.

Side Note 7:

A structure like *Structure 2* in (3) is simply not possible with the string of words in (5):
    *Sue knows [the dog] with the stick.
    Meaning: *Sue uses the stick to know the dog.*
    (We'll use the asterisk * to mark structures which are not possible)
Your mental mechanism for structuring sentences automatically doesn't allow you to use *with the stick* to modify *know*.

So, not all sentences are structurally ambiguous. For some strings of words, you can mentally assign only one structure (like (5), which is like the unambiguous cube in (4b)); in contrast, others can be assigned more than one possible structure. The common denominator is that SENTENCES HAVE STRUCTURE. And as I stated in Side Note 6, this statement must be taken as shorthand for "the human mind unconsciously uses rules to assign structure to words, to create sentences."

1.2 let's start understanding what those unconscious rules that create structure are

Now that we've established the fact that sentence structure comes from your mind, let's spend the remainder of this book using the best methods we know of to discover how you structure sentences. We've already done a bit of this in the first half of this chapter, but it'll be useful to get more "graphic" — literally! So let's talk about **phrase structure rules**. Phrase structure rules are the rules you unconsciously use to form (or, "structure") **phrases** out of words, and to structure sentences out of phrases. Remember that phrases are strings of words which form a coherent meaningful unit; in other words, a phrase is a kind of constituent (Term Box 4). As we'll see later, the structures created from phrase structure rules can be represented in a kind of graph form, which we call **phrase structure trees** (or, **syntactic trees**). Drawing trees of sentences is a handy way to graphically see the ways in which humans assign structure to strings of words.

I'd like us to start by learning about the most basic phrase structure rule, namely, the one which forms a whole sentence. To do this, let's first consider the examples in (6) through (12). Please read each and every one of these examples carefully.

(6) The professor ate the sandwich.

(7) The professor of linguistics ate the sandwich.

(8) The professor of linguistics with brown hair ate the sandwich.

(9) The professor of linguistics with brown hair that Sue had an appointment with yesterday ate the sandwich.

(10) My professor with the big window in her office ate the sandwich.

(11) Maria ate the sandwich.

(12) She ate the sandwich.

Let's assume that in the sentence in (12), *she* refers to the same consistent sandwich-eater who's mentioned in sentences (6) through (11). Now let's do Exercise [3].

EXERCISE [3]

For each sentence in (6) through (11), write down the entire string of words that represents the person which *she* in (12) refers to.
   Example:
In sentence (6), she *refers to* the professor.
In sentence (10), she *refers to* my professor with the big window in her office.

Please do this exercise before you read on.

If you did this exercise, then you likely came up with the following answers:

In sentence X, <u>she</u> *refers to…*

(7')   The professor of linguistics

(8')   The professor of linguistics with brown hair

(9')   The professor of linguistics with brown hair that Sue had an appointment with yesterday

(11')   Maria.

In contrast, here are some strings of words which I'm reasonably sure you did not come up with, as representing the person which *she* refers to:

(6")   professor ate

(7")   professor of

(8")   brown hair

(9")   Sue

(9''')   Sue had an appointment with

etc.

So let's summarize the main accomplishment of Exercise [3]: in each sentence in (6) through (11), you used your instincts to identify a coherent string of words — a phrase — which the word *she* in (12) "stands in for." And you identified this phrase at the exclusion of the words *ate the sandwich*. This is important, as you've noticed a crucial aspect of sentence structure: that a sentence has a "first part" which excludes a "second part." As we'll see in the chapters that follow, identifying these two major parts is a handy first step that we can always rely on as a kind of methodology to help us get at the ever more finely detailed aspects of sentence structure.

Side Note 8: (Another major accomplishment)

Exercise [3] illustrated something else important, namely, that a phrase can consist of one word (like *Maria* in (11)), or fourteen words (like *The professor of linguistics with brown hair that Sue had an appointment with yesterday* in (9)), or anything in between.

Side Note 9: Understanding what humans do vs. learning the tools of analysis

This book has a dual purpose. First, it's meant to show how the human mind structures sentences. At the same time, though, you'll be learning how to use particular tools of analysis, which will help you graphically represent this aspect of human cognition. Sometimes these might seem like two independent things; so, at times it might seem like I'm just instructing you on a method of analysis — a "how-to" on tree-drawing. Whenever we're focused on the "how-to," however, we should not forget that the ultimate point is to capture what it is that humans do unconsciously. You can therefore think of the "how-to" as a way of bringing this unconscious knowledge into your consciousness.

Before I say more about the "second part" of the sentences in (6) through (12) (*ate the sandwich*), let's take stock of the facts we just noted. Basically, our observations lead us to conclude that the most basic phrase structure rule — the one which forms the sentence — states that:

(13) "A sentence is formed out of two major parts."

Now let's give names to our "two major parts" of the sentence. In traditional grammar books, the "first part" we identified in Exercise [3] has been referred to as the **subject** of the sentence. In the field of linguistics, however, where we study sentence structure from a slightly different perspective, this "first part" is often referred to as the **subject noun phrase**. I'll say more about the term **noun phrase** (or **NP**) in a moment, but let's just quickly say something about the "second part" too. As we saw in (6) through (12), the "second part" of the sentence — *ate her sandwich* — is not part of the subject noun phrase. It's a separate phrase, which in traditional grammar has been referred to as the **predicate** of the sentence. In linguistics, however, it's often referred to as the **verb phrase** (or, **VP**). Thus, the phrase structure rule which forms the sentence can be restated as follows:

(14) "A sentence is formed out of a subject noun phrase and a verb phrase."

Term Box 5

We'll talk more about the terms **noun phrase** and **verb phrase** (and **noun** and **verb**) in Chapters 2 and 3. Please be assured that I don't expect you, at this moment, to necessarily know what nouns and verbs are.

To make sure you understand where the major divide is between the subject NP (= the first part of the sentence) and the VP (= the second part of the sentence), please do Exercise [4].

EXERCISE [4]

For each sentence in this exercise, write down on a separate piece of paper what the subject NP is and what the VP is.

Example: *In sentence {4},* her big sister *is the subject NP, and* sang the song at three o'clock *is the VP.*

{1} Maria sang.
{2} The woman sang.
{3} Her sister sang a song.
{4} Her big sister sang the song at three o'clock.
{5} The older sister who lives in New York City sang the song at three o'clock in the cafeteria.

Now that you've done Exercise [4], let's start drawing phrase structure trees out of our phrase structure rule in (14).

First, though, let's further shorten the statement in (14) by using symbols instead of words. Let's use the symbol "S" to mean "sentence," the symbol NP to mean "noun phrase," and the symbol "VP" to mean "verb phrase," as in (15):

(15)   S = "sentence"
        NP = "noun phrase"
        VP = "verb phrase"

Let's also adopt an "arrow" symbol (→), to mean something like "is made up of," or, "is broken down into." In this way, we can transform the statement in (14) into the one in (16):

(16)   S   →   NP   VP

I'd like you to get used to reading statements like that in (16). The phrase structure rule in (16) is simple: it means what (14) says.

To draw our phrase structure tree, we also need to understand how the phrase structure rule in (16) acts as an instruction for drawing a tree. As I said earlier, a phrase structure tree is a kind of graph, a line-drawing that we can use to graphically represent sentence structure. The rule in (16) translates into the phrase structure tree in (17); to make this more concrete, I'll fill in the words from sentence {3} in Exercise [4]:

(17)

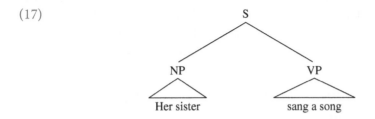

Side Note 10: (A temporary practice)

Notice that in (17), I put triangles above the NP *her sister*, and the VP *sang a song*. I did this as a temporary stop-gap measure, since we haven't yet talked about the internal structure of the NP and of the VP — or as a related matter, *why* these constituents are even called noun phrase and verb phrase in the first place. We'll address these issues in Chapters 2 and 3, where the triangles will be replaced by more articulated tree structures themselves, which will be given to us by the NP and VP phrase structure rules.

The rule in (16) tells us that "S" is made up of two parts, "NP" and "VP," and furthermore, that these two subparts are **subconstituents** of S (see Term Box 4). The tree in (17) captures this in graphic form.

To make sure you understand how to draw this basic phrase structure tree for a sentence, please do Exercise [5].

EXERCISE [5]

For each of the sentences in Exercise [4] (where you've already established the NP and VP of each sentence), draw a phrase structure tree like the one you see in (17).

In this same vein, draw phrase structure trees for the sentences in (6) through (12).

EXERCISE [6]

Just as you did in Exercise [5], draw phrase structure trees (like the one in (17)) for the sentences from Exercise [2]. You'll notice in doing this exercise that you'll come up with only one tree for each sentence. This will be despite the fact that each of these sentences is structurally ambiguous — and therefore, should have more than one structure, as we saw. In Chapter 3, where we'll learn how to break down the internal structure of the verb phrase (VP), we'll learn how to draw the two different structures for each of these structurally ambiguous sentences.

1.3 some conclusions, and what to look forward to in the coming chapters

If you worked your way through each exercise in this chapter as you read along, you should now understand two basic ideas. First, it should be clear that when we say "sentences have structure," we mean that you — as a member our species — have an instinct to structure strings of words into sentences, regardless of the language (or languages) you know. This instinct is there from birth, and it's what's responsible for you learning a language in the first place. Our test investigation of structurally ambiguous sentences showed that you already know how sentences are structured; so now it's just a question of bringing this knowledge you have into your consciousness. That's what this book is for.

Second, you should have gained a very basic understanding of the tools we'll be using in order to bring that knowledge into your consciousness: phrase structure rules and trees. We started using the most basic of phrase structure rules — the one which captures the fact that a sentence consists of two major constituents (the "S" phrase structure rule). In every chapter, we'll be building on this knowledge, developing more and more sophisticated phrase structure rules, which will allow us to see sentence structure in a more and more articulated way. The simple tree in (17) showed us that the words in sentences don't form a flat, linear string; rather, they're **hierarchically organized**, and grouped into meaningful units (constituents or phrases). In fact, even without drawing the internal structure of the verb phrase (VP) in Exercise [6], in Exercise [2] you were already tapping into the different ways that the words in the VP can be hierarchically organized, and how hierarchical organization is more important than linear order. As you saw with the sentence in (3), the single string of words in a structurally ambiguous sentence in fact has only one linear order. But the two different meanings of this single linear order tell us that there's something else hidden behind it. And that hidden thing is hierarchical structure. In sentence (3) (as with all the sentences in Exercise [2]), we saw that *with the stick* can either be associated with *the dog*, or with *poked*. This is regardless of the fact that in linear terms, *with the stick* always follows the word *dog* in (3). This showed us that groups of words which are far apart from one another in linear terms might actually be close together structurally. This will become much clearer in Chapters 2 and 3, when we look more carefully at the internal structure of the noun phrase (NP) and the verb phrase (VP).

We have yet to see the great potential for complexity in the hierarchical organization of sentences that our phrase structure rules give rise to; the plan in this book is to build towards this complexity one step at a time. It won't serve us to try and learn everything at once, but I guarantee you that you'll become a junior **syntactician** by the end of this book, as long as you take each chapter methodically in turn. If you're interested in learning about the origins of the concept of phrase structure rules, you can take a look at Chomsky (1957), though you might want to wait until you're about half-way through this book before you do so.

In meeting the objectives of Chapter 1, you've also learned quite a few new terms. Many of these terms represent sophisticated concepts, so don't be frustrated if at this point in the game you don't feel as if you've fully absorbed the meanings of all of them — though I do encourage you to go back and reconsider the term boxes and the other terms in bold scattered throughout the chapter, as a way to put yourself on firmer ground with these new concepts. The most important thing for now is that you've been familiarized with terms and concepts that are going to reappear again and again in the chapters to come. By the time you get to the end of the book, it'll be like second nature to you!

list of terms/concepts

ambiguous (ambiguity, unambiguous)
cognitive instincts
constituent (subconstituent)
grammar
hierarchy (hierarchical structure, hierarchical organization)
linear distance
modify (modifier; modification)
Necker Cube
noun
noun phrase (NP)
parse
phrases

phrase structure (phrase structure rules, phrase structure trees)
predicate
rules
sentence (S)
sentence structure
structural ambiguity
structure
subconstituents
subject
subject noun phrase
syntax (syntactic trees, syntactician)
verb
verb phrase (VP)

reference

Chomsky, Noam (1957). Syntactic Structures. Walter de Gruyter.

2 The Subject NP — Outside and In

expected outcomes for this chapter

- You'll learn to recognize subjects, noun phrases, and nouns.
- You'll learn to recognize the noun phrase internal categories of determiner, adjective, and prepositional phrase.
- You'll begin to recognize and manipulate greater subtleties of hierarchical structure and will develop more confidence with the concepts from Chapter 1.
- You'll become familiar with the following terms (see words in bold and term boxes): *subject, noun, head, pronoun, possessive pronoun, possessive, nominative case, determiner, definite/indefinite article, demonstrative, quantifier, adjective, preposition, prepositional phrase, optionality, branch, node, immediate dominance, linear order, hierarchical structure, recursion.*

2.1 some introductory words about the *noun phrase* vs. the *subject position*

In the second part of Chapter 1, we tapped into your instincts about sentence structure by showing that you have a natural inclination to conceptualize the "sentence" as being broken up into two major constituents, namely, the subject noun phrase and the verb phrase. You had practice bringing this instinct into your consciousness by dividing sentences up into these two component

Understanding Sentence Structure: An Introduction to English Syntax, First Edition.
Christina Tortora.
© 2018 John Wiley & Sons, Inc. Published 2018 by John Wiley & Sons, Inc.

parts in Exercises 4, 5, and 6. In the latter two of these exercises, you used the sentence phrase structure rule, given here in (1a) to capture this division graphically in tree form, as in (1b):

(1a) S → NP VP
(1b)

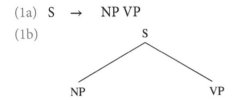

In all of the sentences we've done exercises on so far, we've been consistently identifying the subject as a noun phrase, or, as an NP. Conversely, we've been consistently identifying our one NP of interest as the subject of the sentence. I haven't given you definitions for either of these things yet (NP or subject); this is fine, because it hasn't prevented us from doing important work.

At the same time, I'm concerned that you might have been misled into thinking that "NP" and "subject" are one and the same thing. As it turns out, these two things are not coextensive. So, not all subjects are necessarily NPs, and not all NPs are necessarily subjects.

Side Note 1:

Despite the claim that "not all subjects are necessarily NPs," <u>all</u> of the subjects we will be looking at in this chapter are NPs. But not all NPs in this chapter will be subjects!

In fact, as we'll see in Chapter 3, the verb phrase can itself contain an NP (and even more than one). And as we'll see in Section 2.3, the prepositional phrase (PP) also contains an NP. So before we start picking apart the insides of the NP, it's important for us to understand what a "subject" is, so that we don't incorrectly conflate it with the concept of an NP.

In sum, this chapter is going to help us move towards a more complex understanding of many of the concepts that were introduced in Chapter 1, such as *subject, noun*, and *noun phrase* (NP). In addition, we'll develop a more sophisticated understanding of the concepts of *constituent, modification*, and *phrase structure rules*. We'll develop a more sophisticated understanding of all of these things specifically by taking a closer look at the **NP constituent** in the trees we drew in Chapter 1.

2.2 the subject position

To get started, let's take a look at a phrase structure tree we drew for one of our sentences in Exercise 5 in Chapter 1, and zero-in on the NP on the left branch of the tree (I'm visually highlighting it here with a circle):

(2)

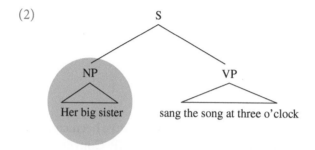

Term Box 1

The lines in a phrase structure tree are called **branches**. In the tree in (2), the NP is on the **left branch** of the sentence tree, and the VP is on the **right branch** of the sentence tree. These two branches meet at the "S." This structure for S is considered a **binary branching** structure, because S only contains two constituents and therefore has only two branches.

Term Box 2

The points in the tree that connect branches are called **nodes**. In this tree then, we can identify three nodes: S, NP, and VP. (This is ignoring the internal structure of the "triangles" for the moment.) Note that we would call the S node a **branching node**, because it splits off into more than one branch. <u>Related words</u>: *nonbranching node, terminal node, nonterminal node, root node* (see Term Box 4).

See Exercise 1 for an example of a nonbranching node. See Exercise 2 for practice on the use of the related words.

Right away, we can see the benefits of defining grammatical concepts structurally. If we focus on the structural concepts just introduced, we can straightforwardly provide a preliminary definition of **subject position**:

(3) Definition of subject: *the subject is the constituent on the left branch of the sentence tree.*

Actually, as we break down the NP into its component parts in Section 2.3, we'll see that the definition in (3) is somewhat imprecise. So from the start, it would be good to have another — more precise — way to define what the subject is. We can do that here by introducing one more concept. This concept is very useful because it will in fact also allow us to talk much more easily about phrase structure in general, in the sections and chapters to come.

In order to understand this new concept, let's look again at the NP **node** on the left branch of the sentence tree in (2) (see Term Box 2). This time, though, let's look at it in relation to the S node. As you can see, if you look at the tree as a **hierarchical structure**, the S node and the NP node are connected by a branch. Furthermore, of these nodes, we can see that one of them is higher in the tree — namely, the S node. This is directly related to the fact that in the sentence phrase structure rule in (1a), the "S" is to the left of the arrow, while the NP is to the right of the arrow.

As we'll quickly see, it's really useful — in our quest to understand sentence structure — to identify which nodes are "higher" in the tree than which other nodes, for nodes that are connected by branches. As we just saw, between the two branch-connected nodes NP and S in the tree in (2), S is higher than NP. You've probably also noticed by now that between the two branch-connected nodes VP and S, S is higher than VP. The technical term we use for this hierarchical relationship between nodes connected by single branches is **immediate dominance**. So now, let's rephrase things a little: in the tree in (2), S **immediately dominates** NP. And as you've surely already concluded, S also immediately dominates VP. Of course, neither NP nor VP immediately dominates S, because although these two nodes are connected to S by branches, they are lower in the tree than S.

Term Box 3

We can define **immediate dominance** as follows: a node (call it "Node A") **immediately dominates** another node (call it "Node B") if A and B are connected by a single branch, and A is higher in the tree than B. (This means that no other node can intervene along that branch between A and B.)

Keep in mind that getting an intuitive feel of this relationship between nodes is far more important than memorizing this definition.

Related words: *dominance, dominate.*

Side Note 2:

The connecting branch between the two nodes in the immediate dominance relation is crucial to the definition. To illustrate, let's consider this: Imagine you draw your sentence tree such that the subject NP is incidentally higher up on the page than your VP, as follows:

There's nothing incorrect about this tree; but in contrast with the structurally identical tree I drew in (2), this one has the NP visually "higher" on the page than VP. This doesn't mean, however, that NP is "higher than" VP, in the sense of **dominance**. The NP doesn't dominate the VP in this tree because it's not connected to VP by a branch.

So now that we have the notion of immediate dominance in place, we can define the concept of **subject** structurally, as follows:

(4) Revised definition of subject: *the subject is the left-branch constituent immediately dominated by the S node.*

EXERCISE [1]

The following is a phrase structure tree that is not unlike our sentence tree in (1b). The two unimportant differences are: (i) it's made up of node labels that we won't identify, and (ii) it's more complex, in that we have not used triangles to obscure the internal structure of X and Y (which we can think of as corresponding to NP and VP). These differences are irrelevant for the questions which follow:

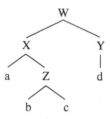

{1} Which node immediately dominates Z?
{2} Which node immediately dominates d?
{3} Does W immediately dominate more than one node?
{4} Does X immediately dominate c?
{5} Which is the one node in the tree that has nothing immediately dominating it?
{6} Which nodes do not immediately dominate anything?

EXERCISE [2]

In Term Box **2**, I defined the term "node," and the related term "branching node." Looking at the tree in Exercise [1] again, answer the following question:

{1} If W, X, and Z are *branching* nodes, which capital-lettered node in the tree would be a *nonbranching* node?

Term Box 4

As a follow-up to Term Box 2, we can define **terminal nodes** as the nodes at the bottom of the tree — the ones that are not expanded any further (or, which do not immediately dominate anything). The **root node** is the one node in the tree that is not dominated by any other node.

EXERCISE [3]

Answer the following questions regarding the tree in Exercise [1]:

{1} Which nodes in the tree are terminal nodes?
{2} Which nodes in the tree are nonterminal nodes?
{3} Which node in the tree is the root node?

2.3 let's get inside that NP triangle

So far, we've only seen one phrase structure rule, namely, the one for the sentence. I'll repeat it here for convenience:

(5)   S → NP VP

In Section 2.2, we discussed the "outside" status of the NP in (5). Specifically, when an NP is the left-branch constituent immediately dominated by the S node, it's a subject. Now it's time to move on to an analysis of the "insides" of the NP. Given that not all NPs are subjects, the extra bit of good news here is that, once we've figured out how to analyze the internal structure of the NP, we'll be able to analyze NPs no matter where they are in the sentence!

So far, the NP has only been represented as an unstructured triangle, but this has just been for temporary convenience. The triangle you see under the NP in (2) is really a placeholder which is obscuring the fact that the NP has internal structure. We therefore need to stop using a "triangle" graph now, and start using branches to represent the internal structure of the NP. Specifically, we need an NP phrase structure rule which will tell us how to draw an NP tree — just like the sentence phrase structure rule in (5) showed us how to draw an S tree.

Rather than give you the entire NP phrase structure rule outright, I'd like to start by reasoning out a few things together with you. Let's begin by looking at some of the subject NPs we isolated in Chapter 1, in Exercises 3 and 4; I'm repeating the relevant sentences here, with the subject NPs <u>underlined</u>:

(6)   <u>Maria</u> ate the sandwich.

(7)   <u>She</u> ate the sandwich.

(8)   <u>The professor</u> ate the sandwich.

Side Note 3:

At this point, I will take it for granted that when you did these exercises in Chapter 1, you made the same decisions as I did here regarding what counts as the subject NP. (If you did not come up with the same answers as I have here, you should go back to Chapter 1 and review Exercises 3 through 6.)

If all of the underlined strings in (6), (7), and (8) are subject NPs, that means that each one is in some sense akin to the NP *her big sister* in the tree in (2) above. So while all of these NPs are different in some way, we also want to be able to generalize across the different types and find out what might be the <u>same</u> about them.

Let's start by looking at the "smallest" NP we can find in this set of examples, namely, an NP that consists of no more than one word. We have two examples of such a subject NP, specifically, *Maria* in (6) and *She* in (7). *Maria* is what we would call a **proper noun**, while *she* is what we would call a **pronoun**. Let's not worry too much right now about how to define these two terms.

Term Box 5

Think of a **proper noun** as a noun that uniquely refers to some entity (so, *Shakira* and *Manhattan* are examples). We'll define **nouns** and **pronouns** in just a little bit. <u>Related words</u>: *common noun*.

Minimally, then, an NP must have <u>at least</u> one word in it. Furthermore, it looks as if that word must be some kind of noun. (I know we haven't defined noun yet, so you might be wondering why I'm making this claim; but just hang in there!)

The following one-word NP shows that this one word can also be a **common noun** (as opposed to a proper noun or a pronoun; see Term Box 5):

(9)   <u>People</u> eat their lunch too early.

So it looks as if we're concluding from all of this that the NP phrase structure rule "breaks down into" (or, "expands into"), at the very least, a noun. (We shouldn't be surprised, then, that this is why it's called a noun phrase!) Much as we abbreviated "noun phrase" as NP, let's abbreviate "noun" as N. So here is our first stab at an NP phrase structure rule:

(10)   NP → N

EXERCISE [4]

Using the NP phrase structure rule in (10), draw the NP phrase structure trees for the subject NPs in sentences (6), (7), and (9). Hint: recall that a phrase structure rule is an "instruction" which tells you how to draw a phrase structure tree. The instruction says that if there are two constituents to the right of the arrow (as in the rule in (5)), then the constituent to the left of the arrow will become a tree node that immediately dominates the two constituents on the right of the arrow (as in the tree in (1)). It follows, then, that a phrase structure rule with only <u>one</u> constituent to the right of the arrow (as in (10)) will result in a tree with a single branch. That is, the constituent to the left of the arrow will become a tree node that immediately dominates only one constituent.

If you did Exercise [4] the way I did, you came up with the following three trees:

(11a)   NP   (11b)   NP   (11c)   NP
         | | |
         N   N   N
       Maria   *She*   *People*

Side Note 4: How can one word be a phrase?

You might be wondering at this point why we should bother calling the subjects *Maria*, *She*, and *People* "noun phrases," as in (11). After all, if each consists only of a single word, then on the face of it, they don't seem to be "phrases" at all! So why not just keep it simple, and call them "nouns" without hypothesizing that they are also simultaneously NPs?

There are actually many reasons why we hypothesize that these words are both single words (at one level), <u>and</u> phrases (at another level). To keep it short, I'll give only one of those reasons here:

Note that if we were to deny "phrasal status" to subjects like *Maria*, *She*, and *People*, we would have to revise our "S" phrase structure rule to include <u>two</u> possibilities for the major sentence divide:

1. S → NP VP   or:
2. S → N VP

That is, if single-word subjects like *Maria*, *She*, and *People* were not analyzed as NPs, then we would need the additional phrase structure rule in 2, in order to account for sentences like those in (6), (7), and (9). In contrast, analyzing a single-word subject as both a single-word (N) <u>and</u> as a phrase (NP) allows us to make our "S" phrase structure rule **general**; that is, we can **generalize** across different NP types, regardless of how many words they have in them.

Now that we've established (10) as a first-pass version of our NP phrase structure rule, it should be immediately obvious that we're going to have to revise it, given that we've already seen NPs which contain more than just one word. In this regard, let's take another look at the NP subject in the sentence in (8) — which I'll repeat here as (12). In fact, let's look at it together with another NP subject from Exercise 4 in Chapter 1 (which I'm giving here as example (13)):

(12)   <u>The professor</u> ate the sandwich.

(13)   <u>Her sister</u> sang a song.

In contrast with the NPs in (11), these are NPs containing two words. A straightforward thing they have in common is that both contain Ns: in (12) the N is *professor*, and in (13) the N is *sister*. This should not come as a surprise to us because, as we've already seen, every NP must contain <u>at least</u> an N. (Once again: I know we haven't defined noun yet, but I'm still going to ask you to just hang in there for now!)

In addition, though, each of these NPs contains a word to the left of the N. In (12) that word is *the*, and in (13) it's *her*. These words belong to a class of items that are called **determiners**. Rather than define what a determiner is, let's just take a look at a few types of determiner for now:

(14) **Determiners:**
  (a) <u>articles</u>: *the* (the **definite article**), *a* (the **indefinite article**)
      examples: *the laptop, a chair*
  (b) <u>demonstratives</u>: *this, that, these, those*
      examples: *this journal, that office, these complaints, those professors*
  (c) <u>possessive pronouns</u>: *my, your, his, her, our, their, its*
      examples: *my concern, your idea, his children, her book, our meeting, their laboratory, its paw*
  (d) <u>quantifiers</u>: *some, no*
      examples: *some Buicks, no students*

Our NP phrase structure rule thus needs to account for the fact that an NP can have a determiner in addition to an N. So let's revise our rule in (10) as follows (with "determiner" abbreviated as "det"):

(15) NP → det N

This rule says "an NP is made up of a determiner and a noun." Note that it also implicitly specifies the **linear order** of the words, such that the det must come first, and the N must come second.

Now, we already learned how to map a phrase structure rule (with two elements to the arrow's right), into a phrase structure tree; recall our sentence phrase structure rule! In other words, we now know everything we need to know in order to straightforwardly draw the tree in (16), from the instruction in (15):

(16)   NP
          ╱   ╲
       det   N

EXERCISE [5]

Using the NP phrase structure rule in (15), draw the NP phrase structure trees for the subject NPs in sentences (12) and (13).

If you did Exercise [5] the way I did, you came up with the following two trees:

(17a) NP — det *the* / N *professor*   (17b) NP — det *her* / N *sister*

Before I move on to more complex NPs, a word is in order here regarding the status of the determiner: as we already saw from the NP possibilities in (11) versus those in (17), it's certainly possible to have a determiner inside an NP, but it's not **obligatory**. In other words, if we abstract away from specific NPs like *the professor*, *her sister*, *people*, or *Maria*, we see that generally speaking, the one thing an NP must have is an N; however, the determiner is a kind of additional element that only comes into play some of the time. In order to capture this difference between **optional** and obligatory elements inside a phrase structure rule, we use **parentheses** as a notational device. The use of parentheses around a particular element inside a phrase structure rule tells us that the element is optional. Thus, we need to revise our NP phrase structure rule in (15) as follows:

(18)   NP   →   (det) N

This rule says that "an NP is made up of an optional determiner and an obligatory noun."

Term Box 6

Putting aside the question of what **heads** the sentence (S) until Chapter 11, it turns out that every phrase has one obligatory terminal node in it. That word is called the **head**.

As we've already seen, the one obligatory terminal node inside the NP is the N; the NP phrase structure rule in (15) reflects this, with a lack of parentheses around the N. That means that the N is the head of the NP.

As we'll see below, the prepositional phrase (PP) has an obligatory preposition (or, P); similarly, in Chapter 3, we'll see that the Verb Phrase (VP) has one obligatory terminal node, and that's the Verb (or, V). In fact, you will have noticed by now that each one of these phrases (NP, PP, VP) is named for its one obligatory terminal node (N, P, V, respectively). So the head of NP is N; likewise, the head of PP is P; and of course, the head of VP is V. Related words: *to head* (as in "The N heads the NP," or, "The VP is headed by the V").

Side Note 5: So what's a *noun*?

At this point, you're actually in a position to start using the tools at your disposal, to try and figure out on your own what a noun is. You can do this without worrying about an actual "definition" of the word noun.

Working forwards from Exercise 3 (Chapter 1), start analyzing the sentences given by using your intuitions (as we did in Chapter 1), to divide the sentence into its two major parts, NP and VP. Then, just focusing on the subject NP (i.e. the left-branch constituent immediately dominated by the S node), limit yourself to considering only those NPs that have two words, namely, a determiner and one other word. Once you've identified the determiner — which for your purposes right now is something from the list in (14) — then it follows that the only other word in the NP must be a noun (i.e. an N).

Similarly, if you limit yourself to considering only those subject NPs that have <u>one</u> word, then by definition the word you are looking at is a noun. If you engage in this exercise enough, it'll begin to become obvious to you what a noun is.

Note that the method I'm suggesting here is not unlike the way babies acquire language! (Note that no one teaches a baby that "a noun is a person, place, thing, or idea." A baby just figures out what a noun is on his or her own.) And since babies are so good at learning grammar quickly, it behooves us to try and use the same method, to bring our own unconscious knowledge of grammar into our consciousness.

Term Box 7

If you'd like a definition for the term **noun**, I'll give you this one: *A noun is the word that heads an NP* (see Term Box 6). Note that often, it's easy to recognize a noun by the fact that you can make it **plural**, e.g., *one laptop* vs. *two **laptops**; that professor* vs. *those **professors**; his child* vs. *his **children***.

2.3.1 getting a bit more complex

If we consider some more NP subjects that we saw in our Chapter 1 exercises, we'll realize that our NP phrase structure rule in (18) doesn't give us everything we need:

(19)   <u>The professor of linguistics</u> ate the sandwich.

(20)   <u>Her big sister</u> sang the song at three o'clock.

(21)   <u>People in this country</u> eat their lunch too early.

(22)   <u>The crazy people in this country</u> eat their lunch too early.

In particular, there are some elements in the underlined NPs in (19) through (22) which we have not accounted for in our NP phrase structure rule. Let's isolate those elements.

Let's first take a look at (20). The one difference between the underlined NP here and the NP in (17b) is the presence of the word *big* in the NP in (20). Let's compare the two NPs directly:

The word *big* is what we call an **adjective** (or, "adj"). Putting aside the definition of "adjective" for now, what we see is that the existence of such an element requires that we revise our NP phrase structure rule to include it. Since the adjective linearly precedes the N (and since the determiner linearly precedes the adjective), our new NP phrase structure rule will have to reflect this fact:

(24)   Revised NP phrase structure rule:

NP   →   (det) (adj) N

EXERCISE [6]

Answer this question: Why is the adj in the phrase structure rule in (24) in parentheses?

This rule says that "an NP is made up of an optional determiner, followed by and an optional adjective, followed by an obligatory noun."

Now let's take a look at the sentence in (21), and compare it with our earlier sentence in (9):

(9)   <u>People</u> eat their lunch too early.

(21)   <u>People in this country</u> eat their lunch too early.

The one difference between the underlined NP in (9) and the underlined NP in (21) is that the latter has the extra words *in this country*. This whole string of words corresponds to a particular kind of phrase, namely, a prepositional phrase (PP). Putting aside the definition of "preposition" and "prepositional phrase" for now, what we see is that the existence of this phrase requires once again that we revise our NP phrase structure rule to include it.

Since the PP linearly follows (i.e. comes after, or, comes to the right of) the N, our new NP phrase structure rule will have to reflect this fact:

(25)   Revised NP phrase structure rule:

NP   →   (det) (adj) N (PP)

Even though we have not yet defined what a PP is, there are actually two ways one can identify a PP inside an NP. First of all, a PP is signaled by the presence of a **preposition**. Again, rather than define what a preposition is, let's just take a look at a few prepositions for now:

(26)   Prepositions: *in, with, of, for, on, from*

Although we'll be decomposing the prepositional phrase with an articulated PP phrase structure rule in Chapter 4, to make your remaining tree-drawing exercises in this chapter a bit easier, I will give you a rudimentary PP phrase structure rule here:

(27)   PP phrase structure rule:

PP   →   P (NP)

What this means is that the rule in (25), taken together with the rule in (27), gives you everything you need to draw the underlined NP in the sentence in (22).

EXERCISE [7]

Before you do anything else, draw a tree for the underlined NP in (22).

If you did Exercise [7] the way I did, you came up with the following tree:

(28)
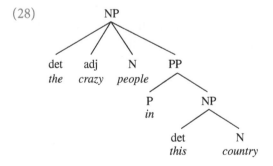

2.3.2 interim summary

Now it's time to stand back and take note of the extent of your ability at this point, to draw phrase structure trees for the sentences in (19) through (22) above.

First, take stock of the fact that you now have three phrase structure rules at your disposal:

(29)   Summary of phrase structure rules used thus far:

S   →   NP VP

NP   →   (det) (adj) N (PP)

PP   →   P (NP)

The first rule tells you to divide the sentence into its two component parts, NP and VP. Keep in mind that at this point in time, you should continue to use the "triangle" for the VP part of the sentence. (In Chapter 3 we'll learn how to get inside the VP.) The second rule tells you to draw the internal structure of the subject NP. This NP phrase structure rule contains a constituent which itself is *not* a terminal node, and as such has to be further broken down. I am specifically referring to the PP here. The phrase structure rule for the PP is now also available to you. Note that in order to draw the PP portion of the tree, all you need to be able to recognize for now are the six prepositions listed in (26).

Because you already know how to draw an NP, that second element in the PP phrase structure rule should not be a problem for you (just go back and look at the NP phrase structure rule). Remember what I said earlier in this chapter: given that not all NPs are subjects, the extra bit of good news is that, once we've figured out how to analyze the internal structure of NP, we'll be able to analyze NPs no matter where they are in the sentence; even when they're inside the PP!

EXERCISE [8]

Using all of the phrase structure rules at your disposal, draw trees for the sentences in (19) through (22). Keep in mind that you will be drawing a triangle for the VP.

EXERCISE [9]

Using all of these phrase structure rules at your disposal, draw trees for the following sentences:

{1} Some interested students came to my office.
{2} They came to my office.
{3} Those ferocious dogs at the kennel got into a fight.

{4} Your old car with the rust on the back door is useless.

{5} It is useless.

{6} The small fridge in the kitchen in the back of the house with the white shutters with flowers on them is broken.

{7} It is broken.

{8} The professor with the big window in her office ate the sandwich.

{9} The students in this class about syntax are working very hard.

2.3.3 the infinity of language

Before we move on, let's take stock of the subject NP in sentence in {6} in Exercise [9].

First of all, as per our work in Chapter 1, you should have started analyzing {6} by first breaking this sentence down into its two major parts, the subject NP and the VP. The sentence in {7} should have served as a hint regarding which string of words in {6} count as the subject NP. In particular, I hope you realized that the pronoun *It* in {7} can refer to the entity represented by entire string of words *The small fridge in the kitchen in the back of the house with the white shutters with flowers on them* in {6}. Then, I hope your NP/VP breakdown of the sentence in {7} resulted in the following major sentence split:

(30)

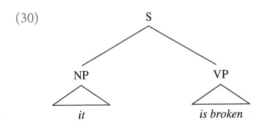

Given this NP/VP split in {7}, and given that *It* in {7} can refer to *The small fridge in the kitchen in the back of the house with the white shutters with flowers on them* in {6}, it follows that the NP/VP split for {6} should be as follows:

(31)

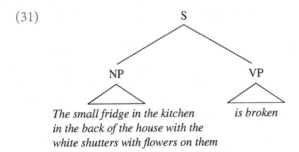

Assuming the NP and PP phrase structure rules in (29), this should have led to the following structure:

(32)

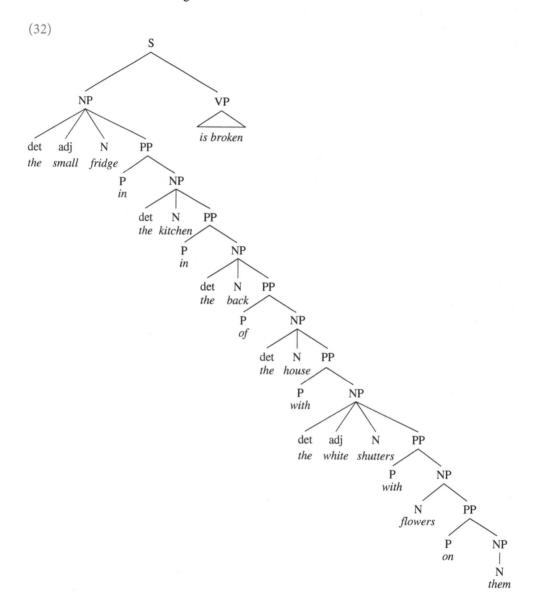

There's something important to be noted about the structure of the subject NP in (32), which illustrates one of the more impressive aspects of the human capacity for language. Specifically, the NP and PP phrase structure rules in (29) together give rise to the possibility of the NP and PP **recurring** over and over again, in a potentially infinite cycle. Thus, an NP can contain — or, **embed** — a PP; given, furthermore, that a PP can embed an NP, it then follows that these phrases can **recur**, and that they can do so **theoretically infinitely**. Thus, a human being could in theory create an infinitely long NP. A corollary of this is that a human being could in theory create an infinite set of NPs; this is because for every NP with *n* PP embeddings, it's possible to add one more embedded PP, creating a distinct NP with *n* + 1 PP embeddings. Let's briefly exemplify this in (33).

Infinite number of NPs:

(33) a. NP1: *The small fridge*
      b. NP2: *The small fridge **in the kitchen***
      c. NP3: *The small fridge in the kitchen **in the back***
      d. NP4: *The small fridge in the kitchen in the back **of the house***
      e. NP5: *The small fridge in the kitchen in the back of the house **with the white shutters***
      f. NP6: etc.

Of course, we say that the phrases recur "theoretically" infinitely (or, we say that we can "theoretically" create an infinite set of NPs), because it is not — in actuality — possible for a speaker to either create an infinitely long NP or to create an infinite set of NPs. But this fact is a mere technicality which simply has to do with our own finite nature. If in an alternate universe a human being could live for an infinite period of time, then that human could create an infinitely long NP. Of course, we must put aside the question of whether that person's infinitely alive interlocutor would be patient enough to sit around listening to this NP for an infinity! Another limitation in this fantasy world of infinitely alive humans is that it might still nevertheless be difficult to create an infinitely long NP, given the limitations on a human being's working memory.

This particular phenomenon, captured in the NP and PP phrase structure rules, is known as **recursion**. We will see a case of recursion again, in Chapter 5, when we look at sentences that embed other sentences. Recursion, as captured in the phrase structure rules, is one example of what linguists call the **creative** or **generative** capacity of human language. If you think about it, it's quite remarkable that a finite being can take a finite number of words, and a (very) finite set of rules, and combine them to create something theoretically infinite!

Side Note 6: Creative capacity and novelty

Note too that the creative capacity of human language is also what allows humans to create completely novel sentences — that is, sentences which have never been uttered before in human history, such as *Groucho ate the cannoli right after chewing on the Australian tea-tree oil chewing stick*. Feel free to create a sentence, right now, that you're certain has never been created in human history!

2.3.4 a final word (for now), on the PP within NP, and the concept of *modification*

There's a sentence from Chapter 1 that we still have not revisited; it's time to revisit it now:

(34)   <u>The professor of linguistics with brown hair</u> ate the sandwich.

It's important to note that, although the underlined NP in (34) contains two PPs, these two PPs do not exemplify the kind of recursion seen in (32). To understand how this is the case, let's take a closer look.

This NP contains the PPs *of linguistics* and *with brown hair*. You might ask how I know that these are PPs. At this point, let me remind you that you your-self have all the tools you need to identify these as PPs; specifically, you've already seen (in example (26)) that *of* and *with* are prepositions. It logically follows that if we have two prepositions in this structure, then we have two prepositional phrases.

The question which arises at this point is how to draw a structure for this NP. Unfortunately, our NP phrase structure rule in (29) forces us to draw the phrase structure tree in (35), which I'll tell you right away is incorrect. I've circled the PP which is the locus of the problem:

INCORRECT TREE:

(35)

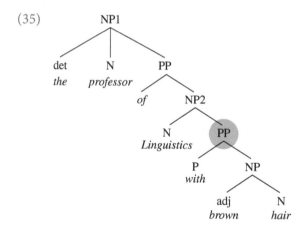

Side Note 7:

You might be wondering how I know that the word *linguistics* is a noun. It's important to remember that even if you don't know off the bat that this word is a noun, you already have the tools to deduce that it is. How so? First, if you look at the list in (26), you see that *of* and *with* are prepositions. Furthermore, if you look at the sentence in (34), you can see that there's only one word that comes after the preposition *of* (before you get to the next preposition, *with*). That word is *linguistics*. Now, if you look at the

PP phrase structure rule, you see that a PP consists of a P followed by an optional NP. So whatever follows *of*, if it's not another preposition, then that thing must be an NP. It's reasonable to conclude that *linguistics* is not a preposition (for one thing, it's not in our list in (26)). Therefore, it must be an NP. Finally, given that it's a one-word NP, then this one word we have here must be an N.

(I have labelled the two different NPs as NP1 and NP2, for the sake of convenience of the discussion to follow.) Why is this structure incorrect? After all, our phrase structure rules in (29) allow us to draw this tree. In fact, this would be the <u>correct</u> tree for the NP *the car with rust on the door* (which is similar in important respects to the subject NP in the sentence in {4} in Exercise [9]):

(36)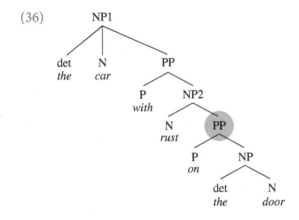

Again, for the purposes of clear discussion, I've labelled the two different NP nodes in (36) with two different numbers, so that we can distinguish between them:

(37) a. NP1 (*the car with rust on the door*)
  b. NP2 (*rust on the door*)

I've circled the PP *on the door* to highlight it, also for the purposes of discussion.

Note that in the correct tree in (36), the PP *on the door* is immediately dominated by NP2, which is headed by the N *rust*. Another way to think of this structural configuration is as follows: the PP *on the door* "branches off of," or, "attaches to" the NP whose head N (*rust*) is **modified** by this PP. (For the term "modify," see discussion around Term Box 3 in Chapter 1.) We say that the PP *on the door* modifies the N *rust* because this PP serves to further describe — or add more information about — the N *rust*. Note that if NP1 were simply *the car with rust*, we wouldn't necessarily know where that rust is on the car. However, when we add the PP *on the door*, we now know where the rust is. So the nature of the location of the *rust* has been further specified by the addition of this PP.

> ## Side Note 8:
>
> Constituents such as this PP are thus called **modifiers**. Note that the adjectives we have seen inside our NPs are also modifiers. For example, if you compare the NP *her sister* with the NP *her big sister*, we see that the adjective *big* serves to provide further information about the noun *sister*. In this case, the modification provides further specification of the noun by specifying a property (bigness), as opposed to a location.

Thus, when we think about the meaning of NP1 in (36), we intuitively conclude that the PP *on the door* says something about the noun *rust*. This is captured by the fact that the string of words *rust on the door* forms a constituent, represented by the NP2 node. In Chapter 4, we'll talk more about how we can actually prove that a modifier forms as syntactic constituent with the word it modifies (a constituent such as NP2 in (36)). But for now, it's important to return to the tree in (35) and see how the present discussion can illuminate our claim that this tree is incorrect.

Again, appealing to your intuition about the meaning of NP1 in (35), you can see that between the two Ns, *professor* and *linguistics*, it is the professor whom we interpret as having brown hair. Indeed, it is completely nonsensical (and for me, impossible) to interpret *Linguistics* as having brown hair. Thus, we would say that the PP *with brown hair* modifies the N *professor*, and <u>not</u> the N *linguistics*. This in turn means that the PP *with brown hair* is attached to the wrong NP in (35). If the PP modifies the N *professor*, then it must be attached to the NP that immediately dominates that N, as follows:

CORRECT TREE:

(38)

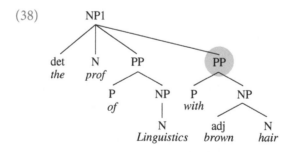

In contrast with the tree in (35), then, the string of words *linguistics with brown hair* does <u>not</u> form a constituent. (Notice how they incorrectly do form a constituent, represented by NP2, in (35)!) Rather, it forms a constituent with *the professor of linguistics*, which is correct, as it is this professor that has the brown hair. Another way to look at this is that the circled PP is immediately dominated by the NP headed by the N *professor*.

EXERCISE [10]

Now double-check the tree you drew for the subject NP in sentence {9} in Exercise [9].

All of this said, now we must take note of the fact that NP1 in (38) immediately dominates <u>two</u> PPs. You might have noticed by now that our NP phrase structure rule, which I'll repeat here, strictly speaking, doesn't allow for this. It only allows for one PP to be immediately dominated by the NP:

(39) NP   →   (det) (adj) N (PP)

Given all of our arguments in favor of the tree in (38), then, we must revise our NP phrase structure rule once again, to allow for the possibility of more than one PP:

Revision of NP phrase structure rule:

(40) NP   →   (det) (adj) N (PP) (PP)

EXERCISE [11]

Now draw a tree for the subject NP in the sentence *Some older cousins of mine in Colombia paid me a visit.*

Note that the revision to the rule in (40) could be simplified, using a notational device that allows us to capture the idea that we're allowed to have zero or more PPs in the NP. The notational device I have in mind is the **Kleene Star** — a superscripted asterisk on the element in question — which means "you can use zero or more of this element."

Another notational way of capturing what (40) says:

(41) NP   →   (det) (adj) N (PP*)

> # EXERCISE [12]
>
> Now consider the following NP:
>
> {1} *The woman with the truck from Brooklyn.*
>
> Using your intuitions, think about what the two meanings of this NP are.
>   Assuming that you've thought of two different meanings for {1} (which I hope you have!), give two possible trees for this NP (keeping in mind our new NP rule in (41)). Hint: look at the two structures in (36) and (38) for the two possibilities.
>   Given our discussion above of modification, which tree do you think represents which meaning?

It's important to make sure we're on the same page regarding what you came up with in Exercise [12], so let's touch base on it.

In our discussion immediately above, we saw that a PP "branches off of" (or, "attaches to") the constituent that we, as speakers, intend it to modify — either when we're creating a sentence, or comprehending a sentence that someone else is creating. For the ambiguous NP *the woman with the truck from Brooklyn*, the issue is that there are two possible attachment sites for the PP *from Brooklyn*. Let's look at the two possible structures for this NP:

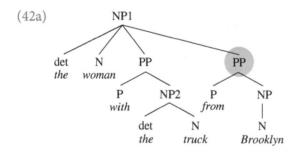

As (42a) illustrates, the PP can attach to the NP headed by the N *woman*. In this case, we interpret the phrase to mean that *the woman* is from Brooklyn.

Side Note 9:

Between two interlocutors (a speaker and a hearer), sometimes the speaker will intend one attachment while the hearer will understand the other, leading to a misunderstanding in conversation. This underscores how structure is not out there in there in the world, but rather, is purely a product of our own individual minds!

(42b)

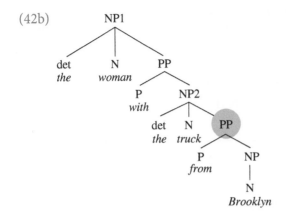

However, as (42b) illustrates, we can also attach the PP to the NP headed by the N *truck*. In this case, we interpret the phrase to mean that *the truck* is from Brooklyn.

Thus, the reason why we humans find the string of words in Exercise [12] to be ambiguous is because we can mentally attach the PP *from Brooklyn* either to NP1 (as in (42a)) or to NP2 (as in (42b)). In (42a), we would say that the PP **modifies** the N *woman* (that is, the head of the NP that the PP attaches to); in (42b), we would say that the PP modifies the N *truck* (again, the head of the NP that the PP attaches to). These two different possibilities reflect how our minds work, which is captured in the phrase structure rules.

Recall from Chapter 1 that, in a case like this, where a string of words can be assigned two possible structures — resulting in two different meanings, we say that the string is **structurally ambiguous**. That is, speakers take it to have two possible meanings, because speakers can assign two possible structures to it (the structure in (42a) and the structure in (42b)). We will see more on structural ambiguity in Chapter 3.

2.3.5 a quick note on adjectives

Now that we know about the possibility of iterating PPs within the NP rule, one final revision to the NP phrase structure rule is in order. Specifically, it turns out that NPs do not limit themselves to one adjective per NP. In this regard, let's revisit the subject NP from sentence {4} in Exercise [9]:

(43) Your **old** car with the rust on the back door

Here, *car* is modified by the adjective *old*. But note that I can add more adjectives:

(44) a. Your **big old** car with the rust on the back door
      b. Your **big old ugly** car with the rust on the back door
      c. Your **big old ugly blue** car with the rust on the back door
      d. etc.

Given that the NP can contain more than one adjective, we should also use our Kleene Star notation on the adjective part of the NP phrase structure rule as well, as follows:

Final revision of NP phrase structure rule:

(45) NP   →   (det) (adj*) N (PP*)

EXERCISE [13]

Draw a tree for the NP in (44c).

2.4 possessive NPs

Before we conclude this chapter, there is one last piece of the NP we should delve further into, to round out our picture. In this regard, let's look back at a subcategory of determiner we saw in example (14), namely, the **possessive pronouns**:

(46) possessive pronouns: *my, your, his, her, our, their, its*

     examples: *my concern, your idea, his children, her book, our meeting, their laboratory, its paw*

I want to revisit the possessive pronoun, with an eye towards gaining a better understanding of (a) what a pronoun is and (b) what the true complexity of the "determiner position" of the NP is.

The NP tree in (47) illustrates the position of the possessive pronoun within the NP:

(47)

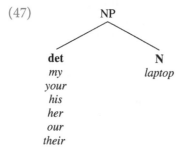

To start the discussion, let's consider the fact that a possessive pronoun is a kind of pronoun.

Term Box 8

The word **pronoun** involves the prefix *pro*, which is Latin in origin. Literally, the whole word, *pro-noun*, means "in place of a noun." Interestingly, though, as we have seen, pronouns do not stand "in place of a noun." Rather, they actually stand "in place of a whole noun phrase." We saw this in Chapter 1, Exercise [3], where the pronoun *she* could stand in for the entire phrase *my professor with the big window in her office.*

Note that *she* is not a possessive pronoun. It is what we would call a **subject pronoun**, because it can only occur in subject position. We say of such pronouns that they are marked with **nominative case**. So a pronoun that is explicitly marked with nominative can only occur in subject position, like *she, he, we,* or *they.* Try putting these pronouns in any other position, and you might find the sentence sounds really funny! How does *They spoke to **she*** sound to you?

Now, we've already seen some examples of pronouns in some sentences that we've already analyzed, which I'll repeat here:

(48)   a.   **She** ate the sandwich.   (e.g., *The professor of linguistics with brown hair*)

      b.   **They** came to my office.   (e.g., *Some interested students*)

      c.   **It** is useless.   (e.g., *The small fridge in the kitchen in the back of the house with the white shutters with flowers on them*)

We saw that words like *she, they,* and *it* "stand in for" entire NPs, like *the professor of linguistics with brown hair* (*she*), or *some interested students* (*they*), or *the small fridge in the kitchen …* (*it*).

Now, returning to the so-called possessive pronouns, let's focus just on the possessive pronouns *her, his,* and *their.* In particular, let's observe the fact that — like the pronouns in (48) — the possessive pronouns also stand in for entire NPs. For the possessive pronouns, though, it's a bit more intricate, because — as elements occupying the determiner position — they happen to stand in for NPs … which occupy the determiner position! To see how this is the case, consider the underlined subject NPs in (49), each of which contains a possessive pronoun in determiner position:

(49)   a.   <u>**Her** book</u> was well received. (e.g., *Maria's*, or, *The professor's*)

      b.   <u>**His** old blue car</u> was useless. (e.g., *That guy's*)

      c.   <u>**Their** room</u> was a mess. (e.g., *The children's*)

As can be seen by the parenthetical examples to the right in (49), each one of the possessive pronouns in bold (*her, his, their*) within the underlined NPs can be replaced by a **possessive NP**:

(50) a. **The professor's** <u>book</u> was well received.

b. **That guy's** <u>old blue car</u> was useless.

c. **The children's** <u>room</u> was a mess.

To make this concrete, let's look at the subject NP *her book* in (51) and compare its structure with the structures of the similar subject NPs *Maria's book* and *The professor's book* in (52) and (53):

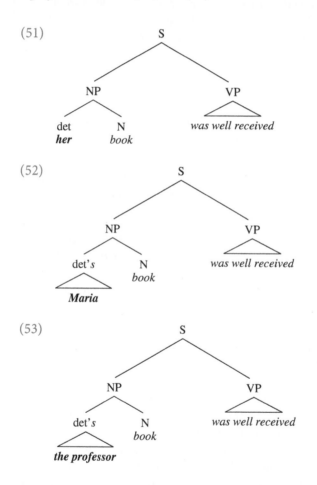

(51)

(52)

(53)

What is important to note here is the det position in (52) and (53). Unlike the det position in (51), the det position in (52) and (53) is complex (hence, the triangle, which for the moment is obscuring the complexity). It doesn't take much, however, to realize that these complex determiners are none other than NPs themselves! So let's start gently, by breaking down the complex-dets in (52) and (53). To distinguish these complex-dets — which as we just noted are NPs — from the "larger" NP in which they are contained, let's give them a special name. Let's call them **PossNP**. As you examine (54) and (55), keep in mind that the PossNPs are none other than the det positions seen in (52) and (53).

(54)

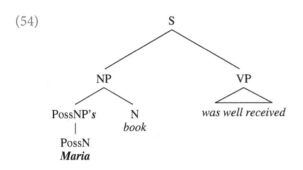

(55)

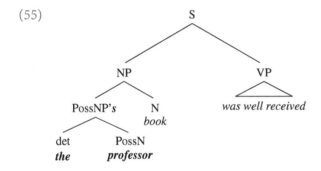

There are three points to immediately note, regarding the fact that a possessive pronoun such has *her* stands in for a PossNP such as *Maria's* or *The professor's* in a noun phrase:

First, this means we have to revise our NP phrase structure rule, to include the possibility of an NP containing a PossNP in determiner position. Consider in this regard the following revision:

NP phrase structure rule (FINAL REVISION for this chapter!)

(56)   NP   → $\left\{ \begin{array}{c} \text{(det)} \\ \text{(PossNP)} \end{array} \right\}$ (adj*) N (PP*)

Here we must introduce a new notational device, namely, the **curly bracket notation**. The curly brackets seen in (56) are meant to capture the fact that the first element in a noun phrase can be <u>either</u> a determiner, <u>or</u> a PossNP. This is really no different than saying that a PossNP is a kind of determiner. (Note that the parentheses around det and PossNP indicate furthermore that these are optional elements; so nothing about the optionality of determiners has changed.)

Second, it is important to immediately note that the PossNP itself has the same exact possibilities for internal structure as the regular old NP. So if you're asking yourself how to draw the internal structure of a PossNP, look no further than the regular old NP phrase structure rule. In fact, we can create a PossNP phrase structure rule simply by mimicking the phrase structure rule for NP (with the added tweak that the head of the PossNP is a PossN):

(57)   PossNP   → $\left\{ \begin{matrix} \text{(det)} \\ \text{(PossNP)} \end{matrix} \right\}$ (adj*) PossN (PP*)

Interestingly, what this means is that an NP can contain a PossNP (in determiner position), which <u>itself</u> can contain a PossNP in <u>its</u> determiner position. This is illustrated in (58):

(58a)   <u>John's mother's friend</u> ate the sandwich.

In (58a), *John's* is a PossNP2 inside the PossNP1 *John's mother*, and *John's mother's* is a PossNP1 inside the NP *John's mother's friend*, as follows:

(58b)

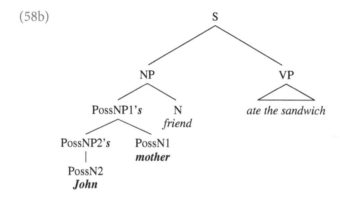

To keep yourself from getting confused, just remember that every NP (including a PossNP) can contain a determiner (and therefore, a PossNP — since a PossNP is a kind of determiner!). If you replace the symbol PossNP's with the symbol "det" in each of these cases, you might find it easier to get used to.

Third, it is important to keep in mind that the suffix *'s* is not a suffix on the last word of the PossNP, but rather, a suffix on the <u>whole PossNP</u>. This is why I placed the *'s* at the level of the phrase (PossNP's) in all of the above trees (and not the level of the word). The fact that the apostrophe-s refers to the head of the PossNP (and not the last word in the PossNP) can be most readily gathered in the following example:

(59)   <u>The king of England's book</u> was well received.

In (59), we interpret the entire underlined subject NP as follows: the book belongs to the king of England. So, this is not about <u>England</u> "possessing" the book; rather, it's about the head of the PossNP — namely, the PossN *king* — being the "possessor" of the book. In other words the *book* belongs to the *King*, not to *England*, as in the tree in (60). Note that this is despite the fact that in the actual spelling, the apostrophe-s goes directly on the word *England* (strangely enough)! But this is just an artifact of the linear nature of spoken language. Even though the possessive *-s* is conceptually associated with the entire NP, the one-word-after-the-other nature of speech requires that we attach this *-s* to something concrete. The linear order of speech gives rise to a convention whereby English speakers seem to attach the *-s* to the last word in the NP-string. This linearity of speech thus doesn't allow us to capture structure the way a tree does!

(60)

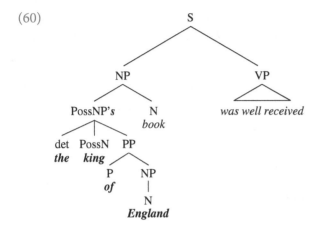

EXERCISE [14]

Draw trees for the NP subjects inside the following sentences:

{1} His mother was a famous woman.
{2} John's mother was a famous woman.
{3} That student's mother was a famous woman.
{4} The student in my class's mother was a famous woman.
{5} Bill's friend's mother was a famous woman.
{6} That guy's friend's mother was a famous woman.

2.5 conclusions

Let's first take stock of the phrase structure rules we've come up with up until this point:

Phrase structure rules at the conclusion of this chapter:

(61) S → NP VP

NP → $\left\{ \begin{array}{l} \text{(det)} \\ \text{(PossNP)} \end{array} \right\}$ (adj*) N (PP*)

PossNP → $\left\{ \begin{array}{l} \text{(det)} \\ \text{(PossNP)} \end{array} \right\}$ (adj*) PossN (PP*)

PP → P (NP)

In the next chapter, we'll provide a rule for the VP, and in Chapter 4, we'll further refine our PP phrase structure rule.

Now, let's look at some of the things we've accomplished. Our analysis of the subject NP allowed us to build on many concepts introduced in Chapter 1. The concept of hierarchical structure has taught us that certain grammatical concepts — such as **subject** and **noun** — can be defined in <u>structural</u> terms. This is a huge bonus, because it helps us get away from outdated descriptions and definitions which are so nebulous and ill-defined, as to lead any alert student into readily finding counter-examples which defy them. To see how problematic these outdated definitions of subject and noun are, let's consider them here:

(62)   A common definition of subject you'll find in "grammar" books:

"The subject is the part of the sentence that indicates what the sentence is about," or

"The subject is who or what performs the action of the sentence."

Now here are six sentences which immediately call into question the usefulness of these definitions of **subject**:

(63a)   <u>My poetry professor</u> wrote that poem.

(63b)   <u>That poem</u> was written by my poetry professor.

(64a)   <u>My house</u> is a mess.

(64b)   <u>Your sweater</u> is sitting right on the chair.

(64c)   <u>The flowers in the garden</u> surround a beautifully carved stone with a dedication on it.

(64d)   <u>You</u> are beautiful.

First of all, for all of these sentences, it is impossible to prove what each sentence is "about." Is the sentence in (63a) "about" *my poetry professor*? Couldn't I just as easily say that it's "about" *my poetry professor's writing of a poem*? In this regard, consider the two sentences in (63) together. If the definition of subject in (62) meant anything, we would have to say that the sentence in (63a) is "about" *my poetry professor*, while the sentence in (63b) is "about" *that poem*, for the simple reason that the subject in the former is *my poetry professor* while the subject in the latter is *that poem*. Yet it's impossible to prove that the "aboutness" of (63a) is completely different from the "aboutness" of (63b). Note that the two sentences have the same meaning.

Similarly, a look at the sentences in (63b) and (64) shows that the subject isn't always "who or what performs the action of the sentence." In (63b), it should be clear that *that poem* is not performing the action; in fact, if anything, you would take *my poetry professor* to be performing the action here (but this is clearly not the subject of the sentence). Likewise, there doesn't seem to be any action going on at all in the sentences in (64).

Thus, any definition of subject that appeals to meaning, or to "aboutness," is doomed to fail in the mission at hand, which is to help us gain a precise definition of subject. In contrast, it's difficult to see how we can defy a definition of subject which relies on purely structural concepts, precisely defined. Given the data we have seen thus far, a subject in English is quite simply the left-branch constituent immediately dominated by the S node.

In a similar spirit, let's take stock of what we've accomplished regarding our knowledge of nouns and noun phrases. Our analysis of the NP, and our discussion of the NP phrase structure rule, has again equipped us with terms that make it easier to talk about hierarchical structure in the syntactic tree. This in turn has taught us that certain grammatical concepts — such as "noun" — can again be defined in <u>structural</u> terms. This also helps us get away from outdated descriptions and definitions which, as we said earlier, are so nebulous that students routinely find counterexamples which defy them! To see how problematic the old outdated definition of noun is, let's consider it here:

(65)   A common definition of noun that you'll again find in "grammar" books:

"a noun is a person, place, thing, or idea"

Now here is a sentence which calls into question the usefulness of this definition of noun:

(66)   Mary put the book <u>on the table</u>.

It is difficult to argue that *on the table* is not a "place." Yet clearly, it's not a noun. It simply cannot be, because "noun" refers to a single word, but *on the table* is an entire phrase (as we shall learn, it is a prepositional phrase, to be precise).

Instead, it can suffice to say that a noun is the word that heads an NP. Of course, there are other clues that help us figure out what a noun is (both as baby humans acquiring English and as adult students consciously learning how English speakers unconsciously analyze English sentences!). For example, as we saw in Term Box 7, nouns are characterized by their ability to be pluralized. In addition, if we know that a noun is the word that heads a noun phrase, then our ability to surmise what a noun is can rest in part on our ability to surmise what an NP is. Needless to say, we want to be careful to not create a set of circular definitions whereby we claim that "a noun is the head of a noun phrase" and "a noun phrase is a phrase headed by a noun." We know that language learners use a combination of syntactic, morphological (= word structure; see Chapter 10, Term Box 3), and semantic knowledge to conclude which words are nouns (versus which words are verbs, prepositions, adjectives, etc.). Regarding the syntactic clues, there are many elements inside the NP which point to where the noun is, like the determiners *the, a, this, that, these, those, my*, etc. And we've already seen that there are all kinds of clues to tell us where the NPs are, in a sentence. This chapter showed that NPs can occur as subjects and also inside PPs. We can determine what a subject NP is by figuring out what the left-branch constituent immediately dominated by the S node is. And we can determine an NP inside a PP by looking first for the Ps. As we'll see in Chapter 3, NPs have a distribution even wider than this, but no matter where they are in the sentence, there are always clues that help us figure out which constituents of the sentence are NPs. Once you've practiced this enough, it'll become second nature to recognize where the nouns are, much like it's second nature to a baby acquiring English.

list of terms/concepts

adjective

binary branching

branch (left branch; right branch; branching node)

creativity

curly brackets

definite article

demonstrative

determiner

dominance (immediate dominance; dominate)

embed

generalization (generalize; general)

generative

head

indefinite article

infinity

Kleene Star

linear order

modification (modifier; modify)

node (branching node; terminal node; nonterminal node; root node)

nominative case

noun (common noun; proper noun)

NP constituent

obligatory

optional

parentheses

phrase

plural

possessive NP (PossNP)

preposition (prepositional phrase)

pronoun (possessive pronoun)

quantifier

recursion (recursive)

structural ambiguity

subject

subject position

subject pronoun

3 The Subject's Better Half: The Verb Phrase

expected outcomes for this chapter

- You'll learn to recognize verbs and verb phrases.
- You'll now recognize that NPs can be both subjects and objects.
- You'll become more adept at manipulating structurally ambiguous sentences.
- You'll begin to recognize and manipulate greater subtleties of hierarchical structure, and develop more confidence with the concepts from Chapters 1 and 2.
- You'll become familiar with the following terms (see items in bold and term boxes): *verb, intransitive, transitive, ditransitive, direct object, indirect object, complement, grammatical function, PP attachment, constituency test.*

3.1 parts of the *verb phrase* we already know about

By now you're ready to discover more about the VP, beyond the unstructured triangle we've been using for the last two chapters:

(1)

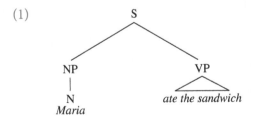

Understanding Sentence Structure: An Introduction to English Syntax, First Edition.
Christina Tortora.
© 2018 John Wiley & Sons, Inc. Published 2018 by John Wiley & Sons, Inc.

In this chapter, we'll "unpack" that triangle, which has until now been a place-holder, obscuring the internal structure of this phrase.

Let's begin by summarizing the phrase structure rules we discovered in Chapters 1 and 2:

(2) Summary of phrase structure rules used thus far (from Chapters 1 and 2):

$$S \rightarrow NP\ VP$$

$$NP \rightarrow \begin{Bmatrix} (det) \\ (PossNP) \end{Bmatrix} (adj^*)\ \mathbf{N}\ (PP^*)$$

$$PossNP \rightarrow \begin{Bmatrix} (det) \\ (PossNP) \end{Bmatrix} (adj^*)\ \mathbf{PossN}\ (PP^*)$$

$$PP \rightarrow \mathbf{P}\ (NP)$$

There are three fundamental things we now know about phrase structure, which already take us halfway through this chapter. This is of course a bit of an exaggeration, as there's still much to be discussed here, but it's important to take stock of the fact that we've actually developed a number of skills and accumulated a lot of knowledge, which is going to take us a long way.

First, we already know how to map phrase structure trees from phrase structure rules; the mapping of a tree from a rule is a general concept which applies across rules, so we know that the VP rule we end up discovering will be the same kind of "instruction" for building a tree as any other phrase structure rule we've seen. Second, as we already saw in Chapter 2 (Term Box 6), every phrase has a head (putting aside the Sentence itself…), which appears in bold in the phrase structure rules in (2) above. That head is the one obligatory element to the right of the arrow in a phrase structure rule, and it's what gives the phrase structure rule its name. So the N heads the NP, the P heads the PP, and the PossN heads the PossNP. It thus follows that, at the very least, the VP has to be headed by an obligatory V:

(3) $VP \rightarrow \mathbf{V}$

Third, as you may have already surmised in considering the many VPs we drew triangle structures for in the previous chapters, VPs can contain NPs and PPs. This means that we already know how to draw trees for any sentences whose VPs contain these phrases. Consider in this regard some of the sentences from our previous exercises. For each underlined VP, let's put the V itself in **bold**; this way, you can try and figure out where the NPs and PPs are in these sentences:

(4) a. The professor **ate** the sandwich.

 b. Her big sister **sang** the song at 3:00.

 c. Many interested students **came** to my office.

 d. She **sang** the song at 3:00 in the cafeteria.

 e. The professor of linguistics **knows** the dog with the stick.

 f. The professor **ate**.

EXERCISE [1]

For each sentence in (4), state what you think the NP(s) and PP(s) are within each VP. Hint: the words *at, in, with, to, on, of, for, from*, and *through* are prepositions. Since you know that a P heads a PP, then, the presence of a P should signal to you that there's a PP in the structure!

3.2 building up the VP

If you did Exercise [1] the way I did, you would have come up with the following breakdowns for each VP:

(5) a. V NP   (NP = *the sandwich*)

   b. V NP PP   (NP = *the song*; PP = *at 3:00*)

   c. V PP   (PP = *to my office*)

   d. V NP PP PP   (NP = *the song*; PP = *at 3:00*; PP = *in the cafeteria*)

   e. V NP PP   (NP = *the dog*; PP = *with the stick*)

   f. V

The sentence in (4f)/(5f), which has a VP that only contains a V, tells us that none of the phrases in (5a–e) are obligatory. It follows that our (preliminary) VP phrase structure rule should be as follows:

(6)   VP   →   V (NP) (PP*)

Just a few comments before we continue. First, recall from our discussion of the Kleene Star in Chapter 2 that the asterisk superscripted on the PP means that more than one PP is possible within the VP. This is evidenced by the sentence in (4d/5d). Also, you should by now be familiar with the parentheses notation, which tells us that anything inside parentheses is optional. And finally, note that you already had plenty of practice with the NP and PP phrase structure rules in Chapter 2, so there is no need to comment on them any further here. (If you feel you need to review NP and PP, go back to Chapter 2.)

EXERCISE [2]

Given the VP rule in (6), draw tree structures for the sentences in (4a–f) and also for the following sentences:

{1} The overworked student put the book on the table.
{2} Some students brought their books to class.
{3} The professor gave her book to the hard-working student.
{4} No students went to the professor's office.
{5} The professor of linguistics with brown hair arrived at the station at 5:00.
{6} They exited the auditorium through the back door at the end of the lecture.

Note that there is no longer any reason to obscure any structure here with the triangle we used earlier. Given the work we did in Chapter 2, you can draw the entire sentence tree, with both subject NP and VP fully structurally articulated.

Term Box 1

In Chapter 2, we defined a subject as the left-branch constituent immediately dominated by the S node. All of our subjects thus far have been NPs, but as we saw — by virtue of introducing the PP in Chapter 2 — not all NPs are subjects.

The NP that is immediately dominated by the VP is called the object.

The terms "object" and "subject" refer to what are often called grammatical functions inside the sentence. Thus, the internal structure of an NP is always going to follow the NP phrase structure rule. However, depending on where the NP is inside the sentence, it has a different grammatical function.

Note that the NP which is immediately dominated by the PP is called the object of the preposition. As we will see in this chapter, there are different kinds of objects. In this term box, we have already noted two types. See Section 3.4.

Now that you've done Exercise [2], let's see what a VP tree looks like; this tree structure is for the sentence in {6} in Exercise [2]:

(7)

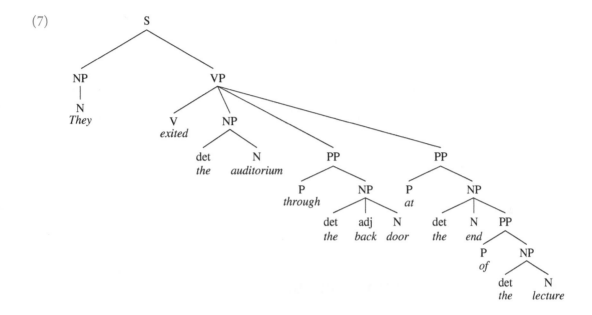

Side Note 1: So what's a verb?

We haven't actually defined what a **verb** is, but at this point you're actually in a position to start using the tools at your disposal, to try and figure it out on your own; you can do this without worrying about an actual definition of the word "verb."

As we did in Chapter 2 for the noun (see Side Note 5), you can work forwards from Exercise 3 in Chapter 1: start analyzing the sentences given by using your intuitions, to divide the sentence into its two major parts, NP and VP. Then, just focusing on the VP (i.e. the right-branch constituent immediately dominated by the S node), limit yourself to considering only those VPs that contain an NP. Once you've identified the NP, then it follows that the only word preceding the NP must be a verb (i.e. a V).

Of course, a much simpler tree would be the one for (4f), while the sentence in (4a) has a VP that is slightly more complex:

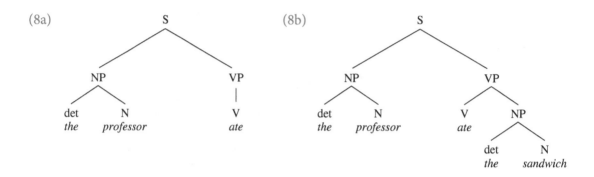

(8a)

(8b)

3.3 revisiting structural ambiguity from Chapter 1

With the VP phrase structure rule in (6) in place, we're now in a position to draw the tree structures for the **structurally ambiguous** sentences from Exercise [2] in Chapter 1, which we can repeat here as Exercise [3].

Before you do Exercise [3], though, you might find it useful to revisit our discussion in Section 2.3.4, on modification, and in particular, Exercise [12]. Recall that a PP "branches off of" (or, "attaches to") the constituent that we, as speakers, intend it to modify. We saw this for the ambiguous NP *the woman with the truck from Brooklyn* in Chapter 2, but recall as well that in Chapter 1, we saw this was also the case for the string of words in (9):

(9)   Sue poked the dog with the stick.

As we discussed in that chapter, in this particular sentence, speakers imagine two possible meanings: either *the dog* has the stick or *Sue* used the stick to poke the dog. The different meanings arise for reasons similar to those we saw in Exercise [12] in Chapter 2, given the way **modification** works. In the case of (9), however, the structural ambiguity arises because of the fact that a VP optionally contains a PP, as we saw in (6). Thus, we have two possibilities for the placement of the PP *with the stick*. Let's look at the two possibilities in detail here.

First, if we take this PP to be immediately dominated by the VP (or, "attached to" the VP), we get the following structure:

(10a)

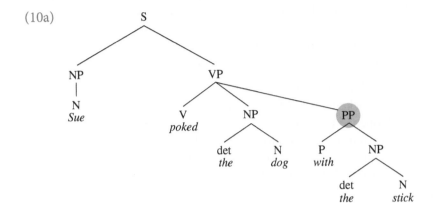

This structure captures the fact that the PP *with the stick* modifies the V *poke*; in other words, the structure in (10a) reflects the meaning where the poking is done with the stick.

In contrast, if we take the PP to modify the N *dog*, then the PP will be immediately dominated by the NP headed by *dog*, as in the following structure:

(10b)

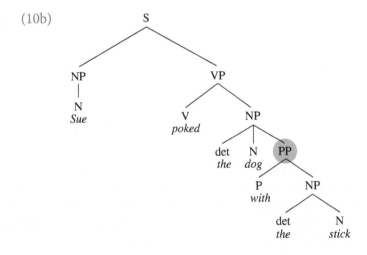

This structure, which has the PP *with the stick* attached to the NP, captures the fact that the PP modifies the N *dog*. This tree thus reflects the meaning where *the dog* has the stick.

EXERCISE [3]

As I did in (10a) and (10b), provide the two different structures for each sentence in this exercise, and for each distinct structure you provide, state which meaning it corresponds to. Note that the meaning you give must be an **unambiguous paraphrase** of the structure you provided.

{1} Steve shot the man with the gun.
{2} Sue attacked the piñata with the ax.
{3} Bill opened the door with the key.
{4} Lisa fixed the refrigerator in the kitchen.
{5} Bob ate the ice cream from the freezer.
{6} Jane painted the tile on the roof.

EXERCISE [4]

For each tree you drew in Exercise [3], state whether the PP is immediately dominated by the VP or by the NP.

If the PP is immediately dominated by the VP, does it form a constituent with the NP? In contrast, if the PP is immediately dominated by the NP, does it form a constituent with the NP?

3.4 VPs with double objects

There are a couple of other possibilities for constituents inside the VP that we should explore, before turning to the more theoretical question of <u>proving</u> that modification works the way we claimed it did in our above discussion of structural ambiguity (which we'll do in Section 3.6). In this section we'll look at double objects, and in Section 3.5 we'll look at adjectives.

Let's take a second look at sentence {3} in Exercise [2].

(11)   The professor gave her book to the hard-working student.

If you drew the tree for that sentence the way that I did, this is what you came up with:

(12)

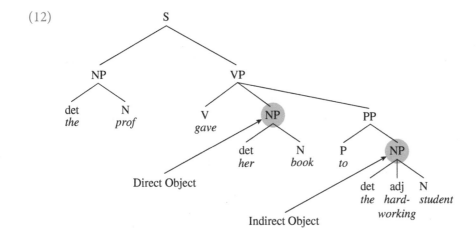

Side Note 2: PP in (12)?

Hopefully it is clear by now why the PP in (12) is not attached to the NP headed by the N *book*. If you think about the meaning, *the hard-working student* is a participant in the act of giving. In Section 3.6, we'll see independent evidence that the PP does not modify the NP.

I've circled the NPs *her book* and *the hard-working student* because I'd like you to focus on them in the following discussion about the structure in (12), and its meaning.

Note that the verb *give* (and the many verbs like it) has a particular meaning that gets reflected in the number and type syntactic constituents that appear in its VP. In particular, this verb's meaning entails (a) that something is given, and (b) that there is a recipient of the thing given. In the structure in (12), the thing that is given, namely, *her book*, is expressed as the **object** (see Term Box 1). In contrast, the recipient of the given thing, namely, *the hard-working student*, is expressed as an object of the preposition *to*. In traditional grammar, this "recipient" (or sometimes, "goal") is called the **indirect object**.

It turns out, however, that the verb *give* (and many verbs like it) allow for an alternative way of syntactically expressing the direct and indirect objects; this can be seen in (13):

(13)   The professor gave the hard-working student her book.

The sentence in (13) certainly does seem to mean the same thing as the sentence in (11). What's different is the structure: in (13), the indirect object NP *the hard-working student* is no longer inside a PP headed by *to*; further-more, it's to the left of the object, as seen in (14):

(14)

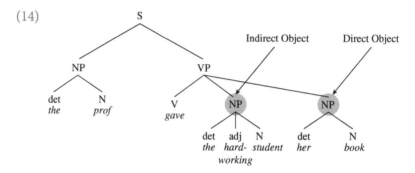

The structure in (13)/(14) is sometimes called the **double-object construction**. Both the **direct object** and the **indirect object** are expressed as NP objects, i.e. NPs which are immediately dominated by the VP.

We must therefore revise our phrase structure rule in (6) to include this possibility:

(15)   **V** → **V** (NP) (NP) (PP*)

The two NPs in (15) are meant to capture the possibility of the double-object construction.

EXERCISE [5]

Draw trees for the following sentences:

{1} John sent a letter to his friend.
{2} John sent his friend a letter.
{3} Bill cooked a nice dinner for Joe.
{4} Bill cooked Joe a nice dinner.
{5} That woman wrote a poem for her sister.
{6} That woman wrote her sister a poem.
{7} Those students lent their book to him.
{8} Those students lent him their book.
{9} Those students gave her homework to the professor.
{10} Those students gave the professor her homework.
{11} They gave her homework to her.
{12} They gave her her homework.

3.5 VPs with adjectives

Our phrase structure rule in (15) is going to require another revision, on account of some VP types that we actually already saw in the exercise sentences in Chapter 2. Consider in this regard the following example:

(16)   It is useless.

This is the tree you would have come up with for this sentence:

(17)

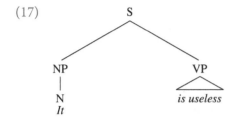

Now let's deduce how to draw the tree structure for the VP in (17). First, we know that a VP must contain at least a V. So since there are only two words in this VP, it follows that one of them must be a V. Furthermore, we saw from the phrase structure rule in (15) that the V is the first element in the VP. So between the words *is* and *useless*, it logically follows that *is* is the V. The final question is, what is *useless*? I'll just give that part away: it's an adjective.

It follows that the fully articulated tree structure for (17) is as follows:

(18)

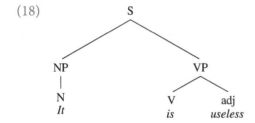

3.5.1 a brief word on the adjective

Now, before we revise the VP phrase structure rule, let's take this opportunity to just say a little more about the structure of the **adjective** itself.

Thus far, we've been treating the adjective as if it is not itself a phrase. Every adjective we've seen until now has been simply given the label *adj*, much as we give determiners the label *det*. That is, we've been treating it as if it's a terminal node (= nonphrasal). If it were truly nonphrasal, however, then it would be the only constituent inside VP that is a terminal element:

VP phrase structure rule containing an adjective (TO BE IMMEDIATELY REVISED in Section 3.5.2):

(19)   VP → **V** (NP) (NP) (adj) (PP*)

Given that all the other constituents inside VP are phrasal, it makes one wonder why the adjective would be any different. As it turns out, there's every reason to consider an adjective to be a phrase. In particular, the following sentences show that adjectives themselves can be modified:

(20) This car is <u>quite useless</u>.

(21) Those students seem <u>very happy</u>.

(22) Those professors are <u>totally angry</u>.

The words *quite*, *very*, and *totally* in (20) through (22) above are called **degree modifiers**. They modify adjectives by expressing the degree of the **property** denoted by the adjective. So, someone can be *happy*, but of course, we can also express the degree of the person's happiness. Here are some degree modifiers:

(23) Degree modifiers: *quite, very, totally, somewhat, extremely, really, too, completely, absolutely*

Thus, a person can be *quite happy* or *very happy* or *really happy* or even *totally* or *completely happy*, or perhaps only *somewhat happy*; there is even such a thing as being *too happy*!

Given the fact that adjectives can be modified by degree modifiers, we must recognize that the adjective itself heads an adjectival phrase (AP), as follows:

(24) AP phrase structure rule:

AP   →   (deg) A

Thus, an AP like *quite useless* would be mapped into a phrase structure tree as follows:

(25)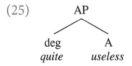

It follows that the tree for the sentence in (20) is as follows:

(26)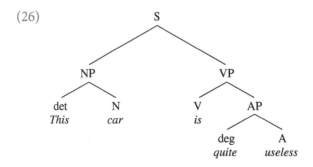

Side Note 3: AP within NP?

Of course, what all of this means is that the NP phrase structure rule must now be revised to take into account this new discovery regarding adjectives:

Old NP rule:

$$NP \rightarrow \left\{ \begin{array}{l} (det) \\ (PossNP) \end{array} \right\} (adj^*)\ N\ (PP^*)$$

New NP rule:

$$NP \rightarrow \left\{ \begin{array}{l} (det) \\ (PossNP) \end{array} \right\} (AP^*)\ N\ (PP^*)$$

EXERCISE [6]

Given Side Note 3, draw a tree for the following NPs:

{1} *That very big car*
{2} *Five extremely happy students*
{3} *My totally wimpy friend*

And it further follows that the tree in (18) should be revised as in (27):

(27)

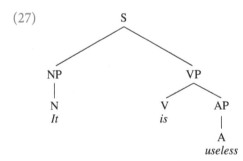

3.5.2 back to the VP

With our digression about the AP out of the way, let's get back to what (16) reveals about the VP phrase structure rule.

The fact that the VP can immediately dominate an AP tells us that we must revise our VP phrase structure rule as follows:

(28)   VP   →   **V** (NP) (NP) (AP) (PP*)

Note that an AP that is immediately dominated by the VP is called a **predicative adjective**. It's called that because it's in the **predicate** part of the sentence (see Chapter 1 for discussion of this concept). This contrasts with the AP within NP (see Side Note 3 and Exercise [6]), which is a **modifier** of N:

EXERCISE [7]

Draw trees for the following sentences:

{1} Those students seem very happy.
{2} My mother was extremely uncomfortable.
{3} That ugly car was too expensive.
{4} Bill arrived quite late.
{5} He was mad.
{6} The blacksmith pounded the metal flat.
{7} The gas rose really high.
{8} We painted the barn red.
{9} We painted the car in the backyard red.
{10} We painted the car red in the backyard.

3.6 constituency test

I'd like to turn now to the question of independent evidence for the **constituent structures** which I've been arguing for.

Recall that in our discussion of modification, I argued that a modifier must be attached to the phrase of the head it modifies. For example, for the string of words in (9), I claimed that the PP *with the stick* should be immediately dominated by the VP headed by *poked* when it modifies this verb (as in (10a)). Similarly, I claimed that the same PP should be immediately dominated by the NP headed by *dog* when it modifies this noun (as in (10b)). This amounts to the claim that each attachment site corresponds to a different meaning.

It's important here to understand that this claim is substantiated by independent evidence; let's look at that evidence here. We'll start by taking a look at the tree structure for {8} in Exercise [7]:

(29)

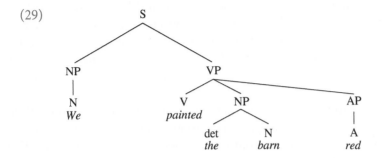

What prompted me to draw the tree this way? Well, there are three clues that tell us the AP is immediately dominated by the VP (and not by the NP headed by the N *barn*). First, if we look at the NP phrase structure rule, we see that the N is not followed by an AP within NP. Thus, the NP headed by the N *barn* in (26) could <u>not</u> have been a possible tree for the NP object:

INCORRECT TREE:

(30)

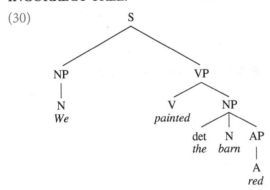

Second, and more importantly, if we pick apart the meaning of this sentence, we understand that the AP *red* expresses a **result** of the act of *painting the barn*, such that the barn was not necessarily red before the painting began. In other words, we take this sentence to mean that (a) there was an event; (b) that event was a painting-of-the-barn event; and (c) the result of that event was that *the barn ended up being red*. Here it is important to note that the entity referred to by the NP *the barn* was, at some point before the painting was finished, not (necessarily) red. Therefore, *red* cannot be considered as a modifier of *the barn*. For this reason, APs (such as *red*) in the structural position in (29) are known as **resultatives**.

3.6.1 third clue

Most importantly, however, there is a third clue which tells us that the AP *red* is not part of the NP headed by *barn*. We have not yet discussed this kind of clue, which, as we will see, clinches the deal. Specifically, it turns out that as speakers of a human language, we have unconscious knowledge of certain rules; these rules perform "operations" on structures, transforming structures such as that in (29) into related (but different structures). These operations are highly sensitive to syntactic structure: in particular, they only operate on constituents.

Let's consider in this regard one such operation, known as **passivization**. Passivization is an operation (or a **transformation**, as it has also been known in the syntax literature), which transforms a sentence such as that in (31a) into a sentence such as that in (31b):

(31) a. John devoured the cake.   ACTIVE
      b. The cake was devoured by John.   PASSIVE

As can be seen, the sentence in (31a) is known as an **active** sentence, while the sentence in (31b) is known as a **passive** sentence. Essentially, the passivization operation on an active sentence does the following:

> ## Term Box 2: Active vs. passive voice
>
> In Section 9.3.4 we'll discuss the difference between active and passive voice in more details. For now, just consider the difference between (31a) and (31b), which gives you an idea of the difference.

Passivization (operation on an active sentence):

a. Starts with an active sentence, and …
b. Removes the original subject from subject position; then …
c. Makes the original object the new subject; then …
d. Gives the verb "passive morphology" (don't worry right now about what this means); then …
e. Puts the original subject in a *by*-phrase, and attaches this *by*-phrase to the VP

To see how this works, let's consider the active sentence in (31a), and how the passivization steps in (a–e) would play out with this example. In the following demonstration, the underlining indicates the eliminated subject, the **bold text** indicates the original object, and anything between two "pipe" symbols (i.e. | ... |) indicates an intermediate stage in the process, leading to the final passive outcome in (e):

(a) <u>John</u> devoured **the cake.**

(b) | ___ devoured **the cake** | >

(c) | **The cake** devoured | >

(d) | **The cake** was devoured | >

(e) **The cake** was devoured by <u>John</u>

What is of utmost importance here is the fact that the passivization operation targets the object, "promoting" it, as it were, to subject position. We can see this depicted in the following two trees:

BEFORE (ACTIVE):   AFTER (PASSIVE):

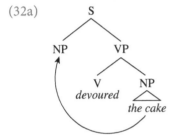
(32a)

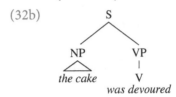
(32b)

Side Note 4:

Let's not worry right now about how to draw a tree with two verbs, like *was devoured.* We'll go over that in detail in Chapter 10. In Chapter 9 we'll cover the concept of passive morphology.

This fact about the passivization operation is directly relevant to our claim regarding the sentence *We painted the barn red,* which I'll repeat here:

(33)   We painted the barn red.

Specifically, recall the claim, represented in the tree in (29), that the NP *the barn* and the AP *red* do not form a constituent; that is, the AP is not a modifier of the NP, but rather is an AP predicate immediately dominated by the VP node. But how can we prove this claim?

As speakers of English, we can simply use our intuitions to create the passive counterpart of this active sentence in (33). The passive of (33) is:

(34)   <u>The barn</u> was painted red.

The sentence in (34) is derived via the unconscious rules we use to form the passive. Let's go through this step by step, as we did for (31a):

(a)   Start with the active sentence: <u>We</u> painted **the barn** red.

(b)   Remove the original subject: | ___ painted **the barn** red |

(c)   Make the original object the new subject: | **The barn** painted red |

(d)   Give the verb passive morphology (Side Note 4): | **The barn** was painted red |

(e)   Put original subject in *by*-phrase: **The barn** was painted red by <u>us</u>.

What is absolutely important in our proof here is the following: in creating the passive, I'm certain that as English speakers you did not come up with the sentence in (35):

(35)   *<u>The barn red</u> was painted.

Side Note 5: The asterisk

It is tradition in Linguistics to use an asterisk notation to the left of a sentence, to indicate that the sentence is not generated by the grammar.

What this proves is that you understand the object in the active sentence in (33) to be *the barn*, as depicted in the tree in (29). In other words, you do <u>not</u> understand the object of the sentence in (33) to be *the barn red*, as incorrectly depicted in the tree in (30).

Put differently: we can think of the tree structure in (30) as a hypothesis for the sentence in (33). Under this hypothesis in (30), the string of words *the barn red* is the NP object of the sentence. However, if this is the NP object of the sentence, then we predict the sentence in (35) to be the correct passive of the sentence in (33). However, given that (35) is in fact not the passive of the sentence in (33), we must conclude that the tree in (30) cannot be correct. That is, the string of words *the barn red* must not be the NP object. Indeed, the correct passive in (34) in fact confirms that the hypothesized structure in (29) — namely, the one in which *the barn* does <u>not</u> form a constituent with the AP *red* — must be the correct one.

EXERCISE [8]

For each of the structures you drew for the sentences in {1} through {6} in Exercise [3], state what the passive sentence would be (no need to draw passive trees).

For example, you drew two structures for the sentence in {1} *Steve shot the man with the gun*, each with a different meaning.

{1a} The passive of one structure is:

The man with the gun was shot (by Steve).

Note that in {1a} this is consistent with the fact that *the man with the gun* is a constituent in the active tree.

{1b} The passive of the other structure is:

The man was shot with the gun (by Steve).

In {1b} this is consistent with the fact that *the man* is a constituent in the active tree (while *the man with the gun* is not).

3.6.2 in conclusion: the test as independent evidence for the constituent structures argued for

In Exercise [8], you used the passivization rule to transform each of the two hypothesized active structures (for each sentence in {1} through {6}) into passive sentences. Let's summarize the results of this constituency test you performed by referring back to the two structures we hypothesized for the sentence *Sue poked the dog with the stick*. We'll start with the structure in (10a), repeated here as (36):

(36)

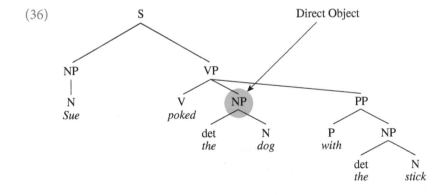

Recall our claim that this structure captures the fact that the PP *with the stick* modifies the V *poke*; in other words, the structure in (36) is claimed to reflect the meaning where the poking is done with the stick. Here, the N *dog* is <u>not</u> modified by the PP. If this is true, then a passivization of this structure, which would target the NP *the dog* as the direct object, should yield the expected meaning unambiguously; the following passive in (36') shows that our expectations are met:

(36')   **The dog** was poked with the stick (by Sue).

In contrast, now, let's look at the structure in (10b), repeated here as (37):

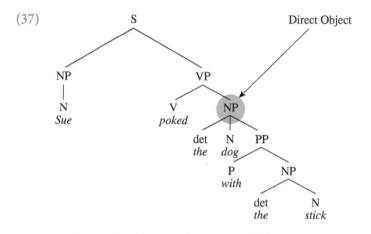

We claimed that this structure captures the fact that the PP *with the stick* modifies the N *dog*. Here, the N *dog* is indeed modified by the PP. Of course, if this is true, then a passivization of this structure, which would target the NP *the dog with the stick* as the direct object, should yield the expected meaning unambiguously; the following passive in (37') shows that our expectations are again met:

(37')   **The dog with the stick** was poked (by Sue).

In conclusion, then, the "passivization test" proves that the different constituent structures we proposed, each one corresponding to a distinct meaning, are in fact correct.

3.7 conclusions

Let's review the VP and AP phrase structure rules we came up with in this chapter.

Summary of revised phrase structure rules:

(38)   S   →   NP VP

NP   → $\left\{\begin{array}{c}\text{(det)}\\\text{(PossNP)}\end{array}\right\}$ (AP*) N (PP*)

PossNP → $\left\{\begin{array}{c}\text{(det)}\\\text{(PossNP)}\end{array}\right\}$ (AP*) PossN (PP*)

VP   →   **V (NP) (NP) (AP) (PP*)**

PP   →   P (NP)

AP   →   **(deg) A**

This chapter's investigation into the structure of the VP gave us a number of opportunities to deepen our knowledge of English syntax. First, we got a much more finely grained understanding of how to analyze the kind of structural ambiguity we first saw in Exercise [2] from Chapter 1. This helped deepen our understanding of the structural representation of modification and the concepts of hierarchical structure and constituent structure. This in turn led us to an introduction to the constituency test, i.e. a methodology for determining which strings of words form constituents and which do not. Here we used the passivization operation as a test for constituency; in Chapter 4 we'll learn about another kind of constituency test (namely, the cleft test), and in Chapter 10 we'll learn more about passivization.

As for the kinds of constituents that can occur within VP, we saw that in addition to PPs, the VP can contain more than one object, namely a direct object and an indirect object. Both kinds of objects can exist in either an NP > PP configuration (where the order is direct object > indirect object), or in an NP > NP configuration (where the order is indirect object > direct object). In addition to these objects (which are selected by the verb — a concept we will examin in depth in Chapter 5), our investigation revealed that VP can also immediately dominate an AP. This AP can either be predicative (as in *My car is **useless***), or it can be a resultative phrase (as in *She painted my car **red***). Our brief foray into adjectives immediately dominated by VP led us to refine our understanding of the lexical category "A" as a head of its own AP.

As with Chapter 2, I avoided giving a definition of verb, preferring instead to get you accustomed to the idea that you can use structural clues to deduce where the verb is in a sentence. But as with the noun in Chapter 2, we have to be careful to avoid circular definitions like "a verb is the head of a verb phrase, and a verb phrase is a phrase headed by a verb." Again, here, language learners use a combination of structural, morphological, and semantic cues to determine which words are verbs. In Chapters 8, 9, and 10 we'll get a better sense of the morphological cues that allow language learners to categorize certain words as verbs. My contention is that once you finish this book, it'll become second nature to recognize where the verbs are, much like it's second nature to a baby acquiring English.

list of terms/concepts

active voice (versus passive
   voice)
adjective (AP)
complement
constituency test
constituent structure
degree modifier
direct object

ditransitive
double-object construction
grammatical function
indirect object
intransitive
modification (modifier)
object (object of the verb; object of a
   preposition)

passive voice   structural ambiguity
passivization operation   subject
predicate (predicative)   transformation
predicative adjective   transitive
property   unambiguous paraphrase
result (resultative)   verb

4

Up Close and Personal with the Prepositional Phrase

---

expected outcomes for this chapter

- You'll learn to recognize different types of prepositions and prepositional phrases.
- You'll begin to manipulate greater subtleties of hierarchical structure.
- You'll develop even more confidence with concepts from previous chapters, such as *constituent, constituency test, structural ambiguity*.
- You'll become familiar with the following terms (see items in bold and term boxes): *functional preposition, locative preposition, lexical category, particle, verb–particle construction, prepositional modifier*.

4.1 aspects of the *prepositional phrase* we already know about

At this point, you've already seen PPs inside both the NP and the VP, as in (1). In this example, the PP *from my class* modifies the N *students*, and the PP *into my office* specifies the location-goal of the students' walking:

Understanding Sentence Structure: An Introduction to English Syntax, First Edition.
Christina Tortora.
© 2018 John Wiley & Sons, Inc. Published 2018 by John Wiley & Sons, Inc.

(1)

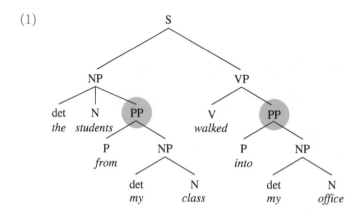

The PPs in (1) reflect the following phrase structure rule that we've been using until now:

(2)   P   →   P (NP)

Given our knowledge of how to read phrase structure rules, we know that this "instruction" means that PP expands into an obligatory P (namely, the head), and an optional NP. This is illustrated in (1), and we've already seen this many times in Chapters 2 and 3.

Two questions which arise at this point are: (i) How do we know what a preposition is? and, (ii) If the NP in (2) is optional, why have we only seen examples of PPs that expand into P <u>and</u> NP? Are there any PPs that have no NP, as in (3)?

(3)   PP
      |
      P
      in

In this chapter, we'll address both of these questions, and more.

Regarding the first question: until now, we've been basing our ability to pick out PPs on the simple "brute force" approach of just providing a list of prepositions. Thus far, we've looked at a limited number of prepositions.

(4)   Prepositions used thus far: *of, with, in, into, on, to, at, from, through, down, over, for, about*

      Examples: The people i<u>n</u> this country eat their lunch too early.

                  The students <u>of</u> linguistics <u>with</u> the highest grades came <u>to</u> my office.

                  Those ferocious dogs <u>at</u> the kennel got <u>into</u> a fight.

                  John put the cake <u>on</u> the table

                  The woman <u>with</u> the truck <u>from</u> Brooklyn fixed my fence.

The students exited the auditorium <u>through</u> the back door.

The police closed the store <u>down</u> the street.

He sent me his homework <u>over</u> e-mail.

The woman bought the car <u>with</u> rust <u>on</u> the fender <u>for</u> a cheap price.

Mary read a book <u>about</u> cavitation.

We used lists like the one in (4) to tell us where to find the Ps — and then, once we found the Ps, we used the phrase structure rule in (2) to build the PPs. In this chapter, we'll consider these and other types of prepositions, and try to get a sense of this particular category, in contrast with Ns, Vs, and As.

For the second question, consider the VP-internal PP in the following sentence, and contrast it with the PP *into my office* in (1):

(5)   The students of Linguistics came in.

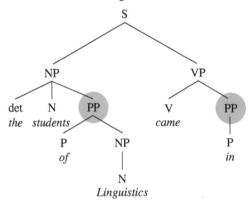

As can be seen in this example, English speakers do indeed allow for PPs with no NP. We'll look at more examples of this type, as well as another possibility still, namely, the PP within the PP!

4.2 it's not just the P and NP anymore!

4.2.1 P with no NP

As just noted in Section 4.1, there's a reason why in the previous chapters we had the NP in parentheses in the phrase structure rule in (2); as we just saw in (5), English allows for many prepositions to appear without an NP **complement**:

(6)   a. John put the blanket <u>on</u>.

       b. Maria walked <u>by</u>.

       c. Sue walked <u>out</u>.

       d. Bill flushed the newspaper <u>down</u>.

Term Box 2: Complement

This is another way of saying **object**. In Chapter 3, we saw that the NPs immediately dominated by the VP are called objects, where **direct object** and **indirect object** were distinguished. We also referred to the NP within PP as the **object of the preposition**. The term **complement** allows us to generalize across types of object, both in terms of where the object is found (VP-internally? PP-internally?), and in terms of what kind of phrase the object is. Until now, we've only seen NP complements (= objects), but in Chapter 5, we'll become familiar with notion of a sentential complement within VP.

EXERCISE [1]

Draw trees for the sentences in (6).

Note that for each of the examples in (6a–d), there is a possible equivalent in which the NP within the PP would be expressed; we can thus think of the PPs in (6a–d) as being the NP-less equivalents of the sentences in (7):

(7)   a. John put the blanket <u>on his back</u>.

       b. Maria walked <u>by our house</u>.

       c. Sue walked <u>out the house</u>.

       d. Bill flushed the newspaper <u>down the toilet</u>.

Side Note 1: Variation across speakers

Is the sentence in (7c) something you would use? It turns out that there is **variation** among English speakers with respect to this structure: some English speakers find it completely acceptable while others prefer the following alternative:

(7c') Sue walked <u>out **of** the house</u>.

This has to do with the fact that different speakers allow for different possibilities, depending on where they're from!
 We'll talk more about the sentence in (7c)/(7c') in a moment.

4.2.2 PP within PP

The example in (7c) raises an important point. As pointed out in Side Note 1, it turns out that not all speakers of English would use the string of words *out the house* here; for these speakers, an extra preposition is required. I'll repeat the variant structures here:

(8) a. Sue walked <u>out the house</u>.
  b. Sue walked <u>out of the house</u>.

The question of when different English speakers require the preposition *of* (and when they don't) is quite interesting; for example, while it's true that some people don't use (8a) (without the preposition *of*), these very same people often find the following — also without *of* — to be completely fine:

(9) Sue walked <u>out the door</u>.

Putting aside the nuances of English-speaker variation here, the fact is, (8b) is possible for many speakers, so our phrase structure has to be able to account for it.
 But now we have a problem: in (8b), we have two prepositions, *out* and *of*. What does this mean? Does this mean that we have two PPs within VP, in the sentence in (8b)? (The answer to arrive shortly is 'No', at least for this example!)
 Sure, we already saw in Chapter 3 that our VP can contain more than one PP; I'll remind you here of the phrase structure rule that encodes this (remember what the Kleene Star means!):

(10) VP → V (NP) (NP) (AP) (PP*)

And we in fact have already seen many examples of a VP node which immediately dominates two PPs; the following was one such example we saw in
Chapter 3:

(11)

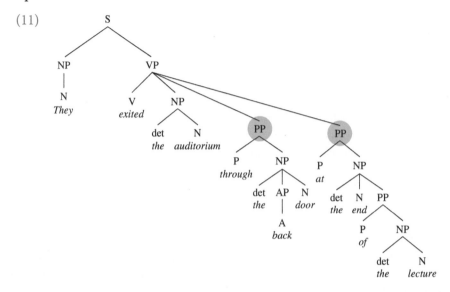

So, let's summarize three things we know:

(i)   A VP can immediately dominate more than one PP,
(ii)   There are two Ps in (8b), *out* and *of* (indicating that there are two
       PPs), and
(iii) A PP doesn't have to contain an NP.

All of the above <u>might</u> make us tempted to think that the correct structure
for (8b) is therefore the following:

INCORRECT TREE:

(12)

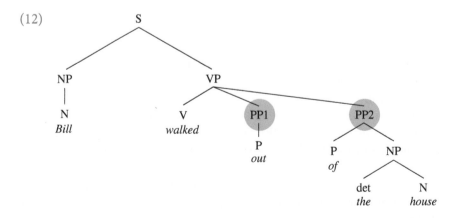

It turns out, however, that there is evidence that the structure in (12) is
not the correct one — <u>at least,</u> not for this particular example. As it turns

out, there are many examples of P + P + NP in English (such as *out of the house* in (8b)), where the correct structure is actually as in (13):

CORRECT TREE:

(13)

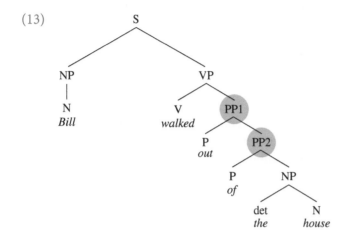

Side Note 2: BEWARE!

We'll see in Section 4.3 that a sequence of two PPs — where the first one has no NP — is in fact possible, IN OTHER CASES! But don't worry: we'll analyze carefully how to distinguish between (i) and (ii):

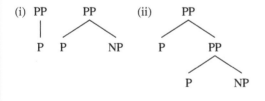

As just noted (see also Side Note 2), we'll soon discuss how we actually know that the PP1 structure in (13) is the correct structure for *out of the house* in (8b). For now, let's just note the following: In the structure in (13), the string of words *out of the house* is represented as a constituent. However, in (12), the string of words *out of the house* is in fact not represented as a constituent. Instead, in (12) this string is broken up into two constituents, namely, *out* (= PP1) and *of the house* (= PP2), where *out of the house* does not all together form a constituent.

The upshot is, we can independently show (with a **constituency test**) that the string of words *out of the house* acts as a single constituent; the discussion will be like the discussion we engaged in in Section 3.6. We will thus be able to support the hypothesis in (13) — namely that PP2 is <u>within</u>

(i.e. immediately dominated by) PP1. This also would mean that the structure in (12) cannot be correct.

Meanwhile, though, let's get back to what the structure in (13) now means for our PP phrase structure rule in (2). If it is indeed possible for a PP to expand into P and PP then we must revise our rule as follows:

Revised PP phrase structure rule:

$$(14) \quad P \rightarrow P \begin{Bmatrix} (NP) \\ (PP) \end{Bmatrix}$$

Recall that the "curly brackets" {...} encode the fact that one or the other item inside these brackets can be chosen, but not both. To summarize, then, this means that there are three possibilities for PP, as follows:

(15a)   PP   (15b)   PP   (15c)   PP
        | ╱╲   ╱╲
        P   P   NP   P   PP

EXERCISE [2]

Draw trees for the following sentences (see (4) above for a list of prepositions; you can add to this list *out, off, inside, outside, up*:

{1} The cat walked out the door.
{2} The cat walked out of the house.
{3} The cat walked out the house.
{4} The cat fell off the bed.
{5} The cat fell off of the bed.
{6} The kite went up.
{7} The boy went up the stairs.
{8} The kite went up into the clouds.
{9} John walked down the street.
{10} John went down into the cellar.
{11} The sound came from inside the house.
{12} The cat ran out into the yard.

4.2.3 evidence for PP within PP

Thus far, all of the P + P + NP sequences we've seen are properly represented by the structure in (15c). Thus, the tree you drew for {11}, for example, should have been follows:

(16)

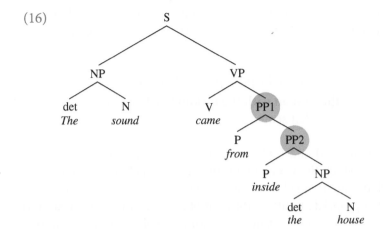

As discussed earlier, you'll notice that the string of words *from inside the house* is represented as a constituent in this tree. The node in the tree representing this constituent is PP1 (as this is the one node that contains all and only the words *from inside the house*). Thus, we can think of the tree in (16) as a kind of "hypothesis" for the sentence; that is, it captures the claim that *from inside the house* should be represented as in (16), and <u>not</u> as in (17):

INCORRECT TREE:

(17)

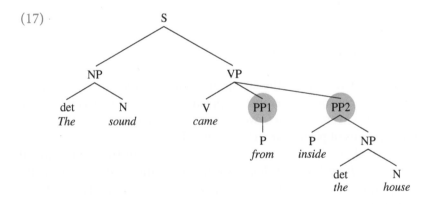

As noted earlier for a similar case (*out of the house*), the tree in (17) does not capture the claim that *from inside the house* is a constituent. Rather, it is an explicit representation of the (incorrect) hypothesis that this string of words does <u>not</u> in fact form a constituent.

But how do we actually prove that *from inside the house* forms a constituent? Much as we did in Section 3.6, we can use a "constituency test," to independently establish the fact. In this case, we cannot use the "passivization" transformation to test this, as this operation only targets NP objects. However, we do have another test at our disposal: the **cleft test**.

What's the cleft test? Well, in order to understand what the cleft test is, it would be helpful to know what a **cleft sentence** is. Consider the sentences in (18):

(18)   a.   The woman with the pickup truck fixed the fence.

      b.   It was **the woman with the pickup truck** that fixed the fence.   cleft sentence

The sentences in (18a) and (18b) mean the same thing: there was a fence-fixing event, in which the woman with the pickup truck was the fixer of the fence. The cleft sentence in (18b), however, has a kind of special status. Unlike (18a), it isn't appropriate to utter (18b) out of the blue; rather, it makes more sense as a kind of response to something someone else said. For example, it could be used in answer to the question *Who fixed the fence?* Or, it could be used as a way to contrast *the woman with the pickup truck* with some other suspected fence-fixer; so imagine (19) as a response to the question "Did you say that <u>John</u> fixed the fence?"

(19)   No, I said <u>it was **the woman with the pickup truck** that fixed the fence</u>.

The important thing to note about cleft sentences such as that in (18b)/(19) is the following: the string of words that appears between the verb *was* and the word *that* is a **constituent**:

Cleft test:

(20)   *It was* [**constituent**] *that....*

So, in the sentence in (19), the string of words *the woman with the pickup truck* must be a constituent because it appears in the "slot" between the words *was* and *that*. Given this fact, we can use cleft sentences to test for the constituent status of particular strings of words.

In this regard, recall our hypothesis, represented in the tree in (16), that the string of words *from inside the house* forms a constituent. If this is true, then this string should be able to appear in the *was* _____ *that* slot (as in (20)), in a cleft sentence.

Let's see if this is true. Imagine you ask me, "Did you say that the sound came from outside the house?" Note that I can answer:

(21)   No, I said *it was* [**from inside the house**] *that the sound came.*

The fact that the sentence in (21) is perfectly well formed proves that the string of words *from inside the house* is a constituent. We know it's a constituent, because it appears happily between the words *was* and *that* in the cleft sentence. Thus, it "passes" the cleft test. This in turn proves that, between the two possible trees presented in (16) and (17), the tree in (17) cannot be correct, as the string of words *from inside the house* is not represented as a constituent.

EXERCISE [3]

For all the <u>PPs immediately dominated by VP</u> in the trees you drew for Exercise [2], see if you can make up cleft sentences that put the PP in question in the "cleft slot" as in (20).
For example:

{2} *It was* [**out of the house**] *that the cat walked.*

4.3 verb–particle constructions

In Sections 4.2.2 and 4.2.3, I spent some time convincing you that the following was the correct structure for the P + P + NP sequences in question (e.g., *from inside the house; out of the house*).

(22)

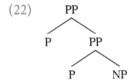

As already alluded to in Side Note 2, however, the preceding discussion shouldn't force us into the conclusion that the following representation for the sequence P + P + NP isn't also possible:

(23)

It turns out that this structural analysis is in fact also possible, even if not for the cases we have analyzed up until now. To see when the analysis in (23) is possible, let's look at **verb–particle constructions**.

What's a verb–particle construction? English is in fact well known for its many **particle verbs**. Let's look at some examples here:

(24)   a. They **ran up** the bill.
       b. I **put out** the candle.
       c. She **threw out** the garbage.
       d. The mayor **shut down** the store.
       e. John **rang up** his friend.
       f. He **turned off** the lights.
       g. The baby **threw up** the formula.
       h. They **ate up** their lunch.

i. He **put up** a fight.

   j. He **turned down** their offer.

   k. They **turned in** their homework.

   l. She **figured out** the solution.

   m. They **blew off** the reading.

   n. She **wrapped up** the chapter.

   o. They **wind down** in the late hours of the night.

   p. I **nodded off** in class.

The few examples in (24) reveal two things: First, particle verbs consist of a verb plus something that looks like a preposition. This preposition, when appearing in constructions like those in (24), is often called a **particle**. As we're just about to see, however, a particle can be analyzed as a PP that contains only a preposition (with no NP or PP object). Second, this verb + particle combination doesn't always yield a meaning that's transparent; that is, the meaning doesn't follow from a composition of the meanings of the verb and the preposition. Compare, for example, the sentence in (24a) with the sentence in (25a):

(24) a. They **ran up** the bill.

(25) a. They ran up the hill.

In (25a), "run up" has a transparent meaning. Here, there is running involved, and the running is going upward. So the meaning of the verb *run* and the meaning of the preposition *up* are both making full contributions to the meaning of the entire sentence. In contrast, in (24a) the verb "run up" has nothing to do with running, and certainly nothing to do with going anywhere, much less going anywhere upward.

Side Note 3: Degrees of idiomaticity

Of course, some particle verbs are more transparent in their meaning than others. Certainly, (24 h) has everything to do with "eating," and in fact, this sentence is almost equivalent in meaning to the sentence *they ate their lunch*; the difference seems to be that in (24 h), it's an absolute certainty that the lunch was finished. The example in (24b) is interesting as it's actually ambiguous between two different meanings: one is "to extinguish" (the flame of the candle); the other is "to place the candle in a location that can be seen." In this case, the second meaning seems to be more transparently related to the notion of "putting," than the first meaning.

Returning to the question of the actual structure of these particle verbs in (24): still comparing (24a) with (25a), we want to be able to distinguish between the string of words *run up the bill* and the string of words *run up the hill*; in the latter, (25a), the P + NP combination seems to form a constituent, while in the former particle construction, (24a), the P + NP string does not seem to form a constituent. This difference actually correlates with a special property that particles have (such as *up* in (24a)): note that a particle, such as *up* in (24a), can be optionally placed after the NP that follows it:

(26)   They ran ___ the bill **up**. (= meaning of (24a))

This ability for a particle to shift (or, "move") to the right of the NP that follows it is a special property of particles in verb–particle constructions. Note that it is only particles that can shift in this way: it's not possible for plain old prepositions that occur with an NP complement. So, as can be seen by the example in (27), this shift is clearly not possible with the preposition *up* in the sentence in (25a):

(27)   *They ran ___ the hill **up**.

Thus, as can be seen by (27), placing *up* after the NP *the hill* leads to disaster.

> ## EXERCISE [4]: Particle shift
>
> For sentences (24a) through (24n), place the particle to the right of the object NP (as I did in (26)). You'll find that there's one example where shifting the particle leads to ungrammaticality. See if you can figure out which one!

Thus, as can be seen by (27), placing *up* after the NP *the hill* leads to disaster.

While the **particle shift** phenomenon allows us to distinguish particles which happen to be followed by NPs, it doesn't allow us to identify particles that are followed by PPs. This is because, for some reason, particles can only shift to the right of following NPs. Note that if we try to shift the particle *off* in (24p) to the right of the PP *in class*, we get a bad result:

(28)   *They nodded ___ in class **off**.

The inability of *off* to shift to the right in (28) does not mean that *off* is not a particle. It just happens to be a particle that's followed by a PP (and not an NP), therefore making particle shift impossible. In these cases, then, how can we be sure we have a particle on our hands?

4.3.1 revisiting the cleft test

Let's see here how we can use our cleft test from our discussion in Section 4.2.3, to determine the difference between verb–particle constructions versus non-particle constructions. To do this, let's first recall our hypothesis that the string of words *up the hill* in (25a) is a constituent. This hypothesis predicts that this string should be possible in the slot between *was* and *that* in the cleft sentence. So let's see if it is: imagine I say "Did you say that they ran up the mountain?" You could answer:

(29)   No, I said *it was* [**up the hill**] *that they ran.*

The fact that it's possible to place *up the hill* in the slot between *was* and *that* in the cleft proves that *up the hill* is a constituent. Thus, the correct structure (unsurprisingly) would be as in (30):

(30)

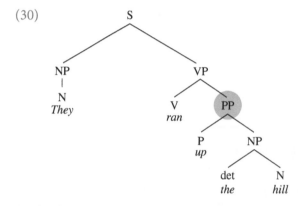

The same however cannot be said for the string of words *up the bill* in (24a). We can again use our cleft test from Section 4.2.3 to show this. The cleft test proves that the string of words *up the bill* in (24a) doesn't form a constituent. That is, this string of words <u>cannot</u> appear in the slot between *was* and *that* in the cleft sentence. So, imagine I say, "Did you say they ran up the tab?" You cannot answer:

(31)   *No, I said *it was* [**up the bill**] *that they ran.*

Side Note 4: *the bill*

You might be thinking right now, "but I can say the following cleft sentence!"

(31') No, I said *it was* [**the bill**] *that they ran up.*

This is perfectly fine, as nothing in this discussion precludes the possibility that the string of words *the bill* is a constituent! See the tree in (32).

The fact that the string of words *up the bill* cannot appear in this slot shows that this string of words is not a constituent. What this means is that the string of words *up the bill* cannot be assigned the structure for PP seen in (30). Our structure must instead capture the fact that *up* is separate from the constituent *the bill*. The following structure does the job (compare this with (30)):

(32)

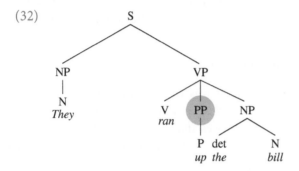

As you can see, in the tree in (32), the string of words *up the bill* is not repre-sented as a constituent — rightly so, since our cleft test in (31) proves that this string of words is <u>not</u> to be represented as such. Rather, the particle (in this case, the PP *up*) is represented as a constituent separate from the NP which follows it. We thus have the following sequence:

(33)

Now that we have introduced the concept of the particle in the verb–particle construction, we can return to our structure in (23), which is reminiscent of the structure in (33):

(23)   PP   PP
         | / \
         P   P   NP

If the structure in (33) is possible (as we just saw in the tree in (32)), then the structure in (23) should also be possible. In fact, this is exactly the correct analysis for the sentence in (24p); here's the tree for that sentence:

(34)

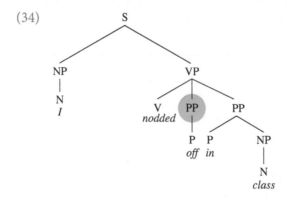

Given that *nod off* is a particle verb, it follows that the particle *off* is to be represented as a PP with no NP complement (as in (23)/(34)). Thus, any PP which follows this particle will be a separate constituent from the PP headed by the particle, as in (34). In other words, the string of words *off in class* in (34) does not form a constituent.

Can we prove this with the cleft test? The answer is Yes. So imagine I ask the question "Did you say they nodded off during the concert?" You cannot answer:

(35)   *No, *it was* **off in class** *that they nodded.*

(Of course, you could answer: "No, *it was* **in class** *that they nodded off*.") The fact that the string of words *off in class* cannot appear in this slot between *was* and *that* in the cleft sentence proves that this string of words is not a constituent. Note that the structure given in (34) correctly represents this fact.

EXERCISE [5]

In the same way I used the cleft test in (35) to prove that *off in class* is not a constituent, use the cleft test to prove that the string of words *down in the late hours of the night* in (24o) does not form a constituent. Likewise, use the cleft test to test the constituent status of all the P + NP strings in (24).

Given the correct structure in (34), we now have to modify our VP phrase structure rule, as we need to allow for the possibility of a particle to precede the NP object. Here is the revised rule:

Revised VP phrase structure rule:

(36)   VP → V (PP) (NP) (NP) (AP) (PP*)

this PP which precedes the NP object is our particle from the verb–particle construction. Note that a particle is a PP which contains only a P (as in (32) and (34)).

EXERCISE [6]

Draw trees for the following sentences:

{1} The baby spit up in the crib.
{2} They ate up their lunch.
{3} They ate their lunch up.
{4} She wrapped it up in three days.

{5} They wind down in the late hours of the night.
{6} She fits in at that school.
{7} He woke up in the morning.
{8} They ate their lunch up in the cafeteria.

4.4 modifiers within PP

Before we conclude, I'd like to make one more important observation about prepositions, which lets us see that at least some of them are a lot more similar to adjectives and nouns than we might think they are, at first glance. This will allow us to say some final words on what prepositions actually are!

Thus far, we've been using the following phrase structure rule for PP:

(37) PP → P $\begin{Bmatrix} (NP) \\ (PP) \end{Bmatrix}$

Side Note 5: Ongoing revisions

I'm sure you've noticed by now that every chapter involves a process of revising the phrase structure rules, as we go along. As you can probably imagine at this point, this is going to continue through to the end of the book. This is where the book serves the second of the two purposes (mentioned in Side Note 9 in Chapter 1), namely, the "how-to" in discovering the ins-and-outs of English sentence structure. Building up the complexity as we go along allows us to piece everything together in a step-by-step fashion (as opposed to becoming overwhelmed by the vast complexity all at once!)

It turns out, however, that much like adjectives, many prepositions can be modified with a spatial or temporal modifier. To draw the analogy with adjectives, let's recall our reason (from Chapter 3) for hypothesizing that adj was not a terminal node by itself, but rather a whole phrase; specifically, as we saw, adjectives can be modified by a degree word (like *quite, very, totally, somewhat, extremely, really, too, completely, absolutely*):

(38) My friend is **totally ecstatic**.

(39) Those professors seem **quite argumentative**.

(40) He baked a **somewhat large** cake.

This is what caused us to hypothesize an entire AP (as opposed to just "adj"); we needed a phrase structure rule that would capture the fact that adjectives seem to head a whole phrase, where the adjective can optionally be modified by a degree modifier (which we abbreviated *deg*):

(41) AP → (deg) A

Thus, we see that an A can have a degree modifier to its left.

Now let's look at the following examples with PPs, which indicate that Ps can also have a modifier of sorts (which I've underlined in (42)):

(42) a. John ran **<u>right</u> up the hill.**
      b. Mary walked **<u>straight</u> to the bookstore.**
      c. The photos were ready **in <u>just</u> under an hour.**
      d. I stood **<u>just</u> to his left.**
      e. They placed the couch **<u>smack</u> in the middle of the living room.**
      f. The baseball flew **<u>clear</u> over the fence.**
      g. That possibility is **<u>flat</u> out of the question.**
      h. He drew the line **<u>plumb</u> down the middle.**
      i. I ate the crackers **<u>right</u> out of the box.**
      j. They came **<u>straight</u> from the station.**
      k. They threw the garbage **<u>right</u> out.**

The words *right, straight, just, smack, clear, flat,* and *plumb* — in these particular contexts — are functioning as modifiers of the prepositions which follow them. Before we say more about these modifiers, let's make this more graphic by taking a look at the structures for (42a) and (42c):

(43a)

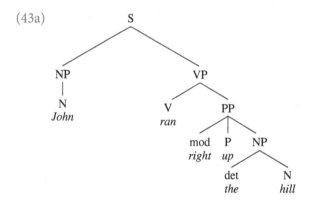

(43b)

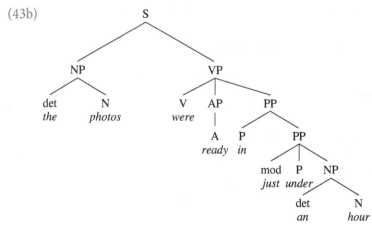

Note that we can confirm that the PPs in (43a) and (43b) are indeed constituents, by using our cleft test from earlier:

(44) a. No, it was **right up the hill** that John ran!

(in answer to: *Did you say John ran down the street?*)

b. No, it was **in just under an hour** that the photos were ready!

(in answer to: *Did you say the photos were ready in two hours?*)

The fact that the underlined string of words can happily appear between *was* and *that* in the cleft sentence tells us that these strings of words are constituents, and that indeed, the structures in (43) must be correct.

The above facts tell us, then, that the following should be the revised phrase structure rule for PP:

(45) PP → (mod) P $\begin{Bmatrix} \text{(NP)} \\ \text{(PP)} \end{Bmatrix}$

EXERCISE [7]

Draw trees for the sentences in (42).

4.4.1 Prepositional modifiers not to be confused with adjectives!

It's important to not confuse the prepositional modifiers in (42) with adjectives. The potential for confusion has to do with the fact that some of our prepositional modifiers can, in a different context, act as adjectives. Consider the examples in (46):

(46) a. [His <u>clear</u> explanation] made the exam easier.
b. His hair is <u>straight</u>.
c. He made [his <u>straight</u> hair] curly.
d. He made [the <u>right</u> decision].
e. His decision was <u>right</u>.

In all of the cases in (46), the underlined word acts as an adjective; in the bracketed NPs in (46a,c,d), the adjective is a modifier within the NP. In (46b,e), the word *right* acts as a predicative adjective. This can be verified by the fact that *right* can be modified by a degree word:

(47)

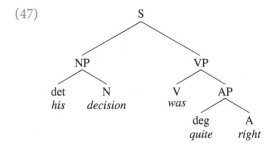

Note that in contrast, in (42a) the word *right* is not functioning as an adjective; we can verify this by showing that in this particular example, where *right* acts as a prepositional modifier, *right* can't be modified by a degree word:

(48)   *John ran **quite right up the hill**.

EXERCISE [8]: (a thought experiment)

Try to think of the differences in meaning between the prepositional modifiers in (42), on the one hand (*right, straight, just, flat*), and the meaning of the adjectives here, on the other:

{1} The coast is **clear**.
{2} His explanation was **clear**.
{3} Her decision was **just**.
{4} The tablecloth was **flat**.
{5} His hair was **straight**.
{6} Her answer was **straight**.

Side Note 6: Ignore the other interpretation

Some of you might be thinking that the sentence in (48) sounds fine; but if it does sound okay to you, I'm sure you're thinking of it with a different interpretation. In the "good" interpretation of the string in (48), we can think of John as running in a *quite right* manner (i.e. he ran *correctly*); in this case, he engaged in this correct manner of running, as he ran up the hill. Under this "good" interpretation, however, we have a completely different structure (which is not the structure we're talking about here!). In this "good" interpretation, *up the hill* is a constituent separate from a constituent *quite right*, as the cleft test shows:

i.   *It was **quite right up the hill** that John ran.
ii. It was **up the hill** that John ran quite right.

The cleft test in (i) shows that the string *quite right up the hill* is not a constituent, under the interpretation we're looking to illustrate in (48).

Indeed, if you think about the meaning of *right* in (42a), versus the adjectival meaning of *right* in (47), we see that in the latter, *right* has the meaning of the synonymous adjective *correct*. In contrast, in (42a), *right* does not have the meaning of "correct." When we say that someone ran *right up the hill*, we're saying that the running-path up the hill was direct, with no deviations from this path. We can see this meaning again in (42i): When you say you're eating crackers *right out of the box*, you're saying that the crackers are going from the box into your mouth, with no deviation from this path; you're not, for example, stopping to put the crackers on a plate (to perhaps put jam or cheese on them).

4.5 lexical vs. functional prepositions

An important thing to note about our prepositional modifiers in (42) is that not all prepositions can be modified by them. Consider, for example, the preposition *of*:

(49) a. He answered both **of** these questions.
     b. I spoke with all **of** the students.
     c. They put the cat outside **of** the house.
     d. They walked out **of** the house.
     e. That's a great book **of** poems.
     f. She bought a book **of** mine.

I'm sure you can see intuitively that *of* is different from the prepositions we see in (42). For one thing, you might have guessed that, unlike the prepositions in (42), it can't be modified by a prepositional modifier:

(50) *He answered both **right of** these questions.

In addition, we see that for many of the above examples, many speakers can do without the preposition *of* altogether; compare in this regard (49a–d) with (51a–d):

(51) a. He answered both __ these questions.
     b. I spoke with all __ the students.
     c. They put the cat outside __ the house.
     d. They walked out __ the house.

Recall our discussion from earlier, regarding *out the house*; this PP without *of* is fine for many speakers. You can compare it with the PP *out the door* (which is fine for many other speakers!)

In sum, there's something about *of* that makes it different. In the linguistics literature, people like to say that *of* is a **functional preposition**. What this means is that it behaves less like a word with rich semantic content, and more like an element that serves a syntactic function. Compare a functional P like *of* with prepositions like those in (52):

(52) Locative prepositions:

     to, from, at, into, in, out, up, down, inside, outside, behind, over, above, below, beside, by, off, beneath

The prepositions in (52) have the label **locative**, because all of these words seem to indicate some kind of location, or location-goal (e.g., *to*), or location-source (e.g., *from*). There are also prepositions which encode **temporal** meaning, like those in (53):

(53)   Temporal prepositions:
      before, after, since

Of course, some locative prepositions can be used temporally, and some temporal prepositions can be used with locative meaning:

(54)   a. John worked **in** his room.   (locative)
        b. John finished his homework **in** an hour.   (temporal)
        c. John did his homework **before** 10:00.   (temporal)
        d. John stood **before** me.   (locative)
        e. John worked **by** my side.   (locative)
        f. John finished **by** 10:00.   (temporal)
      etc.

Despite the fact that many of these prepositions can encode both locative and temporal meanings, the point is, we have a sense that they encode a *meaning* of some sort. This contrasts with *of*, where it's not clear what its meaning is; and notice how removing it from the sentences in (49) (as in (51)) doesn't change the meaning at all, though it does seem to have a function. In (49f), for example, it functions to connect *book* and *mine* (*book of mine*) in some kind of possessive or ownership or authorship relation, giving a meaning like *my book*.

While *of* is thus a functional preposition, we could say that in contrast, the prepositions in (52) and (53), as meaningful locative/temporal prepositions, are lexical. All the word "lexical" means here is that the words have meaning; they're not purely "grammatical" words (see Term Box 1).

Interestingly, the plot thickens, as it turns out that many so-called locative prepositions can also have a purely functional meaning. Consider, for example, the particle *up*, in the following sentences:

(55)   a. He ate **up** his lunch.
        b. He ate his lunch **up**.   (like (55a), only with "particle shift").

Here, the word *up* has no locative meaning. As we noted earlier, in fact, it seems like the only function the particle has, in this context, is to indicate that the lunch is all gone. (This contrasts with the sentence without *up*: *He ate his lunch* doesn't necessarily mean that the lunch was all gone when he stopped eating.) Here, then, *up* is acting as a purely functional preposition.

The same kind of lexical versus functional ambiguity arises with the preposition *at*. The sentence in (56a) shows that it can be used lexically (i.e. to encode a meaning), while the sentence in (56b) shows that it can be used functionally:

(56)   a.   She arrived **at** the station.   (location meaning)
       b.   He worked **at** his dancing.   (functional use)

In (56b), there is no locative meaning of *at*. In contrast with *up* in (55), the preposition *at* here seems to serve the function of indicating that his efforts are ongoing (i.e. over time, he strives to improve his dancing).

In other cases still, we have prepositions which have completely different meanings, depending on the context; consider in this regard *with*:

(57)   a.   That's the man **with** the blue suit.
       b.   The paper was cut **with** the scissors.

In (57a), *with* encodes some kind of possessive meaning (the man **has** a blue suit); in (57b), *with* encodes an instrumental meaning (the scissors are being used as an instrument).

As you can see, then, it's very hard to define preposition, as some preopositions are lexical (i.e. they encode different kinds of meaning, like locational, or temporal, or instrumental), while others are functional (i.e. they only serve to encode some kind of grammatical property, like a possessive relation or a completed event or an ongoing event). What makes it even harder to define them is that many prepositions can be used in different ways, depending on the context.

4.6 English prepositions are not inflected

Unlike nouns and verbs, prepositions can't be inflected. So, a noun like *cat* can be pluralized by adding an inflectional ending -*s* (*cats*). And as we'll see in greater detail in Chapter 8, verbs can also get inflectional endings; for example, a verb like *walk* (*They walk to school every day*) can be turned into a past tense by adding an -*ed* ending (*They walked*). In contrast, there are no inflectional endings to add to prepositions. In some ways, though, prepositions are like verbs, in that they can take objects (or, complements):

(58)

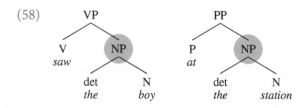

However, in other ways, they're similar to adjectives, inasmuch as they can have modifiers appear to their left within their own phrase:

(59)

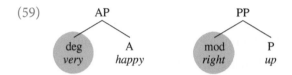

In sum, as English speakers we unconsciously can pick out prepositions as a result of a lot of independent clues, which all point in the direction of an analysis that fits these elements into their place in sentence structure. This can be said both for babies acquiring English and for adult English speakers using their unconscious knowledge of language to form and understand sentences.

4.7 conclusions

First, here's a summary of our latest phrase structure rules (with PP in bold to highlight that this was the phrase we updated in this chapter):

(60)   S   →   NP VP

NP   → $\begin{Bmatrix} \text{(det)} \\ \text{(PossNP)} \end{Bmatrix}$ (AP*) N (PP*)

PossNP   → $\begin{Bmatrix} \text{(det)} \\ \text{(PossNP)} \end{Bmatrix}$ (AP*) PossN (PP*)

VP   →   V (PP) (NP) (NP) (AP) (PP*)

PP   →   **(mod) P** $\begin{Bmatrix} \textbf{(NP)} \\ \textbf{(PP)} \end{Bmatrix}$

AP   →   (deg) A

Our new PP phrase structure rule means that wherever we see the string P + P + NP, there are two possible parses: either (a) we're dealing with a PP headed by a P that takes no object, followed by a PP headed by a P that takes an NP object (as in (23)), or (b) we're dealing with a PP headed by a P that takes another PP as an object (as in (22)). This fact about sequences of P led us to learn about another **constituency test** (namely, the **cleft test**), in order to be able to distinguish between the two cases.

Wherever we have a P that doesn't take a complement, we have a **particle** on our hands. In the VP PS rule in (60), the PP preceding the NP is the particle. Particles themselves provide an important opportunity to test out which string of words within VP is the verb's **object**, given their ability to **shift** to the right of the string of words we parse (as English speakers) as the verb's object (as in (55b)). As such, particle shift itself serves the function of a kind of constituency test (for direct objects).

In contrast with nouns, verbs, and adjectives, prepositions form a **closed class** of items. That is, while it's possible to keep adding new nouns, verbs, and adjectives to the language, this isn't the case with prepositions. They're limited in number compared with Ns, Vs, and As, and the list of prepositions doesn't grow, even if we want it to. Try for yourself to invent a new noun, or a new verb, or a new adjective to your English. Just make something up. You'll see that it won't be that difficult for you to invent a new word for any one of these lexical categories. Now try to invent a new preposition. You'll find that it's quite a challenge!

list of terms/concepts

categories
cleft sentence
cleft test
closed class
complement
constituency test
constituent
degree word
functional category
functional preposition
grammatical words
idiom (idiomatic; idiomaticity)
inflection (inflected; inflectional
    ending)

lexical category
locative preposition
object of a preposition
particle
particle shift
part of speech
preposition (PP)
prepositional modifier
temporal prepositions
variation
verb–particle construction
    (particle verbs)

5

Infinite Wisdom: Sentences Inside the Verb Phrase

expected outcomes for this chapter

- You'll deepen your understanding of the complexity of verb phrases, and will become familiarized with the concept of *selection / subcategorization*.
- You'll manipulate greater subtleties of hierarchical structure.
- You'll become familiar with the following terms (see items in bold and term boxes): *complement clause, embedded clause, complementizer, subordination, subordinating conjunction, selection, optionality / obligatoriness, declarative, interrogative, wh-movement, deep structure, surface structure.*

5.1 aspects of the *verb phrase* we already know about

In Chapter 3, we got a good sense of the kinds of constituents that can appear inside the VP. Let's summarize in (1) some examples which illustrate the variety of possibilities:

(1) a. Mary *read*.   VP → V

       b. Mary *read the newspaper*.   VP → V NP

       c. Mary *handed the newspaper to Sue*.   VP → V NP PP

       d. Mary *handed Sue the newspaper*.   VP → V NP NP

Understanding Sentence Structure: An Introduction to English Syntax, First Edition.
Christina Tortora.
© 2018 John Wiley & Sons, Inc. Published 2018 by John Wiley & Sons, Inc.

e.	Mary *handed Sue the newspaper at 10:00 a.m.*	VP → V NP NP PP
f.	Mary *handed the newspaper to Sue at 10:00 a.m.*	VP → V NP PP PP
g.	Mary *went to the library.*	VP → V PP
h.	Mary *seemed happy.*	VP → V AP
i.	Mary *hammered the metal flat.*	VP → V NP AP
j.	Mary *hammered the metal flat at 10:00 a.m.*	VP → V NP AP PP
k.	Mary *put out the flame with her bare hands.*	VP → V PP NP PP

Given all of the possible VP structures investigated, we decided on the following VP phrase structure rule:

(2) VP   →   V (PP) (NP) (NP) (AP) (PP*)

This rule captures the fact that, within VP, English speakers allow for many different kinds of combinations of NP, PP, and AP, only some of which we see in (1).

Given the way we're building up structure in this book, though, you've surely already guessed that there's more to the VP than our discussion in Chapter 3 let on. In this chapter, we'll continue our discussion of VP by taking a look at the phenomenon of **embedded sentences**.

5.2 building up VP

As it turns out, the VP potentially contains not only NP, PP, and AP; it can also contain another sentence. Here's an example, where the sentence within VP is underlined:

(3)   Mary thinks <u>Sue read the newspaper</u>.

By now you should be able to recognize the subject NP in (3) as *Mary*. That means that the NP–VP split here is as follows:

(4)

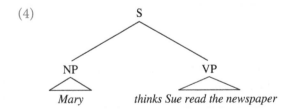

Given what we learned in Chapter 3, you should also now be able to recognize that the word *thinks* is the verb; after all, it's the first word within VP, so given the phrase structure rule in (2), it must be the verb. (See Chapter 3 for more on what makes a verb.)

That said, we have to now identify the nature of the remaining string of words, *Sue read the newspaper*. I'm sure that at this point, you would recognize this string — taken alone — to be a sentence:

(5)   Sue read the newspaper.

Let's take a look at a more articulated version of the tree structure in (4):

(6)

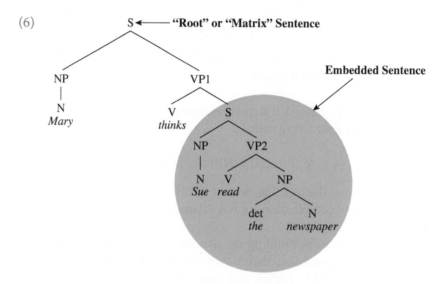

The structure in (6) illustrates in detail the embedded sentence within VP1. Let's temporarily define an embedded sentence as "a sentence that is immediately dominated by a VP." (This will be refined, though, in Chapter 6.) This is in opposition to the notion of a **root sentence** or **matrix sentence**; see Term Box 2.

Term Box 1

Embedded clause, dependent clause, and subordinate clause are all terms equivalent in meaning to "embedded sentence." Clause, by the way, is another word for sentence. I'll use all of these terms interchangeably.

Term Box 2

A **root** or **matrix** sentence (or clause) is a sentence that's <u>not</u> immediately dominated by VP. In fact, it's not dominated by anything.

There are many different verbs which allow for an embedded sentence; here are just a few examples:

(7)   *think, say, claim, prove, believe, assume, realize, know, tell, regret*

In (8), these verbs are in italics, and the sentences that they embed are underlined:

(8) a. Mary *thinks* <u>Sue read the newspaper</u>.
   b. Mary *believes* <u>Sue read the newspaper</u>.
   c. Mary *assumed* <u>Sue read the newspaper</u>.
   d. Mary *realized* <u>Sue read the newspaper</u>.
   e. Mary *knows* <u>Sue read the newspaper</u>.
   f. Mary *told* Bill <u>Sue read the newspaper</u>.

There are many more verbs that allow for an embedded sentence than just those listed in (7); furthermore, embedded sentences come in different types. We'll discuss all of this in Sections 5.3 and 5.4. However, right now let's address the question of the VP phrase structure rule, which has to be modified to account for structures such as that in (6).

5.2.1 revising the VP phrase structure rule

We need to know where the sentence (S) fits into our VP phrase structure rule in (2). In order to better understand where it fits in, let's draw an analogy between the embedded sentences in (8), and the **direct objects** in (9) (which, like the embedded sentences in (8), are also underlined):

(9) a. Mary *devoured* <u>the pizza</u>.
   b. Mary *read* <u>the newspaper</u>.
   c. Mary *saw* <u>that movie</u>.
   d. Mary *painted* <u>the barn</u>.
   e. Mary *wrote* <u>a book</u>.
   f. Mary *gave* Bill <u>the newspaper</u>.

Term Box 3

See Chapter 3 for the concept of **direct object**. Recall too from that chapter that *Bill* in (9f) counts as the **indirect object**.

It'll help you follow the discussion if you draw a tree for one of the sentences in (9) right now. Once you do this, compare your tree with the tree in (6); what you'll see is that there's a structural parallelism between VP1 in (6), on the one hand, and the VP you drew for your sentence in (9), on the other.

   In both cases, let's say that the verb **selects** a particular kind of object, or **complement**. Some verbs, like those in (9), select NP complements. Others, like those in (7)/(8), select S complements.

Term Box 4

As discussed in Term Box 2 in Chapter 4, **complement** is another way of saying **object**; as noted there, the term "complement" allows us to generalize across types of objects, both in terms of where the object is found (VP-internally? PP-internally?) and in terms of what kind of phrase the object is. Here, we see that verbs can **select** either NP complements or S complements.

This just has to do with the nature of the verb itself. Think of the verb as having a kind of "requirement." In fact, when you learned English, you implicitly learned what the requirement of each verb was. For example, as a speaker of English, you implicitly know that the verb *devour* selects an NP, while the verb *think* selects an S. You wouldn't for example use an S complement with the verb *devour*, as in (10a) or an NP complement like *the pizza* with the verb *think*, as in (10b):

(10) a.   *Mary *devoured* <u>Sue read the newspaper</u>.

      b.   *Mary *thinks* <u>the pizza</u>.

The fact that English speakers find both sentences in (10) ungrammatical tells us that the **selectional requirements** of each verb are very particular. In Section 5.2.3, we'll talk about this some more.

Side Note 1: Three types of verb

Not all verbs select an object/complement. The verbs *cry* and *sleep*, for example, can stand by themselves, as in *The baby cried* or *The baby slept*. In addition, as we saw in Chapter 3, some verbs can take two objects, like the verb *give*: *Mary gave <u>Sue the newspaper</u>*. Verbs that don't take any object are called **intransitive verbs**. Verbs that take one object (like the verbs in (9)) are called **transitive verbs**. And finally, verbs that take two objects (like *give*) are called **ditransitive verbs**. See Section 5.2.3 for further comment on this, and on the notion of **selection**.

To summarize: we can think of the underlined sentences in (8) as being like direct objects. So let's treat them like direct objects by putting them in the same place in which we currently have the direct object NP in our VP phrase structure rule in (2). In this way we can capture the fact that, depending on the verb, the "direct object" is either an NP or an S:

(11)   VP → V (PP) (NP) $\left\{ \begin{matrix} (NP) \\ (S) \end{matrix} \right\}$ (AP) (PP*)

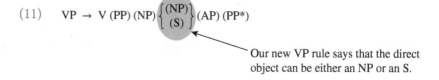

Our new VP rule says that the direct object can be either an NP or an S.

Side Note 2: A curly bracket reminder

Remember that the curly brackets in the phrase structure rules mean that you can pick one or the other item within the brackets (but not both).

Why did I put the optional S in curly brackets together with the <u>second</u> NP in the VP rule (and not the first)? As you might remember from our Chapter 3 discussion of double-object constructions (such as that in (9f) or (12)), it is in fact the second NP — in a string of two object NPs — which is the direct object, not the first. We saw this with example (14) in Chapter 3, which I'm repeating here as example (12), as a reminder:

(12)   The professor gave [the hard-working student] [her book].

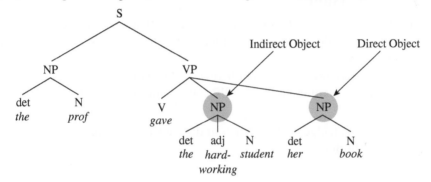

If we look more carefully at the example in (8f), we see that indeed, an embedded sentence is akin to a direct object; (8f) shows that the embedded sentence comes after the indirect NP object *Bill*:

(13)

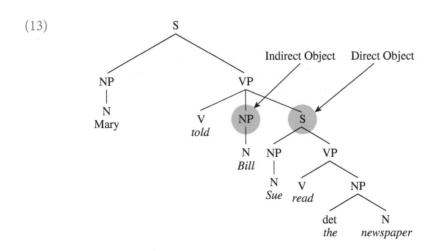

Side Note 3: *give* and *tell*

Why are we claiming that the NP *Bill* is an indirect object, in (13)? The intuition is that *telling something to Bill* is like *giving something to Bill*. See Chapter 3 for a discussion of indirect objects.

EXERCISE [1]

Given the new VP phrase structure rule in (11), draw trees for the sentences in (8).

5.2.2 recursion

In Chapter 2, we talked about **recursion**. Now that we've introduced embedded sentences into our world of sentence structure, recursion has once again become relevant.

Before we see how, let's do a little review from Chapter 2. In that chapter, we saw recursion manifested in NP + PP combinations like the following:

(14)   The fridge in the kitchen in the back of the house with the shutters …

EXERCISE [2]

Refresh your Chapter 2 skills by drawing an NP tree for (14).

Recursion is the possibility of getting a kind of "infinite loop" of phrases; in (14), this infinite loop is possible thanks to the fact that NP and PP can each contain the other. We can illustrate this by giving simplified versions of the NP and PP phrase structure rules in (15):

(15)

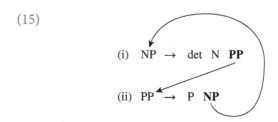

(i)   NP → det N **PP**

(ii) PP → P **NP**

Taken together, the phrase structure rules in (15) say two things: (i) You can embed a PP inside your NP, and (ii) once you have a PP, you can embed an NP inside this PP. And once you have a new NP inside your PP, you once again have the possibility of embedding a PP in this last NP. This looping around and around from NP to PP to NP to PP is what allows us to make our NP longer and longer — in fact, potentially infinitely long.

Now let's go back to our embedded sentences. In particular, let's zero in on the sentence phrase structure rule and the VP phrase structure rule, and let's simplify them for the purposes of illustration, like we did with NP and PP in (15):

(16)

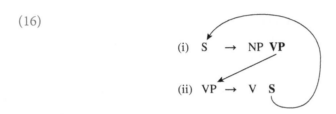

(i) S → NP **VP**

(ii) VP → V **S**

Taken together, the phrase structure rules in (16) say two things: (i) You can embed an S inside your VP, and (ii) once you have another S, you must embed a VP inside this sentence. And once you have a new VP inside your embedded S, you again have the possibility of embedding an S in this last VP. This looping around and around from S to VP to S to VP is what allows us to make our sentences longer and longer. In fact, as with our NP + PP combinations, the VP + S combinations give us the possibility of making an infinitely long sentence, as the result of (16).

We can see this with actual examples, using some of the verbs that we saw in (7):

(17) a. Sue is a great surgeon.
      b. Mary thinks Sue is a great surgeon.
      c. Joe said Mary thinks Sue is a great surgeon.
      d. Sandy claimed Joe said Mary thinks Sue is a great surgeon.
      e. Bill believes Sandy claimed Joe said Mary thinks Sue is a great surgeon.
      f. Janet assumes Bill believes Sandy claimed Joe Said Mary thinks Sue is a great surgeon.

You might think, as I do, that the longer these sentences get, the harder they are to **mentally process**, or to understand. In Section 5.3.1, we'll look more carefully at an alternative way of embedding sentences, which some English speakers claim makes such sentences easier to understand. This other kind of embedded sentence involves the **complementizer** *that*, which in (18) is in **bold type**:

(18) a. Sue is a great surgeon.

b. Mary thinks **that** Sue is a great surgeon.

c. Joe said **that** Mary thinks **that** Sue is a great surgeon.

d. Sandy claimed **that** Joe said **that** Mary thinks **that** Sue is a great surgeon.

e. Bill believes **that** Sandy claimed **that** Joe said **that** Mary thinks **that** Sue is a great surgeon.

f. Janet assumes **that** Bill believes **that** Sandy claimed **that** Joe said **that** Mary thinks **that** Sue is a great surgeon.

The only difference between (17) and (18) is that in the latter, the embedded sentences are preceded by the word *that*. We'll analyze sentences with *that* in Section 5.3.1, which is coming up shortly!

EXERCISE [3]

Draw tree structures for the sentences in (17). For the longer sentences you'll find it easier to turn your paper sideways and plan ahead, because you're going to need a lot of room!

As we said in our Chapter 2 discussion of recursion, it's amazing that a human being — which is finite — has the capacity to take a finite number of words, and a (very) finite set of rules, and combine them to create something theoretically infinite!

5.2.3 more on side note 1: the concept of *selection* and verb *subcategorization*

In Section 5.2.1, we talked about the fact that different verbs **select** different kinds of objects. In Side Note 1, I introduced the terms **intransitive, transitive**, and **ditransitive**, which are meant to capture this idea of **selection**.

Let's get into the details a bit more here. But first, a recap: every verb has a selectional requirement regarding what it "wants" in its VP. Some verbs (like *cry, sleep,* and *dance*) don't select any complements at all; this can be seen by the fact that English speakers are perfectly happy to use such intransitive verbs all by themselves, with nothing following them:

Intransitive Verbs

(19) a. The baby cried.

b. The dog slept.

c. John danced.

Other verbs (like *devour* and *destroy*), by contrast, select a direct object NP:

Transitive Verbs

(20) a. Mary devoured **the pizza**.

      (cf.: **Mary devoured*)

  b. The Romans destroyed **the city**.

      (cf.: **The Romans destroyed*)

Other verbs still (like *give* and *put*; the so-called ditransitive verbs) select two complements, namely, a direct object and an indirect object:

Ditransitive Verbs

(21) a. Mary gave [D.O. **the newspaper**] [to [I.O. **her sister**]]   OR:

  a'. Mary gave [I.O. **her sister**] [D.O. **the newspaper**]

      (cf.: **Mary gave*; **Mary gave the newspaper*)

  b. Mary put [D.O. **the newspaper**] [on [I.O. **the table**]]

      (cf.: **Mary put*; **Mary put the newspaper*)

And as we saw, we have verbs (such as *claim* and *say*) which are "transitive" in the sense that they select a complement; however, this complement must be sentential:

(22) a. Mary claimed **Sue read the newspaper**.

      (cf.: **Mary claimed*)

  b. Mary said **Sue read the newspaper**.

      (cf. **Mary said*).

We even saw a verb — namely, *tell* — which selects a sentential complement much like *claim* and *say* do, but which additionally selects an indirect object (making it analogous to ditransitive *give*):

(23) Mary told [**her brother**] [**Sue read the newspaper**]

  (cf.: **Mary told* **Sue read the newspaper**)

This is the phenomenon of selectional requirements, or subcategorization. What is subcategorization?

  In Chapter 1, we talked about your unconscious knowledge of sentence structure. In a similar way, we can talk about your unconscious knowledge of word meaning, which forms a part of your linguistic knowledge more generally. In order to understand your "knowledge of words," consider the fact that when you learned English, you learned a lot of words — the words that you now know. (In fact, you continue to learn new words throughout your life.) Imagine these words as being in a kind of "mental dictionary," or mental lexicon, as it's sometimes called. For each word entry listed in your mental lexicon, you know at least three things about it:

(i)   how to pronounce the word,
(ii) what the word means (including its lexical category), and
(iii) if its lexical category is verb, its subcategorization.

The verb's subcategorization specifies the number and kinds of complements the verb selects, as in our examples in (19–23) above.

Let's make this concrete by representing the word entries of the verbs *claim* and *destroy* in your mental dictionary as follows:

Mental lexicon:

(24)   word: *claim* (lexical category: Verb)

MEANING: "to assert the truth of something, without necessarily providing evidence"

PRONUNCIATION: /klem/

SUBCATEGORIZATION: a sentential complement

(25)   word: *destroy* (lexical category: Verb)

MEANING: "to end something's existence, through damage or attack"

PRONUNCIATION: /dɪsˈtrɔɪ/

SUBCATEGORIZATION: a direct object NP

It's important to understand that, like sentence structure, this information in (24) and (25) is knowledge which is represented in your mind, not in the world outside of your mind.

The concept of subcategorization will become relevant again, later in this chapter, and then again in our discussion in Chapter 6. For now, though, let's return to the complementizer *that*.

5.3 the complementizer phrase

It's time for us to face a few more complicating facts about embedded sentences in English. In this section we'll introduce the phenomenon of the **complementizer phrase**.

5.3.1 the complementizer *that*

Let's start this discussion by revisiting the sentences in (8). As an English speaker, you might have realized as you were drawing your trees in Exercise (1) that the embedded sentences in (8) can optionally be "introduced" by the word *that*. Let's take a look:

(26)   a.   Mary *thinks* <u>that Sue read the newspaper</u>.

b.   Mary *believes* <u>that Sue read the newspaper</u>.

c. Mary *assumed* <u>that Sue read the newspaper</u>.

d. Mary *realized* <u>that Sue read the newspaper</u>.

e. Mary *knows* <u>that Sue read the newspaper</u>.

f. Mary *told* Bill <u>that Sue read the newspaper</u>.

The sentences in (26) are — for all intents and purposes — equivalent to the sentences in (8). The addition of this little word *that* doesn't seem to change the meaning; compare the two examples in (27):

(27) a. Mary *thinks* <u>Sue read the newspaper</u>.

b. Mary *thinks* <u>that Sue read the newspaper</u>.

This makes it hard to put your finger on what the word *that* even means, or why it's even there! While it doesn't seem to mean anything, it does seem to serve the function of "introducing" the subordinate clause (= embedded sentence). We could in fact think of it as a kind of signal that tells us "a subordinate clause is coming up next." Because of this function, it's often been called a **subordinating conjunction**. As we'll see in just a little bit, English speakers use all kinds of different subordinating conjunctions. The word *that* in (26) is often also referred to as a **complementizer**, or sometimes **C** for short (just like we use N as an abbreviation for noun, V as an abbreviation for verb, etc.). Earlier, we said that the embedded sentences in (8) are complements of the verbs that select them, so this is why we call *that* in (26) a "complementizer." Before we say more about the different types of complementizers, let's establish how the complementizer *that* in (26) is going to figure into our phrase structure in the first place.

For the complementizer, we're going introduce a whole new phrase structure rule, for a phrase that we can call the **complementizer phrase**, or CP for short (just as we use NP as an abbreviation for noun phrase, etc.). The CP phrase structure rule will be very simple; here it is, in (28):

(28) CP → C S

By now we know very well how phrase structure rules map onto phrase structure trees; so we should know that the rule in (28) says that "a CP breaks down into a complementizer (such as *that*), and a sentence," as follows:

(29)

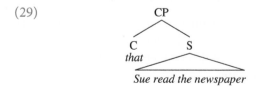

With this phrase structure rule in place, then, we can draw our tree for (26a) as follows:

(30)

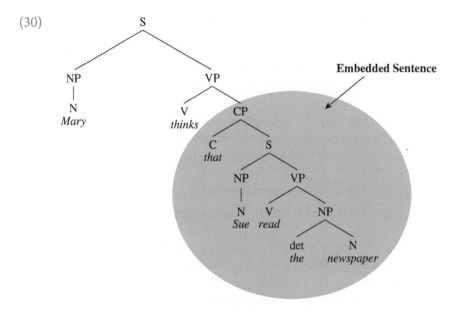

One more thing needs to be added to the phrase structure rules at this point: specifically, now that we've seen that verbs like *think, believe, assume, realize,* etc. can select either an embedded S *or* and embedded CP, our VP phrase structure rule must be modified to reflect this, as follows:

Revised VP phrase structure rule

(31)

$$VP \rightarrow V\ (PP)\ (NP) \begin{Bmatrix} (NP) \\ (S) \\ (CP) \end{Bmatrix} (AP)\ (PP^*)$$

> Our new VP rule says that the direct object can be either an NP, or an S or CP.

EXERCISE [4]

Given the new CP phrase structure rule in (28), and the new VP phrase structure rule in (31), draw trees for the sentences in (26) and (18).

5.3.1.1 Complementizer *that* vs. demonstrative *that*

It's important not to confuse complementizer *that* with the demonstrative determiner *that*, which we learned about in Chapter 2.

Recall from Chapter 2 that our list of determiners in example (14) of that chapter included the four demonstratives:

(32)   demonstratives: *this, that, these, those*

        examples: **this** *journal,* **that** *office,* **these** *complaints,* **those** *professors*

The determiner *that* is a demonstrative, related to the word *those* (e.g., *that student* vs. *those students*); consider the follow sentence:

(33)   That student read the newspaper.

If we now turn the sentence in (33) into an embedded S, we get the sentence in (34a); if we instead turn it into an embedded CP, we get the sentence in (34b):

(34)   a.   Mary thinks <u>that student read the newspaper</u>.
        b.   Mary thinks <u>that that student read the newspaper</u>.

In (34b), the first *that* is the complementizer, and the second *that* is the determiner within the subject NP of the embedded sentence.

EXERCISE [5]

Draw trees for the sentences in (34).

In some cases it can be unclear which *that* we're dealing with; consider the sentence in (35):

(35)   Mary thinks <u>that coffee tastes bad</u>.

Without the benefit of the intonation and gesturing that face-to-face spoken communication is so good at providing, the written sentence in (35) is **structurally ambiguous** (recall Term Box 2 from Chapter 1). In other words, there are two possible structures an English speaker could imagine for this string of words. Let's call these "Structure 1" and "Structure 2." In Structure 1, the word *that* is a complementizer, and the sentence means something like "Mary thinks coffee in general tastes bad; no coffee tastes good, in her opinion." In Structure 2 in contrast, the word *that* is a determiner within the embedded subject NP, and the sentence means something like "Mary thinks *that particular coffee*, as opposed to another coffee, tastes bad." For all we know, other coffees might taste good in her opinion.

EXERCISE [6]

Draw the two different tree structures for the two different meanings of (35).

If you say the two different structures out loud, you'll find that the complementizer *that* has a slightly different pronunciation than determiner *that*: complementizer *that* in Structure 1 tends to have a shorter, more reduced vowel. Furthermore, it can't be accompanied by the pointing gesture. In contrast, demonstrative *that* in Structure 2 can have a long vowel, and you can point at the object that the demonstrative is picking out. In fact, it can be stressed, as in *Mary thinks THAT coffee tastes bad (but she thinks THIS one tastes good)*.

5.3.2 embedded questions

Now it's time to switch gears and talk about a kind of embedded sentence that has a sort of meaning/function which is different from the embedded sentences we analyzed in (8) and (26): the **embedded question**. Because embedded questions have a different function from the embedded sentences we've seen until now, they also have a different kind of complementizer. But before we go into the specifics, let's just briefly talk more generally about what a **question** is.

You might have noticed that all of the sentences we've been analyzing in this book — from Chapter 1 up until now — have had one thing in common: they have all been statements, also known as **declaratives**. The main **discourse function** of a declarative sentence is to give information to your **interlocutor**; for example, if I tell you that *Mary devoured the pizza*, I'm sharing information that for some reason I think will be useful to you as we engage in discussion. This is very different from asking a question; when we ask questions, we are requesting information from our interlocutors. A question actually requires that your interlocutor respond to you.

Term Box 5: Discourse participants

Language doesn't always get used for talking to someone else. We can use it inside our heads, to solve problems or just to think. But often, language is used in conversation with other people. Linguists sometimes refer to the two basic participants in a conversation (or discourse) as the **speaker** and **hearer**. We can also refer to the hearer more generally as the **interlocutor**; this is an especially useful term when talking about signed (as opposed to spoken) languages, like for example *American Sign Language*.

The sentences in (36) are both questions; another term used for this type is sentence is **interrogative**:

(36)   a.   Did Mary devour the pizza?
       b.   What did Mary devour?

The interrogatives in (36) are what we call **root interrogatives** or **root questions**, or alternatively, **matrix questions**. (See Term Box 2 for the definition of root/matrix clause.)

Term Box 6: Two kinds of question

The sentence in (36a) is what is known as a **Yes–No question**. When you ask a Yes–No question, the information you're seeking is minimal; you just need your interlocutor to confirm or deny something, by answering "Yes" or "No." In contrast, the sentence in (36b) involves a request for more information; you're asking your interlocutor to give meaningful content to the question-word *what*. In this case, the content could be something like *the pizza* (where *what = the pizza*). Question words like *what, who, whom, where, when, why, which, whose,* and *how* are called **interrogative pronouns**, or sometimes **wh-words** (because most of them begin with the letters "wh"). This kind of question is called a **wh-question**.

Now that we've established what a question is (and in particular, what a root question is), let's take a look at **embedded questions**.

Just like we can embed declarative sentences (as in (8), (17), (18), (26), (34), and (35)), so can we embed interrogatives. The underlined strings in (37) and (38) are all embedded questions:

(37) a.   Sue is a good surgeon.

 b.   Mary wonders <u>if Sue is a good surgeon</u>.

 c.   Mary wonders <u>whether Sue is a good surgeon</u>.

(38) a.   Sue fixed the sink with a plumbing wrench at lunchtime.

 b.   Bill wondered <u>what Sue fixed</u>.

 c.   Bill wondered <u>when Sue fixed the sink</u>.

 d.   Bill wondered <u>how Sue fixed the sink</u>.

 e.   Bill wondered <u>which sink Sue fixed</u>.

 f.   Bill wondered <u>who fixed the sink</u>.

The embedded questions in (37) are Yes–No questions, while those in (38) are wh-questions (see Term Box 6).

Why do we think of these embedded sentences as questions? Consider the fact that (37b) and (37c) can be paraphrased as follows:

(39)   Mary wonders, Is Sue a good surgeon?

The response to Mary's pondering is going to be either "Yes, Sue is a good surgeon" or "No, Sue isn't a good surgeon." Similarly, we could paraphrase the sentences in (38b–f) as follows:

(40) b.   Bill wondered, What did Sue fix?

 c.   Bill wondered, When did Sue fix the sink?

    d.   Bill wondered, How did Sue fix the sink?

    e.   Bill wondered, Which sink did Sue fix?

    f.   Bill wondered, Who fixed the sink?

The responses to Bill's different ponderings in (40) could be "the sink" (answering the question of *what*), "at lunchtime" (answering the question of *when*), "with a plumbing wrench" (answering the question of *how*), "the BLUE sink" (answering the question of *which sink*), and "Sue" (answering the question of *who*).

    Thus, the underlined embedded sentences in (37) and (38) are not declaratives. But they are also not exactly like the **root** or **direct** questions that we saw in (36) either: specifically, they don't require a response from an interlocutor. When you utter a sentence like that in (38b), for example, you are not requesting that your interlocutor give you information:

(38)   b.   Bill wondered what Sue fixed.

Rather, you're telling your interlocutor that someone has a question (in this case, *Bill*); this is why embedded questions are sometimes called **indirect questions**. They're embedded in declaratives (like *Bill wondered …*), but ultimately, they say that the subject NP of the root clause (like *Bill*) has or had a question.

    In contrast with the long list of verbs that embed declaratives in (7), there aren't many verbs that embed questions. The verb *wonder* is one example; the verb *ask* is another:

(41)   a.   Mary asked <u>if Sue fixed the sink</u>.

       b.   Mary asked <u>whether Sue fixed the sink</u>.

5.3.2.1 The interrogative complementizer in embedded Yes–No questions

Now let's look more closely at the words *if* and *whether* in (37) and (41). You surely noticed by now that embedded Yes–No questions are introduced by one of these two subordinating conjunctions. These words are like the complementizer *that*, in that they "introduce" the embedded sentence. In contrast with *that*, however, *if* and *whether* are specialized to introduce embedded interrogatives. Because of this, we refer to *if* and *whether* as **interrogative complementizers**.

    So now we've seen three different complementizers, summarized in (42):

(42)   <u>complementizers</u>:

      declarative complementizer: *that*

      interrogative complementizers: *if, whether*

Because *if* and *whether* are complementizers, they go under the head of the complementizer phrase (CP), like *that*; let's repeat the CP phrase structure rule from (28) here:

(43)   CP   →   C   S

To illustrate, let's take a look at the syntactic tree for (41a):

(44)

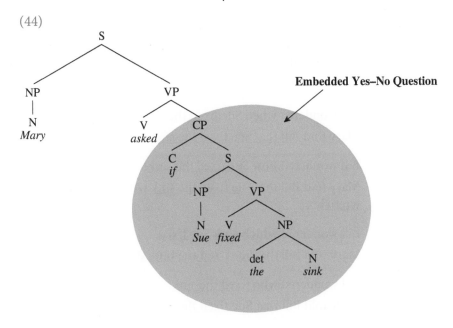

EXERCISE [7]

Draw tree structures for the sentences with embedded questions in (37) and (41).

5.3.2.2 Embedded wh-questions

Now let's examine the sentences in (38), which involve embedded wh-questions (see Term Box 6). Wh-questions are a bit more complicated than Yes–No questions to analyze. To understand why, let's closely compare the underlined embedded wh-question with the embedded declarative in (45a,b):

(45)   a.   Bill wondered **what** Sue fixed. EMBEDDED WH-QUESTION

       b.   Mary said that Sue fixed **the sink**.   EMBEDDED DECLARATIVE

In terms of meaning, the embedded question in (45a) certainly seems related to the embedded declarative in (45b). We also see this relationship in meaning

in matrix (= root) wh-questions versus matrix declaratives, such as in the
following pair:

(46)   a.   **What** did Sue fix?   ROOT WH-QUESTION
       b.   Sue fixed **the sink**.   ROOT DECLARATIVE

With interrogative/declarative pairs such as these, English speakers have the
intuition that an NP like *the sink* in (45b) and (46b) gives meaningful content
to the wh-phrase *what* (again, see Term Box 6). In other words, *the sink* in
(45b) answers the question *what* in (45a), where *what* = *the sink*. In fact,
we see this kind of correlation with the other wh-questions in the sentences in
(38) too; I'll repeat those here:

(47)   a.   Bill wondered **when** <u>Sue fixed the sink</u>.
       b.   Mary told Bill <u>that Sue fixed the sink **at lunchtime**</u>.

       c.   Bill wondered **how** <u>Sue fixed the sink</u>.
       d.   Mary told Bill <u>that Sue fixed the sink **with a plumbing
            wrench**</u>.

       e.   Bill wondered **which sink** <u>Sue fixed</u>.
       f.   Mary told Bill <u>that Sue fixed **the blue sink**</u>.

       g.   Bill wondered **who** <u>fixed the sink</u>.
       h.   Mary told Bill <u>that **Sue** fixed the sink</u>.

In the first pair of sentences in (47a,b), we have the intuition that the
PP *at lunchtime* gives content to the wh-phrase *when*; in the second pair,
we have the intuition that the PP *with a plumbing wrench* gives content to
the wh-phrase *how*; in the third pair, we have the intuition that the NP *the
blue sink* gives content to the wh-phrase *which sink*; and finally, in the
fourth pair, we have the intuition that the NP *Sue* gives content to the wh-
phrase *who*.

Because of these meaning associations that wh-phrases have with their
NP (and PP) counterparts in corresponding declarative sentences, we
assume that wh-phrases actually "start their life" in the same syntactic
position as the NPs (and PPs) that they correspond to. Focusing just on
(45a) for now: what this means is that, even though we can see that the
word *what* appears to the left of the embedded subject NP *Sue*, we suppose
that before it got into that position, it actually started out in the same place
where we find the object NP *the sink* in (45b). Let's make this more concrete
by illustrating with syntactic trees in (49a) and (49b) (which correspond to
the strings in (48a) and (48b)):

(48)   a.   Mary said <u>that Sue fixed **the sink**</u>
       b.   Bill wondered <u>Sue fixed **what**</u>

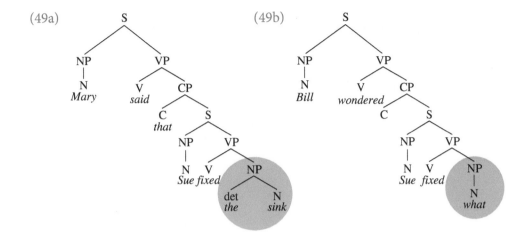

In the tree in (49a), we see an embedded declarative with the direct object *the sink* in the position we expect it to be in — immediately dominated by the VP node headed by the V that selects it. This NP object is, after all, fulfilling the **subcategorizational** or **selectional** requirements of the verb *fix*. In a parallel fashion, in the tree in (49b) we see an embedded interrogative with the wh-phrase *what*. As we saw, the word *what* corresponds to the NP object *the sink* in the embedded declarative in (49a). Because of this, we assume that *what* starts its life in the same syntactic position of the direct object; after all, it too is selected by the verb *fix*. Of course, the structure in (49b) — corresponding to the string of words in (48b) — is not what we actually hear speakers say; what we hear speakers say is represented in (45a). However, it does capture the fact that the wh-phrase *what* in (48b), like the NP object *the sink* in (48a), is selected by the verb.

Given that (48b)/(49b) is not what speakers actually say, how do we progress from the tree structure in (49b) (which captures the fact that English speakers interpret *what* as a direct object inside the VP) to the sentence in (45a) (which has the words in the order we actually say them)? That is, how do we get from (50a) to (50b)?

(50) a. Bill wondered Sue fixed   ⇒ b. Bill wondered **what** Sue
          what   fixed _____

To get from (50a) to (50b), let's propose a "movement rule." In this book, we've already seen two movement rules: in Section 3.7.1 we discussed the **passivization operation**, which moves the direct object of an active sentence to the position of subject in a passive sentence. Then, in Section 4.3, we saw the **particle shift rule**, which moves a particle from the left of the direct object to the right of the direct object. In a similar spirit, we can propose a movement rule for wh-phrases: let's call this **wh-movement**. The wh-movement rule says that a wh-phrase such as *what* moves from its original position (in this case, within VP, as in (50a)) to the position that is normally occupied by the complementizer (as in (50b)). In other words, the rule would take the tree in (49b) and transform it into the tree in (51):

Side Note 4:

Note that in (51), the interrogative pronoun *what* **replaces** the C head. This is a temporary strategy we'll continue to use through Chapter 7. In Chapter 11 we'll revisit the analysis. Also: in your own tree drawings, feel free to use a triangle for the wh-phrase (as it can become too cumbersome to draw out the entire NP when it's in CP).

(51)

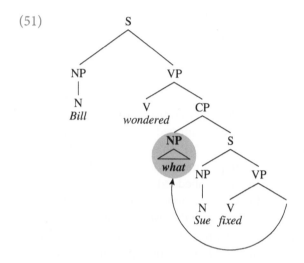

Side Note 5:

What happens to the deep structure object position in wh-movement? It seems to leave a kind of "gap" in the structure. In Section 6.4.3, we'll discuss this in detail.

In this way, the trees in (49b) and (51) are related. We say that the tree in (49b) is the **deep structure** representation of the sentence in (45a)/(50b) and that the tree in (51) is the **surface structure** representation of this sentence. The surface structure, in other words, is the word order as we actually "say" it.

EXERCISE [8]

Draw a tree for (38a); then draw deep structure and surface structure trees for the sentences with embedded wh-questions in (38b,c,d,e,f).
   Some help:
• for (38e): you can put the wh-word *which* of the NP *which sink* in determiner position; in this case, of course, we can't technically call *which* an interrogative pronoun, because here it's not a pronoun.

Rather, it's a determiner (where the head N of its NP is *sink*). Note that the whole NP *which sink* gets wh-moved.

- for (38f): notice that the wh-phrase *who* moves from the embedded subject NP position (not from within the embedded VP). Notice that this movement doesn't actually change the order of the words. That's OK.

Term Box 7: Deep Structure and Surface Structure

Every movement rule takes a tree structure that is created by the phrase structure rules and transforms it into a different tree structure.

A tree that is generated by the phrase structure rules is called a **deep structure**. A tree that represents how a sentence is actually "pronounced" (or, "spelled out") is called a **surface structure**. Thus, a tree such as that in (51), which represents the output of a movement operation that was performed on a deep structure tree, is a surface structure tree.

Note, however, that not every deep structure tree gets a movement rule applied to it; the tree in (49a) is an example. In this case, the deep structure and surface structure trees are identical. In other words, the tree that represents how the sentence is actually pronounced (= the surface structure) is identical to the tree that was generated by the phrase structure rules (= the deep structure).

5.4 embedded adjunct clauses

In addition to the embedded declaratives and the embedded interrogatives examined in Sections 5.2 and 5.3, there's yet another type of embedded sentence; this type, however, is in a class by itself. How so?

Let's think about the embedded declaratives and embedded interrogatives investigated thus far: they're all part of the selectional requirements of the verb (as discussed in Section 5.2.3). That is, they're complements of the verbs which select them. Such **complement clauses** are in direct opposition to **adjunct clauses**. Adjunct clauses are embedded sentences which are not selected by the verb. Let's illustrate with an example:

(52)   John did his homework [**because <u>he wants a good grade</u>**].

Using our techniques from Chapter 1, let's divide this sentence into its two NP/VP parts:

(53)

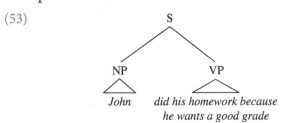

In the VP in (53), we have the verb *did* and the direct object NP *his homework*. So now the question is, what's the remaining string of words *because he wants a good grade*? Note first of all that if we remove that entire string, we still have a perfectly grammatical sentence:

(54)   John did his homework.

The string of words *because he wants a good grade* is not considered to be part of the subcategorization of the verb *do*, which seems to only select a direct object NP (in this case, *his homework*). The phrase *because he wants a good grade* is optional material, which we can choose to include or not, depending on how much information we wish to give. It's not part of what the verb "wants" in its VP (i.e. it's not **selected**); rather, it's extra material that we can optionally add, to give further information. Such phrases that are not selected are called **adjuncts**.

So why are we calling it an adjunct **clause**? In other words, why are we identifying this string as a sentence? Well, notice that if you remove the word *because* in this string, you get the following:

(55)   He wants a good grade.

By now you should be able to recognize this as a sentence. What this means is that the VP in (53) contains the sentence in (55) as an embedded clause. We already know where subordinate clauses go in a syntactic tree, but the remaining question is, what is the word *because*? The most logical conclusion to draw is that it's a kind of **subordinating conjunction**. It's not unlike our complementizers *that*, *if*, and *whether*, in that it serves to "introduce" the embedded sentence.

Given that we already have a syntactic position for subordinating conjunctions — namely, the C head — let's use it for (53):

(56)

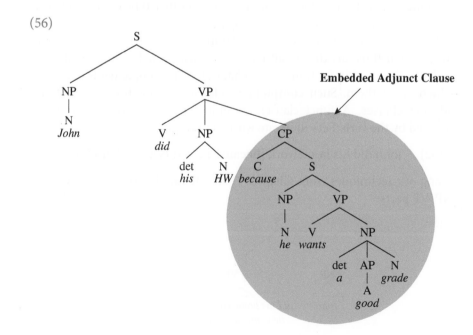

The following sentences show that in addition to *because*, there are other sub-ordinating conjunctions for adjunct clauses, such as *when, whenever, while, unless,* and *if*:

(57) a. John ate the pizza **when <u>he got hungry</u>**.
      b. Sue reads the newspaper **whenever <u>Mary gets a delivery</u>**.
      c. Mary read Wikipedia articles **while <u>John got ready</u>**.
      d. Mary likes her work **unless <u>it gets boring</u>**.
      e. Sue will fix the sink **if <u>John fixes the toilet</u>**.

EXERCISE [9]

Draw syntactic trees for the sentences in (57). For sentence (57e), don't worry for now about where to put the word *will*; we'll talk about this in Chapter 10.

5.4.1 adjunct subordinating conjunctions

There are some differences worth mentioning between the subordinating conjunctions *because, when, whenever, while,* and *unless* on the one hand, and the complementizer *that* on the other.

First, although they all occupy the same syntactic position (i.e. the C head in CP), the adjunct subordinating conjunctions carry much more meaning than the complementizer *that* does. As we saw in Section 5.3.1, it's difficult to see what meaning the complementizer *that* has (if any), given that it can be optionally omitted without changing anything:

(58) a. Mary *thinks* <u>that Sue read the newspaper</u>.
      b. Mary *thinks* _____ <u>Sue read the newspaper</u>.

This contrasts with the adjunct subordinating conjunctions we looked at: note that omitting them from the sentence leads to ungrammaticality (compare the sentences in (57) with those in (59)):

(59) a. *John ate the pizza _____ <u>he got hungry</u>.
      b. *Sue reads the newspaper _____ <u>Mary gets a delivery</u>.
      c. *Mary read Wikipedia articles _____ <u>John got ready</u>.
      d. *Mary likes her work _____ <u>it gets boring</u>.
      e. *Sue will fix the sink _____ <u>John fixes the toilet</u>.
      f. *John did his homework _____ <u>he wants a good grade</u>.

It looks like we can't delete the adjunct subordinating conjunctions because they actually add meaning to the clauses they introduce. We could paraphrase their meanings as follows:

(60)   **Subord. Conj.**   **Meaning**

   a.   when   *at the time at which* (he got hungry)

   b.   whenever   *at all times at which* (Mary gets a delivery)

   c.   while   *during the time at which* (John got ready)

   d.   unless   *but this could change if …* (it gets boring)

   e.   if   *under the condition that …* (John fixes the toilet)

   f.   because   *and the cause of this is …* (he wants a good grade)

Side Note 6:

Don't confuse the adjunct subordinating conjunction *if* (seen in (57e)/(60e)) with the interrogative complementizer *if* (seen in (41a)). If you reflect on their meanings, you'll see that they're two different animals.

In this way, our adjunct subordinating conjunctions are a bit more like our interrogative complementizers *whether* and *if*. Although the meaning of the interrogative complementizers may be more difficult to pin down, note that they cannot be deleted, in contrast with the declarative complementizer *that* (see (58)):

(61)   a.   Bill wondered <u>if Sue fixed the sink</u>.

   b.   Bill wondered <u>whether Sue fixed the sink</u>.

   c.   *Bill wondered _____ <u>Sue fixed the sink</u>

Although the declarative complementizer *that* and the interrogative complementizers *whether/if* differ with respect to their (in)ability to be omitted, it's important to underscore that they are similar to one another — and differ from the adjunct subordinating conjunctions — in an important respect: the embedded sentences introduced by declarative *that* and interrogative *whether/if* are **selected**. That is, they're **complements**. In contrast, our subordinating conjunctions don't introduce complement clauses; rather, the clauses they introduce are unselected **adjuncts**. This difference actually manifests itself syntactically in a significant way: the embedded adjunct clauses can optionally appear to the left of the matrix sentence; take a look at the following pairs of examples:

(62)   a.   <u>John ate the pizza</u> **when he got hungry**.

   a'.   **When he got hungry**, <u>John ate the pizza</u>.

   b.   <u>Sue reads the newspaper</u> **whenever Mary gets a delivery**.

   b'.   **Whenever Mary gets a delivery**, <u>Sue reads the newspaper</u>.

   c.   <u>Mary read Wikipedia articles</u> **while Sue got ready**.

   c'. **While Sue got ready**, <u>Mary read Wikipedia articles</u>.

   d.   <u>Mary likes her work</u> **unless it gets boring**.

   d'. **Unless it gets boring**, <u>Mary likes her work</u>.

   e.   <u>John did his homework</u> **because he wants a good grade**.

   e'. **Because he wants a good grade**, <u>John did his homework</u>.

Side Note 7:

In Section 11.3.2.1, you'll see a new structure for CP which provides a matrix position to which the adjunct clause can move. When you get to this point in Chapter 11, try out the second part of Exercise [3], which will bring us back to (62) here.

In each pair of sentences in (62), we see that English speakers can optionally "move" the adjunct embedded clause (in **bold**) to a position to the left of the matrix sentence (<u>underlined</u>). Interestingly, this movement can't happen with complement clauses; take a look:

(63) a.   Mary thinks **that Sue read the newspaper**.

      a'. *****That Sue read the newspaper**, Mary thinks.

      b.   Bill wondered **if Sue fixed the sink**.

      b'. *****If Sue fixed the sink**, Bill wondered.

      c.   Bill wondered **whether Sue fixed the sink**.

      c'. *****Whether Sue fixed the sink**, Bill wondered.

5.5 conclusions

Here are our latest phrase structure rules, with CP and VP (which are the updated rules) in bold:

(64) **CP**   →   **C S**

        S   →   NP VP

        NP   → $\left\{ \begin{array}{l} \text{(det)} \\ \text{(PossNP)} \end{array} \right\}$ (AP*) N (PP*)

        PossNP → $\left\{ \begin{array}{l} \text{(det)} \\ \text{(PossNP)} \end{array} \right\}$ (AP*) PossN (PP*)

        VP   →   V (PP) (NP) $\left\{ \begin{array}{l} \text{(NP)} \\ \text{(S)} \\ \text{(CP)} \end{array} \right\}$ (AP) (PP*)

        PP   →   (mod) P $\left\{ \begin{array}{l} \text{(NP)} \\ \text{(PP)} \end{array} \right\}$

        AP   →   (deg) A

Let's consider CP for a moment. As we just saw, English speakers exhibit a real difference between complement clauses and adjunct clauses. At the same time, you might have noticed that we're still using the nomenclature "CP" (complementizer phrase) for both. In a way, it doesn't make sense to put an adjunct subordinating conjunction (like *because*) in the head of a "complementizer phrase" when we know quite well that the conjunction heads a clause that is in fact <u>not</u> a complement. Despite this contradiction, we'll continue to use the term "CP," even for adjunct subordinating conjunctions like *because*. One way to think of this is as follows: it doesn't matter what we call it. We could call it "CP" for "conjunction clause," which would capture this phrase's more general use. So we'll just continue to call it "CP" without worrying about the true meaning of "C."

Still on the topic of CP, let's also consider the fact that our analysis distinguished between embedded interrogatives, which are always CP, and embedded declaratives, which are sometimes S and sometimes CP. In the case of interrogatives, it was easy to conclude that there must always be a CP, given the fact that an embedded interrogative always has **overt material** in the CP, either in the form of an **interrogative complementizer** for Yes–No questions (i.e. *if* and *whether*), or in the form of a wh-phrase (for wh-questions). But in the case of embedded declaratives, sometimes we have no complementizer *that*, which is the very phenomenon that caused us to propose the possibility of a "bare" embedded S (with no CP layer dominating it) inside VP. But there's another possibility here: we could instead propose that there is always a CP layer in embedded declaratives, and that in those cases where there is no **overt complementizer** *that*, the C head is empty. Let's leave this issue open for now, but try to think about this when you're reading Chapter 7, which treats **silent categories**.

Let's not lose sight of something else important this chapter introduced us to, namely, **wh-movement** and the concept of **deep structure** versus **surface structure**. Movement rules will rear their heads again in the coming chapters, and as such, deep and surface structures will remain important concepts for the remainder of this book. Watch out for all of this in particular in Chapters 6, 7, 10, and 11.

list of terms/concepts

adjunct clause
adjunct subordinating conjunction
adjuncts
clause (sentence)
complement (sentential complement)
complement clause
complementizer
complementizer phrase (CP)
declarative

deep structure (deep structure tree; surface structure)
dependent clause (subordinate clause; embedded sentence)
direct object
discourse function
discourse participants (speaker, hearer, interlocutor)
ditransitive verbs
embedded clause

embedded question (embedded interrogative)

embedded sentence (dependent clause; subordinate clause)

indirect object

indirect question

interlocutor

interrogative (question)

interrogative complementizer

interrogative pronoun

intransitive verbs

matrix sentence (root sentence)

mental lexicon

movement (movement rule)

optionality/obligatoriness

overt complementizer

particle shift

passivization operation

question (interrogative)

recursion

root question (root interrogative; matrix question; matrix interrogative; direct question)

root sentence (matrix sentence)

selection (select; selectional requirements)

subcategorization (subcategorize)

subordinate clause (embedded sentence; dependent clause)

subordinating conjunction

subordination

surface structure (surface structure tree; deep structure)

transitive verbs

Yes–No question

wh-movement

wh-question

wh-words

6 It's More Complex Than That: The Complex Noun Phrase

expected outcomes for this chapter

- You'll deepen your understanding of the complexity of noun phrases.
- You'll develop more confidence with the concepts from previous chapters (e.g., selection/subcategorization, embedded sentences, wh-movement, lexical categories).
- You'll manipulate greater subtleties of hierarchical structure.
- You'll become familiar with the following terms (see items in bold and term boxes): *complex noun phrase, noun-complement clause, nominalization, derivation, subject relative clause, object relative clause, relative pronoun, gap/trace.*

6.1 aspects of the *noun phrase* we already know about

In Chapter 2, we got a good sense of the kinds of constituents that can appear inside the NP. Let's summarize in (1) some examples which illustrate the variety of possible NPs:

(1)   a.   John   NP → N

         b.   he/him/who   NP → N

         c.   the student   NP → det N

         d.   my student   NP → det N

Understanding Sentence Structure: An Introduction to English Syntax, First Edition.
Christina Tortora.
© 2018 John Wiley & Sons, Inc. Published 2018 by John Wiley & Sons, Inc.

e.	the professor's student	NP →	PossNP N
f.	the talented student	NP →	det AP N
g.	the happy talented student	NP →	det AP AP N
h.	the student with good grades	NP →	det N PP
i.	the very talented student with good grades	NP →	det AP N PP
j.	the talented student of linguistics with good grades	NP →	det AP N PP PP
k.	my happy talented students of linguistics with good grades	NP →	det AP AP N PP PP

Given all of the possible NP structures investigated, we decided on the following phrase structure rule for NP:

(2) $\text{NP} \rightarrow \begin{Bmatrix} (\text{det}) \\ (\text{PossNP}) \end{Bmatrix} (\text{AP}^*)\ \text{N}\ (\text{PP}^*)$

Side Note 1: AP reminder

Recall that we went from a simple **adj** in Chapter 2, to the more complex Adjectival Phrase (**AP**) in Chapter 3.

Side Note 2: Kleene Star reminder

Recall from Chapter 2 that the superscripted asterisk on the right of a parenthetical phrase in a phrase structure rule (the Kleene Star) means "you can use zero or more of this element."

The rule in (2) captures the fact that English speakers allow for many different kinds of combinations of AP and PP (and determiners/PossNPs) inside NP, only some of which we see in (1).

But much as we saw with the VP in Chapter 5, there's actually more to the NP than our previous discussion let on. In this chapter, we're going to continue our discussion of NP by taking a look at the phenomenon of the complex NP.

———————— 6.2 subordinate clauses within the noun phrase

In Chapter 5, we saw that the verb phrase can contain a sentence, represented either as S (as in (3a)) or CP (as in (3b)):

(3) a. They claim <u>Sue read the newspaper</u>.

   b. They claim <u>that Sue read the newspaper</u>.

The tree in (4) will help us recall what a CP embedded within VP looks like:

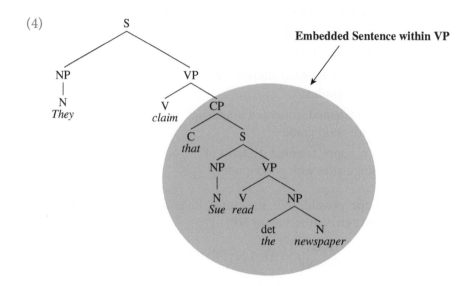

We called such phrases within VP embedded sentences, embedded clauses, dependent clauses, or subordinate clauses (these all mean the same thing). Given structures like that in (4), we defined embedded sentence as "a sentence that is immediately dominated by VP." (This was in opposition to a root or matrix sentence, which isn't dominated by anything.)

It turns out, however, that NPs can also contain embedded sentences. Let's start with the NP example in (5):

Noun Phrase:

(5)   their claim that Sue read the newspaper

The entire string of words in (5) is an NP, the head of which is the N *claim*. The tree in (6) provides a preliminary structure for this NP:

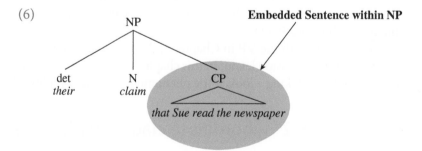

An NP which contains an embedded clause is called a **complex NP**. In this chapter we'll investigate in detail two types of complex NP, namely:

[A]   an NP with a **noun complement clause**, and
[B]   an NP with a **relative clause**

Section 6.3 will be devoted to the noun complement clause, and Section 6.4 to the relative clause. But before we move on to those sections, let's make a couple of preliminary observations about complex NPs.

6.2.1 some preliminary notes on complex NPs

6.2.1.1 Complex NPs are just like any other NP on the outside

The first thing to note is that like any other NP, the one in (5)/(6) can be used either as a subject, an object, or a complement within PP; here are some examples (where the NP is [**bold in square brackets**]):

(7)   a.   [**Their claim <u>that Sue read the newspaper</u>**]   subject NP
             bothered Jill

       b.   Jill refuted [**their claim <u>that Sue read the</u>**   object NP
             <u>newspaper</u>]

       c.   Joe referred us to [**their claim <u>that Sue read</u>**   complement
             <u>the newspaper</u>]   within PP

Side Note 3:

By now you should be able to recognize the subject NP in a sentence like (7a) even if I didn't help you along by giving you the relevant string of words in [**bold in brackets**]. Recalling our exercises from Chapter 1, note, for example, that we can replace the entire string *their claim that Sue read the newspaper* with the pronoun *it*:

{1}   [**It**] bothered Jill.

This tells us that the entire string *their claim that Sue read the newspaper* is a constituent. The simplified structure in {1}, furthermore, makes it easier to see that the remainder of the sentence (namely, the matrix VP) is *bothered Jill*.

As such, on the outside, it's no different from any other NP: it can occupy the same structural positions as any of the other NPs we've seen already (subject, direct object, complement within PP). So in this chapter, let's not lose sight of the fact that everything we learned in previous chapters about the syntactic distribution and behavior of NPs holds for complex NPs as well. There's nothing new in this chapter regarding the "external" behavior of NPs; we're just learning something new about the NP's "internal" composition.

6.2.1.2 Revised NP phrase structure rule

Let's get back to the structure in (6): Given that we already have a phrase structure rule for CP, we actually already have the ability to draw the articulated structure for this NP, as in (8):

(8)

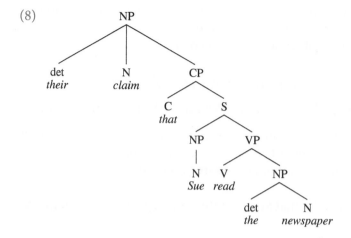

The fact that an NP can contain a CP means we have to revise our definition of "embedded sentence." In Chapter 5 we said that "an embedded sentence is a sentence that is immediately dominated by VP." In order to account for the reality of (8), however, let's now revise that to say "an embedded sentence is a sentence that is immediately dominated by some XP" (where "XP" means an undefined phrase, for example, NP or VP). Another definition that captures the same idea is as follows: "an embedded sentence is a non-root sentence."

We also have to now revise our NP phrase structure rule, to accommodate the possibility of complex NPs. The following will work for our purposes:

Revised NP phrase structure rule

(9) NP → $\left\{ \begin{array}{c} \text{(det)} \\ \text{(PossNP)} \end{array} \right\}$ (AP*) N $\left\{ \begin{array}{c} \text{(PP*)} \\ \text{(CP)} \end{array} \right\}$

Our new NP rule says that either PP or CP can follow the noun.

Side Note 4: PP __and__ CP?

For now let's put aside the question of whether you can get both a PP and a CP following an N within NP.

EXERCISE [1]

Draw syntactic trees for the three sentences in (7).

6.3 the noun complement clause

The structure in (8) is an example of an NP with a noun complement clause. The very term we use for this particular construction already reveals one of its defining properties.

As we saw in Chapters 3, 4, and 5, the term complement refers to a phrase — specifically, either an NP or CP or PP — which is selected by a verb (see Chapters 3 and 5), or by a preposition (see Chapter 4). Revisiting the example in (3), we see that the verb *claim* selects a sentential complement (either an S or a CP):

(10) a.   They claim <u>Sue read the newspaper</u>.

b.   They claim <u>that Sue read the newspaper</u>.

As we also saw in Chapter 5, we can represent this in the entry for the V *claim* in an English speaker's mental lexicon as follows:

(11)   word: *claim* (lexical category: verb)

MEANING: "to assert the truth of something, without necessarily providing evidence"

PRONUNCIATION: /klem/

SUBCATEGORIZATION: a sentential complement

But if the verb *claim* selects a sentential complement, couldn't its noun counterpart do so as well? The NP in (8) can be considered the "noun phrase version" of the matrix verb phrase in (10b), where the noun *claim*, like the verb *claim*, selects a sentential complement. In other words, given the obvious relation between the two, it makes sense to consider the CP in (8) to be a complement of the noun *claim*. So this is why we call the CP in (8) a noun complement clause.

6.3.1 a side note about the head noun

Despite the fact that *claim* is both a verb (as in (10)) and a noun (as in (8)), as an English speaker, you never confuse one for the other in your unconscious knowledge of these words. Your unconscious knowledge is so automatic, that you manipulate the various linguistic concepts, categories, and structures fluidly and without having to consciously think about it.

Despite this fact, the lexical ambiguity between the verb *claim* and the noun *claim* can sometimes cause confusion for students new to syntactic analysis when they try to bring their own automatized, deep-seated knowledge of English to their consciousness. Because of this, it's worth taking a moment to explicitly discuss lexical ambiguity.

This "dual" verb/noun identity seen with *claim* in (10) versus (8) is one of the interesting things about English (and many other languages, in fact): we have a lot of words that are ambiguous in terms of their lexical category.

That is, English speakers use many words — like *claim*, *walk*, *run*, *butter*, and many others — either as nouns or as verbs. Take a look at the pairs of sentences in (12) through (16), where the word of interest is in **bold**:

(12) a. They **claim** that Sue is smart.   VERB
      b. [Their **claim**] is believable.   NOUN

(13) a. They **walk** to school in the mornings.   VERB
      b. [Their **walk**] was enjoyable.   NOUN

(14) a. We **run** every morning.   VERB
      b. We love [our daily **run**].   NOUN

(15) a. They **butter** their bread in excess.   VERB
      b. They like [that **butter**].   NOUN

(16) a. You **jump** quite high!   VERB
      b. [Your **jump**] was quite high!   NOUN

Term Box 1: Lexical category

This is another term we use for the more familiar notion **part of speech**. Noun and verb are two different lexical categories, or parts of speech.

Term Box 2: Lexical ambiguity

When a single word can have more than one meaning/use, we say it's **lexically ambiguous**.

What we see in (12) through (16) should not surprise us: as we already noted in Side Note 5 in Chapter 1, words can be ambiguous; that is, a single word can have more than one meaning or use. For example, the word *bat* has (at least) two different meanings: "baseball bat" or "the flying mammal." We would say, therefore, that the word *bat* is **lexically ambiguous**, which is different from the concept of structural ambiguity (discussed in previous chapters). In the case of *bat*, though, with either meaning the word is a still a noun. In contrast, the ambiguity we see in the pairs of sentences in (12) through (16) derives from the fact that a single word can be assigned to one of two different lexical categories (verb or noun).

EXERCISE [2]

To drive home the fact that the bolded words in the (a) sentences are verbs while the very same words in the (b) sentences are nouns, draw syntactic trees for all the sentences in (12) through (16). This will help make this fact of lexical ambiguity concrete.

The trees you drew for Exercise [2] show that, as speakers, we structurally distinguish between verbs and nouns: the former head VPs, while the latter head NPs — even when the verbs/nouns in question look identical, like those in (12) through (16). Furthermore, the structural distinction we make between verb and noun gets reflected in the kinds of ways we can or cannot transform these words into other related words. Let's compare in this regard the verb *claim* in (12a) with the noun *claim* in (12b). Note that when *claim* is a verb it can be put in the past tense; this can be seen in (12a'):

(12) a'. They **claim<u>ed</u>** that Sue is smart.   (compare with (12a))

In (12a') *claimed* is the verb *claim*, but in the **past tense**, which is expressed by the *-ed* ending on the verb. (As we'll see in Chapter 8, only verbs can be given tenses, like present, past, and future.) This "past tense marker" *-ed* can only go on verbs. By definition, then, it can't go on a noun — even if the noun looks identical to the verb (like *claim*): compare the grammatical NP *their claim* in (12b) with the ungrammatical NP in (12b'):

(12) b'. *[Their **claimed**] is believable.   (compare with (12b))

The NP in (12b') is ungrammatical because in this example we're trying to put the "past tense marker" *-ed* on a noun, something which is impossible — <u>even</u> when the noun looks identical to the verb. Put differently: the fact that the word *claim* can be either a noun or a verb doesn't actually confuse English speakers into doing strange things, like putting *claim* in the past tense when it's a noun (as in (12b')). So, despite the fact that *claim* is ambiguous, as English speakers we know when we're using it as a noun and when we're using it as a verb by virtue of whether we make it the head of NP or the head of VP.

The bottom line is this: just because the word *claim* in (8) "looks like" the verb *claim* in (10) doesn't mean it's a verb.

6.3.2 other head nouns in NPs with noun complement clauses

6.3.2.1 Derived nouns

In addition to *claim*, there are several other nouns in English which are related to verbs which select sentential complements, and which therefore can select noun complement clauses; consider the (b) examples in the following pairs of sentences:

(17)   a.   Jim **believes** that the earth is flat.

　　　 b.   His **belief** that the earth is flat astounds me.

(18)   a.   Mary **proved** that the earth is round.

　　　 b.   Jim ignored Mary's **proof** that the earth is round.

(19)   a.   Mary **realized** that John ate up the last bit of cake.

　　　 b.   Mary's **realization** that John ate up the last bit of cake was heartbreaking.

(20)   a.   Sue **assumed** that Mary disliked the cake.

　　　 b.   Sue's **assumption** that Mary disliked the cake shocked Bill.

EXERCISE [3]

Draw trees for the sentences in (17) through (20).

In all of the (b) sentences, we have an NP whose head noun (*belief, proof, realization, assumption*) is related to a verb which takes a sentential complement (*believe, prove, realize, assume*). Just as we saw with the verb versus noun versions of *claim*, there are two interesting points to make here.

First, there is a clear relationship between the verb and the noun. Let's sketch out this relationship in the following way:

(21)   a. $[\text{believe}]_V$ → $[\text{belief}]_N$

　　　 b. $[\text{prove}]_V$ → $[\text{proof}]_N$

　　　 c. $[\text{realize}]_V$ → $[\text{realization}]_N$

　　　 d. $[\text{assume}]_V$ → $[\text{assumption}]_N$

　　　 e. $[\text{claim}]_V$ → $[\text{claim}]_N$

It's useful to analyze the relationships in (21) in terms of a mental process, whereby we "create" or **derive** nouns from verbs. This "noun derivation rule" represented in (21) basically says that we can take a verb and make a noun out of it. In the example in (21e) (and also in (12–14) and (16)), we see that the conversion from verb to noun doesn't change the way the word actually looks; it's the same word — *claim* — in either case (hence the lexical ambiguity).

Side Note 5: *Butter*?

In example (15) we saw the word *butter* being used as both a verb and a noun. In this case, it's likely that that verb *butter* derives from the noun *butter*, rather than the other way around:

$$[butter]_N \rightarrow [butter]_V$$

However, in (21a–d), the verb → noun derivation changes the **form** of the word. In (21a,b), we can think of these words as kinds of "shapeshifters," whereby they assume a different shape when they become nouns. In (21c,d), the verb → noun derivation involves a combination of shapeshifting and the addition of a **suffix**.

Term Box 3: Suffixes

In the derived nouns in (21c,d) you can see the *-tion* ending (pronounced like the word "shun"), tacked onto the end of the word. This is an example of a **suffix**. There are many kinds of suffixes in English; we already saw an example of the past tense suffix *-ed*, in the example in (12a'). We can think of suffixes as meaningful units that can't stand by themselves but that can be added to a word to change the word's meaning and/or lexical category.

Term Box 4: Derivation

All of these processes of deriving a noun from a verb in (21) are alternatively referred to as **noun derivation** or **nominal derivation** or **nominalization**. The nouns which result from the derivation process are alternatively referred to as **de-verbal noun**s or **derived noun**s or **derivative noun**s or **nominalizations**. And note how the word *nominalization* is a nominalization of the verb *nominalize*!

The second point to underscore is that like with the word *claim*, this derivation from verb to noun doesn't seem to destroy the subcategorizational properties of the verb; if the verb selects a sentential complement (as in the (a) sentences of (17) through (20)), then so does its derived noun (as in the NPs in the (b) sentences in (17) through (20)).

6.3.2.2 Underived nouns in NPs with noun complement clauses

In addition to nouns that are derived from verbs which select a sentential complement, there are also some nouns which <u>cannot</u> be said to be derived from verbs that nevertheless also take noun complement clauses. Here are some examples:

(22) a. The **idea** that John ate the cake on Sandy was upsetting.

b. Bill spread a **rumor** that John ate the cake on Sandy.

c. Bill flipped out over the shocking **fact** that John ate the cake on Sandy.

d. The overwhelming **evidence** that John is guilty disturbed us.

EXERCISE [4]

Draw trees for the sentences in (22). I'll help you get a head start by giving you my own tree for (22d).

Do you think any of the nouns in bold in (22) are related to verbs?

The following structure should help you along in doing Exercise [4]:

(22d)

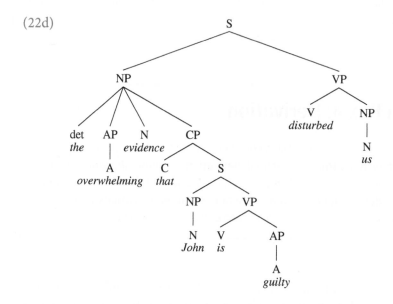

In (22), we have sentences that contain NPs with noun complement clauses, but where the head nouns (in **bold**) can't be said to derive from any verbs. What this tells us is that like verbs (and like prepositions, as we saw in

Chapter 4), some nouns have their own ability to select complements. In Chapter 11, we'll see that adjectives have the same ability to "select" what can and can't appear with them. This shows us that the different lexical categories (see Term Box 1) have a lot more in common than initially meets the eye! In Section 11.4 we'll revisit the idea that lexical categories have a lot in common, structurally.

6.3.3 the optionality of the sentential complement in the noun complement clause

Despite what we just stated in Section 6.3.2.2, something you might have noticed is that the sentential complements of nouns aren't obligatory in the same way that the corresponding complements of verbs are. Let's compare, for example, *prove* and *proof* (see (18)), or *realize* and *realization* (see (19)):

VP:

(23)   a.   Mary proved **that the earth is round**.

   b.   *Mary proved ___.

   c.   Mary realized **that John ate up the last bit of cake**.

   d.   *Mary realized ___.

NP:

(24)   a.   [Mary's proof **that the earth is round**] convinced us all.

   b.   [Mary's proof ___] convinced us all.

   c.   [Mary's realization **that John ate up the last bit of cake**] was heartbreaking.

   d.   [Mary's realization ___] was heartbreaking.

As you can see with the VPs in (23), the selectional requirements of the verbs *prove* and *realize* are exactly that: a requirement. The sentential complement has to be there, otherwise the sentence sounds bad (as in (23b) and (23d)); in other words, the complement is obligatory. With the NPs in (24), in contrast, you can see that the sentential complements are not obligatorily present; rather, they're optional. This doesn't change the fact that they're complements.

6.3.4 noun complement clauses: why CP and not S?

There's another difference between sentential complements selected by V, on the one hand, and sentential complements selected by N, on the other, at least for some English speakers.

As we already saw in detail in Chapter 5, the sentential complement of a verb can be either an S or a CP:

VP:

(25) a. Mary proved <u>the earth is round</u>.

   b. Mary proved <u>that the earth is round</u>.

   c. Mary realized <u>John ate up the last bit of cake</u>.

   d. Mary realized <u>that John ate up the last bit of cake</u>.

In contrast, however, it turns out that many English speakers don't like to eliminate the complementizer *that* when the complement clause is inside an NP:

NP:

(26) a. [Mary's proof <u>that the earth is round</u>] convinced us all.

   b. *[Mary's proof <u>the earth is round</u>] convinced us all.

   c. [Mary's realization <u>that John ate up the last bit of cake</u>] was heartbreaking.

   d. *[Mary's realization <u>John ate up the last bit of cake</u>] was heartbreaking.

There might be some speaker variation here; what do <u>you</u> think of the NPs without *that* in (26b) and (26d)?

I personally find the noun complement clauses without *that* in (26b,d) do sound significantly worse than their CP counterparts in (26a,c). This is why I felt compelled to have the new NP phrase structure rule in (9) only reflect the possibility of an embedded CP:

$$(9) \quad NP \rightarrow \begin{Bmatrix} (det) \\ (PossNP) \end{Bmatrix} (AP^*) \; N \begin{Bmatrix} (PP^*) \\ (CP) \end{Bmatrix}$$

However, if you're the kind of speaker who finds a "bare" embedded S inside NP to sound good, then your mental NP phrase structure rule would have to capture that fact, as follows:

$$(9') \quad NP \rightarrow \begin{Bmatrix} (det) \\ (PossNP) \end{Bmatrix} (AP^*) \; N \begin{Bmatrix} (PP^*) \\ (S) \\ (CP) \end{Bmatrix}$$

If you think all the noun complement clauses in (26) sound OK, then your NP rule would say that the complement clause can be either an S or a CP.

EXERCISE [5]

Whether you find (26b,d) to be grammatical or not, draw trees for these sentences, based on the alternative NP phrase structure rule in (9').

6.4 the relative clause

In Section 6.2 we defined **complex NP** as a noun phrase which contains an embedded clause. In Section 6.3, we analyzed one type of complex NP, namely, the NP with a **noun complement clause**. As we saw, the noun complement clause within NP is a full CP (for English speakers like me), which contains a standard-issue sentence (S) — i.e. the kind of sentence you might see by itself as a root clause, or the kind of sentence that you might also find embedded within VP.

In this section we'll analyze in detail the **relative clause**. The relative clause is another kind of CP within NP; therefore, an NP that contains a relative clause is also a complex NP. But a relative clause differs in some significant ways from a noun complement clause. Let's take a look at the differences, in 6.4.1 and 6.4.2.

6.4.1 a relative clause is not a complement

Let's start by comparing the noun complement clause in (27a) with the relative clause in (27b) (both in **bold** within their respective [NPs in square brackets]):

(27) a. [The claim **that Sue is a great surgeon**] is believable.

  b. [The doctor **that Mary picked**] is reliable.

The noun complement clause in (27a) should by now be familiar to you. It's a sentential complement of the noun *claim*. As we saw, certain nouns — like those in (28) — can select sentential complements, along the lines of verbs like those in (29) (see Chapter 5 for the many verbs that select sentential complements):

(28) *belief, claim, proof, realization, assumption* (derived from verbs); *idea, rumor, fact, evidence*

(29) *believe, claim, prove, realize, assume, think, ask, wonder, regret,* etc.

But now let's consider the head noun of the subject NP in (27b), *doctor*: this noun doesn't select a sentential complement. Its meaning is very different from the kinds of meanings we get with the nouns in (28) in that it doesn't **entail** any statement, or **proposition** (which is expressed syntactically by S or CP). Nevertheless, the string of words *that Mary picked*, which is inside the NP headed by the N *doctor*, is a CP. The tree in (30) helps to illustrate this:

(30)

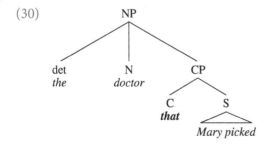

> # Side Note 6: The complementizer as an analytical tool
>
> The presence of complementizer *that* is a very useful analytical tool, when analyzing English sentences: whenever you see it, you can assume (a) that you've got a CP on your hands, and (b) that the string of words that comes after it is a sentence (S). So given the presence of the *that* right after the noun *doctor* in (27b), we can safely conclude that what immediately comes after *doctor* is a CP, and that what immediately follows the C head is an S, as in (30).

Because the CP *that Mary picked* in (27b)/(30) is not entailed by the meaning of the noun *doctor* (i.e. it's not selected), we don't consider it a CP complement; rather, it's what we would call a CP adjunct. As we saw in Section 5.4, an adjunct is "optional material which we can choose to include or not, depending on how much information we wish to give." To better understand this, let's compare the subject NP in (31a) with that in (31b) and (31c):

(31) a. [The doctor] is reliable.

   b. [The doctor **with the degree from Stony Brook University**] is reliable.

   c. [The doctor **that Mary picked**] is reliable.

The sentence in (31a) is perfectly grammatical, but it doesn't give as much information as the sentences in (31b) and (31c) do. In (31b), the PP *with the degree from Stony Brook University* helps us understand more specifically which doctor we might have in mind; in a similar manner, the relative clause *that Mary picked* in (31c) also gives us more information about which doctor we're talking about here. Thus, both the PP inside the NP in (31b) and the CP inside the NP in (31c) are phrases which further specify (= make more specific) the noun that they modify (see Chapters 1 and 2). The only difference between the two in terms of syntax is that one is a PP while the other is a CP.

6.4.2 the "gap" inside the relative clause

Now let's look at another (more significant) way in which a relative clause differs from a noun complement clause. Let's return to a comparison of (27a) and (27b), repeated here as (32a) and (32b):

(32) a. [The claim **that Sue is a great surgeon**] is believable.

   b. [The doctor **that Mary picked**] is reliable.

As we know, the noun complement clause in (32a) is a CP (headed by the complementizer *that*). If we "strip away" the complementizer *that*, the remaining S could stand on its own as a root clause, as in (33):

(33)   Sue is a great surgeon.

But now let's look at the relative clause in (32b). In some respects, it's similar to the noun complement clause in (32a): for starters, it too is "introduced" by the complementizer *that*, indicating that there's a CP inside the NP; this was already illustrated in the tree in (30) (see Side Note 6).

In a certain sense, too, the string of words that follows the complementizer *Mary picked* looks like a sentence. After all, we have an NP + VP string (namely, *Mary* and *picked*). However, if we isolate this string, we find that it can't really "stand on its own" as a root clause the way the string of words in (33) can:

(34)   *Mary picked.

In contrast with the sentence in (33), the string in (34) sounds weird all by itself: notice how something seems to be missing, as though there's a gap of some kind after the verb *picked*. If you recall our discussion on subcategorization in Section 5.2.3, you'll recognize that the VP headed by the verb *picked* is missing the direct object NP that the verb *pick* normally selects.

Side Note 7: The subcategorizational properties of *pick*

Consider what the entry for the verb *pick* looks like in your mental lexicon:

pick (lexical category: verb)
MEANING: "choose something from a set"
PRONUNCIATION: /pɪk/
SUBCATEGORIZATION: a direct object NP

So *pick* selects a direct object NP, but there doesn't appear to be any such direct object in (30)/(34).

On the other hand, if you think about the meaning of the relative clause in (30) in relation to the NP it's embedded in, we have no problem interpreting a direct object NP right after the verb *picked*, even though we can't physically see it or hear it there. (Take a moment to reflect on the meaning of the NP in (30).) In fact, we understand from this entire NP in (30) that *Mary did indeed* *pick **a doctor** —* the very *doctor* that stands as the head noun of the NP in which the relative clause is embedded. Let's sketch out this understood meaning in (35):

(35)

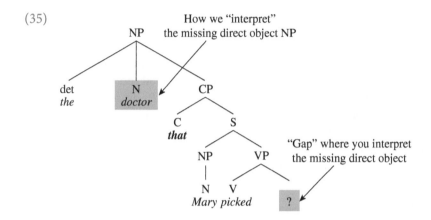

So this is another way in which relative clauses differ from noun complement clauses: as we saw with examples like (32a), noun complement clauses don't contain a gap. The embedded sentence *Sue is a great surgeon* in (32a) has no missing pieces, which is why it can "stand on its own," as in (33).

6.4.2.1 Some practice

As I said in Chapter 1, sometimes this book focuses on the question of how English speakers structure sentences, and sometimes it focuses on the complementary activity of helping you develop the tools of analysis. In this latter regard, it's time for you to get a chance to practice recognizing relative clauses on your own, using the analytical reasoning just presented. Up until now in this section I may have been making it a bit too easy, by pre-identifying for you where <u>exactly</u> the relative clause is in the NP in (30)/(32b). You should learn how to identify a relative clause on your own, so let's take out a moment to go over how to do that.

To learn how to identify a relative clause, let's consider the sentences in (36): one of these contains a noun complement clause, the other contains a relative clause, and the other one still contains a CP embedded within VP (and thus is not part of a complex NP). In no case have I pre-identified any of these for you:

(36) a.   That surgeon hates the fact that the other doctor stole her parking spot.

     b.   That surgeon believes that the other doctor stole her parking spot.

     c.   That surgeon wants the parking spot that the other doctor stole.

Imagine I ask you to find the relative clause. As always, the first thing you should do in analyzing sentences is to recall Chapter 1 and use your intuitions to divide your matrix sentence into its component subject NP and VP:

(37) a. subject NP: That surgeon
   VP: hates the fact that the other doctor stole her parking spot

b. subject NP: That surgeon
   VP: believes that the other doctor stole her parking spot

c. subject NP: That surgeon
   VP: wants the parking spot that the other doctor stole

Next, you'll want to find your relative clause. As we said in Side Note 6, it helps to look for the complementizer *that*. This will at least give you any embedded CP in a sentence. For the sentences in (36), you'll find one CP in each, as follows:

(38) a. CP within NP: **that** the other doctor stole her parking spot
   b. CP within VP: **that** the other doctor stole her parking spot
   c. CP within NP: **that** the other doctor stole

I've identified (38b) as a CP within the VP. Why? Because the CP here immediately follows the word *believes*, which is a verb. Given that the (b) sentence contains a CP embedded directly within a VP, we can rule it out; by definition it can't be a relative clause, because a relative clause is a CP within an NP. So now we're left with the (a) sentence and the (c) sentence.

Next, you'll want to figure out which, out of these two CPs in (a) and (c), has a "gap." You can verify whether you have a gap by "stripping away" the complementizer *that*, leaving yourself just with the remaining S:

(39) a. remaining S: the other doctor stole her parking spot
   c. remaining S: the other doctor stole

Then you can ask yourself whether you think there's a piece "missing" in either of these strings. I don't see a gap in (39a); this string can stand alone as a perfectly good matrix sentence.

However I think there's a gap in (39c), especially if I look at this string in relation to the context in (36c). I think the verb *steal* requires a direct object NP: *the other doctor stole* **what**? Specifically, I think he stole that surgeon's parking spot. In this way, I've identified a relative clause, and can map out my syntactic structure accordingly:

(40)

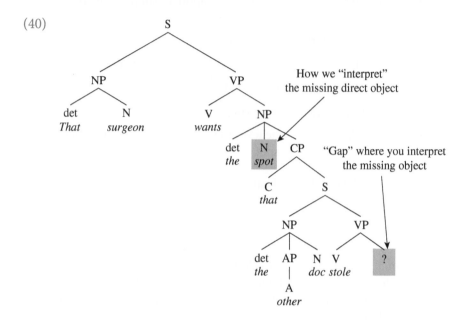

Now you'll be better prepared to do Exercise [6].

EXERCISE [6]

Use the reasoning we just went through above to draw trees for the following sentences, which contain relative clauses. Use the trees in (35) and (40) as a model, identifying the gap, and identifying the head noun that gives you the interpretation of the gap.

{1} I read the book that Mary wrote.
{2} The parking space that that guy stole from me was a good one.
{3} The professor that you reasoned with gave you a good grade.
{4} The homework that his students did was very challenging.
{5} Mary looks for students that she can assign substantive readings to.
{6} The papers that we graded got high scores.

6.4.3 analyzing the gap: the relative pronoun in object relative clauses

In the structures in (35) and (40), I temporarily put a question mark in the position of the "gap" in the relative clause. Now it's time to analyze in detail the nature of this gap.

We can begin solving the "mystery of the gap" by noting a fact about relative clauses that we've been skirting until now. Let's take the sentences in Exercise [6] and repeat them in the (a) sentences in (41) through (46). Reflecting upon the relative clauses in these sentences, you might have noticed that there's an alternative to the complementizer *that*, namely, a **wh-phrase**. Look at the corresponding (b) sentences:

(41) a. I read the book **that** Mary wrote.

      b. I read the book **which** Mary wrote.

(42) a. The parking space **that** that guy stole from me was a good one.

      b. The parking space **which** that guy stole from me was a good one.

(43) a. The professor **that** you reasoned with gave you a good grade.

      b. The professor **who** you reasoned with gave you a good grade.

(44) a. The homework **that** his students did was very challenging.

      b. The homework **which** his students did was very challenging.

(45) a. Mary looks for students **that** she can assign substantive readings to.

      b. Mary looks for students **who** she can assign substantive readings to.

(46) a. The papers **that** we graded got high scores.

      b. The papers **which** we graded got high scores.

In each of the pairs above, we have a wh-phrase, *which* or *who*, that can replace the complementizer *that*. Let's consider the wh-phrase more carefully here. As we'll see momentarily, the wh-phrases in (41–46) are not indicative of interrogatives (there are no questions in these sentences); nevertheless, the wh-phrases here have a similar syntactic behavior to those we examined in Chapter 5.

So let's recall Chapter 5, where we had an introduction to the concept of the wh-phrase, in both matrix and embedded wh-questions (see especially Term Box 6 and Section 5.3.2.2). There, we saw that wh-phrases are subject to a movement rule, **wh-movement**, which says that a wh-phrase moves from its original **deep structure** position to the position which is normally occupied by the complementizer. In a sentence like (47), then (where we have an embedded interrogative), the wh-movement rule takes the deep structure interrogative in (48a), and **transforms** it into the **surface structure** interrogative seen in (48b).

(47) Bill wondered **what** Sue fixed.

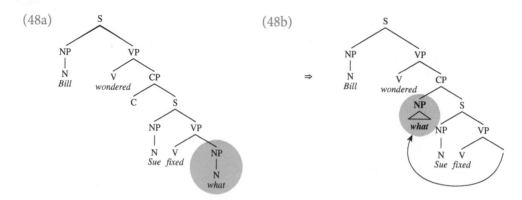

Interestingly, the relative clauses in the (b) sentences in (41) through (46) also have wh-phrases. Clearly, though, in contrast with an embedded interrogative complement like that in (47), these relative clauses are <u>not</u> interrogatives (much less complements). As we saw earlier, they're simply clauses that act to give further information about the head nouns that they modify (see Section 6.4.1). Nevertheless, relative clauses do optionally employ a wh-phrase as part of their structure. Given that the relative clause is not an embedded question, though, we can't consider the wh-phrases in relative clauses to be question words (or interrogative pronouns, as we called them in Term Box 6 in Chapter 5). In a relative clause structure, such wh-words are often referred to as relative pronouns.

What's a **relative pronoun**? Let's think of it as a wh-phrase that provides a "meaning link" between the relative clause and the head noun that it modifies. Although its function differs from that of an interrogative pronoun, as a wh-phrase it's subject to the same wh-movement rule as the interrogative pronoun in (47). Let's take a look at (49), where the wh-movement of the relative pronoun *which* is indicated by the movement arrow:

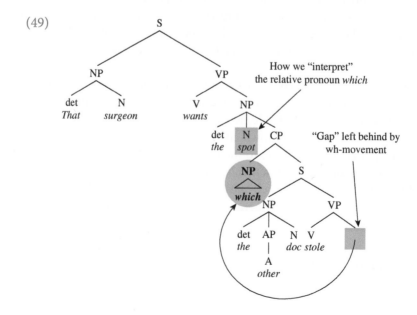

The illustration in (49) allows us to solve the "mystery of the gap" in relative clauses: comparing the structure in (40) with the same structure in (49), we see that the "gap" is none other than the gap left behind by wh-movement.

6.4.3.1 The *trace* left behind by wh-movement

As you can see in the tree in (49), the empty position left behind by wh-movement doesn't disappear. There's still a right branch connecting the embedded VP node with the position that the relative pronoun *which* used to be in, in the deep structure representation (which I haven't actually provided for you). We also left this position intact in our representation of wh-movement in Chapter 5 (see Side Note 5 in that chapter). The reason we leave this position intact is because we want to continue to represent — in the surface structure tree — the position that the wh-phrase is interpreted in (as the direct object of the verb *steal*, in the case of (49)).

This gap which is left behind as the result of movement is sometimes referred to as the **trace of movement**, which in tree structures is often abbreviated as *t* (for *trace*). Furthermore, the trace of movement and the moved element it's related to are often **co-indexed** with an identical subscript. This co-indexing is used as a device to remind us that the two positions (deep and surface) are related to one another. We can pick any index we like (it's arbitrary); as long as the moved phrase and the trace it leaves behind get the same index. Let's illustrate with the subscripted index *k* in (50):

(50)

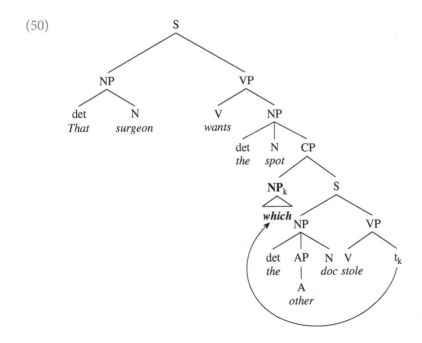

From now on, let's draw any surface structure trees that reflect the application of a movement rule (like wh-movement) in this way: the moved phrase leaves behind a trace (represented as *t* in the tree), and the trace and the moved phrase are co-indexed with the same subscript to indicate their "identity" with each other. Notice that co-indexing renders the "movement arrow" rather superfluous, but personally, I prefer to continue to use it nevertheless, as it helps make the movement path visually much clearer.

EXERCISE [7]

Draw deep and surface structure trees for each of the (b) sentences in (41) through (46). Don't forget to put in a *trace* of movement and to use co-indexing, in your surface structure trees (as I did in (50)).

6.4.3.2 The plot thickens: relative clauses with no complementizer and no relative pronoun

In considering the sentences in (41) through (46), you might have noticed that there's yet another option for the CP of the relative clause — namely, the total absence of a complementizer or relative pronoun altogether. Compare (41) through (46) with the following, where Ø is the symbol for "null" or "empty":

(41')   I read the book Ø Mary wrote.

(42')   The parking space Ø that guy stole from me was a good one.

(43')   The professor Ø you reasoned with gave you a good grade.

(44')   The homework Ø the students did was very challenging.

(45')   Mary looks for students Ø she can assign substantive readings to.

(46')   The papers Ø we graded got high scores.

Term Box 5: Zero relatives

The relative clauses seen in (41') through (46') are often referred to as **zero relatives**. We'll talk more about these in Chapter 7.

The null symbol (Ø) in the examples just given represents the position where we would otherwise find the complementizer *that* or the relative pronoun *who* and *which*. But now the facts in (41') through (46') lead us to another whole series of questions. For example: does the lack of the relative complementizer *that* and lack of relative pronoun force us to conclude that the relative clauses in (41') through (46') are not CPs but, rather, Ss? A related series of questions is: do we have to say that there's no wh-movement in the (a) sentences in (41) through (46), where we only see the complementizer *that*? If so, what do we now make of the "gap" inside the relative clause? Consider the sentence in (50), only with the complementizer *that* or Ø in the C position (instead of *which*), as in (51):

(51)

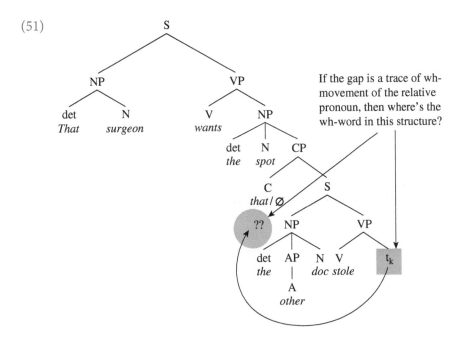

If the gap is a trace of wh-movement of the relative pronoun, then where's the wh-word in this structure?

In other words, *that* or Ø in the C position aside — what happens if we don't see any relative pronoun anywhere in the relative clause structure, as in (41') through (46') and (51)? Does the lack of visible wh-phrase mean the lack of a "gap" in the relative clause? (That can't be.) Or does it mean that the gap is somehow of a different nature? How could we have a trace of wh-movement if there's no visible relative pronoun to be found in the CP in surface structure? We'll reserve discussion of these related questions for Chapter 7.

6.4.3.3 Distinguishing types of relative clauses

All of the relative clauses we've analyzed thus far are specifically called **object relative clauses**. This is because the gap in the relative clause — namely, the trace left behind by movement of the relative pronoun — is in some kind of object position. In (41), (42), (44), and (46), the relative pronouns are the direct object NPs of the verbs *write, steal, do,* and *grade*, respectively. In (43) and (45), the relative pronouns are the objects of the prepositions *with* and *to*, respectively.

The concept of an object relative clause contrasts with that of a subject relative clause, which we'll turn to soon, in Section 6.4.4.

6.4.3.4 Other relative pronouns

The examples in (41) through (46) illustrate the relative pronouns *who* and *which*. Let's talk a bit more about the relative pronouns themselves.

For some English speakers, *who* is used when the head noun (of the NP the relative clause is embedded in) is human, while *which* is used when the head noun (of the NP the relative clause is embedded in) is nonhuman (e.g. *professor* vs. *homework*). Some speakers make yet another distinction, between *who* and *whom*. For these speakers, *who* and *whom* are both used for human **referents** (in contrast with *which*); the difference is that *whom* is used for **object/complement NPs**; in other words, *whom* is like the pronouns *him* and *them*, which are specialized for object position. This contrasts with *he* and *they*, which are specialized for subject position. Compare (52) and (53):

(52)   Mary hired **him/them**.

(53)   [The man **whom** Mary hired] was qualified.

Side Note 8: The *-m* and case

Notice the similarity between *him/them* and *whom*: they all end in the consonant *m*. This contrasts with *he*, *they*, and *who*. As pronouns specialized for object position, the *-m* pronouns are often said to exhibit **accusative case**, which is a "marking" on a word that indicates it's to be used in object position. This contrasts with *he* and *they*, which are "marked" for **nominative case**: they can only be used as subject NPs. For most English speakers, *who* is used both as a nominative (subject) and accusative (object) relative pronoun.

As we just saw in Side Note 8, most English speakers don't distinguish between object and subject when it comes to relative pronouns; these speakers use *who* for human referents in both object and subject position; consider (54), where the relative pronoun *who* is a deep structure object, just like *whom* in (53):

(54)   [The man **who** Mary hired] was qualified.

If most English speakers <u>don't</u> distinguish between subject versus object relative pronouns, then why am I even mentioning it here? My own intuition is that *whom* is used in less natural settings, like in English classrooms with instructors who might like to promote what they believe to be "correct" usage.

Much in the same way that there are English speakers who don't distinguish between subject and object relative pronouns, there are also some English speakers who don't distinguish between human and non-human relative pronouns. Compare in this regard (55) and (56): in (55) we see the human/nonhuman distinction expressed in *who* versus *which*; in contrast, in (56) we see the relative pronoun *what* being used with both human and nonhuman reference:

(55)   a.   I like [the cars **which** they manufacture in Mexico].

   b.   I like [the people **who** they hired last week].

(56)   a.   I like [the cars **what** they manufacture in Mexico].

   b.   I like [the people **what** they hired last week].

Side Note 9: Regional variation

The variation seen in (55) vs. (56) seems to be **regional**. That is, there are some regions where certain speakers (possibly older ones) are more likely to use *what* as a relative pronoun. In the United States, this use can be found for example in the southern Appalachians. It is also found in earlier forms of English.

This difference we see between speakers with respect to *who/which* (= human/nonhuman) versus *what* (= human AND nonhuman) is like the other difference we saw with English speakers, with respect to *who/whom* (= subject/object) versus *who* (= subject AND object).

Other relative wh-phrases are as follows:

(57)   a.   possessive relative *whose*: appears in the determiner position within NP, just like the possessive pronouns *his, their, our*, etc.

   b.   locative *where*: represents a place PP like *in the corner*

   c.   temporal *when*: represents a time PP like *at the time*

Here are some examples:

(58)   a.   Mary admires [the professor **whose students** the college gave honors to ___].

   b.   Mary put the table in [the corner **where** there was room ___].

   c.   We can't wait until [the time **when** we can relax ___].

EXERCISE [8]

Draw deep and surface structure trees for the sentences in (58). Don't forget to put in a *trace* of movement and to use co-indexing, in your surface structure trees. Hints: (i) The ___ indicates the position of the trace; (ii) the relative pronoun *whose* is in determiner position of the NP *whose students*, but it's this whole NP that's wh-moved. (Don't worry about *can* in (58c).)

Now it's time to move on to **subject relative clauses**.

6.5 subject relative clauses

All of the relative clauses we've analyzed thus far (with the exception of (58)) are object relative clauses, where the trace left behind by movement of the relative pronoun is in some kind of object position. Thus, as we saw, an object relative is one in which the relative pronoun is a "deep structure object" of some sort.

As you might have guessed, a **subject relative clause** is one in which the relative pronoun is a "deep structure subject." In other words, in a subject relative, the trace left behind by movement of the relative pronoun is in **subject position**. Thus far, we haven't seen any examples of subject relative clauses. (Even in our discussion of wh-questions in Chapter 5, we only saw one example of wh-movement out of a subject position; can you remember which example that was, from Exercise [8] in Chapter 5?) I've been saving discussion of wh-movement out of subject position for last; in Section 6.5.1 I'll explain why.

But first, let's start by comparing (59) and (60):

Sentence contains an NP with an object relative clause:

(59)   The doctor that they like practices in Manhattan.

Sentence contains an NP with a subject relative clause:

(60)   The doctor that likes them practices in Manhattan.

The relative clause in the sentence in (59) is our familiar object relative. We've had enough practice to help us figure that one out, but let's go over the methodology again here, so that we can then directly apply it to the identification of a subject relative clause in (60):

(59')   i.   The sentence divides into subject NP (*the doctor that they like*) and VP (*practices in Manhattan*);
ii.   The complementizer *that* signals that there's an embedded CP within the subject NP (*that they like*);
iii.   Stripping away the complementizer *that*, we're left with the S *they like*, which contains a gap (*they like* **who**?);
iv.   The gap is in **object** position.

EXERCISE [9]

Draw deep and surface structure trees for the sentence in (59). Don't forget to put in a *trace* of movement and to use co-indexing, in your surface structure trees.

Using the same methodology, we can investigate the relative clause in (60):

(60')   i.   The sentence divides into subject NP (*the doctor that likes them*) and VP (*practices in Manhattan*);

ii.   The complementizer *that* signals that there's an embedded CP within the subject NP (*that likes them*);

iii.   Stripping away the complementizer *that*, we're left with the S *likes them*, which contains a gap (**who** *likes them?*)

iv.   The gap is in **subject** position.

Let's draw a surface structure tree for the subject NP in the sentence in (60), only replacing the complementizer *that* with the relative pronoun *who*:

(61)

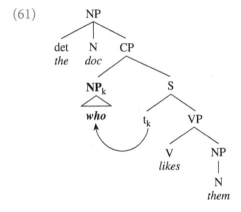

To get more practice, let's consider a few more examples, in (62) through (64). Just focus on the (b) sentences; the (a) sentences are only there to remind you that a relative clause can also be introduced by the complementizer *that*:

(62)   a.   John wants a doctor that specializes in headaches.

b.   John wants a doctor who specializes in headaches.

(63)   a.   The woman that specializes in headaches met with John.

b.   The woman who specializes in headaches met with John.

(64)   a.   They spoke to the doctor that treated John.

b.   They spoke to the doctor who treated John.

EXERCISE [10]

Draw deep and surface structure trees for the (b) sentences in (62) through (64), each of which contains a subject relative clause. Don't forget to put in a *trace* of movement and to use co-indexing, in your surface structure trees.

6.5.1 two special features of subject relatives

Subject relative clauses have two properties that make them different from object relative clauses: **string vacuous movement** and, for some speakers, the **obligatoriness** of the relative complementizer/relative pronoun. Let's take each of these in turn.

6.5.1.1 String vacuous movement

You've noticed by now that in this chapter I used the object relative clause as a way to enter into the discussion on relative clauses in general. I did this for the <u>same</u> reason that in the Chapter 5 discussion on wh-questions, I focused primarily on wh-phrases in **nonsubject position**. So what's the problem with wh-movement of an interrogative pronoun or a relative pronoun out of subject position? Why have I been avoiding examples that involve this kind of movement?

It's because they wouldn't have been very helpful in introducing the concept of wh-movement. To understand why, let's digress for a moment, turning back to our Chapter 5 discussion of interrogatives (and then we'll come back to subject relatives). Let's compare the embedded interrogative in (65) with wh-movement of an object wh-phrase, and the embedded interrogative in (66) with wh-movement of a subject wh-phrase. Recall from our earlier tree structures and discussion that *t* means "trace of movement" (i.e. the gap left behind as a result of movement), and the co-indexing captures the relationship between this deep structure position (where the trace is) and the surface structure position of the wh-phrase:

(65) sentence: Bill wondered what Sue fixed.

      deep structure: Bill wondered [Sue fixed **what**]

      surface structure: Bill wondered [**what**$_k$ Sue fixed **t**$_k$]

(66) sentence: Bill wondered who fixed the sink.

      deep structure: Bill wondered [**who** fixed the sink]

      surface structure: Bill wondered [**who**$_k$ **t**$_k$ fixed the sink]

EXERCISE [11]

Refresh your Chapter 5 knowledge: draw the deep and surface structure trees for the sentences in (65) and (66).

The embedded questions are represented in [square brackets]. As you can see, movement of the object wh-phrase *what* in (65) from its deep structure position to its surface structure position results in a change of word order. This change in word order is in fact the very phenomenon that leads us to believe that there's a wh-movement rule in the first place.

Now imagine we had started our discussion of interrogatives in Chapter 5 just by looking at the sentence in (66): it would've been pretty difficult to convince you, based on an interrogative with a subject wh-phrase, that there's any wh-movement. This is because movement of the wh-phrase is what we call **string vacuous movement**. That is, movement of the subject wh-phrase *who* in (66) from its deep structure position to its surface structure position does <u>not</u> result in a change in word order. This is because there's nothing in between the subject position inside the embedded question (where the *who* originates) and the C position (where the *who* ends up as a result of movement) that the wh-phrase *who* moves around. This is in contrast with the object wh-movement we see in (65), where the wh-phrase *what* moves around the words *Sue fixed*.

Given that we can "see" the wh-movement (or, **displacement** as it is sometimes called) in sentences like (65), we can simply generalize to all wh-phrases, and assume that whenever we have a wh-phrase in the structure, that there has been movement to the C position.

Now back to subject relative clauses: the above discussion also applies to wh-movement of relative pronouns. Compare (67), a sentence with an object relative clause, and (68), a sentence with a subject relative clause:

(67) sentence: The doctor who they like practices in Manhattan.

      deep structure: The doctor [they like **who**] practices in Manhattan.

      surface structure: The doctor [**who**$_k$ they like **t**$_k$] practices in Manhattan.

(68) sentence: The doctor who likes them practices in Manhattan.

      deep structure: The doctor [**who** likes them] practices in Manhattan.

      surface structure: The doctor [**who**$_k$ **t**$_k$ likes them] practices in Manhattan.

EXERCISE [12]

Play along: draw the deep and surface structure trees for the sentences in (67) and (68).

The relative clauses are represented in [square brackets]. Again, as you can see, movement of the object relative pronoun *who* in (67) results in a change of word order; you can physically see (and hear) that *who* moves around the words *they like*. In contrast, wh-movement of the subject relative pronoun *who* in (68) doesn't result in any change in word order. Again, here, the movement is "string vacuous," as there's nothing in between the subject position inside the relative clause and the C position to which it moves, that could give us any evidence of the displacement of *who*. Nevertheless, as with wh-questions, given that we can see/hear the wh-movement in sentences like (67), we simply generalize to all wh-phrases and assume that whenever we have a wh-phrase in the structure, there has been movement to the C position.

6.5.1.2 The obligatoriness of the relative complementizer/relative pronoun

Another difference between subject and object relative clauses has to do with the C position.

As we saw in Section 6.4.3.2, object relative clauses alternatively allow (i) *that*, (ii) a relative pronoun, or (iii) Ø in the C position:

Sentences with object relative clauses:

(69) a. The doctor **that** they like practices in Manhattan.

b. The doctor **who** they like practices in Manhattan.

c. The doctor Ø they like practices in Manhattan.

However, some English speakers don't allow for these three options when it comes to subject relative clauses. For these speakers, the C position has to have <u>either</u> the complementizer *that* <u>or</u> the relative pronoun. In other words, the C position has to be obligatorily "filled" with something:

Sentences with subject relative clauses, for many English speakers:

(70) a. Mary met the doctor **that** practices in Manhattan.

b. Mary met the doctor **who** practices in Manhattan.

c. *Mary met the doctor Ø practices in Manhattan.

Comparing (69c) and (70c), we see that while English speakers universally accept an "empty" C position for object relatives, some don't accept this state of affairs with subject relatives. There are, nevertheless, many English speakers who <u>do</u> allow for all three options in (70), as follows:

(70') a. Mary met the doctor **that** practices in Manhattan.

b. Mary met the doctor **who** practices in Manhattan.

c. Mary met the doctor Ø practices in Manhattan.

For these speakers, (70'c) sounds just as good as (70a,b) (and it means the same thing). Subject relative clauses such as that in (70'c) are sometimes referred to as **subject contact relatives**.

Which kind of speaker are you?

Side Note 10: Regional variation again?

It's not clear to what extent the variation seen with (70) vs. (70') is regional, and to what extent it just has to do with **register**. In the linguistics literature it's often identified as being associated with **Appalachian English** and **African American English**; however, I personally hear all different kinds of New Yorkers using subject contact relative clauses (like that in (70'c)), so perhaps more of a study needs to be made of how widespread this structure is. Sometimes the claims made about the use of a particular construction are based on a genuine lack of understanding of what the real usage facts are, amongst English speakers. One thing we do know is that historical English texts reveal that subject contact relatives have been used by English speakers since the Middle Ages.

6.6 conclusions

In this chapter, we found reason to revise the NP phrase structure rule:

(71) $\text{CP} \quad \rightarrow \quad \text{C} \quad \text{S}$

$\text{S} \quad \rightarrow \quad \text{NP} \quad \text{VP}$

$\textbf{NP} \quad \rightarrow \quad \begin{Bmatrix} \textbf{(det)} \\ \textbf{(PossNP)} \end{Bmatrix} \textbf{(AP*) N} \begin{Bmatrix} \textbf{(PP*)} \\ \textbf{(CP)} \end{Bmatrix}$

$\text{PossNP} \quad \rightarrow \quad \begin{Bmatrix} \text{(det)} \\ \text{(PossNP)} \end{Bmatrix} \text{(AP*) PossN} \begin{Bmatrix} \text{(PP*)} \\ \text{(CP)} \end{Bmatrix}$

$\text{VP} \quad \rightarrow \quad \text{V (PP) (NP)} \begin{Bmatrix} \text{(NP)} \\ \text{(S)} \\ \text{(CP)} \end{Bmatrix} \text{(AP) (PP*)}$

$\text{PP} \quad \rightarrow \quad \text{(mod) P} \begin{Bmatrix} \text{(NP)} \\ \text{(PP)} \end{Bmatrix}$

$\text{AP} \quad \rightarrow \quad \text{(deg) A}$

The NP is now beginning to look a bit more like the VP: just like the VP, N can be followed by a CP. The reader can further their appreciation of the similarities between N and V by reading Chomsky (1970). (In Section 11.4 we'll see how structural similarities across phrases ends up getting played out out in a revised version of phrase structure theory.)

At the same time, the two types of CP that can be embedded within NP illustrate that there are still differences between NP and VP. The **noun complement clause** makes N and those Vs which take embedded sentences look most like one another. At the same time, even here, there are differences: while declaratives embedded under V can appear without the complementizer *that* (see Chapter 5), as we saw in Section 6.3.4, many English speakers find it difficult to embed a bare S (with no CP layer) in the noun complement clause construction. Furthermore, the embedded CP in noun complement clause constructions is not obligatory; the corresponding CP within VP is, as we saw in Section 6.3.3.

Additionally, the **relative clause** seems to be unique to the NP. This highly complicated **modifier** differs from the noun-complement clause in a number of ways. For starters, it's a modifier of the noun, and not a complement to the noun. In addition, in contrast with the noun complement clause — which only allows *that* inside its CP — the relative clause allows relative pronouns (or even nothing) within CP. This is related to the fact that the relative clause involves movement of the relative pronoun to CP, making relative clauses syntactically more similar to embedded interrogatives, even though we must be careful to not analyze them as questions, given that semantically, they are not questions. Examination of this movement operation in turn allowed us to refine our analysis of the deep structure site of the moved element: we now have a theory of a **trace of movement**. In Chapter 7 we'll get a better handle on those relative clauses with a missing *that*/missing relative pronoun and also pursue further study of the trace of movement.

Relative clauses thus gave us the opportunity to analyze another case where a **movement operation** is essential to the syntactic structure under analysis. The gap in the relative clause is perhaps one of the most complex phenomena we've analyzed in this book thus far. In terms of semantics, the wh-pronoun relates to the head noun that the CP (in which the wh-pronoun resides) modifies. If you continue to study syntax beyond this book, you'll learn more about how this interpretation of the relative pronoun in relation to the head N works.

list of terms/concepts

adjunct
African American English
Appalachian English
case (accusative case;
     nominative case)
co-index (co-indexation;
     co-reference)
complement (sentential
     complement)
complex NP
deep structure
derivation (derive)
derivative nouns
derived nouns (underived nouns;
     noun derivation; nominal
     derivation; nominalization;
     verbal noun)
de-verbal nouns
displacement
entailment
form (morphological form)
gap
Kleene Star
lexical ambiguity (lexically
     ambiguous)
lexical category
modifier
movement operation

nominalization
nonsubject position
noun complement clause
object
object/complement
object relative clause
obligatoriness
part of speech
past tense
proposition (sentence)
referent
regional variation
register
relative clause
relative pronoun
selection
string vacuous movement
subcategorization
subject
subject position
subject relative clause
suffix
surface structure
trace of movement
transformation
wh-movement
wh-phrase
zero relatives

7

Making Their Presence Felt: Silent Categories

expected outcomes for this chapter

- You'll deepen your understanding of structural complexity and will become familiar with the concept of *silence* in sentence structure.
- You'll develop more confidence with the concepts from previous chapters (e.g., sentence structure, embedded sentences, subject position, pronominal, relative clauses).
- You'll gain a more in-depth understanding of the *trace* of movement and of co-indexing.
- You'll become familiar with the following terms: wanna-*contraction*, *imperative sentences*, *reflexive pronouns*, *agreement* (*person, number, gender*), *infinitivals*, *silent pro*, *echo-question*, *co-reference*, *zero-relatives*.

7.1 what is a *silent category* in sentence structure?

Up until now, most of the constituents we've been analyzing in this book are pronounced, or uttered — or put yet another way: vocalized. That is, they have been associated with **speech sound**. In order to understand what I mean by this, consider the following very simple sentence:

(1)   The baby cried.

Understanding Sentence Structure: An Introduction to English Syntax, First Edition.
Christina Tortora.
© 2018 John Wiley & Sons, Inc. Published 2018 by John Wiley & Sons, Inc.

In (1) we have an S which breaks down into a subject NP *the baby* and a VP, headed by the verb *cried*:

(2)

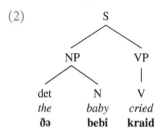

Note that every single phrase and terminal node in this sentence is pronounced with stuff that you can actually hear when spoken (or see when written, or consciously imagine when thought). That is, there is actual speech sound associated with every category in the tree, as follows:

- the entire S has the speech sounds in the words *the* and *baby* and *cried*;
- the subject NP has the speech sounds in the words *the* and *baby*;
- and the VP has the speech sounds in the word *cried*;
- the determiner has the speech sounds in the word *the*;
- the noun has the speech sounds in the word *baby*;
- the verb has the speech sounds in the word *cried*.

The speech sounds are the actual sound you hear coming out a person's mouth when they utter the sentence in (1); these sounds are represented in the bold **phonetic symbols** *ðə bebi kraid* under the words *the* and *baby* and *cried* in (2).

This might at first glance seem like a very odd thing to point out about the elements in a structure: isn't it obvious that when we utter an English sentence, sound comes out of our mouths? Indeed, if the sentence in (2) existed without any perceivable sound when spoken (or words when written, or specific concepts when thought), how would you or anyone else know what you're saying with the tree in (2)? How could you even interpret that tree, without the words, as in (3)?

(3)

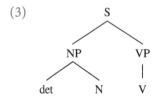

After all, even when you just <u>think</u> the sentence in (1)/(2), there has to be some content there; otherwise, you wouldn't have any way of distinguishing between a sentence like *The baby cried*, in (1), and the sentence *My dog slept* — which like (1), also gets the structure in (3):

(4)

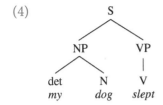

Despite all of this reasoning, in this chapter we're going to explore the idea that sometimes there are some elements in a sentence that are unpronounced, or silent. The idea is this: there are constituents in sentence structure — real entities with real meaning — which, unlike the phrases and words we see in (2) and (4), have no sound associated with them.

Side Note 1: Sentence structure as a product of the mind

In Chapter 1, I introduced this book's approach to sentence structure: structure is not something that's out there in the world. Rather, it's a product of the mind. When we're finished working through this chapter, I hope it'll be clear that the existence of silent categories in English sentences serves as support for our approach to structure. See the conclusions at the end of the chapter, for a follow-up.

7.1.1 a review of the *trace* of movement

To make this idea more concrete, let's start by recalling the **movement operations** that we saw in Chapters 3 through 6. In Chapter 3, we looked at the **passivization operation**, in Chapter 4 we saw the **particle shift** rule, and in Chapters 5 and 6 we looked at **wh-movement**. Each of these movement rules takes a **deep structure** (d-structure) phrase structure tree — namely, a tree that was created by the phrase structure rules, and transforms it into a different tree (called a **surface structure**, or s-structure, tree). Recall that different movement rules "target" different elements within the tree. For example, wh-movement targets a wh-phrase, moving it to the C position in CP. For the purposes of illustration, let's revisit an example of a sentence with an embedded interrogative, such as that in (5):

(5)   Bill wondered [**what** Sue fixed ___]

As we saw in detail in Chapter 6, whenever a wh-phrase gets moved to the C position by the wh-movement operation, it leaves behind a **trace**. This trace represents the d-structure position of the wh-phrase (that is, the position where the wh-phrase started out, before it was moved). This trace, abbreviated t_k, can be seen in (6):

(6)

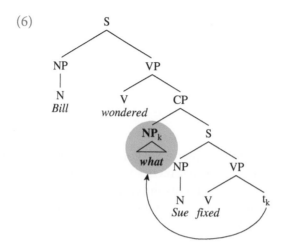

Side Note 2: Co-indexing reminder

Remember that we used a subscript, such as the "k" in (6), on both the trace and the wh-phrase; this subscript serves as an **index**, which allows us to represent the connection between the d-structure and s-structure positions of the wh-phrase. Thus, the two ks we see on *what* and on the trace in (6) serve as co-indices, representing the idea that the two positions are related via movement. (Of course, the movement arrow also makes the relatedness of the two positions explicit.)

Given the presence of t_k in (6), our phrase structure tree can maintain its original deep structure configuration. That is, the binary-branching structure originally created by the VP phrase structure rule is preserved, despite the fact that wh-movement displaces the object NP *what*. So in the case of (6), we don't have to destroy the original binary-branching structure of the VP, once the object has moved from its d-structure position; in this way, our s-structure tree allows us to still see the original position of the object.

In this chapter, I want to work towards an understanding of the trace as something real. In fact, we can think of it as being as real as any other position in the tree — as real, for example, as the position occupied by the NPs *Sue* and *Bill* in (6). The one major difference between t_k on the one hand, and *Sue* and *Bill* on the other, is that t_k is not actually pronounced; that is, there are no speech sounds associated with it. It's as if your mind knows the trace is there within the VP in (6), but you just don't open your mouth to say it. It's a **silent constituent**.

Then, after we talk about the trace of movement, in Sections 7.3 and 7.4 I'll introduce two other kinds of silent constituent, which are different in nature from the trace of movement. For now, though, let's continue to talk about trace.

Term Box 1: Silence

Many different words have been used in the literature for elements in the structure that are silent. Sometimes a trace is referred to as an **empty category**; or as a **covert element** (as opposed to an **overt element**); or as an element that is **phonologically null** (capturing the idea that there is no "sound" associated with it). As we'll see in Sections 7.3 and 7.4, there are other silent (or empty, or phonologically null) categories, which differ from the trace in that they are not something that is left behind by movement.

EXERCISE [1]

In Section 3.6.1 example (32b) illustrates the "after" of the passivization operation. (Note that this "after" is what we would now call the **surface structure**.) Now that we've been introduced to the concept of a "trace," redraw the tree in (32b) with a trace of movement, such that the original binary-branching structure of VP is preserved.

7.2 the reality of the *trace* of movement:
wanna-contraction

I spent some time immediately above trying to convince you that the trace of movement is real — that it's really there in the structure. But what proof do I have?

Let's consider some interesting data which seems to suggest that English speakers do indeed unconsciously recognize the presence of the trace in the sentence, despite the fact that it goes unpronounced — i.e., despite the fact that it's silent.

We'll start by making some basic observations about the words *want to*, which I've put in bold in (7a):

(7a) They **want to** leave early.

Please say the sentence in (7a) out loud a few times. When you do this, what you'll notice is that there's one of two ways to say it: you can either say the words *want to* separately, as in (7a), or you can put them together and pronounce them as one word, *wanna*, as in (7b):

(7b) They **wanna** leave early.

If you say (7a) and (7b) a few times to yourself, I think you'll find that pronouncing *want* and *to* as separate words feels rather unnatural in (7a); it requires you speak unusually slowly (and for me, very unnaturally and self-consciously). It's far more natural, in speaking, to pronounce the two words as *wanna*, as in (7b).

This phenomenon is referred to as ***wanna*-contraction**. What's interesting about *wanna*-contraction is that, despite the fact that it happens so naturally and so regularly, English speakers don't do it in every case where the words *want* and *to* are near each other in the sentence. Consider the sentence in (8a), in which *want* and *to* are clearly not right next to each other:

(8a) They **want** Sue **to** leave early.

In (8a), these two words are separated by the NP *Sue*; notice that in this case, we can't get *wanna*-contraction:

(8b) *They **wan** Sue **na** leave early.

Remember that the asterisk means that the sentence is ungrammatical; therefore, what (8b) shows is that English speakers don't allow for the sequence *wan-na* (i.e. *wanna*-contraction is disallowed), if the words *want* and *to* are separated by an intervening phrase, such as *Sue*. In other words, ***wanna*-contraction is only possible when *want* and *to* are right next to each other**. Clearly, *want* and *to* are not next to each other in (8a).

Now compare the sentence in (8a) with the very similar sentence in (9):

(9) They **want** WHO **to** leave early?

Term Box 2: Echo questions

Echo questions differ from regular questions in that in an echo, the wh-phrase does not move from its d-structure position. Also, an echo question can have a kind of "surprise-disapproval" feeling to it. It isn't just a genuine request for information; rather, it's like a repetition (in question form) of a statement someone has already made.

The sentence in (9) is just like the sentence in (8a), except instead of the NP *Sue*, we now have the NP *who*, in what we would call an **echo question** (see Term Box 2). And just as in (8a), ***want*** and ***to*** are not right next to each other in (9), as WHO is in between them. So expectedly, just as with (8b), *want* and *to* cannot contract:

(10) *They **wan** WHO **na** leave early?

But let's see how the plot thickens: imagine now that we target the wh-phrase *who* in (9) for wh-movement, as in (11):

(11) **Who** do they want __ to leave early?

Side Note 3: *Do* and *to*

In Chapter 8 we'll discuss what the verb *do* is doing in the sentence in (9) (note that it's nowhere to be found in the corresponding declarative in (5)). As for where the *to* goes in the structure: we'll discuss that in Section 7.3.2.1.

The sentence in (11) is a regular wh-question. In this sentence, wh-movement has removed the word *who* from its d-structure position; as a result, in contrast with (8a) and (9), the words *want* and *to* no longer seem to be separated by anything in (11). Since the rule of *wanna*-contraction says that **wanna-contraction is only possible when *want* and *to* are right next to each other**, we might imagine that *wanna*-contraction should be possible in (11), now that *want* and *to* are right next to each other.

Or should it? The question is: are *want* and *to* <u>really</u> right next to each other in (11)? On the one hand, wh-movement has removed *who* from its original position standing between *want* and *to*, so it seems as if *want* and *to* are indeed now right next to each other:

(12) a.   Who do they **want to** leave early?

On the other hand, we argued in Chapter 6, as we have in this chapter, that wh-movement leaves a trace, as in (12b):

(12) b.   **Who**$_k$ do they want **t**$_k$ to leave early?

Under the claim that the trace of movement is a real entity, then as a real entity, it might count as something standing in between *want* and *to* in (12b). On the other hand, if it's <u>not</u> real in the mind of English speakers, then it should <u>not</u> count as something standing in between *want* and *to* in (12b), and *wanna*-contraction should be possible.

So now let's think about what the actual facts are: Do you think *want* and *to* can contract into *wanna* in (12a)?

I don't think so — and neither do many other English speakers. Let's compare the sentences in (7b) and (12a) with the sentence in (13), where I've <u>experimentally</u> forced *wanna*-contraction:

(7b)   They **wanna** leave early.

(12a)   Who do they **want to** leave early?

(13)   *Who do they **wanna** leave early?

The sentence in (13) sounds ungrammatical to the ears of many English speakers, compared with the sentence in (7b) (where *wanna*-contraction is possible) and compared with the sentence in (12a). In fact, we should also compare the sentence in (12a) directly with the sentence in (7a); let's put them back-to-back here:

(7a)   They **want to** leave early.

(12a)   Who do they **want to** leave early?

EXERCISE [2]

Make a real study of (7a) vs. (12a): say each sentence to yourself, and really think about the most natural ways to pronounce each of them. It'll really help your understanding if you engage in this scientific experiment yourself, rather than take my word for it.

As we already said for (7a), you'll find that pronouncing *want* and *to* as separate words in this sentence feels rather artificial; it requires you speak unnaturally slowly. This contrasts with the pronunciation of *want* and *to* in (12a): not only does it feel natural to pronounce these words separately, but it's actually necessary; they can't be contracted into the form *wanna*.

To conclude, the inability of the apparently adjacent words *want* and *to* in (12a,b) to contract into *wanna* tells us that these words are in fact not adjacent: they act as if they are separated by something, just as in (8a) and (9). This suggests that the trace of movement in (12b) is perceived by English speakers as a real entity standing between *want* and *to* (just like the NP *Sue* in (8a), and the wh-phrase WHO in (9)). This is despite the fact that the trace of movement is unpronounced, or silent.

7.3 other kinds of silence: the *null pronoun*

English has a few other kinds of silent categories in addition to the trace of movement. In this section we'll look at the null pronoun found in (i) imperatives and (ii) certain kinds of embedded sentences. Let's begin with imperatives.

7.3.1 imperatives

In Chapter 5, we learned that sentences come in different types, in terms of the kinds of "effect" we want to have on our interlocutors when we speak. So far, we've talked about declaratives and questions: declaratives can be thought of as statements that provide information, while questions can be thought of as requests for information.

In addition to declaratives and questions, there are also imperatives. Unlike declaratives and interrogatives, imperatives neither provide information nor request information. Rather, they serve as commands. Consider the examples in (14):

(14) a. Wash the dishes!
      b. Clean the kitchen!
      c. Eat your dinner!
      d. Eat!
      e. Sleep!
      f. Give that book to Mary!

Side Note 4: The exclamation point

Keep in mind that the exclamation point used in the imperative sentences in (14) is just an artifact of writing; in speaking, there is no punctuation. It's just that in writing, the exclamation point is often used to convey an imperative. (Nevertheless, it's not necessary; each of the sentences in (14) could just as easily be written with a period.)

My guess is that as an English speaker, you would agree that the sentences in (14) are very different from both declaratives and interrogatives. A speaker who utters sentences of the type in (14) is doing so to get a very specific kind of response from his or her interlocutor(s), or, "hearer(s)." If I utter the sentence in (14a) for example, I expect a specific reaction from the person (or people) listening to me — namely, to actually go and wash the dishes.

So in terms of meaning, imperatives are understood as commands. In terms of structure, there is also something very peculiar about imperatives: specifically, you'll have noticed that all the examples in (14) seem to be missing a subject NP. All these sentences surprisingly start with verbs (*wash, clean, eat, sleep, give*), which is unexpected, given that our sentence phrase structure rule says that every sentence has a subject NP:

(15) S → NP VP

But where is the subject NP in the examples in (14)? These apparently "subjectless" sentences lead us to conclude one of two things: either

[A] there are quite simply some sentences that just don't have a subject NP, or
[B] there is a subject NP in these sentences, and we just need to identify what it is.

Let's take a moment to entertain the possibility in [A], though I should warn you that I'm going to immediately reject this possibility!

So, what if [A] were true? What would a sentence with no subject look like? Perhaps it would look like the tree in (16):

(16)

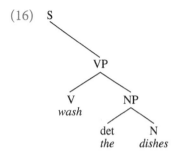

Under this view of imperatives, we would have to admit that in some cases, the subject NP in the phrase structure rule in (15) is optional.

Or are imperatives perhaps "bare VPs," as in (17)? After all, if there is no evidence for a subject, why assume they are sentences at all?

(17)

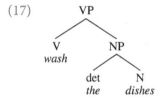

As we're now going on to see, it turns out that [A] cannot be correct — neither as it is manifested in (16), nor as it is manifested in (17). Instead, we'll see that [B] is actually the most promising way to characterize imperative sentences.

But if [B] is true, what would a sentence with such an "unidentified subject" look like? It would have to look something like the tree in (18):

(18)

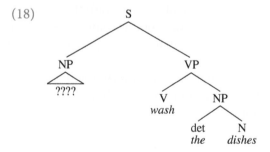

Let's now look at why [A] can't be true, and identify what the subject NP in (18) actually is.

EXERCISE [3]

Using our phrase structure rules (see Section 6.6), draw trees for the sentences in (14). Given the apparent lack of subject NP in these sentences, just use a place-holder NP for now, as I did in (18).

7.3.1.1 Evidence for the silent *you*

What we'll see in this section is that, despite the fact that there is no "pronounced" subject expressed in the imperative sentences in (14), it's counterintuitive to conclude that there is no subject in the structure. Let's look at the reasons for thinking this.

7.3.1.1.1 Interpretation

For starters, in terms of interpretation, we already concluded that imperatives are commands. But who is receiving the command? English speakers agree that imperatives have an understood subject, namely, *you*. In fact, it's even possible to express this *you*, as follows (compare (19) with (14)):

(19)   a.   You, wash the dishes!

     b.   You, clean the kitchen!

     c.   You, eat your dinner!

     d.   You, eat!

     e.   You, sleep!

     f.   You, give that book to Mary!

Side Note 5: Negative imperatives

Use of the pronoun *you* is even more natural when the imperative is in the negative, as in {2}:

{1} Don't go in there!
{2} Don't *you* go in there!

But even if we were to ignore the facts of (19), there is independent evidence from **reflexive pronouns** that there is a silent subject NP in imperatives, and that this silent subject NP has the meaning of *you*. Let's look at the evidence.

7.3.1.1.2 A digression on reflexive pronouns

In order to understand this evidence, we need to digress for just a moment, and get a crash course on reflexive pronouns, such as *myself, yourself, ourselves*, etc. Understanding what reflexive pronouns are, and how they work, will ultimately help us see that we have no choice but to conclude that imperative sentences have a silent subject NP, as in (18).

Let's start by considering the reflexive pronouns in (20):

(20)   a.   **Mary** believes in **herself**.

     b.   **John** believes in **hisself / himself**.

c.   **You** believe in **yourself**.

d.   **You** believe in **yourselves**.

e.   **We** believe in **ourselves**.

f.   **I** believe in **myself**.

g.   **They** believe in **theirselves / themselves**.

Side Note 6: Variation in the "form" of reflexives

Some English speakers use the reflexives **hiss**elf and **theirs**elves, while others use **him**self and **them**selves instead. If you think about the list of reflexives in (20), you'll see that **hiss**elf and **theirs**elves is consistent with the other reflexives, like **yours**elf, **ours**elves, **mys**elf. In all these cases, the pronoun preceding the "self/selves" is a possessive pronoun: his, their, your, our, my. (See Chapter 2 for possessive pronouns.) Speakers who instead use the reflexives **him**self and **them**selves have not regularized the possessive pronoun across the **reflexive paradigm**; note that him and them are not possessive. This is similar to the forms **uss**elves and **mes**elf, used by some British English speakers.

As can be seen in (20), a reflexive pronoun (sometimes just referred to as a reflexive) is a pronoun — such as *her*, *his*, *him*, *your*, etc. — which combines with the form *-self* or *-selves*.

Reflexive pronouns are not like other pronouns: they're very picky about when and where they can occur in a sentence. Specifically, a reflexive pronoun cannot occur by itself; it needs an **antecedent**. What is an antecedent? In (20a), the antecedent of *herself* is *Mary*; in (20b), the antecedent of *himself* is *John*; and so forth. In other words, the antecedent of a reflexive is another NP in the sentence which shares the same **features** as the reflexive — in terms of **person**, **number**, and **gender** (see Term Box 3). When two categories (such as the antecedent of a reflexive and the reflexive itself) are linked with the same features in this way, we say that they **agree** in their features, or that they exhibit **feature agreement**. (In Chapter 8 we'll talk about another type of agreement, namely, subject–verb agreement.) Thus, in (20a), both *herself* and *Mary* are third person singular feminine; in (20b) both *hisself* and *John* are third person singular masculine; in (20c), both *you* and *yourself* are second person singular (no gender specified); and so forth.

EXERCISE [4]

Identify all the different antecedents in (20).

Term Box 3: Person, number, gender

Pronouns of all kinds (nominative, accusative, possessive, reflexive) can be described in terms of at least three features: person, number, and gender. Gender reflects whether the pronoun in question refers to a masculine or a feminine entity (e.g., *he* vs. *she*; *him* vs. *her*; *his* vs. *her*; *himself* vs. *herself*), or even "neuter" (e.g., *it, its, itself*). Number reflects whether the pronoun in question refers to a single entity, or a plurality of entities (e.g., *he* vs. *they*, *him* vs. *them*, *himself* vs. *themselves*). Person refers to whether the pronoun in question refers to the "speaker," which is first person (e.g., *I, me, my, mine, we, us, our, ours*); the "hearer," which is second person (e.g., *you, your, yours*), or neither, which is third person (e.g., *he, she, him, her, they, them*, etc.). See Term Box 8 in Chapter 2, and Side Note 8 in Chapter 6, for additional commentary on case features. See Chapter 10 for the concept of the tense feature.

The following examples show that a sentence with a reflexive pronoun that has no antecedent is ungrammatical:

(21)   a.   ***Himself** is a good person.
          (cf. **He** is a good person.)

      b.   *They believe in **himself**.
          (cf. They believe in **him**.)

      c.   *They believe in **yourself**.
          (cf. They believe in **you**.)

      d.   *They believe in **yourselves**.

The sentence in (21a) is ungrammatical because there is no other NP in the sentence that can act as an antecedent to the reflexive pronoun *himself*. The sentences in (21b,c,d) are ungrammatical for the same reason. Furthermore, these examples show (in comparison with the sentences in (20)) that an antecedent <u>must</u> be an NP that has the same features as the reflexive pronoun. Thus, (21b) is ungrammatical because while *they* is third person plural, *himself* is third person singular; so the reflexive pronoun *himself* thus has no "matching" antecedent in this sentence. Likewise, (21c) is ungrammatical because (again), while *they* is third person plural, *yourself* is second person singular; thus, the reflexive pronoun *yourself* has no "matching" antecedent. The same goes for (21d): even though both *they* and *yourselves* are plural, the reflexive *yourselves* doesn't match with *they*, in terms of person: *they* is third person, while *yourselves* is second person.

EXERCISE [5]

For each of the following grammatical sentences, state what features the antecedent and the reflexive share, in terms of person, number, and gender (if gender is relevant). Likewise, for each of the ungrammatical sentences (those with an asterisk), state the whether the mismatch between antecedent and reflexive is in terms of person, number, or gender.

Example:

{1} **She** admires **herself**.

The reflexive *herself* has an antecedent that matches in **third (person)**, **singular (number)**, and **feminine (gender)**.

{2} ****She** admires **himself**.

The pronoun *she* cannot be an antecedent for *himself*, because it doesn't match in terms of gender (*she* is feminine, but *himself* is masculine).

{3} ****She** admires **themselves**.   {6} **He** admires **himself**.
{4} ****I** admire **herself**.   {7} **We** admire **ourselves**.
{5} ****They** admire **ourselves**.   {8} ****We** admire **themselves**.

The facts exhibited in (20) and (21) reveal to us that English speakers unconsciously follow a rule regarding the use of reflexive pronouns; let's spell out that rule here:

> **Reflexive pronoun rule:** English speakers only use a reflexive pronoun in a sentence if it has an antecedent (where "antecedent" is another NP in the same sentence that has the same features as the reflexive pronoun; see Term Box 3).

7.3.1.1.3 Back to imperatives

So let's come back from our digression. Now that we know about the reflexive pronoun rule, we can see how their special behavior gives us a clue as to how to analyze imperative sentences.

Recall that we were considering two possible ways to analyze imperative sentences such as those in (14): either

[A] imperatives don't have a subject NP, or
[B] there <u>is</u> a subject NP in these sentences, and we just need to identify what it is.

Remember: we've been on the path to rejecting analysis [A], and championing analysis [B].

So now, what can the **reflexive pronoun rule** tell us about the subject in imperative sentences? Well, let's compare the grammatical sentences from (20c,d) (repeated here as (22a,b)) with the ungrammatical sentences in (22c,d):

(22)   a.   **You** believe in **yourself**.

        b.   **You** believe in **yourselves**.

        c.   *They believe in **yourself**.

        d.   *They believe in **yourselves**.

These examples confirm the correctness of the **reflexive pronoun rule**: like all other reflexive pronouns, the reflexive pronoun *yourself* is very picky; it can only occur in the sentence if it has an antecedent which matches it. And that antecedent is the pronoun *you*.

Now let's look at a couple of imperative sentences that we have not yet seen:

(23)   a.   Believe in **yourself**!

        b.   Believe in **yourselves**!

The two imperative sentences in (23) are perfectly grammatical. But how can this be, if the reflexives *yourself* and *yourselves* have no antecedent in (23)?

In fact, what the grammatical sentences in (23) tell us is the following: contrary to outward appearances, these imperative sentences (and therefore all imperative sentences) contain a silent you in subject position. Let's sketch this out in (24), which is very much like the tree for the imperative sentence in (18), only with the subject position identified:

Side Note 7: Why option [A] can't be right

Note that if we assumed that imperative sentences don't have a subject at all (as in (16) and (17)), we would have no way of explaining the grammaticality of the sentences in (23) because we wouldn't have any antecedent for the reflexives *yourself / yourselves*!

---

(24)

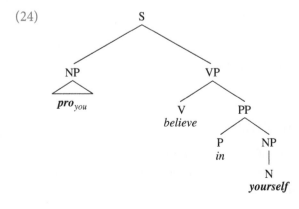

From hereon in, I will identify all silent (or "null") pronouns — such as the silent subject pronoun in imperatives — with the notation **pro**. For imperatives specifically, I will use the notation *pro*~*you*~, to indicate that this silent pronoun is interpreted as *you*. As we'll see in Sections 7.3.2 and 7.4, there are other constructions (besides imperatives) where a silent *pro* is used.

The idea that imperatives contain a silent *pro*~*you*~ in subject position (illustrated in (24)) also allows us to explain the following facts immediately:

(25) a. *Believe in **himself**!

     b. *Believe in **herself**!

     c. *Believe in **themselves**!

     d. *Believe in **myself**!

     e. *Believe in **ourselves**!

The sentences in (25) are all ungrammatical. Why? According to our **reflexive pronoun rule**, English speakers only use a reflexive pronoun in a sentence if it has an antecedent. If we assume that imperative sentences can only contain a silent *pro*~*you*~ in subject position, then no reflexive pronouns other than *yourself* and *yourselves* will be able to "survive" in an imperative sentence, because they are the only reflexive pronouns that "match in features" with the antecedent *pro*~*you*~.

7.3.1.2 Conclusions for imperative sentences

To conclude: in this section we have seen that there are numerous reasons to believe that despite outward appearances, imperative sentences contain a subject, like any other sentence. This subject, which is interpreted as *you*, is as real as any other subject. The imperative sentences with the reflexive pronouns *yourself* and *yourselves* in (23) give us indirect evidence that there is a silent *pro*~*you*~ in the structure.

EXERCISE [6]

Using the model in (24), draw trees for the sentences in (14).

7.3.2 embedded infinitivals with a silent *pro* subject

Now let's take a look at another type of sentence in which English speakers utilize a silent *pro*.

7.3.2.1 Embedded infinitivals

In order to explain the nature of the structure I want to ultimately introduce you to, I need to start by discussing the concept of an **embedded infinitival sentence**, more generally speaking.

To understand what an embedded infinitival sentence is, let's start by recalling our standard-issue embedded sentences from Chapter 5. Here's an example:

(26) a. Mary thinks <u>Sue ate the cake</u>.

b.

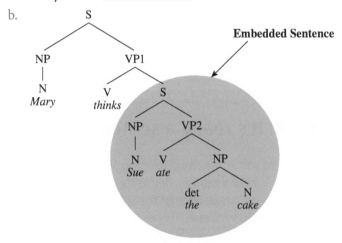

The sentence immediately dominated by VP1 is an embedded sentence. As we saw in Chapters 5 and 6, this particular kind of embedded sentence is selected by the verb (in this case, the verb *think*).

All such embedded sentences that we have so far seen are tensed, or finite. That is, the verb — in this case, *ate* — is specified for a particular tense. In particular, *ate* is a past tense verb. In Chapter 8, we'll go into great detail on what we mean exactly when we say "tensed" or "finite," so don't worry right now if you don't fully understand this idea of tense/finiteness. For the present moment, it simply suffices to recall something we already demonstrated explicitly in Chapter 5: embedded sentences such as the one in (26) can freely stand on their own; witness (27):

(27) Sue ate the cake.

The ability of a sentence to "stand on its own" as a matrix sentence is a particular property of tensed or finite sentences. Consider, by contrast, the following sentence, which contains the embedded sentence *Sue to eat the cake*:

(28) Mary wants <u>Sue to eat the cake</u>.

If we directly compare the sentence in (26) with the sentence in (28), we see a similarity:

(26) Mary **thinks** <u>Sue ate the cake</u>.

(28) Mary **wants** <u>Sue to eat the cake</u>.

In both cases, we have a matrix sentence with a VP headed by a matrix verb which selects an embedded sentence; in (26) the matrix verb is *think*, and in (28) the matrix verb is *want*.

However, there is also a big difference between these two sentences: while the embedded sentence in (26) can stand on its own — as we just saw in (27), note that the embedded sentence in (28) cannot:

(29)   *Sue to eat the cake.

Sentences such as that in (29) can't function as matrix sentences; they can't stand on their own because they aren't finite sentences. Only finite sentences, such as that embedded in (26), can stand on their own, as matrix sentences.

Side Note 8: It's really a sentence

You might be wondering why we would call the string *Sue to eat the cake* a sentence at all, if it can't stand on its own two feet. Despite the fact that the string *Sue to eat the cake* is dependent on another sentence for its existence, our reason for analyzing it as the category S nevertheless is simple: like any other S, it consists of a subject NP (*Sue*) and a VP (*eat the cake*), as per the "S" phrase structure rule in (15).

Sentences which are not finite, such as the embedded sentence in (28), are called **infinitival sentences**. Similarly, the verb *to eat* in (28) is called an **infinitival verb**, or, an **infinitive**. By definition, the verb *to eat* is not finite (it is not tensed).

EXERCISE [7]

Each of the following sentences contains either a finite (tensed) embedded sentence or an infinitival embedded sentence. Identify each by underlining the embedded sentence and stating whether it is finite or infinitival.

{1} Sue believes John finished the exam.
{2} Sue expects Mary to finish the exam.
{3} Sue wants Bill to have finished the exam by 9:00 p.m.
{4} Sue said that Bill finished the exam.
{5} Sue asked Bill to finish the exam.

7.3.2.1.1 *Side note: infinitival* to

One question which we will address more fully in Chapter 8 is the following: what is the word *to*, in embedded sentences like that in (28)?

In Chapter 4, we saw this word several times; in the examples we explored in that chapter, we identified the word *to* as a preposition. As we'll see momentarily, though, the infinitival *to* in (28) is not a preposition. Let's see why.

Consider a typical Chapter 4 example, with the preposition *to*:

(30) Mary sang the song **to John**.

In examples like the one in (30), we analyzed *to* as a preposition, no different from prepositions like *for* and *with*; so compare (30) with (31) and (32):

(31) Mary sang the song **for John**.

(32) Mary sang the song **with John**.

Phrases like the ones underlined in these examples were therefore analyzed in Chapter 4 as prepositional phrases, with the following structure:

(33)

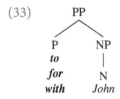

Despite our reasons for analyzing the word *to* as a preposition in examples like those in (30)–(33), we have to be careful not to mistake our infinitival *to* in sentences like (28) for a preposition, as this particular case of *to* does not head a prepositional phrase. How do we know this? Well, for starters, notice how the word *to* in (28) is not followed by an NP or a PP, which are the two kinds of complements that a true preposition can select (see Chapter 4). Instead, it's immediately followed by a verb. This alone gives us a clue that our infinitival *to* does not head a PP.

So where is this infinitival *to* in our embedded sentence in (28)? For now I'll make a preliminary proposal, which we'll revisit in Chapters 9 and 10. Let's say that infinitival *to* is right in between the subject NP and the VP, in the infinitival sentence, as follows:

(34)

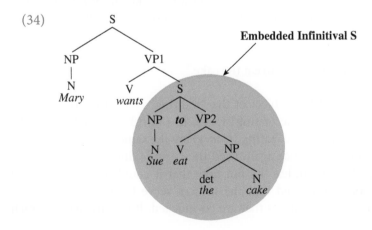

Of course, the (temporary) proposal for the structure of an embedded infinitival sentence means we would have to change our sentence phrase structure rule, to include the possibility of infinitival *to*, as follows:

(35)   S   →   NP (*to*) VP

We'll return to this in Chapter 10.

EXERCISE [8]

Draw trees for the sentences in Exercise [7].

7.3.2.2 Embedded infinitivals with a silent subject

Now that we've reached an introduction to the concept of the embedded infinitival sentence, let's get to our main point of this entire section, which is silent *pro* in infinitivals. To do this, let's revisit our example in (28):

(28)   Mary **wants** <u>Sue to eat the cake</u>.

We've already discussed the idea that *Sue to eat the cake* is an embedded sentence; as we saw explicitly in the structure in (34) (and in Exercise [7]), we have a subject NP *Sue* and a VP *eat the cake* (see also Side Note 8).

So all of that said, let's now compare (28)/(34) to the very similar sentence in (36):

(36)   Mary **wants** _____ to eat the cake.

The sentence in (36) is very similar to the sentence in (28)/(34), except for that fact that in (36) the subject NP of the embedded sentence appears to be missing. At the same time, though, we know what the sentence in (36) means; if we compare it with the sentence in (28)/(34), we see that while in (28)/(34) Mary wants someone else (namely, Sue) to eat the cake, in (36), Mary wants *herself* to eat the cake. In other words, (36) means something like (37):

Meaning of (36):

(37)   "Mary$_k$ **wants** <u>Mary$_k$ to eat the cake</u>."

So, while in (28)/(34) the subject of the "wanting" (*Mary*) is not the same person as the subject of the "eating" (*Sue*), in (36)/(37) the subject of the "wanting" (*Mary*) and of the "eating" (*Mary*) are the same.

Notice that in (37), I once again used the co-indexing device; as before, I arbitrarily picked the index "k," but note that it could be any notational device you choose, provided that the indices serve to show that there is identity between the two items that are co-indexed. It doesn't matter which index we use, as long as we use the same one for the elements that **co-refer**, i.e. elements that refer to the same entity:

(37')   "Mary$_m$ **wants** <u>Mary$_m$ to eat the cake</u>."

(37")   "Mary$_z$ **wants** <u>Mary$_z$ to eat the cake</u>."

In the case of (37), the subject of the matrix clause and the subject of the embedded clause are meant to refer to the same *Mary* (and not two distinct people).

Term Box 4: Co-indexing and co-reference

Keep in mind that the use of indices to indicate identity between two items in the structure is <u>independent</u> of whether those two items are related via movement (see Side Note 2) or whether they are just two independent elements that refer to the same entity. For example, in our discussion of reflexive pronouns in Section 7.3.1.1.2, we could have used co-indexing to capture the fact that a reflexive and its antecedent refer to the same entity, as in *Mary$_k$ believes in herself$_k$*. *Mary* and *herself* are thus said to co-refer in this sentence.

Now, we have to be careful here to keep in mind that the example in (37) is not actually how a speaker would say the sentence in (36): it's just meant to serve as an impressionistic representation of the meaning of (36). In fact, in comparing (36) with its meaning depicted in (37), we see that the actual (36) represents the subject of the embedded sentence as a silent element. This silent element is none other than our silent pronoun *pro*. In the case of (38), the silent *pro* is co-indexed with the matrix subject NP *Mary* to capture the fact that the subject of the "wanting" is in fact the same as the subject of the "eating:"

(38)   Mary$_k$ **wants** <u>pro$_k$ to eat the cake</u>.

Let's look at the tree for (38) (compare it with (34)):

(39)

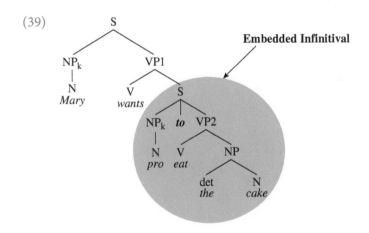

EXERCISE [9]: Draw trees for the following sentences:

{1} John promised to do his homework.
{2} Sue decided to fix the sink.
{3} Mary expected to win the race.
{4} Mary expected Bill to win the race.

In the example in (36) (and in the trees for {1}–{3} you drew in Exercise [9]), the subject NP of the embedded sentence is a silent *pro*. Note that this *pro* is different in nature from the *pro*$_{you}$ we analyzed in imperative sentences in Section 7.3.1. The difference is the following: while the subject NP *pro*$_{you}$ of imperative sentences is always interpreted as a second person pronoun (i.e. *you*), the subject NP *pro* of embedded infinitivals such as that in (36) (and in {1}–{3} in Exercise [9]) gets its reference — or, meaning — from the matrix subject NP.

7.3.2.2.1 *A footnote on embedded infinitival* **pro**

I'd like to make one final observation before turning to the next section. Please consider this subsection to be a kind of a footnote, which you can skip if you just feel like moving on to Section 7.4.

As I just noted, in all of the examples we've seen thus far in Section 7.3.2.2, embedded infinitival *pro* gets its reference from the **matrix subject NP**. However, there are some cases where English speakers interpret embedded infinitival *pro* as co-referent with the **matrix object NP**. I'll give just one example here.

To begin the discussion, let's reconsider sentence {4} from Exercise [9]:

(40) Mary expected <u>Bill to win the race</u>.

My guess is that you (correctly) drew the tree for this sentence as follows:

(41)

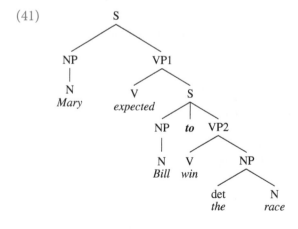

The tree in (41) directly models the structure in (34), which I drew for the sentence in (28). The following sentence speaks to the correctness of the idea that *Bill to win the race* is a sentential constituent:

(42)   Mary expected <u>that Bill would win the race</u>.

The sentences in (40) and (42) mean more or less the same thing: Mary expected something, and that something was Bill's winning the race. The only difference is that in (42), we have an embedded sentence that is not infinitival, and that therefore can stand on its own as a matrix sentence (*Bill would win the race*). It thus makes sense to consider *Bill to win the race* in (40) to be the infinitival equivalent of the embedded finite sentence in (42).

But now let's look at the following sentence:

(43)   Mary told Bill to win the race.

At first glance, it could seem like the string *Bill to win the race* in (43) is a sentential constituent, along the same lines as the underlined string *Bill to win the race* in (40). However, we have reason to believe that it is not. Consider in this regard the following sentence, which is nearly equivalent in meaning to (43):

(44)   Mary told Bill$_k$ that he$_k$ should win the race.

We know from Chapter 5 that *Bill* is the indirect object of the verb *tell*. In fact, as we saw in detail in that chapter, the verb *tell* takes two complements, namely, an indirect object and a sentential object:

(45)

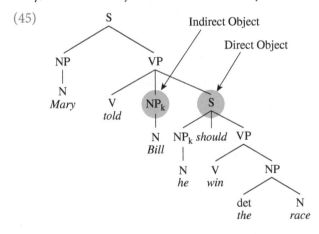

Side Note 9: *Should* vs. *to*

In Chapters 9 and 10 we'll discuss the status of modal auxiliary verbs like *should*.

Given what we've already seen about the verb *tell* in structures like that in (44)/(45), and given that (43) is the equivalent in meaning, then it follows that

Bill in (43) is actually the indirect object of *tell*, and <u>not</u> the subject of the embedded infinitival. In other words, the structure for (43) is as in (46):

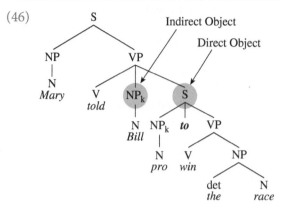

In contrast with (40)/(41), then — where the NP *Bill* is the subject of the embedded infinitival, in (43)/(46) the NP *Bill* is the object of the matrix verb.

In the embedded infinitival in (43)/(46), we have a silent *pro*, which gets its reference from the **matrix object NP**. This contrasts with the silent *pro* (38)/(39), which gets its reference from the **matrix subject NP**.

7.4 the *null operator* in relative clauses

Before we close this chapter, let's talk about one more kind of silent element in sentence structure. Here, we're returning to a mystery that was left open in Section 6.4.3.2.

Let's start with a brief review: as you'll recall, in Chapter 6 we discussed the structure of relative clauses, which are dependent clauses within [NP], such as the clause underlined in (47):

(47)   That surgeon wants [the parking-spot <u>**which** the other doctor stole</u>].

The following is the structural analysis that we argued for in Chapter 6:

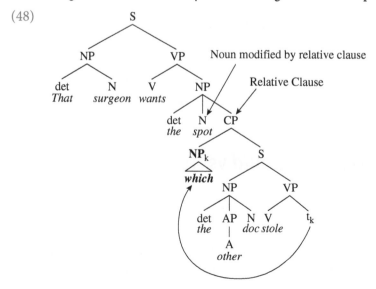

Specifically, we argued that a relative clause is a dependent clause (a) which is immediately dominated by an NP node, and (b) which modifies the noun heading the NP dominating it. Furthermore, a relative clause involves wh-movement of a relative pronoun; in the case of (48), this is the wh-phrase *which*. And as is always the case with the wh-movement operation, movement of the relative pronoun leaves behind a trace. And finally, we noted that the wh-pronoun gets its "semantic content" (i.e. meaning) from the head noun that the relative clause modifies. So, in the case of (48), *which*$_k$ and its associated trace t_k refers to *parking-spot*.

A problem that we raised towards the end of our discussion of relative clauses in Chapter 6 was the following: the relative clause in (47) can optionally have the relative pronoun missing altogether, as in (49):

(49)   That surgeon wants [the parking-spot <u>Ø the other doctor stole</u>].

As we noted in Chapter 6, the null symbol (Ø) represents the position where we would otherwise find the relative pronoun *which*. Relative clauses that have no overt relative pronoun or relative complementizer *that* are sometimes referred to as **zero relatives**. (See Chapter 6.)

The fact of zero relatives led us to a series of questions we left open, such as the following: Does the lack of the relative pronoun force us to conclude that the relative clause in (49) is not a CP but, rather, an S? Do we have to say that there's no wh-movement in (49)? If so, what do we now make of the "gap" inside the relative clause? Does the lack of visible relative pronoun mean the lack of a "gap" in the relative clause? (That can't be.) Or is the gap is somehow of a different nature? How could we have a trace of wh-movement if there's no visible relative pronoun to be found in the CP in surface structure?

All of these questions can be answered now that we understand that English speakers make use of silent categories. In particular, what the possibility of (49) tells us is that English speakers make use of a silent relative pronoun. We can notate this category as *pro*$_{rel-wh}$. The silent *pro*$_{rel-wh}$ behaves just as any other relative pronoun, being subject to the wh-movement rule, as in (50):

(50)

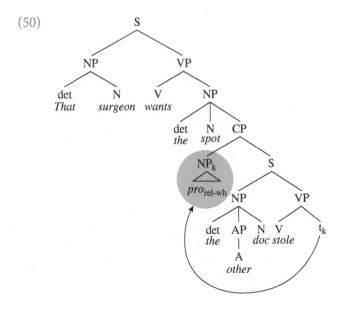

The trace left behind by movement of $pro_{rel\text{-}wh}$ is therefore no different from the trace left behind by movement of the non-silent (or, overt) wh-pronoun *which* in (48).

EXERCISE [10]

Draw trees for the following sentences:

{1} I read the book Mary wrote.
{2} The professor you reasoned with gave you a good grade.
{3} The homework the students did was very challenging.
{4} Mary looks for students she can assign substantive readings to.
{5} The papers we graded got high scores.

7.5 conclusions

This chapter saw a revision to the phrase structure rule for S, as follows:

(51)   CP   →   C S

       S   →   NP (*to*) VP

       NP   → $\begin{Bmatrix} \text{(det)} \\ \text{(PossNP)} \end{Bmatrix}$ (AP*) N $\begin{Bmatrix} \text{(PP*)} \\ \text{(CP)} \end{Bmatrix}$

       PossNP → $\begin{Bmatrix} \text{(det)} \\ \text{(PossNP)} \end{Bmatrix}$ (AP*) PossN $\begin{Bmatrix} \text{(PP*)} \\ \text{(CP)} \end{Bmatrix}$

       VP   →   V (PP) (NP) $\begin{Bmatrix} \text{(NP)} \\ \text{(S)} \\ \text{(CP)} \end{Bmatrix}$ (AP) (PP*)

       PP   →   (mod) P $\begin{Bmatrix} \text{(NP)} \\ \text{(PP)} \end{Bmatrix}$

       AP   →   (deg) A

The revision was made to accommodate **embedded infinitivals**. As we saw, embedded infinitivals gave us the opportunity to explore a type of **silent category**. The idea of a silent subject (and object) *pro*, which we also saw operationalized in **imperative sentences** (as the pro_{you} subject), allowed us to maintain that S always contains a subject, even when we can't "see" (= hear or perceive) it overtly.

The theory of a silent pronoun in embedded infinitivals and imperatives also allowed us to understand the phenomenon of zero relatives, which we can now analyze as involving a silent *pro*. In the case of **zero relatives**, though, the silent pronoun is a relative pronoun (i.e., $pro_{rel\text{-}wh}$), and like all wh-phrases, undergoes movement to CP inside the relative clause. This movement gives rise to a **trace**, which as we saw, is also a silent category, one which is connected to a moved element. In the case of the silent $pro_{rel\text{-}wh}$ then, we have a chain of two silent elements: the moved element and the silent trace it leaves behind.

Our foray into the behavior of reflexive pronouns provided us with an opportunity to become more skilled at the art of hypothesis formation and the testing of predictions. The theory that imperative sentences contain a silent subject pro_{you} correctly predicts that the only reflexive pronouns that imperatives can contain are *yourself* and *yourselves*. Any theory of imperatives which holds that there is no subject "you" at **deep structure** will incorrectly predict that no reflexive will be possible in an imperative sentence, given what we independently saw about the structural requirements on **reflexive pronouns**.

Perhaps the feature of silent categories to be most appreciated is the following: as per Chapter 1, they show us that sentence structure is not something that's out there in the world. You don't see them (in the case of signed languages) and you don't hear them (in the case of spoken languages like English). Yet they are there. And it's the human mind that puts them there.

---

list of terms/concepts

agreement (features; person, number, gender; agree)
antecedent
co-indexing
co-reference (co-refer)
covert element
deep structure
echo questions
embedded infinitivals
embedded infinitival sentence
feature agreement
features (person, number, gender)
finite sentence
finiteness (finite; tensed)
form
imperative sentence (imperatives; negative imperatives)
index
infinitival sentences
infinitival *to*
infinitival verb
infinitive
movement
null operator ($pro_{rel\text{-}wh}$)
null pronoun
overt element

particle shift
passivization operation
person, number, gender (features)
phonetic symbols
pro
$pro_{rel\text{-}wh}$
pro_{you}
reflexive paradigm
reflexive pronoun
selection
silence
silent category (phonologically null element; empty category)
silent constituent
silent *you*
speech sound
surface structure
tense
tensed sentence
trace
trace of movement
wanna-contraction
wh-movement
zero relatives

8

The Main Attraction: Main Verbs and the Simple Tenses

expected outcomes for this chapter

- You'll gain an in-depth understanding of the concept of tense and verb forms.
- You'll gain a more in-depth understanding of what a main verb is in relation to an auxiliary verb.
- You'll develop more confidence with the concepts from previous chapters (e.g., verbs and the verb phrase, agreement, infinitival, tensed/untensed, ambiguity, and variation).
- You'll begin to gain expertise in understanding the English verb system, setting the stage for your understanding of Chapters 9 and 10.
- You'll become familiar with the following concepts and terms: *main verb, auxiliary verb, modal auxiliary, present tense, tensed, untensed, past tense, preterite, simple tense, verb form, subject–verb agreement, infinitive, bare infinitive, verb paradigm, paradigm levelling, inflection.*

8.1 overview: the "main verb" and its entourage

By now you're used to the fact that each chapter of this book revisits some phrase we investigated in an earlier chapter, delving into that phrase more deeply. Here and in Chapters 9 and 10, we'll continue this habit with a further look at the more intricate patterns exhibited by verbs. Unsurprisingly, we're going to see that the VP and the sentence allow for much more complexity than we've so far explored. This complexity reflects the fact that English

Understanding Sentence Structure: An Introduction to English Syntax, First Edition.
Christina Tortora.
© 2018 John Wiley & Sons, Inc. Published 2018 by John Wiley & Sons, Inc.

speakers have highly structured and diverse means for expressing the **times** of **events** and physical / mental **states**. On top of this, much as we've already seen in other areas of the grammar, we'll see that when it comes to verbs, there's a lot of variation among and across English speakers regarding structural (and lexical!) possibilities for expressing the same thing.

It might surprise you to see that in this chapter, I talk less about structure and more about the forms of words, and the kinds of meanings that these forms give to the sentence. This is because in order to understand the syntax of main and auxiliary verbs, it's important to understand some basics about **tense** and **verb forms**. This unto itself involves some discussion (i) of the meanings of tenses, and (ii) of the kinds of **morphological forms** that main verbs can take. (See Term Box 3 in Chapter 10 for a discussion of the concept of morphology.) At a certain level, then, the discussion is outside of the realm of syntactic structure; we'll thus have to wait until Chapter 10 to address syntactic structure again.

Side Note 1: Good timing

If you don't yet have a good sense of what I mean by *times of events and states*, just hang in there. We'll get to this in Section 8.2.

8.1.1 main verb vs. auxiliary verb

To begin to understand the semantic role of the main verb in a sentence, I want to start with a relatively basic point. As always, it helps to take another look at the phrase structure rule of the **lexical category** in question:

$$(1) \quad VP \quad \rightarrow \quad V \ (PP) \ (NP) \left\{ \begin{array}{l} (NP) \\ (S) \\ (CP) \end{array} \right\} (AP) \ (PP^*)$$

As (1) illustrates, V (the actual head of the VP) is obligatory. Given that the sentence phrase structure rule captures the fact that every sentence obligatorily contains a VP, as in (2) (from Chapter 7), we can conclude that *every sentence must have a verb*.

$$(2) \quad S \quad \rightarrow \quad NP \ (to) \ VP$$

The strings in (3) are just a few of the many example sentences we've seen thus far, with the one obligatory verb (one per S) in bold:

(3) a. My dog **slept**.

  b. They **claim** that Sue **is** intelligent.

  c. Bill **wondered** what Sue **fixed**.

  d. Sue **gave** the newspaper to Mary.

  e. Janet **assumes** Bill **believes** that Sandy **claimed** Joe **said** Mary **thinks** Sue **is** a great surgeon.

  f. Bill **expects** Sue to **fix** the sink.

> ## EXERCISE [1]
>
> Draw trees for the sentences in (3), to confirm that you see how each S contains only one verb.

Each one of the verbs in (3) is called a **main verb**. The verbs *slept*, *claim*, *wondered*, *gave*, *assumes*, and *expects* in (a), (b), (c), (d), (e), and (f) (respectively) are all **matrix main verbs**; the verbs *is* in (b) and *fixed* in (c), and the verbs *believes*, *claimed*, *said*, *thinks*, and *is* in (e) and *fix* in (f) are all **embedded main verbs**. You should circle all the Vs in the trees you drew for Exercise [1] to confirm that you know what a main verb is, regardless of whether it's in a matrix or embedded sentence.

A question that arises at this point is, why call these verbs "main verbs"? Is there such a thing as a "non-main verb"? The answer to this question is Yes — though we have a better term than that. We use the term **auxiliary verb** (or, just plain "auxiliary") for any verb that isn't a main verb. In Chapter 9, we'll examine in-depth the various auxiliary verbs. For now, let's take a sneak preview.

> ## Term Box 1: Auxiliaries
>
> Another term you might have heard is **helping verb**. Sometimes **auxiliary** is abbreviated as **aux** (rhyming with "hawks").

8.1.1.1 Auxiliaries: a first pass

Although this chapter is primarily about main verbs, it'll help to make a few preliminary observations about auxiliary verbs to get the ball rolling. Until now, we've barely seen any examples of auxiliaries. I did slip in one example, in Exercise [10] of Chapter 7. I'll repeat that sentence here, with the auxiliary verb underlined, and the main verb in bold:

(4)   Mary looks for students who she <u>can</u> **assign** substantive readings to.

In (4), the embedded sentence containing the embedded main verb *assign* is an object relative clause, which modifies the noun *students* — which itself heads the NP complement of the preposition *for*. (At this point of the book, you should be able to readily understand everything I just said in this last sentence. You should draw a tree of (4), if you need a refresher.)

Let me give you a few more examples of sentences with an auxiliary plus main verb, in (6). As you examine the sentences in (6), please compare them with the one in (5), which contains only a main verb and has no auxiliaries. As with (4), the sentences in (6) have the aux underlined and the main verb in bold.

(5)   Sue **enjoys** her Ford Mustang.

(6)   a.   Sue <u>will</u> **enjoy** her Ford Mustang … (as soon as she finishes fixing the carburetor).

      b.   Sue <u>is</u> **enjoying** her Ford Mustang.   (*is*: a form of the aux *be*)

      c.   Sue <u>has</u> **enjoyed** her Ford Mustang for 25 years now.   (*has*: a form of the aux *have*)

      d.   Sue sure <u>does</u> **enjoy** her Ford Mustang!   (*does*: a form of the aux *do*)

A single sentence with no sentence embeddings can contain quite a few auxiliary verbs: at least up to four in total (and for some English speakers, even five). The sentences in (4) and (6) each have one auxiliary verb. Now let's look at the sentences in (7), each of which contains more than one aux:

(7)   a.   John <u>will</u> <u>have</u> **finished** up his grading by midnight.

      b.   Mary <u>should</u> <u>have</u> <u>been</u> **driving** home by now … (but she got caught up with some last-minute stuff at work).

      c.   The Giants <u>could</u> <u>have</u> <u>been</u> <u>being</u> **beaten** by the Titans in the third quarter already … (if the Titans had only just taken their running game more seriously).

Side Note 2: Don't be passive

Just in case you're wondering whether there's a simpler way to express the thought in (7c): compare this **passive** sentence with its **active** correlate, *The Titans <u>could</u> <u>have</u> <u>been</u> **beating** the Giants in the third quarter already* … (you can revisit Section 3.6.1 if you don't remember what passive vs. active is). Notice that the passive sentence in (7c) has four auxiliaries (*could, have, been, being*), while its active counterpart has only three (*could, have, been*). We'll look at the question of the "extra auxiliary" in passive sentences in Chapters 9 and 10.

The sentence in (7a) has two auxiliary verbs (*will* and *have*); the sentence in (7b) has three (*should, have,* and *been*); and the sentence in (7c) has four (*could, have, been,* and *being*). Perhaps you think the sentence in (7c) doesn't sound very good; if so, I can understand that, because the more auxiliary verbs you pile up, the harder the sentence is to mentally process. But if you listen to English speakers long enough, you'll eventually find someone who produces a sentence with four auxiliary verbs piled up in front of a main verb, like in (7c). In fact, some English speakers actually even allow for five auxiliaries, like in (7d):

(7)   d.   The Giants <u>might</u> <u>could</u> <u>have</u> <u>been</u> <u>being</u> **beaten** by the Titans in the third quarter already …

Side Note 3: Variation again

Not every English speaker uses sequences like *might could*, as in (7d). It depends on where you're from, or at least, what your cultural heritage is. Auxiliary sequences like *might could* or *may should* (*Mary may should go home*) are much more commonly used by English speakers from the southern United States, or English speakers from the North who have southern heritage. But even for speakers who don't actively use these sequences, it's not hard to figure out what they mean. A great resource for exploring all the possible combinations of auxiliaries like *might, could, would*, etc. is the MultiMo website: http://artsandsciences.sc.edu/multimo/. (And now, if you read on, you'll understand immediately what the "Mo" is, in "MultiMo" !)

In Chapter 9, we'll talk in detail about the different kinds of auxiliaries, in terms of their function (what purpose do they serve?) and in Chapter 10 we'll talk in detail about their distribution (what is their syntax?). I'll just give a brief preview here: the auxiliaries themselves come in two types. One type is often referred to as the **modal auxiliaries** (or just **modals**, for short):

Modal auxiliaries:

(8)   *can, could, will, would, shall, should, may, might, must*

EXERCISE [2]

Make up eight of your own sentences, each of which contains just one of the modals in (8) (plus a main verb, of course: every sentence has to have a main verb!). You could start by using the sentence in (6a) as a model.

As for the other type of auxiliary, let's just refer to this class as **nonmodal auxiliaries** for now. These are the auxiliaries *be, have*, and *do*, examples of which can be seen in (6b), (6c), and (6d), and also in (7).

Let's not worry too much about these auxiliaries any further right now. In Section 8.2.1.1 we'll make some use of the modals, just in order to understand some issues revolving around the present tense. But that'll be it for this chapter, as we're going to look at all auxiliaries carefully in Chapter 9, and in Chapter 10 we'll see how they fit into the syntactic structures you've been learning about in this book.

Before we get there, though, I want to return to the main verb. Once we delve into some greater complexities of the main verb, we'll be in a better position to understand the function and syntax of auxiliaries in Chapter 9.

——————   ## 8.2 main verbs: the present, the past, and the future

Let's start this section by revisiting the example in (5), repeated here as (9):

(9)   Sue **enjoys** her Ford Mustang.

Let's focus in particular on the verb *enjoys*. What would happen if we changed the **form** of the verb to *enjoyed*, as in (10)?

(10)   Sue **enjoyed** her Ford Mustang.

Term Box 2: Form and inflection

In Section 6.3.2.1 we talked about the idea that some words are like "shapeshifters." Specifically, we saw that verbs like *believe* or *prove* change their **form**, or assume a different "shape," when being used as the nouns *belief* and *proof*.

With the **verb forms** *enjoys* vs. *enjoyed*, the situation is similar, in that the change in form (*enjoys* < > *enjoyed*) makes the word have a different function. However, notice that both forms (*enjoys* and *enjoyed*) are still verbs. This contrasts with **noun derivation** (e.g., *believe → belief*), where the change in form corresponds to a change in lexical category (V → N). In Chapter 6 we referred to shapeshifting which results in change in lexical category as **derivation**.

In contrast, we refer to shapeshifting which does not result in a lexical category change as **inflection**. The forms *enjoys* and *enjoyed* are still both verbs, related to the verb *enjoy*, but each is inflected. Suffixes like *-s* and *-ed*, added to a verb like *enjoy*, are referred to as **inflectional suffixes** (as opposed to **derivational suffixes**). Read on to get a better sense of what the functions of these inflectional suffixes *-s* and *-ed* actually are!

I'll give you a moment to think about the difference in meaning between (9) and (10).

So, now that you've thought about the meaning of (9) versus the meaning of (10), I'll give my own thoughts on some of the aspects of their different interpretations. Let's start with example (9), which contains the verb form *enjoys* (i.e. *enjoy* plus *-s*): in this sentence, I think of Sue as necessarily *currently* being in the state of enjoyment of her Ford Mustang. She may not be driving her Ford Mustang at the moment I utter the sentence "Sue enjoys her Ford Mustang," but I do know that she currently owns the car (or, is at least somehow in possession of a Ford Mustang), and that there are things about this ownership or possession that currently make her happy, whether she drives the car regularly or not. She might take it out for a spin every morning, or perhaps instead she's never even driven it once, but still, she enjoys owning it. We can't know any of these details for sure, just from the sentence in (9). Whatever Sue's enjoyment of this Ford Mustang derives from, though, there's one common denominator that is of crucial importance, underlying any of the possible scenarios that are consistent with (9): the sentence in (9) with the verb form *enjoys* entails that Sue's state of enjoyment obtains at least *at the moment when I utter the sentence*. **Time of utterance** — the moment that I say or think the sentence — is crucial to understanding when Sue's state of enjoyment holds, in (9).

Oversimplifying for the moment, we can say that the verb *enjoys* in (9) is crucial to our understanding that the time of Sue's enjoyment is contained within the time of my utterance of this sentence. (Again, compare this with the sentence in (10), which has the verb form *enjoyed*.) Let's think of the time of utterance as being in the **present time**, or **now**. Because the verb form *enjoys* gives rise to this "present time" interpretation (in contrast with the verb form *enjoyed*, as we will see), we say that this verb is in the **present tense**. We can also say that *enjoys* is a **present tense verb form**.

Term Box 3: Don't get tense!

The word "tense" in its grammatical meaning here comes from the Latin word *tempus*, which means "time." So when we say a verb is in the **present tense**, or "*enjoys* is the **present tense form** of the verb *enjoy*," we mean that the verb *enjoys* yields an interpretation of the state/event denoted by the verb as happening in present time.

The grammatical term "tense" has a different etymology from the adjective *tense*, which means "not relaxed." The "not relaxed" word comes from the Latin word *tensus*, related to the Latin verb *tendere*, which means "to stretch" (which in turn is where words like *tension*, *extend*, and *extensive* come from).

Since the issue of **time** is relevant to how we interpret the state or event in question, it helps to think of tense in terms of a **timeline**. Let's look at a basic illustration in (11):

(11)   Basic timeline representation of tense:

The **present** overlaps with the time of utterance; so we say of the verb form *enjoys* in (9) that it's in the present tense, or, it's a present tense verb, because this is what gives us the interpretation of (9), in relation to time of utterance.

This idea becomes clearer if we consider the sentence in (10), which in contrast has the verb form *enjoyed* (i.e. *enjoy* plus *-ed*). When I utter the sentence "Sue enjoyed her Ford Mustang," Sue's state of enjoyment was necessarily in the **past**, *with respect to the time I utter this sentence*. The sentence might suggest that Sue used to enjoy her Ford Mustang but she doesn't enjoy it any longer (as in, *Sue enjoyed her Ford Mustang when the carburetor never* *gave her problems, but now she's lost all love for the car*). Or, it could suggest that she used to enjoy this Ford Mustang that she owned, but that she doesn't own it any longer (as in, *When Sue was in Med School, <u>she really enjoyed her Ford Mustang</u>; she should never have sold it*). Or, it could even suggest that she enjoyed taking her Ford Mustang out for a spin late last night — which doesn't necessarily mean that she no longer enjoys her Ford Mustang! (<u>*Sue really enjoyed her Ford Mustang*</u> *last night, when she opened it full throttle on her way home from work! Man, she really enjoys that car, doesn't she?*) So, in this case, Sue may still be in a state of enjoying ownership of the car, such that the sentences in (10) and (9) don't contradict each other. Or, (10) could even suggest that Sue enjoyed taking her Ford Mustang out for a spin last night, but that someone in the neighborhood that she respects yelled out at her as she passed by, "Your car is too loud!", after which she suddenly stopped enjoying it. We can't actually know any of these details, based just on (10). However, one thing we can be sure of is that there is a common denominator for all of these imaginable scenarios: at some point in time *before the time of utterance*, Sue experienced a state of enjoyment of her Ford Mustang. We can therefore say that the verb *enjoyed* in (10) is in the **past tense**, or, that it's a **past tense verb**, because this is what gives us the past time interpretation of (10), in relation to time of utterance. Sometimes grammarians use the term **preterite** instead of the term "past tense," to mean the same thing.

The present tense and the past tense (or preterite) are what we call **simple tenses**. They are "simple" because they are tenses that are expressed through the presence of only a single verb — that is, the main verb by itself, with no auxiliaries to help out with the interpretation. This contrasts with the concept of a **compound tense**, which we'll look at in detail in Chapter 9.

The timeline in (11) also makes reference to the future. Before we discuss future tense, however, we need to stop and consider how present and past tense relate to the concept of verb form (see Term Box 2). Don't worry though — we'll get back to the future soon.

8.2.1 verb forms versus tense interpretations

The discussion so far has introduced some basic ideas about tense as the linguistic means of expressing different times that states can hold (or in which events can occur), in relation to the time of utterance. However, the discussion has thus far been an oversimplification of matters. As a beginner's introduction, there's no way this book can do justice to the real intricacies of how times of states and events can be linguistically expressed, and all the nuanced ways in which English speakers use the so-called present and past verb forms for different tense interpretations (never mind the range of possibilities, once we start talking about auxiliaries in Chapter 9!). In this section I'll take a little time to cover but a few of the complications with respect to the verb forms we just reviewed, but as the reader will soon become aware, the more we delve into the matter, the more complex it becomes.

8.2.1.1 *Bare* form vs. *present* form

Let's consider the sentence in (9) again (repeated here as (12)), which contains a verb form ending in -*s*:

(12)   Sue **enjoys** her Ford Mustang.

Let's stick for the moment with the idea that the form *enjoys* yields a present tense interpretation — in contrast with *enjoyed*, which yields a past tense interpretation. I want to do a little experiment with this verb that uses the inflectional suffix -*s* (see Term Box 2), which we can call **verbal** -*s*, for the sake of discussion. In particular, I want to see what happens if we add a modal auxiliary like *can*, *might*, or *will* to the string of words in (12); so let's look at (13):

(13)   a.   *Sue <u>would</u> **enjoys** her Ford Mustang (… if only it were running well)
        b.   *Sue <u>might</u> **enjoys** her Ford Mustang (… once she fixes the carburetor)
        c.   *Sue <u>will</u> **enjoys** her Ford Mustang (… as soon as she fixes the carburetor)

I tagged all of the examples in (13) with an asterisk, because all of these sentences sound bad to me, and I don't think there's any speaker of English — no matter what English speaking region in the United States or what English-speaking country they come from — who would use a modal auxiliary followed by a verb with verbal -*s*.

Side Note 4: I can has nuther cheezburger?

The weblog *I can has cheezburger* (http://icanhas.cheezburger.com/) depicts all kinds of cats and dogs uttering sentences with a modal aux followed by a verb with verbal -*s*. This seems to contradict my claim that there is no speaker of English that would use the structures in (13). So let me be more precise: there is no **native speaker** of English who uses this construction. I think we can assume that the pets expressing their views on the *cheezburger* weblog are not native speakers!

Instead, what we find is that in the presence of a modal, the verb form has to be **bare**; that is, it cannot have verbal -*s*. Compare (13) with (14):

(14)   a.   Sue <u>would</u> **enjoy** her Ford Mustang (… if only it were running well).
        b.   Sue <u>might</u> **enjoy** her Ford Mustang (… once she fixes the carburetor).
        c.   Sue <u>will</u> **enjoy** her Ford Mustang (… as soon as she fixes the carburetor).

Side Note 5: Verbal -*s*, third person, and variation

The function of verbal -*s* is difficult to pin down, because there's a lot of regional and social variation regarding its use. Perhaps you've noticed that English teachers are generally very concerned about regulating verbal -*s* as a form of **subject–verb agreement**. The consensus, at least for academic English, is that verbal -*s* should be used in the **third person singular** (present tense), so that it's only "correct" to use it with subject NPs like *he, she, it,* and *Sue, the woman, the doctor,* etc. (as you'll see in the verb paradigm in (15) below). (See Chapter 7, Term Box 3, for a refresher on the concept of person and number.) But depending on the region — both in the United States and also in Britain — speakers exhibit distinct patterns. For example, in various areas of the southeastern United States, and also in northern England and Northern Ireland, English speakers use verbal -*s* not only with third singular, but also with certain **third person plural** subjects. In these dialects, then, the rule is ***Sue enjoys*** *her work* and ***The girls enjoys*** *their work.* On the flip side, as discussed, for example, in Green's (2002) book *African American English: An Introduction,* there are English speakers all over the United States who exhibit no verbal -*s*. So, for example, we get things like ***Sue enjoy*** *her work* and ***The girls enjoy*** *their work.* For the sake of exposition, in the text discussion I'll describe the pattern of "academically correct" English, only because it's likely that most readers will be familiar with this pattern!

Now, what is the difference between the verb *enjoys* in (12), and the verb *enjoy* in (14)? Why does verbal -*s* have to disappear in the presence of a modal in (14)? In order to understand this, it helps to understand what the function of this -*s* suffix on the verb is.

Putting aside the complications discussed Side Note 5, let's take the verbal -*s* suffix to be a marker of present tense. So why does this present tense marker go missing in the presence of a modal? Received wisdom tells us the following: there can be at most one **tensed verb** per single S. Of course, if a matrix S contains an embedded S, the entire sentence — which includes both the matrix S and the dependent S — can have at most two tensed verbs; this can be seen for example in (3b) and (3c). The point is, a single S by itself contains at most one tensed verb.

Side Note 6: Coordinated VPs

The claim that a single S can contain no more than one tensed verb seems to be belied by the following example, which involves a single S (with no dependent clause) with coordinated VPs: *John **drank champagne** and **devoured hors d'oeuvres** all night long.* While it is true that this single S contains two tensed verbs (*drank* and *devoured*), this is only possible because of our ability to exploit the coordinating conjunction *and* to coordinate two VPs (*drank champagne* and *devoured hors d'oeuvres*) within a single S. To stay on track, we'll put aside the question of coordination.

Furthermore, if there's more than one verb in a single S like in (14a) (*would* + *enjoy*), then only the leftmost one in the string can be **tensed**, or, can "have tense." This fact will become clearer in Chapter 10, when we examine the special syntactic behavior of the leftmost verb in a sentence with a string of verbs. In (14), the modal (*would, might, will*) is the leftmost verb in each sentence, so this means that the modal is the one tensed verb of each sentence. And it follows from this that the verb *enjoy* must be **untensed** in (14) — which is why verbal -*s* goes missing in the presence of a modal. It may not be clear to you right now what proof we have that the modal is the one tensed verb in each of the sentences in (14); again, we'll get back to this in Chapters 9 and 10. For now, you'd be best off just taking my word for it!

To summarize: verbal -*s* on the main verb is an inflectional suffix (Term Box 2), which signals that the verb is in the present tense. In the presence of a modal, the next verb to the right — which in (14) is the main verb *enjoy* — is untensed. This is why the -*s* is not used. Note that the untensed form of the verb is often referred to as a **bare infinitive**, or also the **root** or **base form** of the verb. See Term Box 6 in Chapter 9 for more discussion of the terms "tense," "untensed," and "infinitive."

8.2.1.1.1 A complication

So *enjoys* is the present tense form, and *enjoy* is the bare infinitive form, right? Well, actually, life isn't so simple, and once again the plot thickens: it turns out that the bare form of the verb happens to be identical to the present tense form of the verb for all subjects except for third-person singular. That is, verbal -*s* is not used for verb forms other than the third person. Let's look at this more closely.

Tacking on third-person verbal -*s* as an inflectional suffix gives the illusion that English speakers have a system of **subject–verb agreement** (see Side Note 5), where the form of the verb changes depending on the person and number of the subject. However, the moment we step outside of the realm of the third-person singular present tense, this illusion disappears. To make this concrete, and to solidify the notion of person and number in Side Note 5, let's look at the **verb paradigm** in (15):

(15)   Present tense paradigm for the verb *enjoy*. (Note that this pattern holds true for every main verb, except for the main verbs *have, be, do*, and *say*, which we'll return to in Chapter 9.)

	singular	**plural**
first person	I **enjoy** work	We **enjoy** work
second person	You **enjoy** work	You all / Y'all / You guys / Youse / Yiz / Yuns / Yins / You'uns **enjoy** work
third person	She (or He) **enjoys** work The professor **enjoys** work Sue **enjoys** work	They **enjoy** work The professors **enjoy** work

If you compare the shaded box with all the other boxes in the paradigm, you'll see that the only place where we find a verb with the suffix -*s* is in the third singular (… though it's useful to recall that many English speakers don't even use -*s* with third singular! See Side Note 5). You can see this again in (16), where I'm comparing and contrasting side by side the third person **singular** verb (which "agrees" with the subject NP *Sue*) in (16a), with the third person **plural** verb (which "agrees" with the subject NP *The girls*) in (16b):

(16) a. Sue **enjoys** her Ford Mustang.

  b. The girls **enjoy** her Ford Mustang.

So, the verbs *enjoys* and *enjoy* in (16a) and (16b) are both claimed to be tensed. As we already saw, if we add a modal, the main verb becomes untensed; compare (16a) with (17a):

(17) a. Sue <u>would</u> **enjoy** her Ford Mustang (… if only it were running well).

  b. The girls <u>would</u> **enjoy** her Ford Mustang (… if only it were running well).

Comparing (16a) with (17a) you can see there's a difference in form between tensed *enjoys*, with verbal -*s*, and untensed (= bare) *enjoy*, with no verbal -*s*; we have already discussed this difference. And again, this difference is one of the factors that influences the received wisdom that verbs appearing with modals are untensed.

But now let's compare (16b) with (17b): here you can see that tensed *enjoy* in (16b) is **identical in form** to the untensed (= bare) *enjoy* in (17b). The entire approach to describing subject–verb agreement in English thus forces us to claim that the verb form *enjoy* in (16b) is tensed, while the (identical-looking!) verb form *enjoy* in (17b) is untensed. In my experience, this is a constant source of confusion for beginning students of English grammar; if we're saying that the form *enjoy* in (17) is untensed (= bare), then why don't we say that about the identical form *enjoy* in (16b)? Indeed, if we just put aside the shaded box in (15), all the tensed verbs in the agreement paradigm in (15) are identical to the bare (untensed) form of the verb.

EXERCISE [3]

Before reading further: confirm your understanding of the immediately preceding discussion by considering the following sentences and then answering the questions that follow. For a list of modals, see (8).

{1} Those very intelligent students want harder classroom assignments.

{2} That very intelligent student likes the homework assignments.

{3} Those very intelligent students might want harder classroom assignments.

{4} That very intelligent student would like the homework assignments (… if there weren't so many of them).

{5} We should ask for longer assignments.

{6} We ask for longer assignments (... whenever we think we haven't gotten enough practice).

For each of these sentences, state whether the main verb is **tensed** or **untensed** (= the bare infinitive = the root form).

Side Note 7: Got milk?

The paradigm in (15) represents the present tense pattern we see with all main verbs in English (with deference to Side Note 5, of course!): all persons except for the third singular are identical to the root (untensed) form of the verb. Then, for the third person singular, you just add -s. But there are a few of exceptions. We'll take a look at those exceptions (*be*, *have*, and *do*) in Chapter 9.

However, let's think right now about one really quirky verb: *get*. The verb *get* means something like "obtain" or "acquire" (as in, *I get the flu every winter*). For many English speakers, the past tense form of *get* is *got* (*I got a new car last week*).

But this form *got* also has a present tense use among many English speakers, meaning something like what *have* means. For example, if a person says to you, "I need a ride to the doctor — *do you have a car?*" it's perfectly reasonable in many regions of the world to answer "Sure, I got a car!" (meaning "I have a car"). This makes sentences like "I got a car" ambiguous between a present tense meaning (*I have a car*) and a past tense meaning (*I obtained a car*). Another funny thing about present tense *got* is that English speakers vary with respect to how it's used in the third person singular. Some people can say *He's got a car*, while other people can say *He got a car*, while others still can say *He gots a car*. Got a problem with that?

8.2.1.1.2 *Making sense of the complication*

In order to make sense of this, we need to think of verb forms like *enjoy* in (16b) versus verb forms like *enjoy* in (17) as follows: the verb form *enjoy* is ambiguous between the bare form, as in (17), and the present tense form, as in (16b). In fact, as we'll see in detail in Section 8.2.1.4, depending on the verb, sometimes English speakers use a form of the verb that is identical to the bare form even with a past tense interpretation! As a preview, let's look at the verb *put*:

(18) a.   I appreciate the fact that my students always   PRESENT TENSE
           put themselves in my shoes.
      b.   I appreciate the fact that my students <u>can</u>   BARE INFINITIVE
           put themselves in my shoes.
      c.   In last night's class, my students **put**   PAST TENSE
           themselves in my shoes.

In (18), we can see that the single form *put* can at once be used as a present tense verb, as a bare infinitive, and as a past tense verb.

One thing we can learn from this discussion, and in particular our examples in (16) and (17), is the following: at the very least, English speakers seem to differentiate between the concept of **tense interpretation** on the one hand and the concept of a **verb form** on the other. As we just saw, in some cases (for example, with the verb *put*), a root form — *put* — can function with both a present tense interpretation and a past tense interpretation (and, of course, also an untensed interpretation).

If we think of things in this way — that is, distinguishing between tense interpretation versus form of the verb — we can say that a verb like *put* has TWO forms which give rise to THREE possible tense interpretations:

Side Note 8: The *-ing* form

For now I'm putting aside another possible form, namely, the form *putting* (as in, *I'm **putting** aside another possible form*). We saw one example of the *-ing* form, in (6b). We'll get back to this in Section 8.2.1.3 and Chapter 9, where we discuss auxiliary *be* in more detail.

---

(19)   Verb: put (2 forms ⇒ 3 interpretations)
    Forms:
        (i) *puts*
            interpretation:
            a. **present tense** (*she **puts** up with it all the time*)
        (ii) *put*
            interpretations:
            a. **present tense** (*they **put** up with it all the time*)
            b. **untensed** (*they might **put** up with it*)
            c. **past tense** (*last night they **put** up with it*)

The verb *enjoy* is different from the verb *put* for many speakers: *enjoy* exhibits THREE forms with THREE possible interpretations:

(20)   Verb: *enjoy* (3 forms ⇒ 3 interpretations)
    Forms:
        (i) *enjoys*
            interpretation:
            a. **present tense** (*she **enjoys** her Mustang*)
        (ii) *enjoy*
            interpretations:
            a. **present tense** (*they **enjoy** her Mustang*)
            b. **untensed** (*they might **enjoy** her Mustang*)
        (iii) *enjoyed*
            interpretation:
            a. **past tense** (*last night she **enjoyed** her Mustang*)

To complicate things further, it turns out that the patterns in (19) and (20) merely represent the "standard English" patterns. The minute we step outside of the realm of "The English Language" as it's regulated by educational institutions, and go into the world of how English speakers actually use English, we find even more possibilities. We're going to look at this in greater detail in Section 8.2.1.4, but for now, I'll just make the passing observation that for many American English speakers, the form *enjoy* (without the *-ed* ending) can also be used with a past tense interpretation, as follows (like the verb *put*):

(21)   Verb: *enjoy* (2 forms ⇒ 3 interpretations)
    Forms:
        (i) *enjoys*
           interpretation:
           a. **present tense** (*she **enjoys** her Mustang*)
        (ii) *enjoy*
           interpretations:
           a. **present tense** (*they **enjoy** her Mustang*)
           b. **untensed** (*they might **enjoy** her Mustang*)
           c. **past tense** (*last night she **enjoy** her Mustang*)

You might not be used to seeing colloquial or regional uses like the example sentence (21c) *in writing*, so perhaps this sounds "wrong" to you upon first reading the example. But if you listen to enough music, watch enough TV, and open your ears to everyday colloquial English speech, it's likely you've heard — or will hear — such use of the bare form with a past tense interpretation, much as it's common to hear the academically sanctioned use of the bare form *put* with a past tense interpretation, as in (18c) and (19c).

Despite the fact that we can distinguish between verb form on the one hand, and the tense interpretation of a sentence on the other, we'll continue to follow tradition in referring to verbs such as *enjoy* in (16b) as "present tense," and verbs such as *enjoy* in (17b) as the "bare infinitive." Basically, despite the fact that the **morphological form** itself is the same in both contexts (i.e. *enjoy*), we traditionally take the actual syntactic context to dictate whether we say a verb is in the "present tense," or whether it's a "bare infinitive." In other words, the context can help us **disambiguate** the actual use of the form. Note, though, that sometimes context doesn't help, and a particular sentence can remain ambiguous, if the context doesn't provide any clues as to the intended meaning! Take, for example, the sentence *They put up with him*: How can you tell whether this has a "present tense" meaning or a "past tense" meaning, without more explicit context?

EXERCISE [4]

Think about the following sentences, which are ambiguous in terms of present tense versus past tense interpretation:

{1} They hit lots of home runs.   {5} My friends upset me.
{2} John and Bill cut carrots.   {6} They hurt you.
{3} We bet on that horse.   {7} We spread our wings.
{4} You quit your job.   {8} They put up with her.

Using your own imagination, try to disambiguate each sentence so that you have two unambiguous examples corresponding to each tense interpretation. Here is an example of what you should do:

4a Every year around this time, **you quit your job**! You have to stop doing that! (present tense)

4b Well, **you quit your job** last week! That's why you have no money now! (past tense)

8.2.1.2 Present form vs. present interpretation

Continuing on the theme of the imperfect line-up between the concepts of "form" versus "interpretation," let's now get back to verbal -*s*. Verbs with -*s* are clearly non-bare, and this -*s* suffix is allegedly a concrete signal of present tense (for third person singular verbs; though see Side Note 5). Nevertheless, even here, we can see that there are ways in which speakers use this "present" form with past and future interpretations. It should be noted, however, that everything we say here about verbs with -*s* holds also for the form without -*s*, used for the other persons and numbers (as we saw in the paradigm in (15)).

8.2.1.2.1 *Future interpretation*

We haven't yet discussed **future tense**, but the timeline in (11) hopefully makes it clear what it is. In a nutshell: future is a tense where speakers interpret the state (or event) denoted by the verb as happening at some point *after the time of utterance.*

Side Note 9: Back to the future

The future is very different from the past. Given that past events have already occurred — before the time of utterance — they are **real**, in the sense that no one can change the fact that something has happened. However, given that future events have not yet occurred (at the time of utterance), future interpretations involve "projections" of the future; this means that projected future events may or may not happen. This is why the future tense is often referred to as an **irrealis** (or, **unreal**) tense. In contrast, the past tense is often referred to as a **realis** tense. As you can probably tell, the word "(ir)realis" is related to the word "real."

There are a few ways to express future tense in English. One is with the modal auxiliary verb *will*, as we can see in the following example:

(22)   The professor of linguistics <u>will</u> **grade** the quizzes the day after tomorrow.

There are other possible ways to express future tense, which I'll discuss more in Chapter 9. For example:

(23) a.   The professor *is going to grade* the quizzes the day after tomorrow.
      b.   The professor *is gonna* grade the quizzes the day after tomorrow.
      c.   The professor *is grading* the quizzes the day after tomorrow.

For now, however, I only want to point out that under the right syntactic circumstances, the alleged present tense verb can be used with a future interpretation. Consider in this regard the following:

(24) When Sue **gets** home from work tomorrow, Mary <u>will</u> **cook** a nice dinner.

The verb *gets* in (24) is an embedded main verb. (Note that the matrix sentence in (24) is *Mary will cook a nice dinner.* See Chapter 5, especially Section 5.4, for a refresher on dependent clauses introduced by *when*.) Formally — that is, in terms of its form — we claim that *gets* is a "present form" because of the presence of verbal -*s*. Nevertheless, in (24) the interpretation of the event denoted by the verb *gets* is future: at the time of utterance of the sentence in (24), Sue has not yet arrived home from work.

Here we thus see a present tense form being used with a future interpretation. Once again, we're reminded that the labels we use for these forms ("present," or "past") don't straightforwardly tell us everything about the range of possible meanings they can be associated with.

8.2.1.2.2 Historical present

Surprisingly, there are also contexts in which the present form can be used with a past interpretation. One of these uses is the historical present. This is a very widespread phenomenon whereby an English speaker will use present tense forms in a narrative, describing to an interlocutor something that happened before the time of utterance (i.e. in the past). Here is an example, from Speaker B:

(25) Historical present:

Speaker A: ... So please continue your story; what happened next?
Speaker B: Well, so then Sue **walks** in, and **hangs** up her coat, and **goes** to the fridge, and **asks** me, "Didn't you buy anything for dinner?"
Speaker A: And then what happened? What did you say?

Side Note 10: Verbal -*s* with the first person singular?

Interestingly, the historical present is one case where English speakers from many different regions use verbal -*s* in the first person singular. Consider a possible response to Speaker A (in (25)) at this point:

Speaker B: Well, so I **says** to her, I **says**, "Are you kidding me? Do you think I had time to go shopping?"

You might find that use of the present forms in (25), with the third person singular subject *Sue*, sounds more "mainstream" than the use of verbal -*s* with the first person singular here. What do you think? (Just consider what you might say in a natural, non-academic setting.)

Side Note 11: Newsflash

Perhaps you've also noticed that news headlines commonly appear in the present tense, even though they describe past events. Here's an example headline from a 3 March 2014 article from the *Chattanooga Times Free Press*:

*Fire **destroys** Mentone Springs Hotel*

The article states that the fire took place on the night of 1 March 2014, so clearly the headline (published 3 March) reports an event that took place in the past, with respect to the writing of the headline. Yet, the present tense verb form is used.

So once again, we see examples of use which suggest that there is a disconnect between the concept of "present tense form" of the verb, on the one hand, and the way that this verb form can be interpreted in terms of times of events, on the other: in the case of the "historical present," we're really dealing with a past tense interpretation.

8.2.1.3 The "present tense" with stative vs. dynamic verbs

Now let's get back to my definitions of "present tense," which I provided around our discussion of the timeline in (11); I'll repeat those ideas here, in (26):

(26)   "The present overlaps with the time of utterance; so we say of the verb form *enjoys* in (9) that it's in the present tense, or, it's a present tense verb, because this is what gives us the interpretation of (9), in relation to time of utterance."

"[In (9)], Sue's state of enjoyment obtains at least at the moment when I utter the sentence."

So the idea of "present tense" should be simple enough, right? (... putting aside the complications in Section 8.2.1.2): A timeline has three times: present, past, and future; each one of these times is associated with a tense; and each one of these tenses is associated with a verb form. For the verb *enjoy*, the forms *enjoys/enjoy* indicate a state overlapping with the time of utterance (see (16)); the form *enjoyed* (see (10)) indicates a state before the time of utterance. We talked a bit about the future tense in 8.2.1.2.1 (and we'll talk a bit more about it in Chapter 9).

Well, once again, things are not actually so straightforward. It turns out that whether or not we get this "state or event overlapping with the time of utterance" interpretation with the "present tense" actually depends on the type of verb. This is related to something you may have noticed already: whenever I've talked about a verb in this chapter, I've repeatedly said something like "the **state** or **event** denoted by the verb." You might have also noticed that I keep referring to the verb *enjoy* as a "state."

Why is it necessary to talk about verbs in English in terms of denoting **states** and **events**? It's necessary because not all verbs are "action words" (contrary to the claims of traditional grammar). In fact, we can think of verbs as falling into two major classes, in terms of the kinds of **situations** they denote. These two classes are sometimes referred to as "states" versus "events"; another way of describing the two verb types is as **stative** versus **dynamic**.

Term Box 4: Situations

This is a technical term that's used to cover the denotation of *any* verb — both stative and dynamic. Having a catch-all term like **situation** allows us to avoid constantly saying "state or event," or "stative or dynamic verb."

8.2.1.3.1 Stative verbs

In (9), the verb *enjoys* expresses a state. Here are some other examples of stative verbs:

(27)   *love, hate, like, want, wish, agree, believe, know, seem*

When used in the present tense, stative verbs are indeed interpreted as denoting a state which overlaps with the time of utterance:

(28)   a.   Sue **loves** coffee.

b.   Sue **hates** it when the train arrives late.

c.   Sue **likes** to arrive on time.

d.   Sue **wants** to talk to Bill.

e.   Sue **wishes** she had a bigger window in her office.

f.   Sue **agrees** with Bill.

g.   Sue **believes** that Bill is right.

h.   Sue **seems** to think that Bill is right.

i.   Sue **knows** how to fix a flat.

j.   Sue **enjoys** her Ford Mustang.

So, for every one of the sentences in (28), we can say that the state of love, hate, belief, etc. is truly holding in present time. This is a reason to think of the verbs in bold as being present tense.

8.2.1.3.2 *Dynamic verbs*

However, at least in English, dynamic verbs behave differently from stative verbs, and their behavior makes the definition of "present tense" in English problematic. Let's look at a few examples of sentences with dynamic verbs in the present tense:

(29) a. Sue **smokes**.

  b. Sue **runs**.

  c. This train **goes** 150 miles per hour.

  d. This camera **takes** both black-and-white and color photos.

Each of the sentences in (29) has a dynamic verb which denotes some kind of **process**, or **activity**, or **achievement**. This contrasts with the verbs in (27)/(28), which all denote emotional or mental states.

Term Box 5: Achievements

Sometimes, the terms used by linguists can be pretty obscure. Perhaps you have a sense of what we might mean by "process" or "activity," but maybe the term "achievement" is a bit harder to figure out? Actually, the term simply refers to verbs which denote events that take place instantaneously; examples of such verbs are *find, break, reach, arrive,* or *recognize*. All of these verbs denote events that happen in an instant. This contrasts with verbs like *run, sleep, cry, dance,* or *write*, which denote activities or processes that occur over time. Things can become complicated, though, because some verbs can be used either as achievements or as activities/processes, such as *punch* or *hit*. A single punch is instantaneous (*Sue punched the bag in a nanosecond!*), but the verb *punch* can also be used to denote a continuous punching activity, where multiple punches are involved (*Sue punched the bag all day long*). Various factors can contribute to our ability to coerce an achievement verb to behave like an activity verb. The verb *arrive*, for instance, is often given as the prototypical example of an achievement verb (*We arrived at the station at 10:00 pm*), but if you use a plural subject, or the right kind of adverb and the right tense, you can use this verb to denote a plurality of arriving events (e.g., *People arrived at the party all night long*, or *Sue always arrives at meetings on time*), making *arrive* seem as though it's an activity verb.

For all of the sentences in (29), we can observe that none of the events denoted by the verbs in question (smoking, running, going, taking) necessarily occur at the time of utterance. Let's look at this fact a bit more closely.

For starters, let's think about the sentence in (29a): it means something like "Sue is a smoker." Similarly, (29b) means something like "Sue is a runner." Interestingly, then, these sentences can be used (and be true!) even if Sue is not smoking or running at the time the sentences are uttered. What necessarily holds at the time of utterance is not the actual activity of smoking or running but, rather, the fact that Sue is a smoker and a runner, that is, the fact that she has these activities as **habits**. Because of this interpretation, we could say that when the present tense is used with dynamic verbs, it actually yields a **property** meaning, and not a true event-at-time-of-utterance meaning. In other words, the habits described in (29a) and (29b) are properties of *Sue*, much as the sentences *Sue is a surgeon* or *Sue has brown hair* or *Sue loves coffee* also describe Sue's many properties.

Now let's turn to (29c) and (29d): Interestingly, (29c) can be true even if the train in question has never gone 150 miles per hour in its existence, or even if the train has never been run on a track! (Think about it.) The sentence could just mean that the train has the **capacity** for going 150 miles per hour. (Again, the sentence just expresses a property of the train in question, like, *The train has 10 cars.*) In the same respect, (29d) is also ambiguous: it can either mean (i) that the camera is habitually used, and when it is used, it takes both black-and-white and color photos — for example, it could be a traffic-light camera that takes both a black-and-white and a color photo every time a car runs a red light; or (ii) that the camera has the capacity for taking both black-and-white and color photos. As such, we could utter (29d) about a camera that's sitting on a store shelf, never having been used once. Or, we could utter (29d) about a camera that has only ever been used to take color photos but that has never been used to take black-and-white photos (even though it could).

What does all of this mean? It means that when English speakers use the present tense with a dynamic verb, contrary to our earlier definition of present tense, it is not the case that the event denoted by the dynamic verb necessarily overlaps with the time of utterance.

Despite this fact, grammarians and linguists alike continue to refer to the verb forms in (29), and also the verb form in (18a), as present tense verb forms.

8.2.1.3.3 What is the "true present" for dynamic verbs?

So does this mean that English speakers have no way of expressing a true present-time meaning (= event occurs at time of utterance) for a dynamic verb? No, not at all. Humans are very good at finding ways to use language to express the things they want to express. And to express a true present-time interpretation for a dynamic verb, English speakers use a present tense form of the auxiliary verb *be* (i.e. *am, is, are*), plus the **-ing form of the main verb** (or, the so-called **present participle**). This combination of *is* (or *am/are*) plus *V-ing* that you see exemplified in (30) is often referred to as the **present progressive tense**:

Present progressive tense:

(30) a. Sue <u>is</u> **smoking**.
      b. Sue <u>is</u> **running**.
      c. This train <u>is</u> **going** 150 miles per hour!
      d. The camera <u>is</u> **taking** a black-and-white photo.
      e. Look at me, I'<u>m</u> **dancing**!
      f. What <u>are</u> they **doing**?
      g. They'<u>re</u> **washing** her Ford Mustang.

Term Box 6: The present participle

Somewhat confusingly (and therefore unfortunately), the *-ing* form of the main verb in (30) is often referred to as "the present participle," or "the present participial form." This term can be quite misleading because actually, the present participle can be used in combination with a past tense form of the verb *be* (i.e. *was/were*), yielding what is called the **past progressive tense**, as in {1} and {2}:

Past progressive tense:

{1} Sue <u>was</u> **smoking**.
{2} They <u>were</u> **running**.

So we say of the sentences in {1} and {2} that they're in the past progressive tense, and the main verb (i.e. *smoking* and *running*) is a present participle! (My personal experience teaching this tells me that it can be a source of great confusion for students.)

We'll talk more about the auxiliary verb *be* (underlined in the examples in (30) and in Term Box 6) in Section 9.3.3.

It's now time to get back to the past.

8.2.1.4 Two kinds of time-travelling shapeshifters: *-ed* suffix vs. other kinds of shapeshifting

Now it's time to revisit the notion of **past tense form**.

8.2.1.4.1 Regular verbs

Until now, I've been pretending that the way we make a past tense form of the verb is by adding the inflectional suffix *-ed*, as in the example in (10), repeated here:

(10)   Sue **enjoyed** her Ford Mustang.

You can revisit Section 8.2 if you would like a refresher on the meaning of "past tense"; as a quick reminder, let's just recall the observation that in (10), Sue experienced a state of enjoyment of her Ford Mustang at some point in time *before the time of utterance* (see timeline in (11)).

Assuming we have a basic understanding of what "past tense interpretation" is: why have I just said that I've been pretending that we make a verb past by adding *-ed*? After all, it is true that the overwhelming majority of verbs in English "shapeshift" to past tense by adding an *-ed* to the **bare form**. Here are just a few examples, for many English speakers:

(31)   a.   walk + ed   ⇒   *walked*
        b.   prepare + ed   ⇒   *prepared*
        c.   study + ed   ⇒   *studied*

d.	claim + ed	⇒	*claimed*
e.	realize + ed	⇒	*realized*
f.	arrive + ed	⇒	*arrived*
g.	paint + ed	⇒	*painted*
h.	punish + ed	⇒	*punished*
i.	pitch + ed	⇒	*pitched*
j.	judge + ed	⇒	*judged*
k.	wade + ed	⇒	*waded*

etc.

Side Note 12: Spelling vs. pronunciation

It's probably worth reminding ourselves that we're not interested in any quirks of spelling, because the object of study here is the language itself (which exists independently of the arbitrary ways we spell things). So you shouldn't be thrown by the fact that, for example, in (31d), the spelling of the past tense is the spelling of the bare form plus the addition of an -*ed*, but in (31c) the spelling convention does not follow this pattern (so, we don't spell the past tense of *study* as *studyed*). You should consider this to be irrelevant.

You might also have noticed that the past tense marker (which we spell as -*ed*) is actually pronounced in different ways, depending on the verb form it attaches to. Although we're going to ignore these pronunciation differences (which are systematic, and which depend on the sound in the bare form that immediately precedes the suffix), I'll make just a few observations. For example, in (31a) and (31h), the suffix is pronounced somewhat like a [t], while in (31b) through (31f), it's pronounced something like a [d]. In contrast, in (31g) it's pronounced somewhat closer to the way it's spelled (a linguist would represent the pronunciation as follows: [ɪd]). I'll leave it as an independent thought experiment, for you to figure out the ways in which these examples differ in pronunciation!

When an English speaker forms a past tense by adding -*ed* to the bare form of the verb (keeping in mind the issues related to pronunciation noted in Side Note 12!), we can say that the speaker is conceptualizing it as a **regular verb**. So the verbs in (31) would be considered "regular." But we also have to keep in mind that not all speakers find it necessary to add an -*ed* to the verbs in (31), to make them past! Recall our discussion in Section 8.2.1.1.2, and see also the discussion immediately following in 8.2.1.4.2.

8.2.1.4.2 The "irregular" verbs

One of the complications of English-speaker knowledge is that for most of us, there is a small subset of verbs (about 150 or so …) where the past tense form of the verb involves a kind of shapeshifting (or lack thereof!) which does not involve the addition of the -ed suffix. We already saw some examples of this in Section 8.2.1.1.2, such as example (18c), repeated here:

(18) c. In last night's class, my students **put** themselves   PAST TENSE
          in my shoes.

For many, many speakers, an -ed suffix is not added to *put* to make it a past tense verb.

   Here are a few more examples of verbs that shapeshift without suffixing -ed; these are known as **irregular verbs**:

(32) a. Sue **went** to the deli this morning to pick up   bare form: *go*
          the newspaper.
      b. John **ate** too much at their Thanksgiving   bare form: *eat*
          dinner last week!
      c. Mary **made** Sue a nice sandwich.   bare form: *make*
      d. Bill **was** happy.   bare form: *be*
      e. John **knew** that Bill went to the movies last   bare form: *know*
          night.

It's rare to hear an adult native speaker of English use the suffix -ed with the bare form of the verbs in (32a–d) in many English-speaking areas of the world; have you ever heard *goed*, *eated*, *maked*, or *beed* as a past tense for these verbs? (As we'll see immediately, however, the form *knowed* is very common in some Englishes!)

   To make things even more complicated — or, more *interesting*, if you're a linguist! — the shape that irregular past tense forms take is an area of English where speakers widely differ from one another, depending on region, gender, social class, ethnicity, etc. (just to name a few ways in which English varies in society). Furthermore, even a single individual speaker may have different past tense forms for a single verb! As a quick example: I notice that I myself can vary in my use of *dreamed* versus *dreamt*, or in my use of *burned* versus *burnt*, or in my use of *shrank* versus *shrunk*, or in my use of *sneaked* versus *snuck*:

(33) a. Last night I **dreamed** that I had a Ford Mustang.
      b. Last night I **dreamt** that I had a Ford Mustang.

(34) a. You **burned** the toast!
      b. You **burnt** the toast!

(35) a. I can't believe I **shrank** my sweater in the wash.
      b. I can't believe I **shrunk** my sweater in the wash.

(36) a. I **sneaked** in while they weren't looking.
      b. I **snuck** in while they weren't looking.

EXERCISE [5]

Using the table you see for the past tense paradigm for the verb *enjoy* in Term Box 7, create past tense paradigms for the following verbs: *have, do, sing, run, give, walk, go, leave, see, drink*. Depending on where you're from, you might have more than one past tense paradigm for a particular verb (because you might have more than one particular past tense form for a verb, such as *shrank* and *shrunk* for the verb *shrink*)!

Term Box 7: Levelling the playing field

No matter what the verb (regular or irregular), and no matter what the variant form a speaker uses, the past tense paradigm in English is different from the present tense paradigm in one important respect: in the past tense, the form doesn't change according to person (first, second, third) or number (singular or plural). So while in (15) we see a distinct form reserved for the third singular, this does not happen in the past tense. When a verb paradigm has the same verb form throughout all persons and numbers, we say that the paradigm is **levelled**:

	singular	**plural**
first person	I **enjoyed** my lunch	We **enjoyed** our lunch
second person	You **enjoyed** your lunch	You all / Y'all / You guys / Youse / Yiz / Yuns / Yins / You'uns **enjoyed** your lunch
third person	She (or He) **enjoyed** her lunch The professor **enjoyed** her lunch Sue **enjoyed** her lunch	They **enjoyed** their lunch The professors **enjoyed** their lunch

We see one exception to this generalization in the examples with *be* (*was/were*) in Term Box 6; we'll return to the past tense of the verb *be* in Chapter 9.

For me, the pairs of examples in (33) through (36) are equally good; let's call these pairs (like *dreamed* and *dreamt*) **variant forms**. A verb that always gives me pause (and where I find myself using different past forms at different times) is *lie down*:

(37)   a.   I **lay** down for a little while.
       b.   I **laid** down for a little while.
       c.   I **lied** down for a little while.

Side Note 13: *lie* vs. *lay*

The standard story about how these two verbs are supposed to differ goes as follows: the former (meaning "to recline") is **intransitive**: *He always* **lies down** *for a rest when he returns from work*. The latter (meaning "to place something down") is **transitive**: *He always* **lays** <u>his bag</u> **down** *on the kitchen table when he returns from work*. Furthermore, each is supposed to have a different form for the past tense: the past tense of intransitive *lie* is supposed to be *lay*, and the past tense of transitive *lay* is supposed to be *laid* (according to the grammar police). Furthermore, note that *lied* is supposed to be the past tense form of yet another verb, *to lie* (meaning, "to deceive").

The truth is, though, that if you ask an English speaker which past tense form belongs to which verb, they'll be hard pressed to feel sure about the answer. I myself always have to think twice about it when I'm writing. Usually, when I'm speaking, I'm too focused on what I'm saying to care about what the grammar police want me to do, especially since I know that most people are themselves unsure about it, like me.

Without doing a systematic, scientific study of my own variation in use of these forms in (33)–(37) (which are but a few examples), I can't say what determines my use of one form over the other. Does it depend on who I'm talking to? Do the different forms mean slightly different things? Are they used in different syntactic contexts? So, am I more likely to say *You* **burnt** *the toast* but *You* **burned** *my finger*? Of course, there are sure to be grammar police who have some very strict rules about how these different verb forms should and shouldn't be used; I'm certain, for example, that there's a grammar cop out there somewhere would tell me that (35b) is "incorrect," or that the only "correct" way to say the thought in (37) is (37a) (see Side Note 13).

But if what we're trying to do is describe English as English speakers world-wide actually speak, then what grammar cops regulate as correct versus incorrect has very little to do with the usage of most speakers. (And it is interesting to note that, in any case, there are instances of variation — such as that in (33) — where most grammar cops would be at a loss as to tell us which one we're "supposed to" use!)

Side Note 14: The cultural capital of educated British speakers

Because of the high prestige of educated British people, English teachers in the United States are less likely to judge British linguistic forms as incorrect, even when those forms are not used by educated Americans. Thus, an American English teacher might find it harder to tell you which is the correct form (if you ask), in pairs like *burned–burnt*, *dreamed–dreamt*, *spelled–spelt*, *leaped–leapt*, and *learned–learnt*. This is because the second of each of these pairs is used in educated British speech. And because the United States has a history of respecting British English, it's less likely that an American teacher will say that the speech of an educated British person is incorrect. So when American teachers let forms like *spelt* and *learnt* off the hook, keep in mind that this is not a linguistically motivated choice. It just has to do with America's culturally and historically based deference to educated British society.

I'm sure that many of you are familiar with (or even yourselves use!) pairs or sets of variant forms, where you've been told — or maybe have heard — that one particular form is the "correct" one, while the other(s) is (are) "incorrect." What do you think of the pairs in (33) through (36), or of the set in (37)? And what do you think of the following pairs?

(38) a. Mary **sung** a beautiful rendition of the Star Spangled Banner at the party last night.
    b. Mary **sang** a beautiful rendition of the Star Spangled Banner at the party last night.

(39) a. I **brought** a delicious cheesecake to the dinner.
    b. I **brang** a delicious cheesecake to the dinner.

(40) a. They **begun** to work on the potholes last week.
    b. They **began** to work on the potholes last week.

(41) a. Who would've **thought** it!
    b. Who would've **thunk** it!

(42) a. He **come** down here yesterday, telling me my sidewalk violated City code.
    b. He **came** down here yesterday, telling me my sidewalk violated City code.

(43) a. He **ran** right out of their house, as soon as he felt the earthquake.
    b. He **run** right out of their house, as soon as he felt the earthquake.

(44) a. He **gave** me a nice haircut this morning.
    b. He **give** me a nice haircut this morning.

(45) a. She **ate** a big breakfast this morning.
    b. She **et** a big breakfast this morning.
    c. She **eat** a big breakfast this morning.

(46) a. John **knowed** Bill went to the movies last night.
    b. John **knew** Bill went to the movies last night.

People interested in regulating other people's English would probably approve of *brought, began, thought, came, ran, gave, ate,* and *knew,* and would probably disapprove of *brang, begun, thunk, come, run, give,* and *et / eat* — though perhaps they'd be less sure of *sang* versus *sung* and *shrank* versus *shrunk* ("which one is the right one?"). Now, if you're trying to get a good grade for a high school or college essay, or if you want to be taken seriously in business and in some other types of professional jobs, I wouldn't suggest trying to fight City Hall on some of these judgments: when it comes to speech — like when it comes to attire — sometimes it can just be easier to learn to use the forms by which others are going to judge you as "smart." I myself learned to use the forms that would cause teachers in high school and in college to judge me favorably — why not? But let's at least understand the total lack of logic behind the judgment of correctness: the arguments that some grammar teachers like to give for the "incorrectness" of one particular form over another can be the very same arguments that you could equally use against the form deemed "correct." And vice versa: very often, the arguments given for the "grammatical correctness" of a particular form are the very arguments you could use to illustrate the "correctness" of a form that some teachers would consider to be incorrect.

For the first issue, consider, for example, the past tense forms *come* and *run* in (42) and (43). I've heard teachers say things like "this is incorrect because you're using the bare form for something that's supposed to be past tense." But notice that this is the exact pattern we saw for the verb *put* in (18), where the "acceptable" past tense form is identical to the bare form:

(18) c. In last night's class, my students **put** themselves in   PAST TENSE
my shoes.

b. I appreciate the fact that my students <u>can</u> **put**   BARE FORM
themselves in my shoes.

(47) a. He **come** down here yesterday, telling me my   PAST TENSE
sidewalk violated City code.

b. He <u>can</u> **come** down here… (but I won't do anything   BARE FORM
about it).

Now, logically speaking, if it's fine for speakers to use the bare form *put* for the past tense, then why isn't it equally fine for the verbs *come* and *run*? Or for any other verb, for that matter? In terms of pure logic, there is simply no way to argue that, "well, for some arbitrarily chosen set of verbs, it's logically and objectively grammatical to use the bare form for the past tense (e.g., *put*), whereas for some other arbitrarily chosen set of verbs, it's ungrammatical (e.g., *come*)." The fact of the matter is, whoever decided many, many years ago that the bare form was all right for the past tense of *put* (but not for the past tense of *come*) was not a linguist; he was just a self-appointed authority who was simply using his own perception of what sounded educated to him; and this itself was based purely on nonlinguistic criteria: he considered only things like the social class and/or region of origin of the people who used the forms that sounded pleasing to him. You really can't get more arbitrary than that.

For the second issue, consider the past tense form *knowed* in (46a) (and also *throwed* and *growed*): I've known teachers to say things like "this is incorrect because you're treating this as if it's a regular verb, but it's not." But who decides which verbs get to follow the regular pattern and which ones don't? As a matter of fact, if we look at the history of English, we find that there are many verbs which are now regular — such as *walked* — which once upon a time were irregular: in fact, the past tense of the verb *walk* used to be *welk*, and there's no doubt that when people started innovating with the form *walked*, using it in variation with *welk* (much like now, when many people in the United States are saying *knowed*, *throwed*, and *growed* in variation with *knew*, *threw*, and *grew*), there were some self-appointed "experts" who started complaining about the form *walked*. Yet despite all of the efforts on the part of the self-appointed experts, the efforts were made in vain, because no one blinks an eye, now that everyone uses *walked*! In fact, if you heard someone use the original *welk* for the past tense, you'd probably be dumbfounded! And here, again, the person who decided that regularization to [bare V + -ed] was fine for *walk* — but not for *know* — had absolutely no logic to back his decision. The decision, again, was just based on preference for a particular social class and region of speakers who were using one form versus the other. And again, you simply can't get more arbitrary and illogical than that.

In contrast with the self-appointed "grammarians" of years past — whose arbitrary, nonlinguistically motivated choices leave us a legacy we're forced to live with — English speakers themselves follow logic. While some self-appointed grammarians may claim that the forms *come* and *run* and *knowed* as past tense forms are "ungrammatical," these forms all follow the logic of patterning that we see many other groups of verbs exhibit. This is why these forms are very widely used in all parts of the United States, Britain, Australia, New Zealand, etc. — in fact, anywhere that the English language has spread to as a native language (so also India, Singapore, Jamaica, Liberia, and so on). In the United States, for example, one frequently hears these forms in New York City, Chicago, Detroit, Appalachia, the South — and many other places.

8.3 conclusions

8.3.1 fighting city hall?

My purpose here is not to convince English teachers or anyone else that they should stop coming up with arbitrary and illogical reasons for why some forms should be considered correct, while others should be considered incorrect. In fact, since I've noticed it's very hard to change people's minds about such things (I'm sure I have many readers right now who aren't convinced), I would just as soon advise students to do what the teachers say — *in an academic context or other context which calls for respect of the academic form.* After all, we also can't deny that it's useful to learn which forms are considered to be correct in more formal contexts — arbitrary and illogical though the reasons for considering them correct may be! There can be times when it's in your best interest to avoid being judged negatively — for example by someone who is in a position to make important decisions about you.

8.3.2 time marches on

Two facts remain, however. First, if a verb has two or three different past tense forms, learning to use the form that an English teacher says is the "correct" one does not entail that the other form is "incorrect." You may not want to use *brang* instead of *brought* in a college essay, or in a job interview, or on the job as the CEO of a major corporation, but that doesn't mean that *brang* is objectively incorrect, or that we have to devote ourselves to eradicating it from the face of the earth, or that you can't acceptably use it in certain other social contexts. After all, people who grew up using the variant past tense forms like those in (33) through (46) did so because they found that these were actually the *correct* forms for the social contexts in which they were using them. Otherwise, why would everyone in that particular social context be using these forms? For *that* context, *this* is the norm. And following different social norms — depending on the social context — is just what we humans do. It's like clothing: just because it's socially bizarre and unacceptable for me to wear a nightgown to teach class doesn't mean I have to stop wearing nightgowns completely. I just need to know when other people think it's acceptable for me to wear one. This is how respect for social conventions works.

Another fact which remains is the following: Regardless of the **prescriptivist** rules that teachers and others appeal to in order to try and regulate which verb forms we use (e.g., (42a) vs. (42b)), these regulators are on the losing side of history. It's a 100% certainty that language changes, and that it changes in the direction that the majority of people make it change — not in the direction that a handful of regulators and teachers want it to change. Little do many grammar cops realize that at a certain point in the history of English, all the forms they currently consider to be the "correct" ones were once-upon-a-time considered to be incorrect by one of their regulating predecessors. As we saw above, even something as simple and innocuous as the form *walked* (as in *John **walked** to campus*) was at one point considered incorrect by regulators; yet notice that not only did the form *walked* survive, but it survived as the currently accepted form: nowadays no one would say *John **welk** to campus.* For the same token, although (46a) (*John **knowed** that Bill went to the movies*) is probably considered incorrect by most English teachers, the fact is, it's extremely likely that in the future, this form will sound correct to English teachers, and no one will any longer say (46b) *John **knew** that Bill went to the movies*. Indeed, at some point in the future, *John **knew*** may sound as weird as *John **welk*** sounds today. In the end, the force of popular linguistic knowledge always overrides the self-appointed regulators who want language to remain static. We know one thing for sure: no human language has ever remained unchanged. Like all things in the natural world, English is ever-evolving.

EXERCISE [6]

Here are some verbs: *prove, get, sink, dive, spell, drink, tell, hang, sit, see, weave, shine*. For each of these, think about what you think the possible past tense forms are. In some cases, you might only be able to think of one form, while in others you might be able to think of more than one. Or maybe you can think of more than one form for all of them. Even if the second (or third) form you think of is something you don't think you would personally use, jot it down anyway; you might have heard other people using it.

list of terms/concepts

achievement verb (dynamic verb)
active
activity verb (dynamic verb)
ambiguous
auxiliary verb (aux; helping verb)
capacity
compound tense (simple tense)
derivational suffixes
dynamic verbs
embedded main verbs
events
form (bare form; bare infinitive; root form; base form; morphological form; present tense form; past tense form)
future tense
habit
helping verb (aux; auxiliary verb)
historical present
inflection (inflectional suffix)
infinitive
-*ing* form of the main verb
irrealis (unreal)
irregular verb (vs. regular verb)
lexical ambiguity (disambiguate)
lexical category
main verb
matrix main verbs
modal auxiliaries (modals)
morphological form
native speaker

nonmodal auxiliaries (nonmodals)
noun derivation
number (singular, plural)
paradigm levelling
passive
past progressive
past tense (preterite)
past tense verb
person (first, second, third)
prescriptivist (prescriptive rules)
present participle
present progressive (true present)
present tense
present tense verb form
preterite (past tense)
process
property
realis (real)
regular verb (vs. irregular verb)
simple tense (compound tense)
situation
states
stative verbs
subject–verb agreement
tense (tensed; finite; untensed; infinitival; nonfinite; bare infinitive)
tense interpretation
timeline (present time; past time; future time)

time of utterance
transitive/intransitive
utterance
variant forms

variation
verbal -*s*
verb form
verb paradigm

reference

Green, Lisa J. (2002). African American English: A Linguistic Introduction. Cambridge: Cambridge University Press.

9

The Support System: Auxiliaries and the Compound Tenses

expected outcomes for this chapter

- You'll deepen your understanding of tense interpretation.
- You'll gain a more in-depth understanding of auxiliary verbs.
- You'll develop more confidence with the concepts from previous chapters (e.g., word order, verbs and the verb phrase, verb forms, subject–verb agreement, tense, active voice, passive voice, ambiguity, paradigm levelling, and variation).
- You'll become familiar with the following terms: *auxiliary verb, modal auxiliary, auxiliary* have, *auxiliary* be, *progressive* be, *passive* be, *auxiliary verb contraction, present perfect, past perfect, future perfect, present progressive, past progressive, future progressive, present participle, past participle, subjunctive, conditional, mood, aspect, finiteness, nonfiniteness,* and *affix hopping.*

9.1 auxiliary verbs: the support in the English verb system

In Chapter 8, we focused primarily on main verbs and the simple tenses, namely, **present tense** and **past tense**. But it was impossible to talk about main verbs without at least mentioning auxiliary verbs in that chapter. For example, we saw that to understand the form of the present tense of main verbs (as opposed to the bare infinitival form), it was necessary to observe that the presence of the **modal auxiliary** determines the form of the verb

Understanding Sentence Structure: An Introduction to English Syntax, First Edition.
Christina Tortora.
© 2018 John Wiley & Sons, Inc. Published 2018 by John Wiley & Sons, Inc.

which follows it. Repeating (16a) and (17a) from Chapter 8 as examples (1a) and (1b) here, recall that when we use a <u>modal</u> (as in (1b)), the main verb appears in its bare infinitival form:

(1)   a.   Sue **enjoys** her Ford Mustang.   present form
      b.   Sue <u>would</u> **enjoy** her Ford Mustang (... if   bare infinitival form
           only it were running well).

So while *enjoys* in (1a) is considered a present tense form, *enjoy* in (1b) is considered a **bare infinitival form**. This means that *enjoy* in (1c) is also considered a present tense form, because it's not preceded by a modal (or any other auxiliary for that matter):

(1)   c.   They **enjoy** their Ford Mustang.

As we'll see, modals form part of a larger system of auxiliary verbs in English. In this chapter, we'll sharpen our focus on the auxiliary verb system in English and get a fuller appreciation of the extent to which auxiliaries interact with main verbs. We'll also see how auxiliaries interact with each other, and how each auxiliary has its own special properties with respect to its contribution to the tense interpretation of the sentence, as well as with respect to its influence on the **morphological form** of the verb that it selects. (See Chapter 5, Side Note 1 and Section 5.2.3, for the concept of **selection**. See Term Box 3 in Chapter 10 for the concept of **morpheme**.)

You'll notice that this chapter is like Chapter 8 in that I talk less about structure and more about the forms of words and the kinds of meanings that these forms give to the sentence. In Chapter 10, I'll bring together Chapters 8 and 9 to discuss the complexity of sentence structure that the English verb system gives rise to.

9.1.1 modal versus nonmodal auxiliaries

As we already previewed in Chapter 8, we can conceptually divide the world of auxiliaries into two categories: **modal auxiliaries** versus **nonmodal auxiliaries**. It'll become clearer as we forge ahead (and also in Chapter 10) how the two types are different. We've already seen examples of the modals in Chapter 8; we'll repeat our list here in (2):

(2)   *can, could, will, would, shall, should, may, might, must*

In Section 9.4 we'll take a look at the modals in greater detail.

As for the nonmodal auxiliaries, there are only three to worry about: *have, be,* and *do*. These three auxiliaries have a number of properties that differentiate them from the modals, something we'll understand bit by bit, as this chapter unfolds. For starters, note that the auxiliaries *have, be,* and *do* distinguish themselves by the fact that they can also act as **main verbs**. Take a look at the examples in (3), (4), and (5). The (a) examples illustrate these verbs in their main verb use; the (b) examples, on the other hand, illustrate their use as auxiliaries:

have

(3) a. Sue **has** a lot of friends.   main verb

     b. Sue **has** enjoyed her Mustang for years now.   auxiliary verb

be

(4) a. Sue **is** my favorite colleague.   main verb

     b. Sue **is** working very hard these days.   auxiliary verb

do

(5) a. Sue **does** her homework every day.   main verb

     b. Sue **does**n't like that idea.   auxiliary verb

In the (b) examples, the auxiliaries *have* (3b), *be* (4b), and *do* (5b) are each followed by a main verb (*enjoyed, working,* and *like*).

If you think carefully about the meanings of these verbs in their main versus auxiliary verb uses, you'll notice some differences. For example, the verb *have* in its main verb use in (3a) has what we can call a "possessive" meaning; this possessive meaning seems to be missing with *have* in its auxiliary verb use in (3b). Likewise, the verb *do* in its main verb use in (5a) means something like "to engage in" or "to work at"; again, this meaning seems to be missing with *do* in its auxiliary verb use in (5b). The auxiliaries *have* and *do* in (3b) and (5b) don't contribute a meaning, so much as they act as "helpers" to the main verb, which is why **auxiliary verbs** are sometimes referred to as **helping verbs**.

It's less clear what the main verb *be* in (4a) means. It's therefore unsurprising that a lot of languages simply do without the verb *be* in the present tense. Even many English speakers eliminate this verb altogether in the present tense; compare the examples in (4) with the examples in (4'):

Some varieties of English (cf. (4)):

(4') a. Sue my favorite colleague.

      b. Sue working very hard today.

The fact that many languages do without the verb *be* in the present tense, as in (4'), underscores that this verb doesn't add any clear meaning to the sentence, either in its main verb or in its auxiliary verb uses. As we'll see in Chapter 10, the syntax of the verb *be* also sets it apart from all other verbs.

Notice how — in contrast with the nonmodals *have, be,* and *do* — the modal auxiliaries can never function as main verbs:

(6) a. *John **will** his book.   (cf. *John will finish his book*)

     b. *Sue **might** her Mustang.   (cf. *Sue might drive her Mustang*)

     c. *The professor **can** her   (cf. *The professor can help her*
        students.   *students*)

There are also syntactic differences between modals and nonmodals which we'll explore in detail in Chapter 10.

We'll start this chapter by looking at the nonmodal auxiliaries *have* and *be* in Sections 9.2 and 9.3, taking each in turn. Then in Section 9.4 we'll revisit the modals, and in Section 9.5 we'll summarize all the possible verb combinations in English with the auxiliaries *have*, *be*, the modals, and main verbs. We'll reserve a discussion of auxiliary *do* for Chapter 10, where it'll become most relevant.

9.2 auxiliary *have*

As we just saw in example (3), *have* can function either as a main verb or as an auxiliary verb. Let's take a look at the present and past tense paradigms of the verb *have*, in both its main verb and auxiliary verb incarnations.

9.2.1 present tense form of *have*

The present tense paradigm of *have* is a bit quirky compared with the present tense paradigm of all other verbs. Consider (7):

(7)   Present tense paradigm for the verb *have* (both main verb and auxiliary verb)

	singular	**plural**
first person	MAIN VB: I **have** a lot of friends AUX: I **have** enjoyed my Mustang for years	MAIN VB: We **have** a lot of friends AUX: We **have** enjoyed our Mustang for years
second person	MAIN VB: You **have** a lot of friends AUX: You **have** enjoyed your Mustang for years	MAIN VB: You **have** a lot of friends AUX: You **have** enjoyed your Mustang for years
third person	MAIN VB: She **has** a lot of friends AUX: She **has** enjoyed her Mustang for years	MAIN VB: They **have** a lot of friends AUX: They **have** enjoyed their Mustang for years

At first glance, present tense *have* (either main verb or auxiliary, it's irrelevant) appears to have the same characteristics of the present tense of all other main verbs (like *enjoy*): the only form that's different in the entire paradigm is the one for the third person singular. But let's focus on this form in the third person singular in the shaded box in (7) carefully: if you're a native English speaker, it probably seems natural to you that the form is *has* (though of course for many speakers another possibility is *have*; see Side Note 5 in Chapter 8). However, the form *has* is unexpected, given the pattern we've seen for every other verb until now! Think about it: every other verb examined until this point forms the third person singular simply by suffixing verbal -*s* onto the bare form of the verb (again, with the caveat in Side Note 5 in Chapter 8). Look for example at (8):

(8)　a.　walk + s　⇒　*she walks*

　　b.　enjoy + s　⇒　*she enjoys*

　　c.　put + s　⇒　*she puts*

　　d.　love + s　⇒　*she loves*

　　e.　sip + s　⇒　*she sips*

　　f.　catch + s　⇒　*she catches*

Side Note 1: Inflectional suffix behavior revisited

In Side Note 12 in Chapter 8, we noticed that the past tense marker which we spell as -*ed* is actually pronounced in different ways, depending on the verb it suffixes to. As we saw, these pronunciation differences are systematic and depend on the last speech sound in the verb that immediately precedes the suffix. Well, just like with the past tense suffix, present tense verbal -*s* is also pronounced differently, depending on the speech sound in the verb that immediately precedes it. For example, in (8a,c,e) the suffix is pronounced somewhat like an [s], while in (8b,d) it is pronounced something like a [z]. Furthermore, in (8f) it is pronounced rather more like it's spelled (a linguist would represent the pronunciation as follows: [ɪz]). As with Side Note 12 in Chapter 8, I'll leave it as an independent thought experiment for you to think about the ways in which the last speech sound in each verb form differs in pronunciation and how this affects the pronunciation of verbal -*s*. For example, compare the last sound in *walk* with the last sound in *love* (ignore spelling and think about pronunciation). Why might the -s in *walks* be pronounced like [s] while the -s in *loves* is pronounced like a [z]?

The pattern we see for every other verb (like in (8)) would actually lead us to expect the third person singular form of *have* to be *haves*:

(9)　have + s　⇒　**she haves*

The asterisk in (9) is a reminder that this expected form **haves* is actually not possible. So the verb *have* is an exception to the rule we see in (8): If we take *have* and add verbal -*s* to it, we get the completely quirky form *has*:

(10)　have + s　⇒　*she has*

It's as if verbal -s suffixes onto a root form "*ha-*" (with the missing "v"). In this sense, the verb *have* has an irregular present tense paradigm, compared with all other verbs. (See Term Box 4 in Chapter 10 for the concept of **spell-out rules**.)

There's something else about present tense auxiliary *have* that's important to note that makes it different from the present tense of main verb *have* — something that's not reflected in the paradigm in (7). Take a look at the examples in (11), and compare those with the auxiliary *have* examples in (7):

(11) a. I'**ve** enjoyed my Mustang for years.   first person singular

b. You'**ve** enjoyed your Mustang for years.   second person singular

c. She'**s** enjoyed her Mustang for years.   third person singular

d. We'**ve** enjoyed our Mustang for years.   first person plural

e. You'**ve** enjoyed your Mustang for years.   second person plural

f. They'**ve** enjoyed their Mustang for years.   third person plural

The examples in (11) all contain a **contracted** form of auxiliary *have*. The contracted form might actually be the more common form used in speech (as opposed to writing). For many English speakers, however, contracted *have* is only possible with the auxiliary — not with main verb *have*.

> ## EXERCISE [1]
>
> To see whether you allow main verb *have* to be contracted, just take the sentences with main verb *have* in the paradigm in (7), and replace the uncontracted *have* with contracted *have*. Judge for yourself whether these sentences with contracted main verb *have* sound grammatical.

9.2.2 past tense form of *have*

In contrast with the present tense paradigm for *have*, there's nothing out of the ordinary with past tense *have*. Like the other so-called irregular verbs (see Section 8.2.1.4.2), the past tense of *have* isn't formed by adding the *-ed* suffix to the bare form (*have + ed). But like all regular and irregular past tense verbs (except for *be*, as we'll see in Section 9.3), *have* exhibits a **levelled past tense paradigm** (see Term Box 7 in Chapter 8). That is, all forms are the same, no matter what the person or number:

(12)   Past tense paradigm for the verb *have* (both main verb and auxiliary)

	singular	**plural**
first person	MAIN VB: I **had** a lot of work yesterday AUX: I **had** already spoken with him	MAIN VB: We **had** a lot of work yesterday AUX: We **had** already spoken with him
second person	MAIN VB: You **had** a lot of work yesterday AUX: You **had** already spoken with him	MAIN VB: You **had** a lot of work yesterday AUX: You **had** already spoken with him
third person	MAIN VB: She **had** a lot of work yesterday AUX: She **had** already spoken with him	MAIN VB: They **had** a lot of work yesterday AUX: They **had** already spoken with him

Also, like present tense auxiliary *have*, past tense auxiliary *have* has a contracted form, which is usually spelled *'d*. Take a look at the examples in (13) and compare those with the past tense auxiliary *have* examples in (12):

(13)   a.   If only I**'d** spoken to him earlier …   first person singular
        b.   If only you**'d** spoken to him earlier …   second person singular
        c.   If only she**'d** spoken to him earlier …   third person singular
        d.   If only we**'d** spoken to him earlier …   first person plural
        e.   If only you**'d** spoken to him earlier …   second person plural
        f.   If only they**'d** spoken to him earlier …   third person plural

EXERCISE [2]

As with Exercise [1], you can check to see whether you allow main verb *had* to be contracted to *'d*: just take the sentences with main verb *had* in the paradigm in (12), and replace the uncontracted form *had* with contracted *'d*. Judge for yourself whether these sentences sound grammatical.

9.2.3 the compound tenses with *have*

We just saw the present and past tense paradigms for auxiliary *have* in (7)/(11) and (12)/(13). Now it's time to take a closer look at the function of *have* as an auxiliary, in both its present and past tense forms.

9.2.3.1 present tense auxiliary *have*: the present perfect

We already saw some examples of present tense aux *have*, which I'll repeat here (with *have* underlined):

(14) a. Sue <u>has</u> **enjoyed** her Ford Mustang for years.   (*has*: 3rd present sing. of *have*)

     b. She<u>'s</u> **enjoyed** her Ford Mustang for years.   (contracted *has*: 3rd present sing. of *have*)

     c. They<u>'ve</u> **enjoyed** their Ford Mustang for years.   (contracted *have*: 3rd present pl. of *have*)

     d. They <u>have</u> **enjoyed** their Ford Mustang for years.   (*have*: 3rd present pl. of *have*)

The sentences in (14) contain examples of **compound tenses** (see Term Box 1). A compound tense is a tense which contains a form of an auxiliary plus a main verb. This particular kind of compound tense (present tense form of *have* plus main verb) is known as the **present perfect**. Let's explore both the meaning and the form of this tense.

Term Box 1: Compound tense vs. simple tense

A **compound tense** is a tense resulting from the combination of more than one verb in a single S — i.e. an auxiliary plus a main verb. The **present perfect** is therefore one example of a compound tense. In Term Box 6 in Chapter 8 we saw two other examples of compound tenses: the **present progressive** (*Sue is smoking*) and the **past progressive** (*Sue was smoking*), which we'll explore in more detail in Section 9.3. In contrast, the present tense (*Sue loves New York*) and the past tense (*Sue loved New York*) are considered simple tenses. These are the only two simple tenses in English.

9.2.3.1.1 *The present perfect: meaning*

As we just saw, the present perfect tense involves a present tense form of the auxiliary verb *have* plus the *-ed* form of the **main verb**, if the verb is **regular**. (I'll get to the **irregular** main verbs in just a moment.)

The present perfect is a funny tense: it presents a lot of variation in its possible uses/interpretations, depending, for example, on whether we're talking about British English or American English (and even within British English, depending on what region of Britain we're talking about). Its meaning also depends on what kinds of adverbs are used in conjunction with it — adverbs like *already*, *always*, *never*, and *just*. (We'll discuss adverbs in Chapter 11.) The possibilities and the variation are in fact so complex and so vast that we won't be able to cover it all in this book. So I'll just make a few observations.

Side Note 2: Negatives and interrogatives

For the present purposes, in the discussion I'm putting aside sentences with negation and also interrogatives (though you'll see a couple of examples with negation in Exercise [4]). Here are some examples of interrogatives and sentences with negation:

{1} Sue **has** never **watched** a hockey game in her life.
{2} Sue **hasn't fixed** the sink yet.
{3} **Has** Sue ever **climbed** Mt. Everest?

We'll talk about this in Chapter 10.

For many American English speakers, the present perfect is neither a present nor a past, but rather, it expresses a kind of hybrid between the two. In my own spoken English, for example, I use this construction to express at least one of two things.

First, just focusing on states: English speakers can use the present perfect to express a state that started holding at some point in the past and which has held continuously ever since — up to and including present time. This can be seen in the examples in (14), and also in the following examples:

(15)   a.   Sue <u>has</u> always **loved** New York City.

     b.   Sue <u>has</u> **respected** Mary ever since she successfully fixed the sink.

Term Box 2

For stative vs. dynamic verbs, see Section 8.2.1.3.

Even though the sentences in (14) and (15) are not in the present tense — they are in the present perfect — Sue's enjoyment of her Mustang, Sue's love for New York City, and Sue's respect for Mary all include the time of utterance. What makes the tense in these sentences different from the present tense is that here, the present perfect expresses that the state in question (enjoyment, love, respect) started to hold at some point in the past.

Another possible use of the present perfect — which is prevalent with dynamic verbs — is similar: when using the present perfect with a dynamic verb, English speakers interpret the activity/process denoted by the verb to have held at least one time (if not on multiple occasions), throughout a certain time period. And again, this time period starts at some (possibly unspecified) point in the past, and holds up to and including the present time. For example:

(16)   a.   Sue <u>has</u> **watched** *The Big Lebowski* 102 times.

     b.   Sue <u>has</u> **played** baseball before!

The present perfect in (16) tells us that at some point in the past, a time period began — a time period which is still relevant at the time of utterance; furthermore, in this time period, there have been *Big Lebowski* watching events and baseball playing events (at least one).

Now, what I just described is representative of American English speakers. Yet there are other English speakers still, for example in Britain, who use the present perfect also to indicate a recent past event. Compare (17a) with (17b):

(17) a. John **has** just **finished** his dinner.   PRESENT PERFECT TENSE

      b. John just **finished** his dinner.   PAST TENSE

There are many British English speakers who find (17b) to be unacceptable and who would only use the present perfect to express an event of the recent past, as in (17a). However, there are many American English speakers who would sooner use the past tense in (17b) to indicate a recent-past event than they would the present perfect in (17a). This is an example of regional variation, where the regions in question are two different countries.

9.2.3.1.2 *The present perfect: form*

The range of possible meanings that can be associated with the present perfect, the many ways in which it can be used, and the extent of the variation across English speaker types, are all too much for us to do justice to it here. For the purposes of this book, I'd like to limit myself at this point just to some questions about the **form** of the present perfect.

As we already saw (or, as we have already seen …), when used with regular verbs, the present perfect involves a present tense form of the verb *have* plus what seems to be the *-ed* form of the verb. Now, in Chapter 8, we identified the *-ed* form of the verb as the **past tense**. However: despite the fact that the main verbs in (14) through (17) all look like past tense verbs (*enjoyed*, *loved*, *respected*, *watched*, *played*, *finished*), it's actually standardly claimed that in the present perfect, these are <u>not</u> past tense forms. Instead, whenever we find such a verb in the present perfect (or any compound tense with a form of *have*, as we'll see below for the past perfect and the future perfect), the form of the verb following auxiliary *have* is taken to be a **past participle**. Thus, in (17a) the main verb *finished* would be in its **past participial form**, while in (17b) the main verb *finished* would be in its **past tense form** (sometimes referred to as the **simple past form**), as in (18):

(18) a. John <u>has</u> just **finished** his dinner.   *finished*: past participial form

      b. John just **finished** his dinner.   *finished*: simple past form

Now, I'd like to acknowledge immediately that this can be very confusing for students: note that the two forms are identical —*finished* and *finished*! So why should we make this terminological distinction seen in (18a) versus (18b)?

There are at least two main factors that have led grammarians and linguists alike to make this distinction between the concept of a simple past form on the one hand (as in (18b)) and the concept of a past participle on the other, as in the present perfect in (18a). First of all, the centuries-old descriptions of English grammar have always been influenced by the way Latin grammar works. And since Latin (a very different language from English) shows a clear difference between a past tense form and a past participial form, this had some influence on the way grammarians chose to describe English. This is despite the fact that, generally speaking, Modern English doesn't always overtly exhibit the same kinds of distinctions that Latin exhibits. As a thought experiment: those readers who know Spanish can think about the difference between a simple past form like *caminé* 'I **walked**' and a past participial form like *caminado* (in the sentence *he caminado* 'I have **walked**'), to see how different the forms are in a language other than English.

Side Note 3: Distinguishing indistinguishable things

Related to the concept of (not?) distinguishing between *finished* (simple past form) and *finished* (past participial form) in (18b) and (18a) is the concept of "subject–verb agreement" in English. As we saw in Chapter 8, the present tense of all verbs only has a distinct verb form in the third person singular (with the exception of *be* and the modals, as we'll see) — and even here, we saw that there are many speakers who don't use verbal *-s* at all (Side Note 5 in Chapter 8)! Furthermore, if we put aside the verb *be*: in the past tense, verbs do not distinguish form according to person and number (see Term Box 7 in Chapter 8). This raises the question of whether there is such a thing as "subject–verb agreement" in the English past tense at all! What does it mean for the subject and the verb to agree in terms of person and number if every form of the verb is the same for the past tense, no matter what the person and number?

EXERCISE [3]

For each of the following sentences, state whether the main verb is a simple past or a past participle. Remember: if the main verb is preceded by some present tense form of the auxiliary verb *have*, then it logically follows that the tense of the sentence is the present perfect, and therefore that the main verb is in its past participial form.

{1} I haven't **walked** to campus once this week!
{2} They **arrived** at my house at 9:00 p.m.
{3} We have never **presented** a paper at a conference later than 11:00 a.m.
{4} Sue's **walked** to campus four times already this week.
{5} We **presented** our paper at that conference really early in the morning.
{6} They've always **arrived** late to our parties.

9.2.3.1.3 *The present perfect form and irregular verbs revisited*

There is, however, another factor which has led grammarians and linguists alike to want to describe English as a language that distinguishes between a simple past form and a past participial form in tenses like the present perfect. This factor has to do with irregular verbs. Let's see how.

As we saw in Section 8.2.1.4.2, especially in examples (32) through (47), there's a small subset of verbs in English which are **irregular** — let's say around 150, where the number will vary according to regional and individual variation. These are verbs which don't follow the regular pattern for the past tense. Whatever the differences among speakers, what remains constant is the fact that every English speaker has a small subset of irregular verbs in their **mental lexicon** (or, mental vocabulary). It may not always be the same verbs that are irregular for all speakers, but all speakers have irregular verbs.

Second, it's important to observe that, of these irregular verbs, the overwhelming majority are *also* irregular in the present perfect. To start with, let's just look at two examples of the present perfect with irregular main verbs; these are the (b) examples in (19) and (20):

put:

(19)   a.   In last night's class, my students **put** themselves in my shoes.
         form of main verb: *simple past*
         tense of sentence: *past tense*

       b.   They <u>have</u> always **put** themselves in other people's shoes.
         form of main verb: *past participle*
         tense of sentence: *present perfect*

buy:

(20)   a.   John **bought** Bill a nice gift last night.
         form of main verb: *simple past*
         tense of sentence: *past tense*

       b.   John <u>has</u> always **bought** nice gifts for people.
         form of main verb: *past participle*
         tense of sentence: *present perfect*

Side Note 4: *Morphological form* vs. *tense interpretation*: the reckoning

In Section 8.2.1 we talked about the difference between the concept of a verb form, on the one hand, and that of tense interpretation, on the other. When we talk about **verb form**, we're talking about the **morphological form** of the word itself. When we talk about tense, we're talking about the interpretation of the time that a particular event takes place (e.g., present, past, future). In this section, we introduced the present

230 AUXILIARIES AND THE COMPOUND TENSES

perfect tense, which we should think of as an interpretation regarding the time (or time period) in which a state holds or an event takes place. The present perfect tense consists of two verb forms: the present tense form of the verb *have*, and the past participial form of the main verb. In the examples in (19) and (20), I've made explicit this distinction between the form of the main verb on the one hand, and the tense interpretation of the sentence on the other.

We already saw in Chapter 8 that *put* is an irregular verb in the past tense (19a); what (19b) shows us, however, is that this verb is also irregular in the present perfect. That is, as in the past tense, the main verb in the compound tense is not formed by adding *-ed* to the root. Similarly, we see in (20b) that the form of *buy* is not an *-ed* form, much like the irregular simple past form. (Though see Side Note 5!)

Side Note 5: *Putted* and *buyed*: caveat lector!

Although I claim that the past tense and past participial forms of *put* and *buy* are not *putted* and *buyed*, I actually couldn't swear that there aren't some adult native speakers of English in some English-speaking community somewhere, who use the forms *putted* and *buyed*. I just personally haven't seen this attested anywhere in the literature on the topic. But this doesn't mean it doesn't happen!

So why did I just observe the fact that irregular verbs are also irregular in the present perfect? What does this observation tell us about the fact that grammarians and linguists alike make a distinction between the simple past form on the one hand and the past participial form on the other? After all, the examples in (19) and (20) show that, despite the irregular status of the verbs *put* and *buy* in both past tense and compound tense contexts, these nonpresent forms are still identical in both contexts (*put* and *put*; *bought* and *bought*), just like the regular verb forms *finished* and *finished* in (18). Thus, we still see no distinction in form, despite their irregular status.

Term Box 3: Nonpresent forms

To avoid the sometimes cumbersome formula "simple past form and past participial form," I find it convenient to use the cover-all term nonpresent form. This term allows us to refer to simple past and past participial forms as a set, at the exclusion of the present tense form and the bare infinitival form.

The key fact to observe here about irregular verbs is the following: despite what we just saw about the irregular verbs *put* and *buy*, there are also many irregular verbs which have distinct forms for the simple past tense vs. the compound tenses (like, for example, the present perfect), for many speakers of English. That is, there are numerous irregular verbs which have distinct nonpresent forms which specialize for one of these two contexts. The verb *go* is one very clear example:

go:

(21) a. John **went** to the store only once this morning.
form of main verb: *simple past*
tense of sentence: *past tense*

    b. John <u>has</u> **gone** to the store five times this morning already!
form of main verb: *past participle*
tense of sentence: *present perfect*

As can be seen in (21), for the verb *go* it is very common for English speakers to use one form for the simple past (*went*), and another in the present perfect tense (*gone*).

Let's refer to the English speakers who exhibit the distinction seen in (21) as "Type-X Speakers" (my own terminology here). For Type-X Speakers, the verb forms *went* and *gone* in (21) — both nonpresent forms — are specialized for these two different contexts, past tense versus present perfect. There are actually quite a few verbs for which Type-X Speakers make this distinction between past tense and present perfect contexts (over 100, in fact). Here are a few more examples:

Type-X Speaker (distinct nonpresent forms which specialize for past tense versus compound tense contexts):

see:

(22) a. Sue **saw** Bill this morning.
form of main verb: *simple past*
tense of sentence: *past tense*

    b. Sue <u>has</u> **seen** Bill five times this morning already!
form of main verb: *past participle*
tense of sentence: *present perfect*

take:

(23) a. John **took** Bill to dinner for his birthday.
form of main verb: *simple past*
tense of sentence: *past tense*

    b. John <u>has</u> **taken** Bill to dinner for his birthday four
times this week so far.
form of main verb: *past participle*
tense of sentence: *present perfect*

give:

(24) a. John **gave** Bill a beautiful gift.
form of main verb: *simple past*
tense of sentence: *past tense*

      b. John <u>has</u> **given** Bill three gifts for his birthday so far.
          form of main verb: *past participle*
          tense of sentence: *present perfect*

eat:

(25) a. John and Bill **ate** some sushi on the first night.
          form of main verb: *simple past*
          tense of sentence: *past tense*

      b. John and Bill <u>have</u> **eaten** sushi four times this week so far.

          form of main verb: *past participle*
          tense of sentence: *present perfect*

As you might have already noticed, this difference that some English speakers exhibit in the main verb's form in simple past versus compound tense contexts — for the verbs *go*, *see*, *take*, *give*, and *eat*, and many others — happens to be a pattern that is also sanctioned by the grammar police. So whatever kind of speaker you may be (Type-X, or another type, as we'll address immediately), you may have learned at some point in school that the distinctions made in (21) through (25) are the "correct" ones to make.

EXERCISE [4]

For each of the following sentences, state whether the main verb is a simple past form or a past participle. Remember: if the main verb is preceded by some form of the auxiliary verb *have*, then it logically follows that the main verb is in its past participial form.

  {1} They've **eaten** sushi four times this week so far.
  {2} They **came** to our party last night.
  {3} He **sang** that cantata so beautifully!
  {4} I've **ridden** my bike five times already this week.
  {5} You **swore** that you would eat healthy from now on.
  {6} He's never **sung** that before.
  {7} They **ate** some sushi last night.
  {8} I **rode** my bike this morning.
  {9} We have **sworn** off of sugary drinks.
  {10} They haven't **come** to a single party of ours this year!

There are five simple past / past participle pairs scattered throughout these sentences. Group these pairs together, and state for each pair what the bare form of the verb is. For example: "Sentences {1} and {7} contain the forms *eaten* and *ate*, which are the past participial and simple past forms (respectively) of the verb *eat*."

But let's get back to the main point: the existence of this distinction for Type-X Speakers between the two nonpresent verb forms — in past tense versus present perfect contexts — is precisely what influences linguists and grammarians alike to posit the two different concepts of simple past form on the one hand and past participial form on the other. Thus, for the verb *go*, for example, we distinguish between *went* as a simple past form and *gone* as a past participial form, and this concept gets generalized to all verbs. So even in those cases where there's only one nonpresent form for both contexts — such as *finished* in (18) or *put* in (19) — we still distinguish between the concept of a past participle (*finished* in (18a)) and a simple past (*finished* in (18b)).

Now, there are two things that make this conceptual distinction between "simple past form" versus "past participial form" so difficult to remember for the many students of English grammar who are asked to learn these concepts in school. First of all, there's the fact I just noted: the overwhelming majority of verbs in English don't exhibit distinct nonpresent forms for simple past versus compound tense contexts in the first place. I've taught this material enough times to know that no amount of reviewing these terms with students will lead everyone to the conclusion that "Oh, of course! It totally makes sense to say that the instance of *finished* in (18a) is a past participle and the instance of *finished* in (18b) is a simple past, even though they're identical." It just seems counterintuitive to recognize that *finished* and *finished* are different forms. It's also hard for students because both terms contain the word "past" in them (simple past and past participle). Also, it's not as if the term "participle" has any intuitive value for students new to the study of language.

And second: not every English speaker is a Type-X Speaker, something which would make the distinction even less obvious, for many people. Let's talk about this more.

Not every English speaker makes the kinds of distinctions we see in (21) through (25). First, it's important to remember that, as is always the case with linguistic variation, what the actual facts are will depend on region, social class, gender, ethnicity, and — just as importantly — the individual. Here, we have to recall our discussion of Chapter 1 where we established the fundamental approach taken in this book: structure is ultimately the product of the individual mind. Because of this, it's impossible to successfully make blanket generalizations about "English," and nowhere is this clearer than in the case of variation with nonpresent verb forms, and in particular, with which verbs will be "irregular," and how English speakers will use the various irregular forms in simple past and compound tense contexts. On the other hand, the truth is that there have been relatively few scientific studies of the phenomenon of variation in use of irregular verb forms in simple past and compound tense contexts amongst English speakers, so it's hard to say exactly what the possible patterns are for different speakers. Nevertheless, I'll make a few observations which are based in part on my own research.

One factor which seems to play a role in how speakers treat the different irregular verb forms is the verb itself. So not all irregular verbs may exhibit the same kind of variation. For example: the verb forms *seen* and *done* are commonly used by many speakers in past tense contexts (alongside present perfect contexts) as follows:

(26) a. She **seen** him just this morning.

      b. Sue <u>has</u> **seen** Bill five times this morning already.

(27) a. They **done** it again.

      b. They'<u>ve</u> **done** that five times this morning already!

These uses of *seen* and *done* in both simple past and compound tense contexts are extremely common worldwide, in the United Kingdom, Ireland, Australia, and the United States (including New York and Appalachia, among many other places). They seem to be as widely used as the forms *come* and *run*, for both contexts:

(28) a. He **come** down here yesterday, telling me that my sidewalk violated City code.

      b. He <u>has</u> **come** down here to complain before, but I won't do anything about it.

(29) a. She **run** the NYC marathon yesterday.

      b. She <u>has</u> **run** the NYC marathon ten times already.

Now, from the perspective of the academic norm, (28a) and (29a) might look as though such speakers "are using the past participle for the simple past." However, it's not clear that these speakers themselves really see it that way! Note that the very same speakers who use (28a) and (29a) may be less likely to use the forms *gone*, *given*, or *eaten* in simple past contexts:

These examples are in question (it's not clear how common they are, compared with (28a) and (29a)):

(30) a. John **gone** to the store only once this morning.

      b. John **given** Bill a beautiful gift this morning.

      c. John and Bill **eaten** some sushi on Bill's birthday.

Another issue is **intraspeaker variation**, which — although we may not think about it much — is the reality of human linguistic behavior (see Term Box 4). We already saw examples of intraspeaker variation in (33) through (37) in Section 8.2.1.4.2. I'll repeat two examples here in (31) which, as I said, are both possible for me in the past tense:

(31) a. Last night I **dreamed** that I had a Ford Mustang.   simple past form (past tense)

      b. Last night I **dreamt** that I had a Ford Mustang.   simple past form (past tense)

Term Box 4: Intraspeaker variation

The use by a single speaker of different linguistic forms to mean the same thing is called **intraspeaker variation**. We've already seen a few examples of intraspeaker variation in this book. For example, in Chapter 6, we saw that embedded declaratives within VP can either contain — or not — the complementizer *that*. The presence or absence of *that* furthermore does not change the meaning of the sentence: *Sue thinks (that) Bill is smart*. We also saw an example of intraspeaker variation in Chapter 4, with particle shift: so alongside *Mary **ate up** her sandwich*, we get the semantically equivalent *Mary **ate** her sandwich **up***, with the particle *up* appearing to the right of the direct object, with no change in meaning.

In other words, I vary in my use between the two forms *dreamed* and *dreamt* for the past tense. What's important here is that a single individual speaker (such as myself) will also use both these forms *dreamed* and *dreamt* in the present perfect as well:

(32) a. Sue <u>has</u> always **dreamed** of owning   past participial form (pres.
          a Mustang.   perfect tense)

      b. Sue <u>has</u> always **dreamt** of owning   past participial form (pres.
          a Mustang.   perfect tense)

So given (31) and (32), it's clear that neither form, *dreamed* or *dreamt*, specializes for past tense versus compound tense contexts. This means that the existence of the two nonpresent forms cannot be attributed to the simple past versus past participle distinction.

To generalize even further, this may mean that there are even more cases of variant nonpresent forms than we realize, which many English speakers do not treat as specialized for past tense versus compound tense contexts. In other words, the kind of variation seen in (31) and (32) may actually be common wherever there exists more than one nonpresent form related to a single verb. Consider forms like *saw* and *seen*: there may be speakers who use the two different forms, each in both contexts, as follows:

Possible for a single speaker (for some speakers):

(33) a. I **saw** him just this morning.   simple past form (past tense)
      b. I **seen** him just this morning.   simple past form (past tense)

(34) a. Sue <u>hasn't</u> **saw** that movie in a   past participial form (pres.
          long time.   perfect tense)

      b. Sue <u>hasn't</u> **seen** that movie in a   past participial form (pres.
          long time.   perfect tense)

Thus, the forms *saw* and *seen* may be used in both contexts, much as we see with *dreamed* and *dreamt* in (31) and (32). As we'll see in Side Note 18, this variation may be more common in **infinitival perfects**, i.e. *have* + nonpresent structures in which aux *have* follows a modal (which we'll see in Section 9.5). Thus, speakers might be more likely to use forms like *saw* or *went* (instead of *seen* or *gone*) in strings such as *Bill would have saw that movie* or *Mary would have went*.

If this kind of variation is more widespread across a speaker's lexical inventory of verbs than we think, it would become difficult to sustain the hypothesis that the two distinct nonpresent forms (e.g., *saw* and *seen*) exist to distinguish between simple past versus past participle, for all English speakers.

EXERCISE [5]

Here are some verbs: *prove, get, sink, dive, spell, drink, tell, hang, sit, see, weave, shine.* Come up with your own present perfect example sentences for each of these. Think about what the possible past participial forms are for you. In some cases, you might only be able to think of one form, while in others you might be able to think of more than one. Or maybe you can think of more than one form for all of them. Even if the second (or third) form you think of is something you don't think you would personally use, jot it down anyway; you might have heard other people using it in the present perfect. Then compare your results with Exercise [6] from Chapter 8.

9.2.3.2 The past perfect

In Section 9.2.3.1 we examined the form and the meaning of the present perfect tense. We saw that this tense consists of a present tense form of the auxiliary verb *have* plus a past participle. Indeed, the <u>present</u> tense of the verb *have* in this construction is what leads us to call it the <u>present</u> perfect.

But there are other perfect tenses. As you might have already guessed from the title of this section, there is also a tense that we call the **past perfect**. And as you can easily surmise at this point, the past perfect consists of the past tense form of the auxiliary verb *have* (namely, *had* or *'d* as per Section 9.2.2), plus a past participle. So really, the past perfect is just like the present perfect (as in Sections 9.2.3.1.2 and 9.2.3.1.3), except instead of present tense *have*, we use past tense *have*. Take a look at the two examples in (35) and (36), which compare and contrast the present perfect and the past perfect:

Side Note 6: Form of the past perfect

Although we talked extensively about the form of the present perfect in Sections 9.2.3.1.2 and 9.2.3.1.3, we won't spend any time on the form of the past perfect, beyond what we note at the beginning of Section 9.2.3.2.

Just assume that everything we say about the past participle in Sections 9.2.3.1.2 and 9.2.3.1.3 also holds for the past perfect. So in terms of the question of the form of the past perfect, all our work has already been done!

(35)   John **has** always **eaten** his dinner at 5:00 p.m.   present perfect
(36)   <u>John **had** already **eaten** his dinner</u> by the time that   past perfect
        Bill got home.

Let's talk about the meaning of the past perfect. To do this, I want you to first think about the tense interpretation of the underlined part of the clause in (36): *John had already eaten his dinner.* In particular, I want you to think about when this dinner-eating event could have taken place in relation to the time at which Bill got home. Take a moment to think about it.

Term Box 5: Pluperfect

In case you've ever heard the word **pluperfect** and wondered about it: sometimes in grammar books this is the term that's used for the past perfect. So just assume pluperfect and past perfect refer to the same thing.

EXERCISE [6]

For the sentence in (36), assume that John ate his dinner at 5:00 p.m. Now think about the meaning of the entire sentence and ask yourself, What time could Bill have gotten home? Was it before John ate his dinner or after John ate his dinner? Make up a time that Bill might have gotten home, based on your interpretation of the past perfect in the (36).

Now that you've thought about the interpretation of *had eaten* (the **matrix tense** — see Chapter 5 Term Box 2 for a definition of "matrix sentence"), you've probably noticed that that John's dinner-eating took place <u>before</u> Bill's getting home. You get this interpretation even if you eliminate the adverb *already*. (Do this as a thought experiment.)

This is the defining characteristic of the past perfect tense: the past perfect indicates a past event which took place <u>before</u> another event — which itself is also in the past. The timeline in (37) illustrates the sequence of events.

(37)   Timeline representation of **past perfect tense** (compare with the timeline in (11) in Chapter 8):

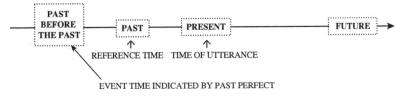

Using the sketch in (37), we can imagine a timing for the events expressed in (36) in which Bill arrived home in the past; this past time is the **reference time** in (37). Before this reference time, John ate his dinner ("past before the past"). The past perfect is thus a tense that we can use in English, to talk about the time at which a past event occurred in relation to another past time.

Many English speakers feel equally comfortable using the simple past (see Chapter 8) to indicate the same thing that the past perfect indicates in (36). Do you find the sentence in (38) to be an acceptable equivalent to the sentence in (36)?

(38)   <u>John already **ate** his dinner</u> by the time that Bill got home.

Side Note 7: The compound preterite

Don't confuse the idea of past perfect tense with another tense which happens to have the same form of the past perfect (that is, *had* + participle) — but, which has a different tense interpretation. Consider this example:

{1}   John **had** just **called** me five minutes ago.

Not all English speakers use this particular tense, which we can call the **compound preterite** (though in the linguistics literature the construction goes by different names, such as "preterite *had*" and "pre-verbal *had*"). In Chapter 8, we saw that "preterite" is a term sometimes used instead of the term "simple past," to indicate a past tense interpretation. Thus, the compound preterite in English has the same tense interpretation as a past tense, as in {2}:

{2}   John just **called** me five minutes ago.

Linguists consider the compound preterite to be a vernacular form; therefore, it's not found much in formal writing, and the grammar police tend not to like it.

Side Note 8: The past subjunctive

You should also not confuse the past perfect tense interpretation with another use of the compound tense consisting of *had* + participle, known as the **past subjunctive**. Here is an example of the past subjunctive (underlined):

{1}   <u>If only John **had eaten** breakfast this morning</u>, he wouldn't be so hungry right now.

The **subjunctive** is considered an **irrealis mood**. (See Side Note 9 in Chapter 8 for "irrealis tense"; see Term Box 8 in this chapter for "mood.") The past subjunctive is the **subjunctive mood** in the past tense. The tense interpretation of *had eaten* in {1} is therefore not a past perfect; rather, the interpretation of *had eaten* in {1} involves a present wish about something that should have happened in the past but which did not. In fact, a lot of speakers use the simple past form for the past subjunctive interpretation (instead of the compound *had*+participle in {1}), as in {2}:

{2}   If only John **ate** <u>breakfast</u> this morning, he wouldn't be so hungry right now.

Do you think {2} can mean the same thing as {1}? For many speakers, it can; but for many speakers, it cannot. For me, the underlined form in {2} can only be interpreted as a **present subjunctive** — that is, as involving a present wish about something that should happen now or in the future:

{3}   If only John **ate** <u>breakfast on a regular basis</u>, then he wouldn't be such a skinny person; it's too bad he won't do it.

And as if variation in the use of these different forms with the different possible meanings isn't already interesting enough …: there are some speakers who don't like to use the past form (like *ate*) with a present subjunctive interpretation, as in {3}. Instead, they like to use the modal auxiliary *would*+verb, as in {4}:

{4}   If only John **would eat** <u>breakfast on a regular basis</u>, then he wouldn't be such a skinny person; it's too bad he won't do it.

9.2.3.3 The future perfect

We've already seen examples of two kinds of perfect: present perfect and past perfect. As we saw, both of these perfect tenses involve the auxiliary verb *have* in either the present or past form (respectively) plus the past participial form of the main verb.

In addition to the present and past forms, the verb *have* also has a future form, namely, *will have*. As a result, English also has a perfect tense known as the **future perfect**. We actually already saw an example sentence containing a future perfect, in Chapter 8 (example (7a)), when we introduced the concept of the modal auxiliary. Let's take a look at that example again, repeated here as (39):

(39)   John **will have finished** up his grading by midnight.

As we already noted in Chapter 8, the example given here in (39) contains the bare infinitival form of aux *have*, followed by the main verb *finished*. Recall from Chapter 8 that the verb following a modal auxiliary like *will* is a bare infinitive. And recall from this chapter that the verb following auxiliary *have* is a past participle. I'll illustrate this sequence of verb forms more explicitly in (40) (though see Section 9.5.2 for a complete sketch):

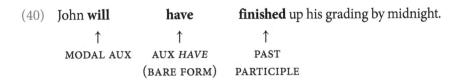

(40)   John **will**   **have**   **finished** up his grading by midnight.
               ↑   ↑   ↑
         MODAL AUX   AUX *HAVE*   PAST
                            (BARE FORM)   PARTICIPLE

Side Note 9: The modal aux *will*

Will is a modal auxiliary which can be used to indicate a future event, as we saw in example (22) from Chapter 8:

*The professor of linguistics **will grade** the quizzes the day after tomorrow.*

Keep in mind that *will* also has a contracted form, spelled *'ll*. We**'ll talk** more about modal auxiliaries in Section 9.4, so just hang tight for now! And by the time you're done reading this chapter, you**'ll have read** all about them!

The example in (40) summarizes the form of the future perfect.

Now what about the meaning? Take a look at the three examples in (41), (42), and (43), which compare and contrast the present perfect and past perfect (already examined in Sections 9.2.3.1 and 9.2.3.2), with the future perfect:

(41) John **has** always **eaten** his dinner at 5:00 p.m.   present perfect

(42) John **had** already **eaten** his dinner by the time that   past perfect
      Bill got home.

(43) John **will have** already **eaten** his dinner by the time   future
      Bill gets home.   perfect

Just as I asked you to do with the past perfect in Section 9.2.3.2, I want you to think about the tense interpretation of the underlined part of the clause in (43), *John will have already eaten his dinner*. In particular, I want you to think about when this dinner-eating event will take place, in relation to the time at which Bill gets home. Take a moment to think about it.

EXERCISE [7]

For the sentence in (43), assume that it's morning at the time this sentence is uttered, and that John will eat his dinner at 5:00 p.m. Now think about the meaning of the entire sentence, and ask yourself, What time will Bill get home? Will it be before John eats his dinner or after John eats his dinner? Make up a time that Bill might get home, based on your interpretation of the future perfect in the (43).

Now that you've thought about the interpretation of *will have eaten* (the matrix tense), you've probably noticed that that John's dinner-eating will take place in the future, but **before** Bill gets home. You get this interpretation even if you eliminate the adverb *already*. (Do this as a thought experiment.)

This is the defining characteristic of the future perfect tense: the future perfect indicates a future event which takes place <u>before</u> another event — which itself is also in the future. The timeline in (44) illustrates this.

(44)   Timeline representation of future perfect tense (compare with the timeline in (11) in Chapter 8 and the timeline in (37) of this chapter):

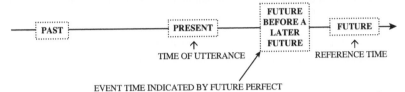

Using the sketch in (44), we can imagine a timing for the events expressed in (43) in which Bill arrives home in the future; this future time is the reference time in (43). Before this reference time, John eats his dinner ("a future before the further future"). The future perfect is thus a tense that we use in English to talk about the time at which a future event occurs which is in the past only in relation to another time which is even further into the future.

EXERCISE [8]

For each of the following sentences, state whether the tense for the matrix sentence is present perfect, past perfect, or future perfect. Beware: there are embedded sentences in some examples which are irrelevant to the question.

{1} By the end of this chapter, you'll have read all about modal auxiliaries.
{2} John had learned a bit about them before Bill gave him this chapter to read.
{3} They'd already been to the bookstore by the time I arrived.
{4} We've believed his story since the beginning.
{5} Bill will have heard all about John's new ideas by the end of the week.
{6} Bill hasn't read that book for years.

Side Note 10: Main verb *have*

Don't forget that *have* also functions as a main verb, as we saw in (3a):

Sue **has** a lot of friends.

As a main verb, it can appear in the perfect tenses, just like any other main verb. Note that the past participial form of main verb *have* is *had*:

{1}   Sue **has** always **had** lots of friends.
{2}   Sue **had** already **had** her temperature taken by the time the doctor came in.
{3}   Sue **will have had** her temperature taken by the time the doctor comes in.

Thus, in {2}, the first instance of *had* is auxiliary *have* (in the past tense), and the second instance of *had* is main verb *have* (in its past participial form).

9.2.3.4 Summary of the three perfect tenses

In this section we've explored the form and meaning of three perfect tenses, namely the present perfect, the past perfect, and the future perfect. And in Section 9.4.4 (in my discussion of modals), I'll discuss the concept of an infinitival perfect. (I'm saving this one for later for a reason.)

Think that's enough? Well, it's not. There are actually three more forms of the perfect to discuss: namely, these three that we discussed in 9.2.3.1, 9.2.3.2, and 9.2.3.3 — but in the progressive aspect. But before we dive into the present perfect progressive, the past perfect progressive, and the future perfect progressive — all of which involve the auxiliary verb *be* — let's first explore *be* in its own right. Once we have a handle on some basics about auxiliary *be*, then we can return to the our three additional perfect tenses, in Section 9.3.3.

9.3 auxiliary *be*

The verb *be* is unique in English (and the most unique verb in other languages as well). It has many different functions in both its main verb and auxiliary verb capacities; it's the most frequently occurring verb in actual linguistic usage; and it's the most irregular, in terms of its paradigms and its forms. In Chapter 10, comparing it with the other verbs, we'll further see that it stands alone in its syntactic behavior. In this section, we'll explore both the form and the function of this verb, to fully appreciate its role in the English verb system.

We already saw some examples of *be* as an auxiliary verb in Sections 8.1.1.1 and 8.2.1.3.3. We'll see in this section that auxiliary *be* comes in two types: progressive *be* and passive *be*. It'll become clearer in Sections 9.3.3 and 9.3.4 what the difference is, between these two types of auxiliary *be*.

But let's start by taking a look at the present and past tense paradigms of the verb *be*, in both its main verb and auxiliary verb incarnations.

9.3.1 present tense form of *be*

The present tense paradigm of *be* is quirky, compared with the present tense paradigm of all other verbs. Consider (45):

(45)   Present tense paradigm for the verb *be* (both main verb and auxiliary verb)

	singular	plural
first person	MAIN VB: I **am** happy AUX: I **am** enjoying my Mustang	MAIN VB: We **are** happy AUX: We **are** enjoying our Mustang
second person	MAIN VB: You **are** happy AUX: You **are** enjoying your Mustang	MAIN VB: You **are** happy AUX: You **are** enjoying your Mustang
third person	MAIN VB: She **is** happy AUX: She **is** enjoying her Mustang	MAIN VB: They **are** happy AUX: They **are** enjoying their Mustang

Side Note 11: Progressive *be* vs. passive *be*

I just noted that there are two different uses of auxiliary *be*. To keep things simple for now, the paradigm in (45) only contains examples of **main verb** *be* and **progressive** *be*. We'll save **passive** *be* for later.

These present tense forms of the verb *be* of course reflect "mainstream" or "standard" use; we'll put aside other ways in which different English speakers use present tense *be*.

A look at the present tense paradigm for *be* (either main verb or auxiliary, it's irrelevant) reveals that this verb is unique. All other verbs (except modal auxiliaries, which we'll talk about in Section 9.4) have a distinct form only in the third person, namely, the form with verbal *-s* (see Chapter 8, and also example (8) above). In contrast, *be* has three distinct present tense forms, namely *am*, *are*, and *is*. Furthermore, the first singular form of the verb (*am*) is distinct from the forms of the plural (*are*): a contrast that you don't see with any other English verb.

Side Note 12: *That ain't the whole story*

As we'll see more clearly in Chapter 10, the present tense paradigm for both main verb *be* and auxiliary *be* can be levelled to *ain't* in the presence of the negative marker *n't*. Thus, alongside forms like *isn't* and *aren't* (*She **isn't** happy, We **aren't** happy*), the form *ain't* is commonly used, for all persons and numbers in (45). Check for yourself by plugging in *ain't* into each example in the paradigm (in place of each form you see there in bold).

But this still ain't the whole story! As we'll see in Chapter 10, the life of *ain't* is more complex than this, and for some speakers, it implicates the auxiliaries *have* and *do* as well.

There's another feature which distinguishes *be* from all other verbs, including *have*. First, note that all of the present tense forms of *be* can be contracted — something which is not reflected in the paradigm in (45). As with *have*, the contracted form might in fact be the more common form used in speech (as opposed to writing):

(46) a. I**'m** happy.   first person singular MAIN VB
     b. I**'m** enjoying my Mustang.   first person singular AUX

(47) a. You**'re** happy.   second person singular MAIN VB
     b. You**'re** enjoying your Mustang.   second person singular AUX

(48) a. She**'s** happy.   third person singular MAIN VB
     b. She**'s** enjoying her Mustang.   third person singular AUX

(49) a. We**'re** happy.   first person plural MAIN VB
     b. We**'re** enjoying our Mustang.   first person plural AUX

(50) a. You**'re** happy.   second person plural MAIN VB
     b. You**'re** enjoying your Mustang.   second person plural AUX

(51) a. They**'re** happy.   third person plural MAIN VB
     b. They**'re** enjoying their
        Mustang.   third person plural AUX

Interestingly, though, in contrast with *have* (see Exercise [1]), the forms of *be* can be contracted in both their auxiliary <u>and</u> in their main verb incarnations, as you see in (46) through (51). The fact that main verb *be* can be contracted (just like auxiliary *be*) suggests that main verb *be* acts like an auxiliary verb. In Chapter 10 we'll see how main verb *be* also behaves like an auxiliary in syntactic terms as well!

Side Note 13: The ambiguity of *'s*

If you compare (48) with (11c), you'll notice that third person singular *has* and third person singular *is* both contract to *'s*. This means that the following sentence is ambiguous between *She has gone* and *She is gone*:

{1} She's gone.

Can you think of other similarly ambiguous examples?
    And of course, the contracted verb *'s* (= *is* or *has*) shouldn't be confused with possessive *'s* (Chapter 2), as in the noun phrase **John's book** in *John's book won a prize*. The existence of possessive *'s* can give rise to ambiguity between the possessive and auxiliary *be*, as in the string *John's singing*: this string can either be an NP containing possessive *John's* as in {2}, or it can be a sentence equivalent to *John is singing*, as in {3}:

{2} **John's singing** is beautiful.   NP

{3} **John's singing** right now.   aux *be*

9.3.2 past tense form of *be*

In addition to the present tense, the verb *be* exhibits distinct behavior in the past tense as well.

Recall from Term Box 7 in Chapter 8 that all main verbs in English have a levelled paradigm in the past tense. This means that the form of the verb doesn't change according to person (first, second, or third) or number (singular or plural). We saw this with the past tense of the verb *enjoy*, and you can verify for yourselves that this is true for every other verb in English, including *have*. The verb *be*, however, is an exception to this generalization for many speakers. The paradigm in (52) illustrates the distinct forms *was* and *were*, for past tense *be* in "mainstream" or "standard" English:

(52) Past tense paradigm for the verb *be* in "standard" English:

	singular	**plural**
first person	MAIN VB: I **was** happy AUX: I **was** enjoying my Mustang	MAIN VB: We **were** happy AUX: We **were** enjoying our Mustang
second person	MAIN VB: You **were** happy AUX: You **were** enjoying your Mustang	MAIN VB: You **were** happy AUX: You **were** enjoying your Mustang
third person	MAIN VB: She **was** happy AUX: She **was** enjoying her Mustang	MAIN VB: They **were** happy AUX: They **were** enjoying their Mustang

As you can see, *was* is used for first and third singular, and *were* is used for everything else. Because there is no other verb in English that has different forms in the past tense whose use depends on person and number, it's not at all surprising that many speakers actually prefer not to make the distinction between *was* and *were* seen in (52). The following **levelled past tense paradigm** for *be* is found in a wide variety of English speaking regions across the world:

(53) Levelled past tense paradigm for the verb *be* for many English speakers:

	singular	**plural**
first person	MAIN VB: I **was** happy AUX: I **was** enjoying my Mustang	MAIN VB: We **was** happy AUX: We **was** enjoying our Mustang
second person	MAIN VB: You **was** happy AUX: You **was** enjoying your Mustang	MAIN VB: You **was** happy AUX: You **was** enjoying your Mustang
third person	MAIN VB: She **was** happy AUX: She **was** enjoying her Mustang	MAIN VB: They **was** happy AUX: They **was** enjoying their Mustang

---

Side Note 14: *That weren't the whole story*

Less commonly found — but still possible for some English speakers — is a levelled past tense paradigm for *be* where the form is *were* throughout (instead of *was*). You can make up this paradigm for yourself by just replacing *was* in (53) with *were*. Furthermore, there are varieties of English (for example, the English spoken on Ocracoke Island in North Carolina) where the paradigm is levelled to *were* only when it's contracted with the negative marker *n't* (i.e. *weren't*). In Chapter 10 we'll talk more about *n't* with the verb *be* and with the auxiliary verbs *have* and *do*.

The levelled paradigm in (53) is a logical extension of the fact that all other verbs in English have a levelled paradigm in the past tense. As a thought experiment, ask yourself whether you use the forms seen in (53) or whether you know someone who does or at least whether you've heard examples like *you was, we was,* or *they was,* in the movies, in literature, or in music.

Interestingly, unlike what we find with present tense *be* (and unlike what we find with the present and past tense forms of auxiliary *have*), not all English speakers have contracted forms for the past tense of *be*. Thus, for many speakers, neither *was* nor *were* have a contracted version. This contrasts with the present tense forms *am, are,* and *is,* which as we saw in (46) through (51) contract to *'m, 're,* and *'s.*

EXERCISE [9]

Think about whether you would contract past tense *was* in the same way you contract present tense *is* in (48): can the *'s* in the sentence *She's happy* serve as a contracted form of *was* for you? If you're from the southern Appalachians (eastern Kentucky, northeast Tennessee, southwest Virginia, or western North Carolina), your answer might be Yes!

9.3.3 progressive *be*

We just saw the present and past tense paradigms for auxiliary *be* in (45) and (52)/(53). Now it's time to take a closer look at the function of *be* as an auxiliary. In this section (9.3.3) we'll explore progressive *be* in all six of its tenses. Then, in Section 9.3.4, we'll examine a different case of auxiliary *be*, namely, passive *be*.

Simply put, the progressive in English is a compound tense that consists of the auxiliary verb *be*, followed by a verb which ends in the inflectional suffix *-ing* (such as *eat + ing > eating*). A verb that ends in the suffix *-ing* is called a present participle, or also a present participial form. See Term Box 6.

We already saw examples of the present progressive and the past progressive in Section 8.2.1.3.3. But there are more types of progressive than just these two. In fact, there are as many types of progressive tense as there are tenses in English. What are the tenses in English? Thus far, between Chapter 8 and this chapter, we've seen six different tenses. Let's summarize these six tenses in (54), with the main verbs *drive, take, enjoy, prepare,* and *eat* (as a preamble to our subsequent discussion of the six progressive tenses).

(54)   Summary of the six tenses covered thus far, with verbs other than *be*:

tense	example
present tense	Sue **drives** her Ford Mustang every day.
past tense	Sue **took** her Ford Mustang out for a spin last night.
future tense	Sue **will enjoy** her Ford Mustang once she fixes the carburetor.
present perfect tense	Sue **has taken** her Ford Mustang out every night this week.
past perfect tense	Sue **had** already **prepared** dinner by the time Bill got home.
future perfect tense	Sue **will have** already **eaten** dinner by the time Bill gets home.

EXERCISE [10]

Identify the tense of each sentence (for {7}, focus just on the matrix S):

{1} They've scrubbed the windows clean.
{2} Rick has worked on that project for hours.
{3} Their work went really well.
{4} We will have worked on our projects for hours by lunchtime.
{5} Walter and Bill plan on a tricky job.
{6} They'll be on break in an hour.
{7} Rick had considered a different strategy before Walter and Bill changed his mind.

Now, for each tense you identified, pick out (a) the main verb; (b) any past participles; (c) any bare infinitives.

Since the verb *be* is like any other verb in terms of what tenses it can appear in, it follows that there are six different tenses for the verb *be* as well. Let's first look at all six tenses for **main verb** *be* in (55) (with an eye towards setting the stage for progressive *be*, which we'll look at in a moment). Compare (55) with (54):

(55)   Summary of the six tenses covered thus far, with main verb *be*:

tense	example
present tense	Sue **is** happy with her Mustang.
past tense	Sue **was** happy with the car's performance last night.
future tense	Sue **will be** happy once she fixes the carburetor.
present perfect tense	Sue **has been** happy with the car for years.
past perfect tense	Sue **had** already **been** out to dinner by the time Bill got home.
future perfect tense	Sue **will** already **have been** out to dinner by the time Bill gets home.

Side Note 15: *Add* been *to the list*

Note that *been* is the past participial form of *be*. This means that the verb *be* has 8 uncontracted forms: *be, am, are, is, was, were, being,* and *been.*

This doesn't include the contracted forms *'s* and *'re*, nor does it include the most famous negated version of *be*, namely *ain't*, which we'll talk about in Chapter 10.

Now, because *be* can appear in all six tenses (as we see in (55)), it follows that there are also six different progressive tenses. This is because the progressive consists of *be* (in some tense), followed by a verb in its present participial form (i.e. V + *ing*). Thus, six tenses for progressive *be* plus a present participle = six progressive tenses. All six progressives are illustrated in (56). For each example, the entire tense is in bold (as in (54) and (55)). In addition, I have underlined the part of the tense that just involves a tense of *be*, so that you can compare the underlined string with the identical strings in bold in (55):

The six progressive tenses

(56)   a.   present progressive   *am, is, are* + present participle
              Sue **_is_ working** right now.

        b.   past progressive   *was, were* + present participle
              Christina **_was_ working** when Bill walked through the door.

        c.   future progressive   *will be* + present participle
              Sue **_will be_ working** when Mary gets home.

        d.   present perfect progressive   *has/have been* + present participle
              Sue **_has been_ working** on this problem for hours.

        e.   past perfect progressive   *had been* + present participle
              Sue **_had_** already **_been_ digging** into her dinner when Bill arrived.

        f.   future perfect progressive   *will have been* + present participle
              Sue **_will_** already **_have been_ digging** into her dinner by the time Bill arrives.

Term Box 6: Present participle, past participle, and nonfiniteness

As we saw in Term Box 6 in Chapter 8, the -ing form of the main verb in (56) (working, digging) is confusingly referred to as a **present participle**, or the present participial form. Again: this term can be misleading because use of the word "present" incorrectly suggests that it has something to do with present interpretation. But as we can see in (56b), the present participle can be used in combination with a past tense form of auxiliary be (i.e. was/were), yielding what is called the **past progressive tense**. Thus, (56b) is in the past progressive tense, with the main verb (working) in its present participial form. As I said previously, my personal experience teaching this material tells me that it can be a source of great confusion for students.

For students who find this confusing: my advice would be to just ignore the fact that the term for the V + ing form following auxiliary be has the word "present" in it. Just think of this term as meaningless for now. Similarly, for past participle, you might want to ignore the fact that this term for the verb form following auxiliary have has the word "past" in it. Technically, the past participial form is not a past tense.

In fact, the present participle and the past participle — despite their names — do not contain any tense at all. That is, they are **untensed**, or, **nonfinite**, just like the bare infinitive we saw in Chapter 8. Like the bare infinitive (which is preceded by a modal auxiliary), the nonfinite present and past participles must also be preceded by auxiliaries (progressive be and have). Note that the words "nonfinite" and "infinitive" (discussed in Chapter 7) are very similar (both mean "not finite"), and the term "untensed" can also be used to describe nonfinite verbs in English. All three terms — nonfinite, infinitive, untensed — refer to verbs that do not have tense. In contrast, verbs that have tense are considered **finite** or **tensed**.

EXERCISE [11]

Identify the tense of each sentence (for {7}, focus just on the matrix S):

{1} They're scrubbing the windows clean.
{2} Rick has been working on that project for hours.
{3} Their work is going very well.
{4} We will have been working on our projects for hours by lunchtime.
{5} Walter and Bill were planning on a break.
{6} They'll be taking a break in an hour.
{7} Rick had been considering a different strategy before Walter and Bill arrived.

Now, for each tense you identified, pick out the present participle.

In Section 8.2.1.3.3, we saw that the **present progressive** functions as a "true present tense" (= event occurs at time of utterance) for dynamic verbs. In addition, in Section 8.2.1.2.1 we talked about the various ways that English speakers express future tense. The modal auxiliary *will* provides one possibility (*Walter will take a break in 5 minutes*); however, as we saw, the present progressive can also be used express a future event (*Walter is taking a break in 5 minutes*). This is despite the fact that the true present interpretation expresses a **continuous aspect**. That is, events encoded in the progressive are conceptualized as ongoing (as opposed to punctual). Thus, compare (56b) with a simple past, like *Christina worked*. In (56b), use of the past progressive captures the idea that Christina was in the process of working (in the past); this processual quality of the event contrasts with the simple past (*Christina worked*), which expresses a **punctual** or "discrete" quality to the event. See Term Box 8 for the concept of aspect.

9.3.4 passive *be*

In the previous section we explored the use of auxiliary *be* as a component in the progressive tense. As we saw, the progressive is composed of (some tense of) auxiliary *be* plus a present participle (V + *ing*), as in (56).

But auxiliary *be* in English is also used in another construction. In this case, *be* is not used to form a new tense. Instead, *be* is used to convert a sentence from **active voice** to **passive voice**, *staying within the same tense*. We already explored active vsersus passive in Chapter 3. As a brief review, recall that we talked about a movement operation called passivization which transforms an active sentence such as that in (57) into a passive sentence such as that in (58):

(57)   John **ate** the cake.   ACTIVE

(58)   The cake **was eaten** by John.   PASSIVE

We saw that this passivization operation on an active sentence does the following:

(59)   (a)   It starts with an active sentence, and ...

      (b)   ... it removes the original subject from subject position; then ...

      (c)   ... it makes the original object the new subject; then ...

      (d)   **... it gives the verb "passive morphology;"** then ...

      [optional step]:

      (e)   ... it puts the original subject in a *by*-phrase, and attaches this *by*-phrase to the VP.

To see how the passivization steps in (59a–e) work on a real example, in Chapter 3 we started with an active sentence like that in (57) and applied each step in (59) in turn, as follows:

(59')   (a)   <u>John</u> ate the cake.

      (b) | ___ ate the cake | >

      (c) | The cake ate | >

      (d) | The cake was eaten | >

      (e)   The cake was eaten by <u>John</u>

Thus, in a passive sentence like that in (58), the structural subject has "object-like" properties, in terms of being something that is "acted upon" (like a **patient**), rather than being the "actor" or **agent**, as it is often called. This is why we use the term "passive" to refer to such a construction: the subject in a passive sentence is passive, like an object.

For the present discussion, it's important to compare the tense in (57) with the tense in (58). What you'll note when you compare the two is that they have the same tense, namely, the past tense. This can be seen in the form *ate* in (57), and in the form *was* in (58). However, despite the fact that they're both past tense, they do have different forms: *ate* versus *was eaten*. This difference is a result of the cryptically worded step (59d), "give the verb passive morphology."

So, how exactly do we give "passive morphology" to an active verb like *ate*? It's actually something quite simple, which we can think of in two micro-steps, as in (60) (See Term Box 3, Chapter 10, for the concept of **morphology**):

(60)   Going from active verb morphology to passive verb morphology:
    a.   Identify the tense of original active verb (e.g., past tense *ate* in (57)), and replicate that tense with passive *be* (e.g., past tense *was* in (58))

    b.   Then, take the original main verb (*ate* in (57)), and convert it to its past participial form (*eaten* in (58))

I'll illustrate the two-step conversion from active verb morphology to passive verb morphology with all six non-progressive tenses we saw summarized in (54). Note that in (61) the tenses are in bold. The past participle in the passive version of each sentence is in blue font.

(61)   The six non-progressive tenses in (54), in both active and passive form:

	column A	column B	column C	column D
	ACTIVE	main V tense	PASSIVE (past participle in blue)	tense of passive *be*
a	Sue **drives** her Mustang every day.	pres.	That Mustang **is** driven every day.	present
b	Sue **took** the car out for a spin.	past	The car **was** taken out for a spin.	past
c	Sue **will drive** the car once we fix it.	fut.	The car **will be** driven once we fix it.	future
d	Sue **has taken** the car out for a drive.	pres. perf.	The car **has been** taken out for a drive.	present perfect
e	John **had** already **prepared** dinner.	past perf.	Dinner **had** already **been** prepared.	past perfect
f	John **will have prepared** dinner.	fut. perf.	Dinner **will have been** prepared.	future perfect

As you can see, the tense of *be* in the passive version of each sentence in (61) is the same as the tense of the main verb in the active version of each sentence. For example, the present perfect *has taken* in row (d) is replicated in *has been*, also a present perfect. For this reason, we consider the passive version of any corresponding active sentence to not involve a change in tense. Of course, since the passive version of each sentence contains the main verb in its past participial form (in addition to some tense of passive *be*), the passive version of an active sentence always contains one more verb than its active counterpart. You can verify this for yourself with Exercise [12].

EXERCISE [12]

Focusing on the table in (61), count up the number of verbs in each example in column A and compare this with the number of verbs you count up in each example in column C.

EXERCISE [13]: Active to Passive

Using the steps in (59) and (60), and also the table in (61) as a model, convert the active sentences below into passive voice.

{1} The owl has eaten the chipmunks.
{2} The chipmunk devoured the acorns.
{3} The chipmunk had collected 50 acorns before the day's end.
{4} The owl will have caught the chipmunk by night's end.
{5} The owl freaks out the chipmunks every night.
{6} The owl will catch the chipmunk by night's end.

For example:

{1} The owl **has eaten** the chipmunks. > The chipmunks **have been eaten** by the owl.

9.3.5 passive *be* combined with progressive *be*

By now, our discussion should have made it clear that passive *be* (whatever tense it appears in, as in (61)) is always followed by a past participial form of the main verb (e.g., *driven, taken, prepared*). This contrasts with progressive *be*, which as we saw in Section 9.3.3 is always followed by a present participial form of the main verb. Let's highlight this distinction in (62) and (63):

(62)   The chipmunk *was* **eating**.   **progressive *be*** followed by **present participle**

(63)   The chipmunk *was* **eaten**.   **passive *be*** followed by **past participle**

This is an important grammatical distinction between progressive *be* and passive *be*. As we'll summarize in Section 9.5, every auxiliary verb — including modals — ensures that the immediately following verb is of a particular form. Keeping in mind this distinction between progressive *be* and passive *be* helps us tease apart complicated situations when progressive *be* combines with passive *be*. Let's see how this works.

As we saw in (56), there are six progressive tenses. Let's start by examining the present progressive, for the purposes of illustration:

(64)   The owl **is eating** the chipmunk.   present progressive, ACTIVE

Like any of the other (non-progressive) tenses we saw in (61), it's perfectly possible to convert the present progressive in (64) into passive voice, by simply following the steps in (59) and (60). Following those steps, we get (65) as a resulting passive:

(65)   The chipmunk **is being** eaten by the owl.   present progressive,
                                                        PASSIVE

How did I derive *is being eaten* (passive) from *is eating* (active)? I just followed the steps in (60), repeated here with the relevant verbs:

(60')   Going from active verb morphology to passive verb morphology
        in (64) > (65):

      a.   Identify the tense of original active verb. This is present progressive in (64) (*is eating*); replicate that tense with passive *be*. This gives you present progressive *is being* in (65).

      b.   Then, take the original main verb (*eating* in (64)), and convert it to its past participial form (*eaten* in (65))

Let's now map this out for all six progressive tenses in (56).

(66)   The six progressive tenses in (56), in both active and passive form; tenses in bold:

```
              ┌---------- IDENTICAL TENSE ----------┐
              ↓                                     ↓
```

	column A	column B	column C	column D
	ACTIVE	main V tense	**PASSIVE** (past participle in blue)	tense of passive *be*
a	Sue **is driving** that Mustang.	present progr.	That Mustang **is being** driven by Sue.	present progr.
b	Sue **was taking** the car out for a spin.	past progr.	The car **was being** taken out for a spin.	past progr.
c	Sue **will be driving** the car soon.	future progr.	The car **will be being** driven soon.	future progr.
d	Sue **has been taking** the car out.	pres. perf. progr.	The car **has been being** taken out.	pres. perf. progr.
e	John **had been preparing** dinner.	past perf. progr.	Dinner **had been being** prepared.	past perf. progr.
f	John **will have been preparing** dinner.	fut. perf. progr.	Dinner **will have been being** prepared.	fut. perf. progr.

EXERCISE [14]: Active Progressive to Passive Progressive

Using the steps in (59) and (60), and also the table in (66) as a model, convert the active sentences below into passive voice.

{1} The owl has been eating the chipmunks.
{2} The chipmunk was devouring the acorns.
{3} The chipmunk had been collecting all kinds of acorns (before the owl stopped him).
{4} The owl will have been catching all the chipmunks before you know it.

{5} The owl is freaking out the chipmunks.

{6} The owl will be catching all the chipmunks before you know it.

For example:

{1} The owl **has been eating** the chipmunks. > The chipmunks **have been being eaten** by the owl.

9.4 modal auxiliaries

Let's start our exploration of modals — and all the ways in which they differ from the nonmodal auxiliaries — by revisiting our list of nine modals in (2), repeated here as (67):

(67) *can, could, will, would, shall, should, may, might, must*

Side Note 16: Contracting modals

As we wend our way through the discussion on modals, keep in mind that *will* (He **will** lend a hand) and *would* (He **would** lend a hand) also have contracted counterparts (He**'ll** lend a hand and He**'d** lend a hand).

In Sections 9.2 and 9.3 we took a close look at the auxiliaries *have* and *be*. One feature that sets these nonmodals apart is that they have main verb counterparts, as we saw in (3) and (4), just like the verb *do* (which we saw in (5) and which we'll cover in Chapter 10). Just like their main verb counterparts — and just like all main verbs — *have* and *be* inflect for person and number in the present tense: we saw this in the present tense paradigms for these verbs in (7) and (45). Specifically, there's a distinct form for the third person singular (i.e. the verb plus the -*s* inflectional suffix, also known as **verbal** -*s*).

These properties set nonmodals apart from modals in a number of ways. In the next five subsections (9.4.1, 9.4.2, 9.4.3, 9.4.4, and 9.4.5), I'll go over the differences.

9.4.1 modals don't have main verb counterparts

First, as we already saw in (6) (repeated here), in contrast with *have*, *be*, and *do*, none of the nine modals have a main verb counterpart:

(6) a. *John **will** his book. (cf. *John will finish his book*)

b. *Sue **might** her Mustang. (cf. *Sue might drive her Mustang*)

c. *The professor **can** her students. (cf. *The professor can help her students*)

This fact leads to a number of other differences between modals and nonmodals. Let's look for example at the fact that modals don't inflect for person and number.

9.4.2 modals don't inflect for person and number

None of the modals in (67) have any overt marking for the third person singular. Thus, we never find examples in English such as the following:

(68) a. *Sue **cans** drive the car. (cf. *Sue **can** drive the car*; *Sue **drives** the car*)

  b. *Mary **mays** help Sue. (cf. *Mary **may** help Sue*; *Mary **helps** Sue*)

  c. *John **wills** lend a hand. (cf. *John **will** lend a hand*; *John **lends** a hand*)

  d. *Bill **musts** leave by 5:00. (cf. *Bill **must** leave by 5:00*; *Bill **leaves** by 5:00*)

In all of the examples in (68), we have a third person singular subject, yet we can see that the modals *can*, *may*, *will*, and *must* don't allow verbal -*s*. This contrasts with all nonmodal verbs in English (with the exception of present tense *got* — see Side Note 7 in Chapter 8). It's clear, then, that every one of the modals in (67) has a **levelled present tense paradigm** (see Term Box 7 in Chapter 8), where the form of each modal does not change according to person and number. Here's a sample paradigm, for the modal *will*. (As a thought experiment, make a paradigm like the one in (69) for each of the modals in (67).)

(69) Paradigm for the modal *will*

	singular	**plural**
first person	I **will** lend a hand	We **will** lend a hand
second person	You **will** lend a hand	You **will** lend a hand
third person	He **will** lend a hand	They **will** lend a hand

9.4.3 modals are always tensed

Third, the modals are never untensed. This is in contrast with the auxiliaries *have* and *be*, which can be untensed. We've already seen several cases of untensed auxiliary *have* and *be* throughout this chapter. I'll repeat some of the examples here, which you can review in conjunction with Term Box 6 above:

(70) Sue will **be** working when Mary gets home. progressive *be* in its bare infinitival form (cf. (56c))

(71) Sue has **been** working on this problem for hours. progressive *be* in its past participial form (cf. (56d))

(72)	The car will **be** driven once we fix it.	passive *be* in its bare infinitival form	(cf. table (61), row c)
(73)	The car has **been** taken out for a drive.	passive *be* in its past participial form	(cf. table (61), row d)
(74)	That Mustang is **being** driven by Sue.	passive *be* in its present participial form	(cf. table (66), row a)
(75)	John will **have** prepared dinner.	aux *have* in its bare infinitival form	(cf. table (61), row f)
(76)	**Having** fixed it before, I was confident.	aux *have* in its present participial form	

Side Note 17: Knowing your verb forms

How can I be so sure that the **be** and the **been** of (70) and (71) are progressive *be* (and not passive *be*)? Easy: the verb which follows them (*working*) is a present participle (V + *ing*). Checking the form of the following verb is a surefire way of knowing which *be* we're dealing with. Likewise, we know that the **be**, **been**, and **being** of (72), (73), and (74) are passive *be*, simply by virtue of the fact that the verbs which follow them (*driven*, *taken*) are past participles. In sum: if aux *be* is followed by a present participle, then you're dealing with progressive *be*. If aux *be* is followed by a past participle, then you're dealing with passive *be*.

Furthermore: recall from Chapter 8 that the verb following a modal is a bare infinitive, and recall from Section 9.2 that the verb following aux *have* is a past participle. We'll go over all of this in Section 9.5.

Term Box 7: Participial clauses

We haven't actually seen yet in this book an example like that in (76). In this example, the matrix S is *I was confident*, and *having fixed it before* is an adjunct clause (see Section 5.4). An adjunct clause containing only a participle (and no tensed verb) is called a participial clause. Thus, *having fixed it before* is a participial clause — where *having* is a present participle. We can also have participial clauses with past participles, such as the underlined phrase in {1}:

{1} **Encouraged** <u>by her previous successes</u>, Sue fixed the sink.

In this example of a participial clause (which contains no tensed verb), *encouraged* is a past participle. The clause is related to a passive sentence like *Sue was encouraged by her previous successes*.

Given that modals are never untensed, as per Section 8.2.1.1, it follows that if there is a modal in the sentence, it will always be the leftmost verb in the string of verbs within the same S, because the leftmost verb in the string is always tensed. (And of course anything to the right of it in the same S is untensed.) We can see this in (77a), which contains five verbs (cf. row (f) in (66)):

(77) a. Dinner **will** have been being prepared.

See also (7c) from Chapter 8, which we'll repeat here:

(77) b. The Giants **could** have been being beaten by the Titans in the third quarter already … (if the Titans had only just taken their running game more seriously).

The fact that the modals are always tensed is also evidenced by the fact that in contrast with *have* and *be*, modals can never co-occur with infinitival *to*. Let's take a closer look at this.

9.4.4 infinitival *to* and modals do not co-occur

In Section 7.3.2 we discussed embedded infinitivals with infinitival *to*. Recall for example sentence {3} from Exercise [7] of that chapter, repeated here as (78):

(78) Sue wants Bill **to have** finished the exam by 9:00 p.m.

Here we see a compound tense *to have finished*. Thinking back to Section 9.2.3.4 (where we summarized our three different perfect tenses), the fact that the underlined string in (78) contains a form of *have* plus a past participle confirms that we're dealing with a kind of perfect. The presence of infinitival *to* indicates that this is a fourth type of perfect — namely, the **infinitival perfect**. (More specifically, this is an **infinitival-*to* perfect**, as opposed to a **bare infinitival perfect**, which we'll see in Section 9.5.) This construction is called the infinitival perfect because auxiliary *have* is in its infinitival form, *to have*.

What the infinitival perfect tells us is that auxiliary *have* is perfectly compatible with infinitival *to*. Unsurprisingly, both progressive *be* and passive *be* are also compatible with infinitival *to*. Consider the examples in (79):

(79) a. Sue wants Bill **to be** finishing up the exam by   progressive *be*
9:00 p.m.
b. Mary wants the sink **to be** fixed by Sue in time   passive *be*
for the party.
(cf. corresponding ACTIVE: *Mary wants* Sue to fix the sink in time for the party)

Thus, auxiliary *have*, and both types of auxiliary *be* (progressive and passive) can occur with infinitival *to*. However, as noted above, in contrast with *have* and *be*, modals never occur with infinitival *to*. This can be seen in (80):

(80) a. *Sue wants <u>Bill **to can** finish the exam by 9:00 p.m.</u>
(cf. *Sue wants <u>Bill to be able to finish the exam by 9:00 p.m.</u>*)

   b. *Sue expects <u>Bill **to may** finish the exam by 9:00 p.m.</u>
(cf. *Sue expects <u>Bill to be allowed to finish the exam by 9:00 pm</u>*)

   c. *Sue believes <u>Bill **to must** finish the exam by 9:00 p.m.</u>
(cf. *Sue believes <u>Bill to be obligated to finish the exam by 9:00 pm</u>*)

The fact that modals cannot co-occur with infinitival *to* confirms — along with the facts discussed in 9.4.3 above — that modals are always tensed, and never infinitival. The fact that modals are always tensed will become even more clear in Chapter 10, when we examine the special syntactic behavior of the leftmost verb in a sentence with a string of verbs.

9.4.5 tense and the semantic ambiguity of modals

The auxiliaries *have* and *be* can occur in both the present tense and past tense: *has* versus *had*, or *is* versus *was*, for example. In contrast, each of the nine modals listed in (67) do not obviously have present versus past tense forms. Consider for example the modal *must* in (81):

(81) Bill **must** leave by 5:00 p.m.

How can we possibly make the modal auxiliary *must* a past tense? There doesn't seem to be any way to transform this modal into a meaning along the lines of (81'):

(81') *Bill **musted** leave by 5:00 p.m.

This doesn't mean that there isn't a way to say something like what (81') is trying to say; the following is a close approximation to the desired meaning of a past tense of *must*:

(82) Bill **had to** leave by 5:00 p.m.

The sentence in (82) is a translation of the concept of a past *must*, using a different kind of verb — *to have to X* — which allows us to put it in the past tense (*had to X*). Thus, we have a way of expressing the concept of an obligation in the past, but we cannot accomplish that by putting the modal *must* in the past tense as there is no past tense form of *must*.

However, things start to get murky when we look at other modals, like *will* and *would*. On the one hand, there are uses that make these two modals seem completely unrelated to one another. Then again, there is a use of *would* that makes it seem as if it were the past tense of *will*.

Two particular interpretations of *would* which make it seem unrelated to *will* are the conditional (which is a mood; see Side Note 8) and the

past habitual (which combines the concept of past time with the concept of **habitual aspect**). Take a look at (83):

(83) a. Christina **would gut-renovate** her house   conditional *would*
if only she had the money.

    b. When we were kids, we **would eat** ice-cream   past habitual *would*
every day.
(cf. *When we were kids, we **used to eat** ice-cream every day*)

On the other hand, there is one use of modal *would* which makes it look a lot like it could be the past tense version of *will*. Consider first the sentence in (84a):

(84) a. Sue says that she **will fix** the sink.

The matrix sentence in (84a) (*Sue says*) is in the present tense, while the embedded sentence (*that she will fix the sink*) expresses a future event using modal *will*. Thus, Sue is speaking now about an event to take place in the future. Interestingly, though, we can put *say* in the past tense, so that Sue is speaking in the past, about an event to take place in the future — but a future in the past. The example in (84b) shows that the modal *would* appropriately expresses a future time, in relation to past tense *said*:

(84) b. Sue said that she **would fix** the sink.

In other words, *would* in (84b) acts like the past tense of *will* in (84a), because if we think about what Sue said in the past in (84b), it was something like, "I will fix the sink."

For this reason, *would* is sometimes analyzed as a past tense form of *will*, at least in one of its uses. On the other hand, the uses of *would* in (83) show that it doesn't always act like the past tense of *will*. Indeed, each of the nine modals listed in (67) has more than one semantic interpretation, making it impossible to pin down each modal to any one function or meaning. The complexity is too much to go into for the purposes of this chapter, but to illustrate, let's just look at one more case: *could*. Like *would*, modal *could* can have a past habitual meaning, indicating something like "used to be able to," as in (85a):

(85) a. When I was young, I **could sing** really well.   past habitual *could*
(Now I'm a bad singer.)
(cf. *When I was young, I used to be able to sing really well*)

This past habitual use of *could* makes it look like the past tense version of a present tense *can* (*I can sing*). On the other hand, *could* can also be used as a conditional (like *would* in (83a)), making it look nothing like the past tense of *can*. Consider (85b):

(85) b. John **could drive** Bill to work, if only he   conditional *could*
could find the car keys.

These kinds of **tense** and **mood** ambiguities for each of the modal auxiliaries is another property that makes them very unlike the nonmodal auxiliaries *have* and *be*.

Term Box 8: Mood and aspect

In Side Note 8 above, we talked a bit about the subjunctive mood, and here we're talking about the **conditional mood**. Like the subjunctive, the conditional is an **irrealis mood**: it is "not real," in the sense that the events or states that it encodes have not taken place, and where the speaker is expressing some desire or wish for them to exist. In contrast with the subjunctive and the conditional moods, the **indicative** mood is a **realis mood**. That is, verbs in the indicative (like the past tense) express events or states that are an empirical reality.

   Aspect, on the other hand, refers to the fact that we have different grammatical means for conceptualizing how events denoted by verbs are structured. Consider, for example, the difference between *Sue ate ice cream for breakfast this morning* and *Sue would eat ice cream all the time when she was a kid*. These two sentences both describe eating events that took place in the past. However, in the former, *ate* encodes an event that took place at a single moment in time (**punctual** or **perfective aspect**), while in the latter, *would eat* encodes eating events that take place over the course of time (**habitual** or **imperfective aspect**). Similarly, the progressive (as we saw in Section 9.3.3) is considered to be a kind of **continuous aspect**: that is, events encoded in the progressive are conceptualized as ongoing (as opposed to **punctual**).

9.5 verb selection and word order

Now that we've gotten a handle on the different auxiliary verbs, it's time to bring everything together and appreciate how orderly the English verb system actually is. Our discussion of word order in this section will serve as a backdrop for Chapter 10, where we'll be able to fully appreciate how this complex system of auxiliary verbs and main verbs fits together in terms of syntactic structure.

9.5.1 selection

Let's first take stock of the fact that each auxiliary verb we've seen (*have*, progressive *be*, passive *be*, and the modals) **selects** for a particular verb form (see Side Note 16). Thus, each auxiliary requires that the verb which follows it appear in a particular form.

   To review: modals are always immediately followed by a bare infinitive, regardless of whether this following verb is a main verb or an auxiliary. Take a look at (86), where the modal is underlined and the immediately following verb is in bold:

(86)   Modals must be followed by a **bare infinitive**:

     a. Rick <u>will</u> **put** a third coat of paint on   modal + main V
        the window sill.

b. Bill <u>would</u> **have** worked today, but   modal + aux *have*
    Walter was on break.

c. John <u>could</u> **be** helping out in the   modal + progressive *be*
    kitchen.

d. The wall <u>should</u> **be** given a second coat   modal + passive *be*
    of paint.

Side Note 18: *Coulda, shoulda, woulda*!!

Take a close look at (86b) and (87f) and think about how you would normally pronounce the sequence [modal + aux *have*] in examples like these. The standard orthographic representation of aux *have* following a modal is "have." Despite the spelling, though, English speakers exhibit an overwhelming tendency to pronounce *have*$_{bare-inf}$ in this context like the preposition "of" [əv], or even like "uh" [ə], just as you might pronounce the word *of* in phrases such as *a bunch **of** coconuts* or *he's kind **of** nice* or *he's sort **of** my friend*. This is why, very frequently, English speakers actually spell phrases like *should have known* as *should of known* or even *shoulda known*, and as they may spell *bunch of* or *kind of* or *sort of* as *buncha* or *kinda* or and *sorta*.

There's another interesting feature of such infinitival perfects — i.e. [*have*$_{bare-inf}$ + past participle] embedded under a modal (as in (86b) and (87f)): it seems that this is the one perfect construction where English speakers exhibit a greater tendency to use nonpresent forms variably, as we discussed in Section 9.2.3.1.3. Thus, English speakers worldwide may be just as likely (or even more likely) to use *coulda went* in place of *coulda gone*, or *shoulda ate* instead of *shoulda eaten*, or *woulda took* instead of *woulda taken*, and so forth.

Something which is also captured in (86b) is the fact that **auxiliary** *have* is always followed by a past participle, again, regardless of whether this following verb is a main verb or an auxiliary — <u>and</u> *regardless of whether aux have itself is a bare infinitive or tensed*. This can be also be seen in (87), where aux *have* is underlined, and the immediately following verb is in bold:

(87) Aux *have* is followed by a past participle:

a. Bill would <u>have</u> **worked** today, but   aux *have* + main V
    Walter was on break.

b. They'<u>ve</u> **worked** all week long.   aux *have* + main V

c. Bill would <u>have</u> **been** working today,   aux *have* + progressive *be*
    but Walter was on break.

d. Bill'<u>s</u> **been** working all week long.   aux *have* + progressive *be*

e. The wall <u>has</u> **been** given a second   aux *have* + passive *be*
coat of paint.

f. The wall should <u>have</u> **been** given a   aux *have* + passive *be*
second coat of paint.

EXERCISE [15]

For each sentence in (87), state whether aux *have* itself (i.e., the underlined verb) is a bare infinitive or tensed.

Also captured in (86c) and in (87c,d) is the fact that **progressive *be*** is always followed by a **present participle**, once again, regardless of whether this following verb is a main verb or an auxiliary — <u>and</u> *regardless of whether progressive be itself is a bare infinitive, a past participle, or tensed*. This can be also be seen in (88), where progressive *be* is underlined, and the immediately following verb is in bold:

(88) Progressive *be* is followed by a **present participle**:
a. Bill <u>is</u> **working** today.   prog. *be* + main V
b. John could <u>be</u> **helping** out in the kitchen.   prog. *be* + main V
c. Bill has <u>been</u> **working** the entire week.   prog. *be* + main V
d. Bill would have <u>been</u> **working** today, but   prog. *be* + main V
Walter was on break.
e. Bill <u>is</u> **being** paid today.   prog. *be* + passive *be*
f. Bill could <u>be</u> **being** paid out in the kitchen.   prog. *be* + passive *be*
g. Bill has <u>been</u> **being** paid the entire month.   prog. *be* + passive *be*
h. Bill would have <u>been</u> **being** paid today,   prog. *be* + passive *be*
but he left town.

EXERCISE [16]

For each sentence in (88), state whether progressive *be* itself (i.e. the underlined verb) is a bare infinitive, a past participle, or tensed.

And finally: also captured in (86d), (87e,f), and (88e–h) is the fact that **passive *be*** is always followed by a past participle. *This is regardless of whether passive be itself is a bare infinitive, a past participle, a present participle, or tensed.* In this case of passive *be*, the following verb is <u>always</u> going to be the main verb.

I'll repeat all of the relevant examples in (89), where passive *be* is underlined, and the immediately following verb is in bold:

(89)   Passive *be* is followed by a past participle:

    a.   The wall should <u>be</u> **given** a second coat of paint.   passive *be* + main V

    b.   The wall has <u>been</u> **given** a second coat of paint.   passive *be* + main V

    c.   The wall should have <u>been</u> **given** a second coat of paint.   passive *be* + main V

    d.   Bill is <u>being</u> **paid** today.   passive *be* + main V

    e.   Bill could be <u>being</u> **paid**, if he were here to pick up his check.   passive *be* + main V

    f.   Bill has been <u>being</u> **paid** the entire month.   passive *be* + main V

    g.   Bill would have been <u>being</u> **paid** today, but he left town.   passive *be* + main V

EXERCISE [17]

For each sentence in (89), state whether passive *be* itself (i.e. the underlined verb) is a bare infinitive, a past participle, a present participle, or tensed.

9.5.2 word order

In the 9.5.1, we saw that each auxiliary verb (modal, *have*, progressive *be*, and passive *be*) selects for a particular verb form. In the case of modals, *have*, and progressive *be*, this is regardless of whether the verb it selects is a main verb or an auxiliary. In the case of passive *be*, the selected verb will always be the main verb.

These facts add up to the following, in case you haven't already noticed: all of these verbs occur in a specific order. If you take a look at the sentence in (89 g), for example — which has the maximum number of verbs (namely, five) — from left to right we get the order seen in (90):

(90)   **Order of verbs:**

    modals > aux *have* > progressive *be* > passive *be* > main verb

Note that the order in (90) explains a number of things. First, it explains the fact that passive *be* is always followed by the main verb (and never by a modal or aux *have* or progressive *be*). Likewise, it explains the fact that modals can be followed immediately by aux *have* (as in (86b)), or by progressive *be* (as in (86c)), or by passive *be* (as in (86d)), or by the main verb (as in (86a)). It also explains why aux *have* can be immediately followed by progressive *be* (as in (87d)), or by passive *be* (as in (87e)), or by the main verb (as in (87b)). And finally, it explains why no other combination is possible (that is, why progressive *be* is not followed by aux *have*, and so forth).

The order in (90) can also be used as a way to remember the selectional properties of each auxiliary. That is, we can use (90) to remember which verb form each auxiliary requires the following verb to be, if we just add this information to the sketch:

(91)   Order of verbs plus summary of each verb's selectional requirements

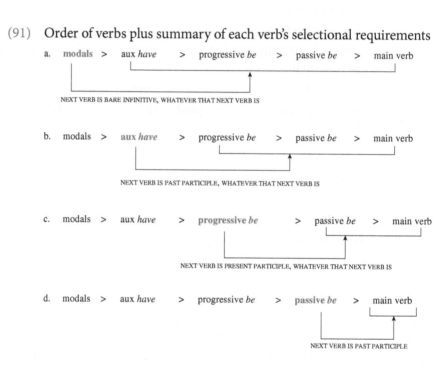

9.6 conclusions: all 16 possible combinations

Given the four types of auxiliary verb above (modals, aux *have*, progressive *be*, and passive *be*) plus the main verb, it follows that English provides us with 16 possible combinations, which I've laid out in the table in (92). Note that for the purposes of illustration, I arbitrarily chose *will* as my modal (though for Exercise [18] you can choose another modal); for tensed *have/be* and the tensed main verb, I arbitrarily chose the third person singular present tense (though for Exercise [18] you can choose the past tense and/or another person/number); and for the main verb, I arbitrarily chose *see* (though for Exercise [18] you can choose another main verb). Take note of the fact that the table replicates the facts about selectional requirements summarized in (91).

(92)   Possible combinations of modal, *have*, progressive *be*, passive *be*, main V

	modal (always tensed)	*aux* **have**	*prog.* **be**	*passive* **be**	*main verb*
1					sees
2	will				see
3	will	have			seen
4	will	have	been		seeing
5	will	have	been	being	seen
6				is	seen
7			is	being	seen
8		has	been	being	seen
9	will			be	seen
10	will		be		seeing
11		has	been		seeing
12		has		been	seen
13	will		be	being	seen
14	will	have		been	seen
15		has			seen
16			is		seeing

EXERCISE [18]

For each possible combination in (92), make up your own sentence (that's 16 sentences altogether). Feel free to use any of the nine modals (you don't have to limit yourself to *will*), and for the tensed verbs in rows 1, 6, 7, 8, 11, 12, 15, and 16, feel free to use the past tense (you don't have to limit yourself to the present tense). Also, feel free to use a subject other than the third person singular.

Once you have created your 16 sentences, for each sentence, using (91) as a guide, identify the form of each nonmodal verb. For example, in row 5 in (92): *have* is a bare infinitive; *been* is a past participle; *being* is a present participle; *seen* is a past participle. In row 10, *be* is a bare infinitive; *seeing* is a present participle.

list of terms/concepts

affix
agent vs. patient
aspect (punctual, perfective; imperfective, continuous, habitual)
auxiliary *be*
auxiliary *have*
auxiliary verb (aux; helping verb)
auxiliary verb contraction
bare infinitival form (bare infinitive)
compound preterite
compound tense (vs. simple tense)
conditional
conditional mood
contraction (contracted modals; contracted nonmodal auxiliaries)
dynamic verb
finiteness vs. nonfiniteness (tensed vs. untensed)
form vs. meaning
future perfect (tense)
future perfect progressive (tense)
future progressive (tense)
indicative (mood)
infinitival perfect (bare infinitival perfect)
infinitival-*to* perfect
inflectional suffix
intraspeaker variation
irregular verbs
levelled paradigm
main verb
main verb *be*
matrix tense
mental lexicon
modal auxiliary (modal)
mood (realis; irrealis; subjunctive; conditional)
morphological form (form; morpheme)

nonmodal auxiliary
nonpresent forms (simple past form; past participial form)
participial clauses
passive voice vs. active voice
past habitual
past participle (past participial form)
past perfect (tense)
past perfect progressive (tense)
past progressive (tense)
present tense
past tense
pluperfect
present participle (present participial form)
present perfect (tense)
present perfect progressive (tense)
present progressive (tense)
progressive aspect
progressive *be* vs. passive *be*
punctual
reference time
regional variation
regular verbs (vs. irregular verbs)
selectional requirements (selection)
spell-out rules
state (stative verbs)
subjunctive (mood; irrealis mood; present subjunctive; past subjunctive)
tense
untensed forms (nonfinite forms; infinitive; bare infinitive; present participle; past participle)
verbal -*s*
verb form
voice (active and passive)
word order

10

It Takes a Village: Main Verbs, Auxiliaries, Tense, and Negation

expected outcomes for this chapter

- You'll deepen your understanding of structural complexity, and recognize and manipulate much greater subtleties of hierarchical structure.
- You'll gain an in-depth understanding of the syntax of auxiliary verbs and main verbs.
- You'll gain an in-depth understanding of *negation*.
- You'll gain an appreciation of the negative auxiliary verb *ain't*.
- You'll develop more confidence with the concepts from previous chapters (e.g., phrase structure, sentence structure, word order, hierarchical structure, recursion, tense, features, interrogatives, movement).
- You'll become familiar with the following terms and concepts: *verb movement, negation, tense head, paradigm levelling in the presence of* n't, *affix lowering,* do-*support.*

10.1 the syntax of the English verb system

In the previous two chapters, we examined the English verb system in great detail. In Chapter 8 we focused on main verbs and the simple tenses (present and past), and in Chapter 9 we explored how the modal auxiliaries and the nonmodals *have* and *be* interact with main verbs, to create all kinds of compound tenses (perfects, progressives, the future), with different interpretations. In that chapter we also saw that the combination of all of these verbs (a modal, *have*, progressive *be*, passive *be*, and the main verb) respects

Understanding Sentence Structure: An Introduction to English Syntax, First Edition.
Christina Tortora.
© 2018 John Wiley & Sons, Inc. Published 2018 by John Wiley & Sons, Inc.

a strict word order, which we saw illustrated in (90) through (92); let's take a look at that word order again here:

(1) **Order of verbs:**

modals > aux *have* > progressive *be* > passive *be* > main verb

In this chapter, we'll see in detail how this word order reflects a much more complex sentence structure that we had previously seen in Chapters 1 through 7.

10.2 auxiliaries and the syntactic expression of tense

In Chapters 8 and 9 we became familiar with the concept of **tense**, focusing primarily on the verb forms and how they relate to tense **interpretation**. On the one hand, the discussion might have made it appear as if tense interpretation is dependent on the form of the verb. On the other hand, we saw that tense interpretations which we think of as "present" (= overlapping with the time of utterance), or as "past" (= before the time of utterance), or as "future" (= after the time of utterance) don't always line up neatly with the verb forms (or strings of forms) that we think of as present, past, or future. For example, we saw that the verb we call the "present form" can sometimes be used to indicate a past event (e.g., *Fire destroys hotel*), or that the "present progressive" can be used to indicate a future (*Walter is taking a break in an hour*). In other words, the particular forms seem somewhat independent of the tense interpretation, making it seem as if tense has a life of its own.

Well, actually, tense does have a life of its own — in fact, a syntactic life of its own. Thus, in addition to providing a way of interpreting events in relation to the **time of utterance** (Section 8.2), tense is represented in the syntactic structure, just like any grammatical word we've seen in Chapters 1–7, like determiners or prepositions (with just a little twist, as we'll see). And we actually already have a few clues available to us from Chapters 7, 8, and 9 in order to determine where tense resides, structurally speaking. Let's take a look at these clues to determine where tense is found in the syntax.

Let's start with two related generalizations we made in various discussions in the last two chapters: First, recall that in a single finite S, there is only one tensed verb, no matter how many verbs there are in the sentence. (See Term Box 6 in Chapter 9 if you need a refresher on the concepts of tense and finiteness.) This means that there is only **one tense** per single finite S, no matter how many verbs there are in it.

> ## EXERCISE [1]
>
> Confirm for yourself that each finite S contains only one tensed verb, by identifying the tensed verbs in the sentences you made up for Exercise [18] in Chapter 9, for rows 1, 2, 7, and 11. Additionally, identify the tensed verbs in examples (88d) and (88h) in Chapter 9; note that each of these examples contains more than one finite S. Also review sentences (3a–e) in Exercise [1] in Chapter 8, to confirm your understanding of what I mean by a "single finite S."

Now that you did Exercise [1], you remember that in sentences like those in (2), although there are six finite sentences each (one of which is the matrix sentence, and five of which are embedded sentences), each one of these contains only one tensed verb:

(2) a. Janet **assumes** that Bill **believes** that Sandy **claimed** that Joe **said** that Mary **thinks** that Sue **is** a great surgeon.

b. Janet **had** assumed that Bill **will** believe that Sandy **has** claimed that Joe **had** said that Mary **will** think that Sue **could** be a great surgeon.

In (2a), each one of these six finite sentences in fact contains only one verb (so, six verbs altogether), and since each sentence is finite, then by definition each verb is finite. In (2b), each one of these six finite sentences contains more than one verb (six sentences times two verbs each = 12 verbs). But only the six verbs in bold are tensed (*had, will, has, had will, could*). The sentence in (3) consists of only one finite sentence (that is, there are no embedded sentences, unlike (2)), but it contains five verbs. Again, only one is tensed (namely, the modal *should*):

(3) The window sills **should** have been being given a second coat of paint.

Similarly, the sentence in (4) (which also consists only of one finite sentence) contains three verbs, but again, only one is tensed (namely, the auxiliary *have*, which is third person plural present tense, agreeing with the third person plural subject *the window sills*):

(4) The window sills **have** been given a second coat of paint.

Second, recall that in a single finite S, the tensed verb will always be the leftmost verb in the string. Thus, in (3) the tensed verb *should* is the leftmost verb in the string, and in (4) the tensed verb *have* is the leftmost verb in the string. Likewise, in each of the six finite sentences in (2a), each verb is by definition the leftmost verb within its own S. You can also review Section 8.2.1.1.1 to confirm all of this, and the 16 possible combinations of modals, nonmodal auxiliaries, and main verb, in (92) in Chapter 9.

EXERCISE [2]

As a follow up to Exercise [1], confirm for yourself that the tensed verb in each finite S is the leftmost verb in each example you examined in Exercise [1]. (Note that if the finite S contains only one verb, then that verb is, by default, the leftmost verb.)

Now that you've done Exercise [2], you'll have solidified the idea that while *have* in (3) is untensed (it's a bare infinitive), *have* in (4) is tensed. The fact that the leftmost verb is always associated with tense suggests that in addition to there being only one tense per single finite S, that <u>structurally,</u> <u>tense is the first element in a string of verbs</u>. Let's summarize these two under-lined generalizations here:

[A]   *There is only one tense per single finite S, no matter how many verbs* *there are in it.*

[B]   *Structurally, tense is the first element in a string of verbs.*

The above two generalizations can be combined with a proposal we made in Chapter 7, regarding infinitival *to*, in order to help us understand where tense is, structurally speaking. Recall first that in addition to finite sentences like the underlined string in (5a), as per Chapter 7 we can also have infinitival sentences (with infinitival *to*), like the underlined string in (5b):

(5)   a.   Mary believed that <u>those kids would eat the cake</u>.

b.   Mary wants <u>those kids to eat the cake</u>.

In example (34) in Chapter 7, we proposed that infinitival *to* is right between the subject NP and the VP, as follows:

(6)

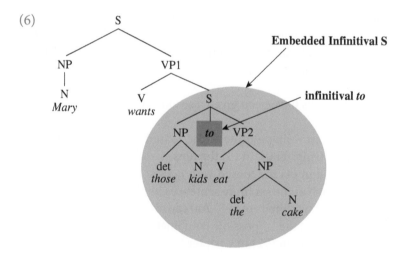

This is what led to our revision of the PS rule for the sentence, as follows:

(7)   S   →   NP (*to*) VP

Now, in order to get closer to understanding where tense resides in the struc-ture, let's think about the function of infinitival *to*: by definition, it represents the lack of tense. That is, any **infinitival** sentence is **nonfinite**, or **untensed** (again, see Term Box 6 of Chapter 9). This contrasts with **finite** sentences, which have **tense**. So let's say that infinitival *to* is an overt expression of a sen-tence's lack of tense. Furthermore, let's think of the infinitival sentence's lack of tense in terms of a **feature**. We can abbreviate this feature as [-tense], or [-tns] for short, which you should read as "minus tense."

Term Box 1: Features

In previous chapters we talked about **features** of different kinds. In Chapter 7 we talked about **agreement** with reflexive pronouns in terms of the features **person**, **number**, and **gender**. We also talked in Chapter 8 about **subject–verb agreement** in terms of the features person and number. In Chapter 2 (Term Box 8) — and again in Side Note 8 in Chapter 6 — we talked about **case features** (**nominative**, **accusative**).

As we saw, all of these features are syntactically relevant. Agreement features link distant syntactic entities (for example, a subject with a reflexive pronoun, or a subject with a verb). Case features indicate the grammatical function of a pronoun (e.g., whether it is a subject or an object). Our discussion of the **tense feature** in this chapter is bringing us even closer to the realization that all features have syntactic import. If you take a more advanced syntax course, you might learn more about how agreement and case features are syntactically expressed. For the purposes of this book, we'll just stick with a discussion of the syntax of tense.

The example in (8) illustrates the [-tns] feature as part of the syntactic structure:

(8)   ...

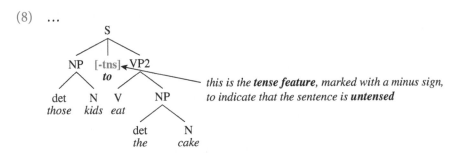

*this is the **tense feature**, marked with a minus sign, to indicate that the sentence is **untensed***

The configuration in (8) encodes the idea that this embedded sentence itself is untensed, and that the word we call "infinitival *to*" serves as the overt expression of this [-tns] feature.

Side Note 1: The syntactic expression of features

Imagine the idea in (8), except we're talking about the plural number feature inside an NP like *these books* instead. This would involve the words *these* and *books*, and a plural feature encoding the fact that each word overtly expresses plurality:

{1}

```
              NP
             /  \
        [+pl]    [+pl]
        those    kids
```

The idea in {1} isn't actually that far off from how syntacticians think about the expression of **number** inside the NP! I hope this makes the proposal in (8) look a little less strange to you. (See Term Box 1.)

EXERCISE [3]

Redo Exercise [8] from Chapter 7 (sentences {2}, {3}, and {5}), modifying your trees to include the [-tns] feature illustrated in (8).

So what about a [+tns] feature? The tense feature marked with a plus sign indicates — as you might have guessed — a sentence which is **finite**, or **tensed**. I'll illustrate this in (9):

(9)

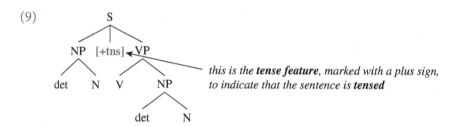

*this is the **tense feature**, marked with a plus sign, to indicate that the sentence is **tensed***

Notice how the structure in (9) reflects a specific syntactic position for tense, inside S. This in fact captures the two generalizations we just summarized in [A] and [B], namely: [A] there is only one tense per single finite S, no matter how many verbs there are in it; and [B] structurally, tense is the first element in a string of verbs. Regarding [B], since the VP follows the syntactic position for tense, by definition tense will always be the first element in a string of verbs. Regarding [A], since the syntactic position for tense is unique, it follows that there will only ever be one tense per single finite S.

All of this means that we have to revise our PS rule in (7) to take into account the fact that infinitival *to* is simply the overt expression of a [-tns] feature (found in infinitival, or nonfinite, sentences), and furthermore, that the tense feature can also have a "plus" value, as follows:

(10)   S   →   NP [±tns] VP

We can read the '±' symbol as "plus or minus." Using this "plus or minus" symbol in front of the [tns] feature in our new PS rule for S allows us to take into account that a sentence can be either [-tns] (an infinitive, or a nonfinite, or an untensed sentence), or it can be [+tns] (a finite, or tensed, sentence).

Note how in contrast with (7) (where we had infinitival *to* in parentheses, to indicate its optionality), in (10) I did not put the feature [±tns] in parentheses. This is because [±tns] is not optional: every sentence is either [+tns] or [-tns]. In other words, under this new way of looking at things, we have to accept that every S immediately dominates three branches, like in (11):

(11)   S

The million-dollar question now is this: if infinitival *to* is the overt expression of the [-tns] feature, then what is the overt expression of the [+tns] feature?

The answer to this question is complex — in a good way, though, as it'll help us understand a multitude of other facts about sentence structure. The ultimate answer all depends on which type of verb we're talking about (modal auxiliary, nonmodal auxiliary, or main verb), and whether or not there are any auxiliaries in the sentence to begin with. Given the complexity of the situation, I'll break the answer down into parts, in Sections 10.2.1 (modals), 10.2.2 (sentential negation), 10.2.3 (aux *have*), and 10.2.4 (aux *be*). Thus, we'll start with modals and then work our way rightward and downward in the structure after that. The story will unfold in such a way as to also reveal how we can get a total of five verbs to coexist in a single sentence (as per, e.g., row 5 in (92) in Chapter 9).

We'll reserve our discussion of [+tns] and main verbs for Section 10.3, since main verbs are in a class all by themselves.

10.2.1 modals are born in the tense position

We already know from Sections 9.4.3 and 9.4.4 that modals are always tensed, and as such, they never co-occur with infinitival *to*. In other words, if a single sentence contains any one of our nine modals (*can, could, shall, should, will, would, may, might,* and *must*), then that S by definition is [+tns].

From this fact, it's reasonable to conclude the following: if there is a modal in the sentence, then that modal is born in the tense position, and the tense feature is necessarily [+tns]. This is depicted in (12):

(12)

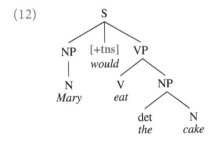

EXERCISE [4]

Using the immediately foregoing discussion and (12) as a guide, draw trees for the following sentences:

{1} Bill must leave by 5:00 p.m.
{2} Christina should gut-renovate her house.
{3} Sue will fix the sink.
{4} John can drive Bill to the office.

Side Note 2: The competition between modals and infinitival *to*

The fact that modals and infinitival *to* never occur together (see Section 9.4.4) is what suggests that they compete for the same syntactic position. This is similar to the case of the definite article *the* vs. demonstratives (*this, that, these,* and *those*), which we saw also compete for the same syntactic position, namely the determiner position. The proposal that the definite article and demonstratives both occur in the same position allows us to account for the fact that a single NP can never contain both simultaneously (compare *the woman* and *this woman* with *the this woman* or *this the woman*). Likewise, a single S can never contain a modal and *to* simultaneously (*Sue expects Bill to can finish the exam;* see (80) in Chapter 9).

Given that there is only one tensed verb per single S, it follows that the verb *eat* in (12) (and the verbs *leave, gut-renovate, fix,* and *drive* in Exercise [4]) are all untensed. Previous discussions in Chapters 8 and 9 remind us that these verbs are in their bare infinitival form (see e.g., (91a) in Chapter 9); the fact that they do not end in verbal *-s* (despite the fact that the subject is a third person singular) confirms this. This means that the VP in (12) is headed by a nonfinite verb. As we will see in Section 10.2.3.1.1, all VPs are headed by verbs in their nonfinite forms.

For the next section, though, let's take a look at the syntax of the adverb *not.* The syntax of this adverb serves as an essential diagnostic in establishing the syntactic position of our other verbs. This in turn will help us understand what the overt expression of [+tns] is, in the absence of a modal auxiliary.

10.2.2 the negative markers *not* and *n't*

Until now, this book has barely discussed adverbs. Now it's time to introduce the most useful adverb of them all, when it comes to determining the syntax of the English verb system. The sentential **negative marker** *not* — and its contracted version *n't* — are really useful as a diagnostic tool for verb syntax because these words have a rigid syntactic position. That is to say, they have their own position in the syntax in which they like to stay put, something which allows us to test the position of verbs around it.

We'll start with a look at **sentential negation** in relation to modals. Consider the sentences in (13), which contain *not* and *n't* in a string of modal plus a bare infinitive:

(13) a. Bill can**not** come to John's party.

    a'. Bill ca**n't** come to John's party.

    b. Mary should **not** take Sue's help for granted.

    b'. Mary should**n't** take Sue's help for granted.

c. Sue would **not** fix the sink a fourth time.

c'. Sue would**n't** fix the sink a fourth time.

Side Note 3: Spelling vs. language

Keep in mind that the quirks of English orthography shouldn't detract you from the fact that *cannot* is simply *can* plus *not*. The fact that it's conventionally spelled as a single word is just an artificial rule of orthography, not a rule of natural language. Similarly, *can't* is *can* plus *n't*, which if you put them together should be spelled *cann't* (if English orthography weren't so quirky).

In contrast, the modals *will*, *shall*, and *may* present a whole different ball game when it comes to their combination with contracted *n't*. Affirmative **will** contrasts with negative **won't**, which is more than just a difference in spelling — it's a notable difference in pronunciation. If this modal were regular, you would expect the negated form *****willn't**. Similarly, for those readers who use the modal **shall**, you'll notice that this contrasts with negative **shan't**, which again is more than just a difference in spelling; if this modal were regular, you would expect the negated form *****shalln't**. See Term Box 4 for the concept of a **pronunciation spell-out rule**, which can explain a form like *won't*, which is not predictably derived from the combination of *will* + *n't*. Along the lines of (24) in Section 10.2.3.1.1, we can imagine a spell-out rule that says "pronounce *willn't* (which is the composition of *will* plus *n't*) as *won't*." See Section 10.2.6 for *ain't*.

For many speakers, *may* is in a class by itself, as it doesn't combine with the contracted *n't* at all: *****mayn't**. Thus, for many English speakers, the only sentential negation possible in combination with modal *may* is *not* (*may not*).

Compare the sentences in (13) with their corresponding affirmative counterparts in (14):

(14) a. Bill can come to John's party.

b. Mary should take Sue's help for granted.

c. Sue would fix the sink a fourth time.

In terms of meaning, you can see that the sentential negators *not* and *n't* serve to reverse the **truth value** of a **proposition** (encoded in a sentence), like the propositions you see in (14). For example, you can think of (14b) as meaning something like "It's true that Mary should take Sue's help for granted," while you can think of (13b) as meaning something like "It's false that Mary should take Sue's help for granted." Negation is like responding to a statement such as that in (14b) with the statement "opposite!" If you say *Mary should take Sue's help for granted* and I respond with *opposite!*, this means that Mary should **not** take Sue's help for granted.

In terms of syntax, the modal auxiliary can help us determine what the fixed position of the sentential negative marker is. As you can see in (13), with a modal present, the natural place for sentential negation is between the modal and the next verb. If you try to put *not* any place else, you get an ungrammatical sentence (compare (15) and (16) with (13)):

(15)   a.   *Bill **not** can come to John's party.

       b.   *Mary **not** should take Sue's help for granted.

       c.   *Sue **not** would fix the sink a fourth time.

(16)   a.   *Bill can come **not** to John's party.

       b.   *Mary should take **not** Sue's help for granted.

       c.   *Sue would fix **not** the sink a fourth time.

Term Box 2: Sentential negation vs. constituent negation

The concept of sentential negation — which is what we're concerned with here — should not be confused with **constituent negation**. Under the right interpretation, the sentence in {1} is grammatical:

{1}   *Bill can come <u>not</u> to John's party.* (cf. (13a))

In this case, *not* doesn't appear between the modal and the main verb. But we have to be careful to not confuse this with a sentence like that in (13a). In (13a), the entire proposition is negated (hence, "sentential negation"). In {1}, on the other hand, the negative marker *not* negates the constituent *to John's party* (hence, "constituent negation"). The sentence in {1} does not involve negation of the entire proposition. Instead, it means something like *Bill can come, but NOT to John's party… (but, he can come, for example, to Sue's party).*

Let's take the facts in (13), (15), and (16) to indicate that the fixed syntactic position of sentential negation is right after the modal, and right before the following verb. We thus have to revise our PS rule for S in (10) to account for the position of the negative marker, which we'll abbreviate as NEG. Our revised PS rule is in (17):

Revised PS rule for S:

(17)   S   →   NP [±tns] (NEG) VP

Notice how I put the NEG in parentheses. This is to indicate that sentential negation is not obligatory. The revised PS rule in (17), which now accounts for the fixed position of the negative marker, gives rise to the following possibility for sentence structure:

(18)   S   (with *not*)

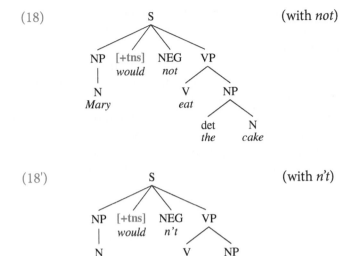

(18')   S   (with *n't*)

EXERCISE [5]

Using the immediately preceding discussion and (18)/(18') as a guide, draw trees for the sentences in (13).

Now that we've established the fixed position of the negative marker, we can move on to the question of the overt expression of the [+tns] feature. In Section 10.2.1, we saw that when the sentence contains a modal (as in (18)/(18')), the modal itself serves as the overt instantiation of the [+tns] feature. This makes sense, because modals are never untensed.

But what happens if there's no modal in the sentence, like in (19)?

(19)   Rick has given the window sill a third coat of paint.

As we saw earlier, the question of what resides in the [+tns] position is complex, and it depends on which type of verb we're talking about. Let's now talk about auxiliary *have* (as in (19)), which will teach us something new about the [+tns] position.

10.2.3 auxiliary *have* and verb movement

Everything we've said about tense up until now points to the fact that the verb *has* in (19) is tensed. It's the leftmost verb in this (single) sentence, and we can see that it agrees with the third person singular subject *Rick*, by virtue of the presence of verbal *-s*.

Given this fact, should we conclude that, like the modal in (12), tensed aux *have* is born in the [+tns] position? Perhaps surprisingly, the answer to this question is No. Let's see why.

As we already saw in Chapter 9, aux *have* is different from the modals. It can co-occur with infinitival *to* (i.e. it can be untensed; see (78) in Chapter 9 for confirmation). Additionally, as we saw in (90) through (92) of that chapter, if a modal is present, aux *have* always comes after the modal. These facts suggest that even when there is no modal, aux *have* has its own place in the syntactic structure, independent of the [±tns] position — regardless of whether it's tensed, as in (19), or untensed, as in (78) in Chapter 9, or as in (20):

(20)   Rick could have given the window sill a third coat of paint.

If aux *have* is born in a different syntactic position than the modal, then where is this position?

Let's propose that aux *have* is born within its own VP, whether it's tensed (as in (19)), or untensed (as in (20)). This is depicted in (21) and (22):

untensed *have* (cf. (20)):   tensed *have* (cf. (19)):

In the tree in (21), the modal auxiliary *could* is the overt instantiation of the [+tns] feature. But what is the overt instantiation of the [+tns] feature in (22)? Or is there one? There's a twist here. To understand this twist, take a look at the negated versions of (19) versus (20):

(19')   Rick <u>has</u> **not** given the window sill a third coat of paint.
Rick <u>has</u>**n't** given the window sill a third coat of paint.
(cf. *Rick **not** <u>has</u> given the window sill a third coat of paint.)

(20')   Rick could **not** <u>have</u> given the window sill a third coat of paint.
Rick could**n't** <u>have</u> given the window sill a third coat of paint.

Side Note 4: The verb following aux *have*

In Section 10.2.3.2 we'll take a look at the syntactic position of the past participle following aux *have* in (19) and (20).

The negated versions of (19) and (20) show us that tensed aux *have* appears to the left of the negative marker (*has > not*), while untensed aux *have* appears to its right (*not > have*). In other words, tensed aux *have* (which is realized as *has* in (19)) appears in the same position that the modal appears in, in (20)/(21), namely, the [+tns] position itself. Using the negative marker as a diagnostic as in (19') allows us to see clearly that tensed aux *have* must appear in the [+tns] position. But make no mistake: even when we don't have a negative marker in the sentence (as in (19) and (20)), we must still conclude that tensed aux *have* appears in the [+tns] position.

This means that tensed *have* in (19) is actually in the [+tns] position, despite what we just said about tensed *have* heading its own VP, as depicted in (22). So how can tensed *have* appear in the [+tns] position, when we're saying that it's born as the head of its own VP, as the tree in (22) depicts?

Easy! Remember **movement rules**? As we saw with wh-movement in Chapter 5, a movement rule operates on some constituent at **deep structure**, moving it to a **surface structure** position. In the case of wh-movement, we move a wh-phrase from its deep structure position to a position within CP. Similarly, in the case of passivization, we move the object NP to subject position (as in Chapters 3 and 9). Here, I'd like to introduce the notion of **verb movement**, which is sometimes also called **verb raising**.

10.2.3.1 Verb movement

Verb movement (or verb raising) is a syntactic operation that moves a verb from its deep structure position to a surface structure position. In the case of a sentence like (19), tensed aux *have* starts out its life (at deep structure) as the head of its own VP, as in (22). But [+tns] has a requirement: if there's a tensed auxiliary in the structure, it requires that that tensed auxiliary come to reside in its position. And let's remind ourselves how we know that the [+tns] position requires a tensed auxiliary in it: again, take a look at (19'): the very fact that the tensed verb *has* appears to the left of *not/n't* is evidence that the [+tns] position — which is to the left of the negative marker — needs to be filled by a tensed auxiliary.

This requirement on the part of the [+tns] position forces movement of the tensed aux *have* from its deep structure position to [+tns], the tensed aux's surface structure position. The trees in (23) illustrate this.

DEEP STRUCTURE: SURFACE STRUCTURE:

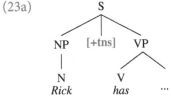

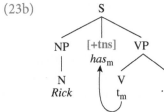

Remember from Chapters 5, 6, and 7 that any moved constituent leaves a trace of movement in its deep structure position, which is co-indexed with the moved element; in (23b) I arbitrarily chose the index subscript "m".

10.2.3.1.1 The inflectional suffix in [+tns]

Now that we've covered the basics of verb movement, I can turn to a somewhat more complicated issue. It may not be clear at this very moment why we have to finesse things in this way, but I guarantee you that the motivation for this particular analysis becomes clearer in Section 10.3, when we talk about main verbs. (Feel free to jump ahead to that section, if you want to take a peek at what's going on with main verbs.)

The issue relates to a question we asked slightly earlier, namely, what is the overt expression of the [+tns] feature in (22)/(23a)? Or is there one? We said that there was "a twist," and thus far, the twist has involved verb movement in the absence of a modal — in particular, movement of the nonmodal aux *have* from its base position in V to the [+tns] position. But why exactly does the tensed aux *have* have to move to the [+tns] position?

In order to understand this better, let's hearken back to Section 9.2.1 and Chapter 8 (Term Box 2), where we saw that we create present tense and past tense forms of regular verbs by suffixing verbal -*s* (for the third singular present tense) and -*ed* (for the past tense). Since these **inflectional suffixes** are the markers of present and past tense, let's **morphologically** decompose the present and past tense versions of aux *have* — namely, *has* and *had* — into their component parts:

(24) a. *have* + -*s*   >   "haves"   >   **has**
      b. *have* + -*ed*   >   "haved"   >   **had**

Term Box 3: Morphemes and morphology

Morphology is the study of **morphemes** and word structure. A morpheme is a minimal unit of meaning in language. We say "minimal unit" to capture the idea that the element in question cannot be broken down into any further meaningful parts. For example, the word *eat* is a single morpheme, as it can't be broken down into any meaningful component parts. The word *eats*, however, is composed of two parts, *eat* and -*s*. Both of these parts are morphemes, because they are minimal units of meaning; *eat* means something, and so does -*s* (specifically, third singular present tense). We would also say that the word *eats* is **bimorphemic**, because it consists of two morphemes. The word *eat* on the other hand is **monomorphemic**.

The sketch in (24a) tells us that in terms of its meaning, the verb form *has* is composed of the bare infinitive *have* plus the inflectional suffix -*s*, which marks third singular *have* as a present tense verb. But when you put these two morphemes together, you get the form **haves*, which is not how English speakers actually pronounce the word. Instead, there is a kind of **pronuncia-tion spell-out rule** that tells English speakers something like "pronounce *haves* (which is the composition of *have* plus *-s*) as *has*."

Term Box 4: Pronunciation spell-out rules

Be careful here! The linguistic concept of a spell-out rule has nothing to do with spelling. It refers to pronunciation, not orthography. The pronunciation spell-out rule discussed in the text is one of the many linguistic rules that exist below our level of consciousness, which we internalized as babies when we were learning English, with-out realizing it. It's not a rule you learned in school — you didn't have to, because you already unconsciously knew it by the time you got there. English speakers are not alone as humans in their unconscious knowledge of pronunciation spell-out rules. Every word in our mental lexicon, no matter what the language, has to follow a spell-out rule in order to be uttered. The output of a spell-out rule (= pronunciation of a word) is either **predictable** or **unpredictable**. In the latter case, when learning the language as babies, we have to memorize the unpredictable form. In the former case, by definition the form is predictable. For example, the pronunciation of the word *walked* is predict-ably surmised from the composition of *walk*+ *-ed*. However, the pronunciation of the word *ate* can't be predicted from the composition of *eat*+ *-ed*. As babies learning English, we would expect this word to be pronounced *eated* (from *eat*+ *-ed*), not as *ate*. And anyone who hangs around with English learners knows that *eated* is actually something they might produce! But over time, an English learner memorizes that *eat*+ *-ed* is conventionally pronounced (= "spelled out") as *ate*. Every language in the world has spell-out rules that give rise to either predictable or unpredictable forms.

We can say the same for the sketch in (24b): in terms of its meaning, the verb *had* is composed of the bare infinitive *have* plus the inflectional suffix *-ed*, which marks *have* as a past tense. Furthermore, when you put these two morphemes together, you get the form **have-ed*, which is not how English speakers actually pronounce the word. Instead, a pronunciation spell-out rule tells us something like "pronounce *have-ed* (which is the composition of *have* plus *-ed*) as *had*."

So to conclude: tensed aux *have* is composed of the bare form *have* plus some inflectional suffix which marks tense.

Given that these suffixes mark tense, it makes sense to say that they are the overt expression of the [+tns] feature in the absence of a modal. This idea is depicted in (25); compare with our first-pass hypothesis in (23a):

DEEP STRUCTURE:

(25)

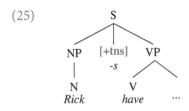

Side Note 5: Past *-ed* vs. participial *-ed*

Remember from Chapter 9 that we must not confuse the *-ed* of the past participle in {1} with the *-ed* of the simple past in {2}:

{1} John has **finished** his dinner.   past participial form
{2} John **finished** his dinner.   simple past form

We know that *finished* in {1} is a past participle, because it follows aux *have*. Furthermore, we know that past participles are nonfinite (i.e. untensed). Therefore, we do not consider the *-ed* of *finished* in {1} to be a tense marker. (In contrast, the *-ed* in {2} is.)

The tree in (25) captures the idea that *has* is, at deep structure, broken down into the bare form *have* (which heads its own VP) and the present tense marker *-s*, which is the overt instantiation of the [+tns] feature, immediately dominated by the S node. Even though aux *have* starts out its life as a bare form, the entire deep structure ensures this is a tensed sentence, given the [+tns] feature.

And now we have the real reason why verb movement takes place: in order to become the form *has* (as in (24a)), aux *have* must move up to the [+tns] position, to join up with the inflectional suffix *-s*. This is depicted in (26), which you should compare with our first-pass attempt in (23b).

SURFACE STRUCTURE (= (19)):

(26)

The surface structure in (26) reflects movement of *have* from its deep structure position within VP to the [+tns] position; and as always, this movement leaves behind a co-indexed trace, which I've notated as t_m. The normal spell-out rules of English (as per (24a)) ensure that [*have$_m$* + *-s*] is pronounced as *has*.

Now what would happen if instead of the present perfect in (19), we had a past perfect, as in (27)?

(27)   Rick had given the window sill a third coat of paint.

The only thing that would change is the nature of the inflectional suffix in the [+tns] position. Thus, instead of (25) and (26), we would get (28) and (29):

DEEP STRUCTURE:

(28)

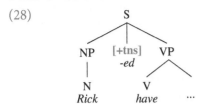

SURFACE STRUCTURE (= (27)):

(29)

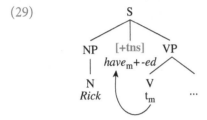

Side Note 6: Present vs. past interpretation

Notice that in both the present tense version of aux *have* in (26) and the past tense version of aux *have* in (29), the [+tns] feature itself doesn't distinguish present versus past tense. To be more precise, we really should add this information to the feature, to distinguish the two. So the tense feature in (26) should really look like {1}, and the tense feature in (29) should really look like {2}:

{1} [+tns, present]
{2} [+tns, past]

Keep in mind that it makes sense for the tense feature to include this extra specification in order to truly capture the tense interpretation of the sentence. Note that this difference is what underlies the distinct temporal interpretations of *put* (present) and *put* (past) in (18) in Chapter 8, repeated here (in Section 10.3 we'll look at the [+tns] feature with main verbs):

{3} My students always [+tns present] **put** themselves in my shoes.
{4} Last night, my students [+tns past] **put** themselves in my shoes.

To keep the trees from becoming too busy looking, though, I'll forego this extra notation in the actual tree illustrations. But please keep it in mind!

Again, the surface structure in (29) reflects movement of *have* from its deep structure position within VP to the [+tns] position, which leaves a co-indexed trace. The normal spell-out rules of English (as per (24b)) ensure that [*have*$_m$ + -ed] its pronounced as *had*.

Also, let's not forget that in the present tense, first and second singular and all the plural persons do not have an overt inflectional suffix for tense — look back at the present tense paradigm for *have* in (7) in Chapter 9. Compare (19) (repeated here) with (30):

(19)   Rick **has** given the window sill a third coat of paint.

(30)   They **have** given the window sill a third coat of paint.

The form *have* in (30) is the third plural present tense form of *have*, as per the paradigm in (7) in Chapter 9. We know it's tensed because it's the leftmost verb in this particular S, agreeing with the third person plural subject *they*. Just because the form *have* in (30) isn't marked with verbal -*s* doesn't mean, therefore, that it's not tensed. As such, it involves the same process of verb movement for the purposes of tense interpretation that we see in (26). The word order in the sentence in (30') proves that the tensed aux *have* in (30) moves to the [+tns] position:

(30')   They <u>have</u> **not** given the window sill a third coat   (have > not)
of paint.

They <u>have</u>**n't** given the window sill a third coat of   (have > n't)
paint.

(cf. *They **not** <u>have</u> given the window sill a third   (*not > have)
coat of paint.)

Note how this verb appears to the left of *not*, just like we saw for the tensed verb *has* in (19'):

(19')   Rick <u>has</u> **not** given the window sill a third coat of   (has > not)
paint.

Rick <u>has</u>**n't** given the window sill a third coat of   (has > n't)
paint.

(cf. *Rick **not** <u>has</u> given the window sill a third   (*not > has)
coat of paint.)

The negated version of (30) in (30') shows us that present tense aux *have* appears to the left of the negative marker (*have > not*) — just like *has* in (19) — even when it's in its third plural form, even without inflectional -*s* to overtly mark the present tense. You can compare the example in (30') with (20'), which shows untensed aux *have* appearing to the right of (*not > have*); I'll repeat that example here:

(20')   Rick could **not** <u>have</u> given the window sill a third   (not > have)
coat of paint.

Rick could**n't** <u>have</u> given the window sill a third   (n't > have)
coat of paint.

In other words, third plural present tense aux *have* in (30)/(30') appears in the same position in which the modal appears in (20)/(20'), and in which aux *has* appears in (26) (namely, the [+tns] position) — even if there is no overt inflectional suffix. Given the word order facts, we must assume this.

(Remember: we're just using the syntax of *not* in relation to the auxiliaries in order to diagnose the position of the auxiliary verbs, in the surface structure. Our diagnosis leads to the conclusion that — even in those sentences without the negative maker, such as (30) — we have tensed auxiliary movement.)

To capture the fact that tensed aux *have* always moves to the [+tns] position, even when there's no inflectional suffix, let's hypothesize the existence of a silent inflectional suffix -Ø. This silent inflectional suffix -Ø encodes the tense information that verbal *-s* encodes for the third singular, except it does so for all the other persons and numbers, i.e. first and second singular, and all the persons of the plural in (7) in Chapter 9. The examples in (31) and (32) illustrate this.

DEEP STRUCTURE:

(31)

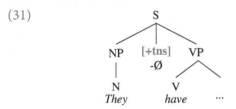

SURFACE STRUCTURE (= (30) *They **have** given the window sill a third coat of paint*):

(32)

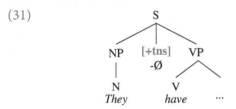

EXERCISE [6]

Reinforce your understanding of the tensed aux's position in relation to the negative marker by using the PS rule in (17) to draw a tree structure like that in (32), but with the negative marker included, as in the sentence in (30'). In your tree, does [*have*$_m$ + -ø] appear to the left or to the right of *not*?

Along the lines of Side Note 6: this analysis allows us to capture the interpretive distinction between tensed *have* in (30) and untensed *have* in (20) and (21), repeated here for comparison:

(30)   They **have** given the window sill a   tensed *have* (see tree (32))
       third coat of paint.

(20)   Rick could **have** given the window   untensed *have* (see tree (21))
       sill a third coat of paint.

untensed *have* (= (20) *Rick could* **have** *given the window sill a third coat of paint*):

(21)

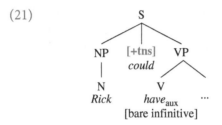

10.2.3.2 Past participle following *have*

In order to have the tools to draw full-blown tree structures for the example sentences in this section (such as (19), (20), (30), and the like), we have to address one more matter.

If aux *have* is born within its own VP in (25), (28), and (31), then where is the main verb *given* born? Within its own VP, of course! In other words, structures like (12) and (18)/(18'), coupled with the idea that aux *have* is born within its own VP, lead us to conclude that we must allow for more than one VP in a single sentence, to accommodate both aux *have* and the main verb. Take a look at the tree in (33), which corresponds to the sentence in (19):

DEEP STRUCTURE:

(33)

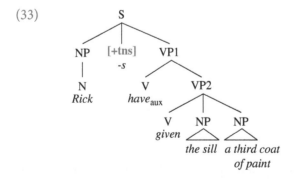

Side Note 7: Double objects

See Section 3.4 if you've forgotten about the **double-object construction** (which is what VP2 contains, in (33)).

In the structure in (33), we see that aux *have* heads its own VP (which I've labelled as VP1), while the main verb *given* (which is a past participle; see (91b) in Chapter 9) also heads its own VP (which I've labelled as VP2 to distinguish it from VP1). Note that although there are two VPs, the phrases that are selected by the main verb (the NP *the sill* and the NP *a third coat of paint*) — and any additional locational or temporal PPs that we might want to add, like those we've seen in Chapters 3 through 7 — **are all attached to the VP headed by the main verb. They do not attach to the VP headed by the auxiliary verb**.

The idea that syntactic structure accommodates strings of multiple verbs in this way means we have to slightly revise our PS rule for the VP. Until now, our VP rule has been structured as follows (see the end of Chapter 7 for the last revision):

$$(34) \quad VP \quad \rightarrow \quad V \text{ (PP) (NP)} \left\{ \begin{matrix} \text{(NP)} \\ \text{(S)} \\ \text{(CP)} \end{matrix} \right\} \text{(AP) (PP*)}$$

However, this rule does not take into account the fact that a verb like *have* in (33), which heads the highest VP, can select another VP, such as VP2 in (33), which is headed by the past participle *given* (i.e. the main verb of the sentence). But we can easily fix this with the following revision:

Revised VP rule:

$$(35) \quad VP \quad \rightarrow \quad V \text{ (VP) (PP) (NP)} \left\{ \begin{matrix} \text{(NP)} \\ \text{(S)} \\ \text{(CP)} \end{matrix} \right\} \text{(AP) (PP*)}$$

The PS rule in (35) encodes the idea that a verb can select another VP (just as it can select a PP, or an NP, or an S, or a CP, or an AP). The VP is thus **recursive** — it allows for the **recursion** of the VP, as depicted in (36) (see Section 5.2.2 for a review of the concept of recursion):

(36)

$$VP \rightarrow V \textbf{ VP}$$

This recursive property results in the following hierarchical structure for VPs:

(37)

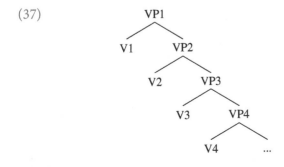

EXERCISE [7]

Using (i) the discussion in this section; (ii) the PS rules in (17) and (35); (iii) the structures in (26), (29), and (32); and (iv) the idea of recursion depicted in (36)/(37) — all as your guides: draw **surface structure trees** for the sentences below. Remember: if there is verb movement, your tree will have to contain a co-indexed trace of the moved verb. Hint: If there's a modal auxiliary in the sentence, then there is no verb movement.

{1} Bill would have worked this morning.
{2} Bill has worked the entire week.
{3} She should not have put a fourth coat of paint on the wall.
{4} I've been really happy with his work.
{5} They've given too many coats of paint to that wall!

Challenge sentences: given the new PS rule in (35) and what we know about passives, see if you can draw trees for the following two sentences. Give it your best shot!

{6} The fireplace mantel has not been given its third coat of paint.
{7} The fireplace mantel should have been being given a third coat of paint.

10.2.4 auxiliary *be* and verb movement

If you successfully drew surface structure trees for sentences {6} and {7} in Exercise [7], then you've already tested out the kind of configuration in (37), which allows us to accommodate strings of upwards of 4 verbs in a single S. Let's take a look at a first pass of the surface structure tree for {6} from Exercise [7] in (38):

SURFACE STRUCTURE of {6} (= *The fireplace mantel has not been given its third coat of paint*):

(FIRST PASS)

(38)

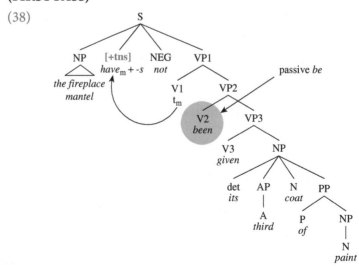

The tree in (38) captures the fact that the sentence is tensed (= finite), and as such, *have* has to move to the [+tns] position. The past participle *been* following *have* heads its own VP, which I labelled VP2, to notationally distinguish it from the VP headed by *have*. And the past participle *given* — which is the main verb — also heads its own VP.

But as I hinted at in Exercise [7], we're dealing here with a passive sentence. This can be verified by the fact that the main verb (*given*) is in its past participial form, and is preceded by aux *be*. This aux *be*, furthermore, must be none other than **passive *be***, because as per Chapter 9 (see especially (90) through (92)), if aux *be* is followed by a past participle, then we know it's passive *be* (and not progressive *be*). But think also about the meaning of the sentence: Someone should be giving the fireplace mantel a third coat of paint. Thus, *the fireplace mantel* is really a deep structure object. The active counterpart of this sentence would be as in (39):

(39)   Rick has not given <u>the fireplace mantel</u> its third coat of   ACTIVE
       paint.
       (cf. <u>*The fireplace mantel*</u> *has not been given its third coat*   PASSIVE
       of paint)

This means that our surface structure in (38) is not quite right, because it doesn't capture the passivization movement rule, which moves the deep structure object to subject position; see Exercise [1] in Chapter 7. So let's revise our tree to capture this other movement operation taking place inside of this sentence:

SURFACE STRUCTURE of {6} (= *The fireplace mantel has not been given its third coat of paint*):

(SECOND PASS)

(40)

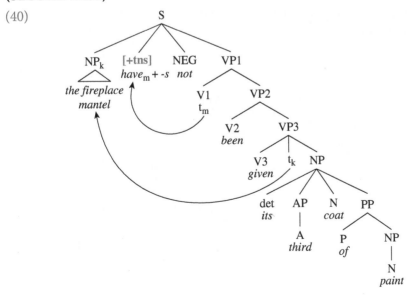

EXERCISE [8]

Now check to see if the tree you drew for the passive sentence in Exercise [7] was correctly drawn with the trace of the deep structure object as a sister to the main verb *given*, as in (40).

Now that we've grasped the detail of the passivization movement operation: let's get back to passive *be* in the example in {6}/(40). In this example, passive *be* (which is an auxiliary) is untensed. Specifically, as we just noted, it's a past participle. It's in its past participial form because it follows aux *have*, and as per (90) through (92) in Chapter 9, we know that the verb which follows aux *have* is always a past participle. The PS rule in (35) (which is broken down in (36) and (37)) allows us to accommodate this untensed (= nonfinite) form of auxiliary *be*. We can further confirm that *been* is untensed, by virtue of the fact that it follows the negative marker *not* (*not > been*). This means that it couldn't possibly be occupying the [+tns] position, which is to the left of *not* (*has > not*).

But what about tensed passive *be*? How does it fit into the structure? Consider the sentence in (41):

(41)   The fireplace mantel **was not** given a third coat of paint.   (was > not)

   (cf. *The fireplace mantel **not was** given a third coat of paint)   (*not > was)

In (41), the first verb in the string is passive *be* in a tensed form, namely past tense *was*. Note that *was* precedes the negative marker *not* (*was > not*). This tells us that when passive *be* is tensed, it behaves just like tensed aux *have*: it must move from its deep structure position to the [+tns] position. Thus, the surface structure tree for (41) is as in (42):

SURFACE STRUCTURE (= (41) *The fireplace mantel **was** not given a third coat of paint*):

(42)

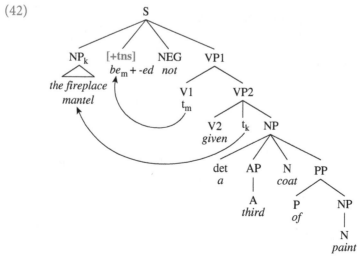

In (42) we're dealing with past tense *be*, namely, *was*. In terms of its morphological structure (see Term Boxes 3 and 4), *was* is composed of *be* plus the past tense inflectional marker *-ed*. This yields *be -ed*, which of course is not how this form is actually pronounced. As we saw with *has* and *had* in (24), English speakers pronounce the verb *be* plus the past tense suffix *-ed* as *was* (compare the following with (24)):

(43)   *be* + *-ed* > "beed" > *was* (or *were*, if the subject is plural)

In sum, if passive *be* is untensed (like the past participle *been*), it stays inside its own VP. If it's tensed (as in (41)/(42)), then it moves from its deep structure position to the [+tns] position, to join up with the tense marker.

Predictably, when untensed passive *be* is a present participle (as in (44a)) or a bare infinitive (as in (44b)), we once again see that it follows *not*, just like the past participle *been* does (44c):

(44)   a.   The fireplace mantel will **not be** given a   (not > be)
             fourth coat of paint.
             (cf. *The fireplace mantel will **be not** given a*   (*be > not)
             fourth coat of paint)

       b.   The fireplace mantel is **not being** given a   (not > being)
             fourth coat of paint.
             (cf. *The fireplace mantel is **being not** given a*   (*being > not)
             fourth coat of paint)

       c.   The fireplace mantel has **not been** given its   (not > been)
             third coat of paint.
             (cf. *The fireplace mantel has **been not** given its*   (*been > not)
             third coat of paint)

This is because — as we've already noted numerous times — the bare infinitive, the present participle, and the past participle are all untensed. (See Term Box 6 in Chapter 9 for a refresher.) Thus, neither the present participle *being*, nor the bare infinitive *be*, nor the past participle *been* move to the [+tns]. We can see this by virtue of the fact that they do not appear to the left of the negative marker.

Now let's take a closer look at the example in (44b): as should be clear by now, the present participle *being* is passive *be* — witness the fact that it's followed by a past participle, *given* (and also, think about the meaning). But what about the form *is*? As we saw in Section 9.3.1, this is the third person singular present tense form of the verb *be*. Which *be* is it? Well, since it's followed by a present participle, as per (90) through (92) in Chapter 9, we know that it has to be progressive *be*.

As you've probably surmised by now, progressive *be* doesn't behave any differently from passive *be* or from aux *have*: it's born within its own VP; if it's the leftmost verb, it's tensed and therefore must move to the [+tns] position; if it's not the leftmost verb, then it's untensed and it stays put. Let's take a look at a few examples:

(45) a. Rick **isn't** giving the fireplace mantel a fourth coat of paint.   progressive *be*, tensed

b. The fireplace mantel **is** being given a third coat of paint.   progressive *be*, tensed

c. Rick will **be** giving the fireplace mantel a third coat of paint.   progressive *be*, untensed

d. The fireplace mantel will **be** being given a third coat of paint.   progressive *be*, untensed

e. Rick hasn't **been** giving the fireplace mantel a third coat of paint.   progressive *be*, untensed

f. The fireplace mantel has **been** being given a third coat of paint.   progressive *be*, untensed

EXERCISE [9]

State which of the sentences in (45) are active and which are passive. Also, for each passive sentence, underline passive *be* (in order to be sure that you know how to distinguish progressive *be*, which is bolded in the examples in (45), from passive *be*). Hint: passive *be* is always followed by a past participle, as per (90) through (92) in Chapter 9.

EXERCISE [10]

Draw **surface structure trees** for the sentences in (45). Remember that for each passive sentence (there are three of them), you have to have a trace of movement of the deep structure object, like you see in (42).

10.2.5 summary of discussion on [+tns] and verb syntax

In this section, we've made progress on three important points: First, we saw that tense is syntactically represented, in the form of a [tns] feature, which is immediately dominated by S in our new PS rule in (17). This feature can either have a "plus value," i.e. [+tns], or a "minus value," i.e. [-tns]. The overt expression of the [-tns] feature is infinitival *to*. The overt expression of the [+tns] feature depends on the auxiliary verb in question. If a modal is present in the structure, then it is born in the [+tns] position. The auxiliaries *have* and *be*, on the other hand, are born within their own VPs. If there's a modal present, then by definition any following auxiliaries will be untensed and therefore do not move. However, if there is no modal present, then the left-most auxiliary will need to move to the [+tns] position.

Second, we established the fixed syntactic position of the negative markers *not* and *n't*, also seen in our new PS rule in (17). Like the [+tns] feature, NEG is immediately dominated by the S node. In terms of linear order, it occurs to the immediate right of [+tns]. We also saw that the negative marker serves as a very handy diagnostic for determining the position of the nonmodal auxiliaries. If the nonmodal is to the left of the negative marker, then we know it must be tensed.

Third, our revised VP rule in (35) captured the idea that the maximum string of verbs within a single S, repeated here (from Chapter 9), can be accommodated within the structure of the sentence:

(46)   Order of verbs:

      modals > aux *have* > progressive *be* > passive *be* > main verb

A sentence like the {7} in Exercise [7] (repeated here), which contains all five verbs seen in (46), can thus be accommodated:

(47)   The fireplace mantel should have been being given a third coat of paint.

For your reference, here's the structure, in (48):

(48)

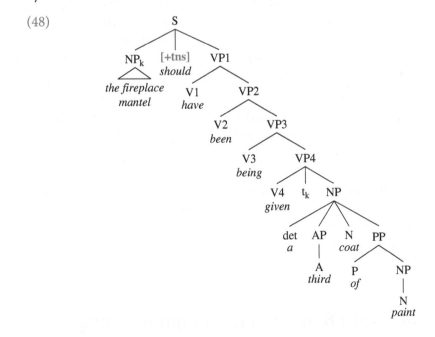

EXERCISE [11]

Draw **surface structure trees** for the sentences in (88) from Chapter 9.

10.2.6 ain't that something! auxiliaries *be* and *have* with *n't*

In Side Note 3 we talked about the modals in combination with the contracted form of the negative marker, namely *n't*. When combined with *n't*, the modals *will* and *shall* are unpredictably pronounced as *won't* and *shan't*. We say that these pronunciations are "unpredictable" because, for example, the string of sounds in *won't* isn't derived in any obvious way from the combination of *will* + *n't*. (See Term Box 4 for the concept of **pronunciation spell-out rules**.)

In this spirit, I want now to turn to the negated forms of the nonmodal auxiliaries *be* and *have*. These nonmodals also exhibit a negated form — in the present tense — which isn't predictable from any combination of the present tense forms plus *n't*. Let's take a closer look, starting with *be*.

English speakers worldwide commonly use the form *ain't* as a negated present tense form of *be*, for all persons and numbers. This is illustrated in the paradigm in (49), which you can compare with the affirmative present tense paradigm for *be* in (45) in Chapter 9:

(49) Present tense paradigm for negated *be* (both main verb and auxiliary verb)

	singular	**plural**
first person	MAIN VB: I **ain't** happy AUX: I **ain't** enjoying my Mustang	MAIN VB: We **ain't** happy AUX: We **ain't** enjoying our Mustang
second person	MAIN VB: You **ain't** happy AUX: You **ain't** enjoying your Mustang	MAIN VB: You **ain't** happy AUX: You **ain't** enjoying your Mustang
third person	MAIN VB: She **ain't** happy AUX: She **ain't** enjoying her Mustang	MAIN VB: They **ain't** happy AUX: They **ain't** enjoying their Mustang

This levelled paradigm contrasts with what we find for the affirmative present tense paradigm of *be* — the one without *n't*: as we saw in (45) in Chapter 9, it exhibits distinct forms in the first and third singular (*am* and *is*), compared with all the other persons and numbers, where we find yet another form, *are*.

Side Note 8: *n't* and paradigm levelling

In Side Note 14 in Chapter 9, we had a preview of this common phenomenon, **paradigm levelling in the presence of *n't***. Depending on the dialect and on the auxiliary verb, an otherwise nonlevelled paradigm will level when *n't* attaches to the verb. We'll see in Side Note 15 of this chapter that paradigm levelling in the presence of *n't* is in fact very common for the present tense paradigm of auxiliary *do* as well.

If we attempt to morphologically decompose the form *ain't*, we can certainly identify the *n't* part as the contracted form of the negative marker. But once we take away the *n't*, what we're left with is *ai-* (pronounced as the mid tense vowel [e], as in *pay*), which is not an obviously recognizable auxiliary verb by itself (see Term Box 3 for **morpheme**). But this is reminiscent of the case of *won't*. If we take away the *n't*, what we're left with is *wo-*, which by itself is not obviously a recognizable morpheme. In Side Note 3, I talked about a way around this problem, namely, a pronunciation spell-out rule that converts a predictable form into an unpredictable form.

For *won't*, we proposed something along the lines of the sketches in (24a) and (24b), namely, that we start with *will + n't*, which composes into *willn't*. But then a spell-out rule converts the predictable form *willn't* to the pronunciation *won't* (compare with (24)):

Pronunciation spell-out for *won't*:

(50)   *will + n't*   >   "willn't"   >   ***won't***

In a similar way, we could view *ain't* as the output of a pronunciation spell-out rule operating on the affirmative forms *am*, *is*, and *are* combined with *n't*, as follows:

Pronunciation spell-out for *ain't*:

(51)   a.   *am + n't*   >   "amn't"   >   ***ain't***   first person singular
     b.   *is + n't*   >   "isn't"   >   ***ain't***   third person singular
     c.   *are + n't*   >   "aren't"   >   ***ain't***   second sing; all plural numbers

The spell-out rules in (51) derive *ain't* from *amn't*, *isn't*, and *aren't*, just like the rule in (50) derives *won't* from *willn't*. But *ain't* is different in one important respect. You might have noticed that in (50), the pre-spell-out form *willn't* doesn't exist as an alternative to *won't*. However, in (51), the pre-spell-out forms *amn't*, *isn't*, and *aren't* actually do exist as variant forms of *ain't*. In fact, the grammar police out there who don't like the fact that we use *ain't* would claim that these pre-spell-out forms are the "correct" ones!

Side Note 9: Aren't I making you think about *amn't*?

There are actually many English speakers who don't have the first singular form *amn't* as part of their grammar:

{1}   *I amn't happy.

For these speakers, a first singular affirmative declarative like *I'm happy* or *I am happy* is negated either (i) by avoiding *n't*, as in {2}, or (ii) by using *ain't*, as in {3}:

{2}   I'm not happy. / I am not happy.
{3}   I ain't happy.

Interestingly, though, such speakers allow the form *aren't* for the first person singular, in **matrix interrogatives** (which we'll discuss in depth in Chapter 11), as in {4}:

{4}   Aren't I happy?

But for many of the speakers who allow {4}, the form *aren't* isn't grammatical in the corresponding declarative:

{5}   *I aren't happy.

What kind of speaker are <u>you</u>?

Side Note 10: Elephant in the room

As you might have noticed from our many examples, negated *be* (*isn't*, *aren't*, *ain't*) is usable as a main verb in addition to an auxiliary (take a look at (49)). We'll talk about main verb *be* shortly, when we talk about main verbs (Section 10.3). As a preview: main verb *be* is unique in being the only main verb which behaves like an auxiliary verb

Another important difference between *won't* and *ain't* is that the former serves as the negated form of only one auxiliary, namely, modal *will*. But for many speakers, *ain't* serves as the negated form of auxiliary *have* as well as auxiliary *be*. Think about what the negated forms of the following sentences with auxiliary *have* might be for you (see present tense paradigm for aux *have* in (7) in Chapter 9):

(52)   a.   I've worked out one time this week.
      b.   You've worked out one time this week.
      c.   Sue has worked out one time this week.
      d.   We've worked out one time this week.
      e.   You've worked out one time this week.
      f.   They've worked out one time this week.

Perhaps you thought of the following negated forms for auxiliary *have*:

(53)   a.   I haven't worked out one time this week.
      b.   You haven't worked out one time this week.
      c.   Sue hasn't worked out one time this week.
      d.   We haven't worked out one time this week.
      e.   You haven't worked out one time this week.
      f.   They haven't worked out one time this week.

But hopefully, this discussion about *ain't* also made you think of the following possibilities for auxiliary *have*:

(54)   a.   I ain't worked out one time this week.

   b.   You ain't worked out one time this week.

   c.   Sue ain't worked out one time this week.

   d.   We ain't worked out one time this week.

   e.   You ain't worked out one time this week.

   f.   They ain't worked out one time this week.

Side Note 11: What contracts?

There's another possibility for contraction of aux *have* with the subjects *I, you, Sue, we,* and *they* which doesn't involve *n't*. Instead, it involves *not* for the sentential negation. Compare {1a} through {1f} with (53) and (54):

{1}   a.   I've not worked out one time this week.

   b.   You've not worked out one time this week.

   c.   Sue's not worked out one time this week.

   d.   We've not worked out one time this week.

   e.   You've not worked out one time this week.

   f.   They've not worked out one time this week.

There is regional variation between the usage in {1} and that in (53) and (54): {1} is more common in the southern Appalachians and also in Britain. However, as is always the case with linguistic variation, individual speakers will vary in their use between (53)/(54) and {1}. How do the forms in {1} sound to you?

   This regional variation with aux *have* contrasts with *be*, where contraction of *am, is,* and *are* with the subjects *I, Sue,* and *we–you–they* followed by *not* is as regionally widespread as contraction of the aux with *n't*. Compare for example *Sue's not working out* with *Sue isn't working out*, or compare *They're not working out* with *They aren't working out*. Do these pairs sound as common to you as the pair *They've not worked out yet* and *They haven't worked out yet* ?

Not every speaker uses *ain't* as the negated form of aux *have*. However, if you do use *ain't*, you most definitely use it as the negated form of *be*. In other words, those speakers who use *ain't* for *be* may or may not use *ain't* for *have*; however, those speakers who use *ain't* for *have* definitely also use it for *be*. This kind of grammatical organization is sometimes referred to as a **unidirectional entailment**, which we can sketch out as follows:

(55) $ain't_{have}$ $\Rightarrow$ $ain't_{be}$

The **entailment** in (55) can be read like this: "If you use *ain't* for *have*, then you also use it for *be*, but not vice versa; so, if you use *ain't* for *be*, then it doesn't necessarily follow that you'll use it for *have*."

As we'll see in the following section, some speakers also use *ain't* as the negated form of auxiliary *did*, as in (56b):

(56) a. John **didn't** eat breakfast this morning. =

      b. John **ain't** eat breakfast this morning.

Those speakers who use *ain't* as a form of *didn't* also use *ain't* for *have* and for *be*. This means that the cross-dialectally, the entailment of usage is as follows:

(57) $ain't_{did}$ ⇒ $ain't_{have}$ ⇒ $ain't_{be}$

The entailment in (57) can be read like this: "If you use *ain't* for *did*, then you also use it for *have* and *be*; if you use *ain't* for *have*, then you also use it for *be*, but not necessarily for *did*; if you use *ain't* for *be*, then it doesn't necessarily follow that you'll use it for *have* or for *did*."

The entailment rule regarding *ain't* in (57) reveals that this auxiliary form has a remarkably organized behavior across dialects. Thus, far from being ungrammatical, it represents the quintessence of grammaticality: perfectly rule-governed.

10.3 main verbs: in a class by themselves

Our discussion in Section 10.2 on the syntactic expression of tense focused exclusively on auxiliary verbs (with the exception of main verb *be*). Now it's time to move to the topic of main verbs, which in Modern English have a completely different behavior from auxiliaries — except for main verb *be*! Let's see how.

We'll start by revisiting the position of the negative marker as a diagnostic for the position of verbs:

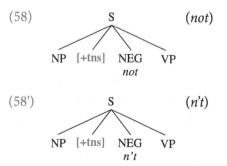

As we've already seen, modals always appear to the left of the negative marker (see (13) versus (15)/(16)), because they're always tensed. The auxiliaries *have* and *be* appear to the left of the negative marker when they're tensed (as in (19') and (41)), and to the right of the negative marker when they're untensed (as in (20') and (44)). All the main verbs we saw in Section 10.2 were untensed (with the exception of main verb *be*, which was sometimes tensed), so of course, they all appeared to the right of the negative marker. (To avoid repeating the statement "with the exception of main verb *be*," from here on my discussion of tensed main verbs will exclude main verb *be* until Section 10.3.1.)

But what about a structure with a tensed main verb? We haven't yet seen an example of negation with a sentence that contains only a main verb, like the following example:

(59)   John likes pizza.

I'll let you think for a moment of what the negated version of the affirmative sentence in (59) would be.

Now that you've thought about it, you've likely come up with the two possibilities in (60):

(60)   a. John does **not like** pizza.   (not > like)
       b. John does**n't like** pizza.   (n't > like)

That is, despite the fact that the main verb *likes* in (59) is tensed, unexpectedly, it doesn't appear to the left of the negative marker (*like > not). So the sentence in (61) is not what a Modern English speaker would commonly use as the **sententially negated** version of (59):

(61)   *John **likes not** pizza.

Side Note 12: Ignore constituent negation

Put aside any ideas you might have about (61) under a **constituent negation** interpretation, where *not* modifies *pizza*. See Term Box 2 for a refresher.

Thus, in contrast with the tensed auxiliary verbs in (40) and (42), the tensed main verb does not move to the [+tns] position. The surface structure tree in (63) depicts the fact that raising of the main verb is prohibited in Modern English, even when it's the only verb in the sentence and the sentence is [+tns]:

(62)   DEEP STRUCTURE:

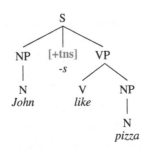

(63) INCORRECT SURFACE STRUCTURE (*John likes pizza*)

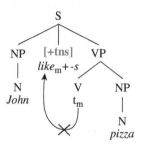

Side Note 13: *Ask not what your country can do for you...*

It's important to emphasize that movement of the main verb to the [+tns] position as in (63) is not in common use in Modern English. But if you've read any Shakespeare (Early Modern English) or Chaucer (Middle English), you'll know that main verb movement to the [+tns] position was once upon a time a rule of English grammar. In fact, even in modern times, speechmakers will sometimes use movement of the main verb to the [+tns] position for rhetorical effect, to sound compelling and erudite. Consider, for example, John F. Kennedy's famous speech, where he said "**Ask not** *what your country can do for you — ask what you can do for your country*" (ask > not). This movement of the main verb *ask* (which is part of an imperative sentence, as in Chapter 7) to the [+tns] position contrasts with lack of verb movement, in the corresponding **Do not ask** *what your country can do for you* (not > ask), which is not the sentence Kennedy chose for his speech. If you listen to speeches by Barack Obama, you'll notice that he frequently adopted this style of main verb movement to the [+tns] position.

For the remainder of this book, we'll gloss over the question of <u>why</u> the main verb differs from auxiliary verbs in this way in Modern English — though see Side Note 13 for commentary on historical English. For our purposes, let's just accept it as a point of fact that Modern English grammar doesn't allow raising of main verbs to the [+tns] position. (If you want the real story, you'll have to study more linguistics!)

10.3.1 affix lowering

But then how does our poor little inflectional marker *-s* join up with a verb, if not through verb movement as depicted in (63)?

The answer to this question depends on whether the sentence is affirmative (as in (59)) or negative (as in (60)). Let's start with (59).

The fact that the main verb cannot appear to the left of the negative marker (as in (61)) tells us that main verbs do not raise to the [+tns] position. Yet, in the affirmative sentence in (59), the inflectional suffix *-s* somehow makes its way onto the verb. It seems, then, that if we can't "raise the bridge," we must "lower the river." In other words, since the verb can't raise up, then the inflectional marker will have to lower down. This movement, known as **affix lowering**, is depicted in (64) (compare with the ungrammatical (63)).

(64) Affix lowering (CORRECT SURFACE STRUCTURE for *John likes pizza*)

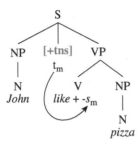

Term Box 5: Affixes

The term **affix** covers the concept of **prefixes** and **suffixes**. Since verbal *-s* is a suffix, the lowering operation could also have been called "suffix lowering." I've chosen the term "affix lowering" to remain consistent with the syntax literature.

As you can imagine, this affix lowering operation applies the **silent inflectional suffix** *-Ø* as well, which we saw depicted in the tree in (31). Recall that this silent inflectional suffix *-Ø* encodes the tense information that verbal *-s* encodes for the third singular, except it does so for all the other persons and numbers, i.e. first and second singular and all the persons of the plural. As such, at deep structure it resides in the [+tns] position, just like third singular *-s*. The examples in (65) and (66) illustrate the deep and surface structures for the sentence *They like pizza*, with the third person plural subject *they* and the agreeing third plural verb *like*, which the affix *-Ø* is suffixed to at surface structure:

DEEP STRUCTURE (*They like pizza*):

(65)

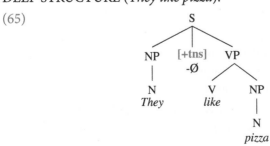

SURFACE STRUCTURE (*They like pizza*):

(66)

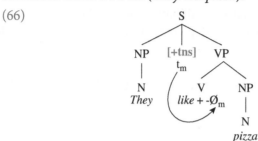

Similarly, affix lowering applies to past tense *-ed* when the only verb in the structure is a main verb. We saw *-ed* as the overt expression of [+tns] in (28). Now take a look at (67) and (68), which illustrates the deep and surface structures for the sentence *They liked the pizza*.

DEEP STRUCTURE (*They liked the pizza*):

(67)

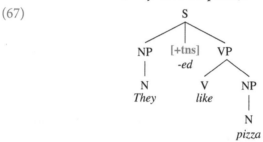

SURFACE STRUCTURE (*They liked the pizza*):

(68)

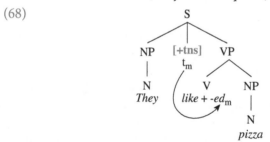

EXERCISE [12]

Using the trees in (64) through (68) as a guide, draw **surface structure trees** for the following sentences:

{1} Rick finished the mantel.
{2} Bill helps us out with difficult jobs.
{3} They ate their lunches in the afternoon.
{4} We drink our coffee in the morning.

I'm sure you can figure out {3}, if you keep in mind the discussion of pronunciation spell-out rules discussed in Term Box 4! (Hint: *eated*).

10.3.2 *do*-support

Now let's return to the negated versions of (59), seen in (60). If nothing else is stated, we should expect affix lowering to take place even in the presence of a negative marker, as in the sentence in (69), and in the corresponding tree in (70):

(69) *John **not likes** pizza.

SURFACE STRUCTURE TREE FOR THE UNGRAMMATICAL (69):

(70)

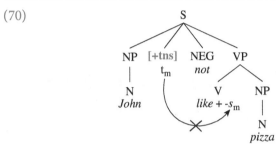

If we compare the ungrammatical tree in (70) with the grammatical tree in (64) for *John likes pizza* (which correctly captures lowering of the affix *-s*), the only difference between the two is the following: (70) contains the negative marker *not*, while (64) does not. Thus, for some reason, affix lowering cannot take place in the presence of the negative marker, as is confirmed by the ungrammatical (69).

Once again: for the remainder of this book, we'll gloss over the question of why the presence of the negative marker prevents affix lowering onto the main verb in this way. For our purposes, let's just accept it as a point of fact that English grammar doesn't allow it. (And once again, if you want the real story, you'll have to study more linguistics!)

But then how does our poor little inflectional marker *-s* join up with a verb, if not through affix lowering like in (70)? And if not through verb movement, as depicted in (63)?

As can be seen in (60) (repeated here), in order for the inflectional marker to have something to attach itself to, the [+tns] position is filled by the auxiliary verb *do*, which comes to the inflectional suffix's rescue:

(60) a. John **does** not like pizza.

  b. John **doesn't** like pizza.

Auxiliary *do* doesn't have any particular meaning in this structure. Rather, it's just a semantically empty verb which serves the function of "verbal material" that the suffixes *-s*, *-Ø*, and *-ed* can attach to. For this reason, this auxiliary is sometimes referred to as **dummy *do*** or **pleonastic *do***. The phenomenon seen in (60) is referred to as *do*-**insertion** or *do*-**support**.

Let's propose that *do* is not present at deep structure, but rather is inserted via the operation known as *do*-insertion. As such, the deep structure for the sentence in (60a) is as you see in (71).

DEEP STRUCTURE for (60a) (*John does not like pizza*)

(71)

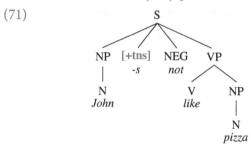

Side Note 14: An unpredictable spell-out

The pronunciation of *does* is unexpected. While *do* rhymes with *too*, when you add verbal -*s* to this verb, the quality of the vowel changes from [u] to [ə]. Thus, unpredictably, *does* doesn't rhyme with *dues*, but rather, with *fuzz*. Hence our transcription [dəz] in (73).

Once *do*-insertion takes place, we get the resulting surface structure:

SURFACE STRUCTURE for (60a) (*John does not like pizza*)

(72)

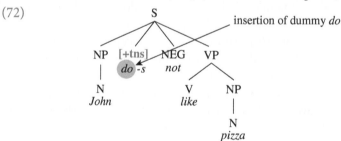

The verb *do* combined with the inflectional suffix -*s* is pronounced according to the following pronunciation spell-out rule:

(73)   *do* + -*s*   >   "do-s" [du + z]   >   ***does*** [dəz]

Keep in mind that this *do*-insertion operation also applies when there's a silent inflectional suffix -Ø, which I illustrated in the tree in (31). As we saw, this silent inflectional suffix -Ø encodes the tense information that verbal -*s* encodes for the third singular, except it does so for all the other persons and numbers, i.e. first and second singular, and all the persons of the plural (Chapter 8). The examples in (74) and (75) illustrate the deep and surface structures for the sentence *They don't like pizza*, with the third person plural subject *they* and the agreeing third plural aux *do*:

DEEP STRUCTURE (*They don't like pizza*):

(74)

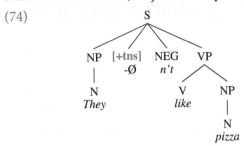

SURFACE STRUCTURE (*They don't like pizza*)

(75)

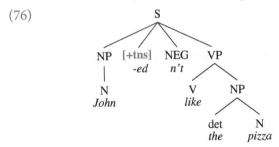

Similarly, *do*-insertion applies in the presence of the past tense suffix *-ed*, which was depicted for auxiliary *have* in (28) and (29). Take a look at (76) and (77):

DEEP STRUCTURE (*John didn't like the pizza*):

(76)

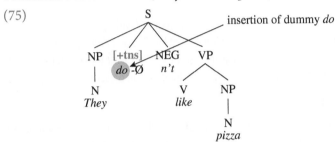

SURFACE STRUCTURE (*John didn't like the pizza*)

(77)

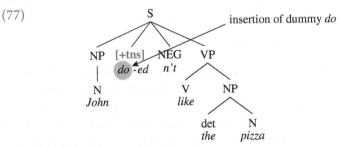

In (77), the verb *do* combined with the inflectional suffix *-ed* is pronounced according to the following pronunciation spell-out rule:

(78) *do + -ed* > "do-ed" [du + d] > ***did*** [dɪd]

Side Note 15: Levelling in the presence of *n't*

In Section 10.2.6, we talked about *ain't* as the a levelled negated auxiliary that stands in for the verb *be*, and for some speakers, for the verb *have*, and for some speakers still — also for auxiliary *do*, as in {1}:

{1}   John ain't eat breakfast this morning. (= John didn't eat breakfast this morning)

Interestingly, *ain't* as the negated form of auxiliary *do* is only used for the past tense form, *didn't*. This contrasts with *ain't* as the negated form of *be* and aux *have*, which can only be used for the present tense (*isn't, aren't, amn't, hasn't,* and *haven't*), as in (51) and (54).

It is very common in English, no matter what the regional variety, to level negated aux *do* in the present tense, to the form *don't*. This use of levelled aux *don't* (present tense) is far more common across Englishes than the use of levelled *ain't* for past tense *didn't*. Consider the following example with *don't* in the third person present tense singular:

{2}   He don't like pizza.

The form *don't* in {2} is considered to be part of a levelled paradigm for present tense *do*, because in contrast with third person present tense *doesn't*, it's identical to the form used for the first and second singular, and all the persons of the plural. Note that many speakers who level to *don't* (i.e. in the presence of *n't*) exhibit nonlevelled *does* in the affirmative:

{3}   He DOES like pizza!

10.3.3 the beauty of the hypotheses put forth in this chapter

Let's stop and smell the roses here to appreciate two facts of English syntax that the analysis of [+tns] allows us to capture very neatly.

First, think about the fact that in the affirmative sentence in (79a), the tensed main verb is *liked* (i.e. in the past tense), but in the corresponding negative sentence in (79b), the main verb is untensed *like* (i.e. a bare infinitive):

(79)   a.   John **liked** the pizza.   (cf. (68))

        b.   John didn't **like** the pizza.   (cf. (77))

This difference between the affirmative (tensed *liked*) and the negative (untensed *like*) in (79a) and (79b) follows directly from the idea that the inflectional marker *-ed* resides in the [+tns] head at deep structure, as depicted in the trees in (67) and (76). When the sentence is affirmative, as in (79a), the suffix *-ed* lowers to join up with the main verb *like*, as we already saw in the surface structure tree in (68). The result is a combination of *like* + *-ed*, spelled out as the tensed main verb *liked*. However, when the sentence is negative, the negative marker prevents affix lowering. As such, the suffix *-ed* stays put, and *do*-insertion takes place, as we saw in the surface structure tree in (77). Thus, without the following three hypotheses, it would be difficult to explain why the verb is tensed *liked* in (79a) but untensed *like* in (79b):

(80) a. **Hypothesis 1:** there is a [+tns] position inside S;

     b. **Hypothesis 2:** the inflectional marker is the overt instantiation of [+tns] (when there's no modal);

     c. **Hypothesis 3:** the suffix lowers to the verb in (68) but stays put when there's a negative marker, as in (77).

Second, think about the fact that we still get *do*-support with main verbs, even in the absence of an overt inflectional marker like *-s* or *-ed*. Compare (81a) and (81b):

(81) a. They like pizza.   (*like* is tensed)

     b. They do not like pizza (cf. the trees in   (*like* is untensed)
        (74)/(75))

As we said earlier, auxiliary *do* doesn't contribute any meaning (hence the term "dummy *do*"). So if it doesn't add any meaning, why is it inserted in (81b)? Why isn't the negative counterpart of (81a) simply what we see in (81c)?

(81) c. *They not like pizza.   (*like* is tensed)

Without the following two hypotheses, it would be difficult to explain why the auxiliary *do* has to be inserted in (81b) (and thus, why (81c) is ungrammatical):

(82) a. **Hypothesis 4:** even in the absence of an overt tense marker like *-s* and *-ed*, if the sentence is tensed (and there is no modal), there is a silent inflectional suffix -Ø in the [+tns] position, encoding the tense features for those persons and numbers where the verb doesn't have an overt marker;

     b. **Hypothesis 5:** dummy *do* is inserted in the structure when the inflectional suffix cannot lower to the main verb (i.e. in the presence of a negative marker), even if the inflectional suffix is silent -Ø.

Thus, the fact that *do* is inserted in (81b) proves that even a **silent suffix** needs a word to attach to — which in turn proves that the silent suffix exists. If it didn't, there would be no reason to insert *do* in (81b), and (81c) should be grammatical. The silent suffix also distinguishes between tensed *like* in (81a) (i.e. *like* + -Ø, which is spelled out as the tensed main verb *like*), and untensed *like* in (81b), which has no inflectional suffix, silent or otherwise. This analysis can help you understand our discussion back in Section 8.2.1.1 when we distinguished between the present tense verb form for the first and second singular and all the persons of the plural on the one hand (*like*), and the bare infinitive (*like*), on the other.

EXERCISE [13]

Explain why each of the following sentences is ungrammatical. Hint: two of the sentences have the same reason for their ungrammaticality (see (81c)).

{1} *They not eat their lunches until the late afternoon.
{2} *John likesn't pizza.
{3} *John -s not like pizza.
{4} *John not wants the pizza.

EXERCISE [14]

Using all the examples in this section as a guide, draw **deep** and **surface structure trees** for the following sentences:

{1} Bill doesn't want to leave us in a lurch.
{2} They don't eat their lunches until the late afternoon.
{3} I don't drink coffee before 10:00 a.m.
{4} They ate their lunch at 3:30 p.m.
{5} They didn't eat their lunch until 3:30 p.m.
{6} They don't do homework on Sundays.

10.3.4 main verb *do*

Now, it's important to not confuse auxiliary *do* with main verb *do*, the latter of which we had a preview of in example (5a) in Chapter 9. The examples in (83) illustrate the verb *do* in its main verb capacity:

(83)   a.   They do their homework every night.

　　　b.   Mary does her homework every night.

The verb *do* in its main verb use means something like "to engage in" or "to work at" or "to make," and like any main verb, it can stand as the only verb in a sentence (like in (83)). This contrasts with auxiliary *do*, which doesn't have any meaning, and which exists alongside a main verb. Furthermore, we can show that syntactically, main verb *do* behaves just like all other tensed main verbs: it cannot appear to the left of the negative marker *not*. Compare (83) with (84):

(84)   a.   *They **do not** their homework every night.   (*do_{main} > not)

　　　b.   *They **don't** their homework every night.   (*do_{main} > n't)

　　　c.   *Mary **does not** her homework every night.   (*$does_{main}$ > not)

　　　d.   *Mary **doesn't** her homework every night.   (*$does_{main}$ > n't)

The sentences in (84) are ungrammatical for the same reason that (61) is ungrammatical (*John **likes not** pizza): tensed main verbs do not move to the [+tns] position. As with every other tensed main verb, when there is a negative marker in the structure with main verb *do*, then *do*-insertion must take place, as in (85) (compare with (83)):

(85)   a. They **do not do** their homework every night.   (do$_{aux}$ > not)
       b. They **don't do** their homework every night.   (do$_{aux}$ > n't)
       c. Mary **does not do** her homework every night.   (does$_{aux}$ > not)
       d. Mary **doesn't do** her homework every night.   (does$_{aux}$ > n't)

EXERCISE [15]: The do's and don'ts of *do* and *do*

To make sure you understand the difference between auxiliary *do* and main verb *do*, identify which is which in the sentences in (85), and draw **deep** and **surface structure trees** for (85a) and (85c).

10.3.5 main verb *be*

It's finally time to talk explicitly about the unusual behavior of main verb *be*, which I've been hinting at all along, but which we have yet to investigate in full force.

As we've already seen, the tensed auxiliary verbs *have* and *be* differ from all tensed main verbs: the former exhibit verb movement to the [+tns] position, while the latter do not. In (84), we saw ungrammatical examples of main verb *do* to the left of the negative marker, confirming that main verbs don't raise to the [+tns] position. For American English speakers, this is true even for main verb *have* (86b,c) which differs from auxiliary *have* (86a), precisely in not exhibiting verb movement:

(86)   a. John **has not** eaten his pizza.   (has$_{aux}$ > not)
       b. *John **has not** the pizza with him.   (*has$_{main}$ > not)
       c. *John **hasn't** the pizza with him.

In (86b,c), we see that despite the verb movement behavior of auxiliary *have* in (86a), American English speakers treat tensed main verb *have* as a completely different kind of syntactic entity. Thus, the **categorial** difference between aux *have* and main verb *have* is syntactically real to many English speakers. Main verb *have* appears to the right of *not* (and requires *do*-support), just like any other main verb:

(87)   a. John has the pizza with him.
       b. John does **not have** the pizza with him.   (have$_{main}$ > not)

This means that even in the sentence in (87a) (without *not*) we get affix lowering onto the verb *have*, which stays put in its deep structure position heading its own VP.

EXERCISE [16]

Draw **surface structure trees** for (86a) and (87a), and a **deep** and **surface structure tree** for (87b).

Side Note 16: *I haven't the time for this*

In the text, I'm emphasizing <u>American English</u> speakers, because there are other Englishes worldwide where main verb *have* has the same syntax as auxiliary *have*, just like main verb *be*, as we'll see immediately!

But the verb *be* is different. In contrast with *have* — where we make a syntactic distinction between its main verb versus its auxiliary verb incarnation — tensed *be* always behaves like an auxiliary verb, **even when it's a main verb**. Let's take another look at some examples we've already seen throughout this chapter and Chapter 9:

(88)   a.   Sue **is** my favorite colleague.   main verb
       b.   Sue **is** working very hard these days.   auxiliary verb

If we negate both of these sentences, we see that the tensed verb must appear to the left of the negative marker, in both cases:

(89)   a.   Sue **is not** my favorite colleague.   main verb *be*   (is > not)
       a'. *Sue **not is** my favorite colleague.   main verb *be*   (*not > is)
       b.   Sue **is not** working very hard   auxiliary verb *be*   (is > not)
            these days.
       b'. *Sue **not is** working very hard   auxiliary verb *be*   (*not > is)
            these days.

We expect this syntax for tensed auxiliary *be*, but it's surprising to find it with tensed main verb *be*, given that no other main verb in English has this auxiliary-like property. Note that this property of main verb *be* is also what allows us to use *ain't* as a main verb, when it stands in for *be*:

(90)   a.   Sue **ain't** my favorite colleague   main verb *be*
       b.   Sue **ain't** working very hard these days.   auxiliary verb *be*

This contrasts with *have*: *ain't* can only be used in place of aux *have* (91b) but not main verb *have* (91a):

(91)   a.   *John **ain't** the pizza with him.   *main verb *have*
            (cf. (86b,c))

       b.   John **ain't** made dinner yet.   auxiliary verb *have*
            (cf. (86a) and (54))

This is consistent with what we see for aux *have* versus main verb *have* in (86) and (87).

To conclude: of all the verbs we've talked about in this book, the only main verb in English that has the syntactic behavior of an auxiliary verb is *be*.

Side Note 17: *We needn't cover everything in a single book*

There are other kinds of verbs (besides the nine modals, aux *have* and *be*, and the main verbs) which we haven't covered in this book. For example, there's the verb *need*, which is ambiguous between a main verb (as in {1}) and what is called a **semi-modal**, as in {2}:

{1}   They need a break from work.   main V
{2}   They need to fix the sink.   semi-modal

The verb *need* in {1} exhibits exactly the syntactic behavior you would expect from a main verb; witness {3} and {4}:

{3}   They do**n't need** a break.   (not > need)
{4}   *They **needn't** a break   (*need > not)

Semi-modal *need* is a bit trickier, though. Depending on the speaker, it can act like a main verb (as in {5}), or like an aux (as in {6}):

{5}   They do**n't need** to fix the sink.   (not > need)
{6}   They **needn't** fix the sink.   (need > not)

The sentence in {6} is further complicated by the fact that embedded infinitival *to* goes missing when there's no *do*-support (compare with the example with *do*-support in {5}, where we have *to fix* instead of simply *fix*).

What all of this shows is that English syntax is endlessly interesting, with many, many more phenomena to be understood than this book has been able to cover. As I've already said a few times in this chapter, the only remedy is to study more linguistics!

EXERCISE [17]: *be* vs. *have*

To make sure you understand the difference between *be* (aux or main verb) on the one hand, and aux *have* vs. main verb *have* on the other: draw **surface structure trees** for the sentences in {1} through {5}.

{1} Rick has finished his work for now.
{2} Walter has very strong skills.
{3} They're very good at their jobs.
{4} Bill is running a very good business.
{5} Walter had another job which called him away.

10.4 conclusions

This chapter saw important revisions to the phrase structure rules for S and for VP, as follows:

(92) CP   →   C   S

S   →   NP [±tns] (NEG) VP

NP   → $\begin{Bmatrix} (det) \\ (PossNP) \end{Bmatrix}$ (AP*) N $\begin{Bmatrix} (PP*) \\ (CP) \end{Bmatrix}$

PossNP → $\begin{Bmatrix} (det) \\ (PossNP) \end{Bmatrix}$ (AP*) PossN $\begin{Bmatrix} (PP*) \\ (CP) \end{Bmatrix}$

VP   →   V (VP) (PP) (NP) $\begin{Bmatrix} (NP) \\ (S) \\ (CP) \end{Bmatrix}$ (AP) (PP*)

PP   →   (mod) P $\begin{Bmatrix} (NP) \\ (PP) \end{Bmatrix}$

AP   →   (deg) A

This revision to the S rule is the culmination of the work we front-loaded in Chapters 8 and 9, which was all leading up to this conclusion. This is perhaps the single most exciting thing about the complexity of English verb syntax: all of the facts regarding main verbs, auxiliary verbs, negation, and verb word order lead to the conclusion that at the heart of the sentence, we have [±tns]. You can read up on the origins of the ideas discussed in this chapter in Emonds (1976) and Pollock (1989).

How can something so small and abstract as a mere **feature** be big enough and important enough to be at the heart of our most major phrase? This is a question that you'll ask yourself less and less, as the reality sets in. There is no turning back on all of the conclusions that the many facts discussed in these last three chapters have led us to: all roads lead to Rome. In the first section of Chapter 11, we'll see how this conclusion (i.e. that [±tns] is at the heart of S) finally allows us to propose that S, just like all the other phrases, has a head.

list of terms/concepts

affix lowering
agreement (subject–verb agreement)
ain't
auxiliary contraction
auxiliary verb syntax vs. main verb
   syntax
case feature
categorial
constituent negation
deep structure
do-support (*do*-insertion; dummy
   do)
double-object construction
entailment (unidirectional
   entailment)
features
finite (tensed)
gender
infinitival sentence
inflectional suffix (-*s*, -*ed*, -Ø)
interpretation
main verb *be* as aux
matrix interrogative
morphology (morphemes; monomorphemic; bimorphemic)
movement rules
negation (sentential negation;
   negating a proposition; reversing
   truth value)

negative marker
nonfinite
number
paradigm levelling in the presence
   of *n't*
passive movement operation
person
pleonastic *do* (dummy *do*)
prefix
pronunciation spell-out rules
   (predictable pronunciation;
   unpredictable pronunciation)
proposition
recursion (VP recursion)
recursive
semi-modal
sentential negation (vs. constituent
   negation)
silent inflectional suffix
surface structure
syntactic expression of tense
tense
tense feature ([±tns])
tense head
time of utterance
truth value
untensed (nonfinite)
verb movement (verb raising)
word order

references

Emonds, Joseph E. (1976). *A Transformational Approach to Syntax: Root, Structure-preserving, and Local Transformations*. New York: Academic Press.

Pollock, Jean-Yves (1989). "Verb movement, universal grammar, and the structure of IP," *Linguistic Inquiry* 20(3): 365–424.

11 Unfinished Business

expected outcomes for this chapter

- You'll deepen your understanding of structural complexity and recognize and manipulate much greater subtleties of hierarchical structure.
- You'll gain an understanding of the consequences of the many proposals put forth throughout the previous 10 chapters.
- You'll become familiar with *adverbs*.
- You'll develop more confidence with the concepts from previous chapters (e.g., phrase structure, sentence structure, word order, hierarchical structure, interrogatives, movement, *do*-support, binary branching).
- You'll become familiar with the following terms and concepts: *verb movement, negation, negative phrase* (NegP), *tense head, tense phrase* (TP), *matrix questions,* do-support in matrix questions, *V-to-T movement, T-to-C movement, head-to-head movement, phrasal movement, bar-levels, projections, intermediate projection, maximal projection, landing sites, binary branching, X-bar theory, adverb phrase* (AdvP), *adverb.*

11.1 overview

This book started with a very basic concept: the sentence can be parsed into two major constituents, namely the subject NP and the VP. We've come a long way since this simple idea in Chapter 1, in our exploration of how complex these major sentential constituents can become. In the process, we've learned about the complexity of other phrases (PP, AP, CP); we've learned how to model movement operations; we've learned how to relate surface structure with deep structure; we've learned how to identify silent elements

Understanding Sentence Structure: An Introduction to English Syntax, First Edition.
Christina Tortora.
© 2018 John Wiley & Sons, Inc. Published 2018 by John Wiley & Sons, Inc.

in grammar; we've learned how to model the ways in which English speakers interpret tenses and how the morphological forms of verbs interact with other elements in the syntax to create such interpretations; we've learned about features and agreement; and we've learned how to test the predictions of particular hypotheses in order to see if our analyses are on the right track (among many other things). In addition, we gained a greater appreciation of the linguistic details particular to English grammar, and also a greater appreciation of grammatical variation across Englishes worldwide.

Expectedly, though, the more complex things become, the more that further questions arise. In this sense, this book is just the beginning. The various aspects of syntax that we've explored have led us to a number of outstanding questions that you can pursue in your future studies. In this chapter I'll cover just a few of these outstanding questions, with an eye towards preparing you for your next step in your journey.

In Section 11.2 we'll see how our analysis of tense as a syntactic entity in Chapter 10 leads us to completely reanalyze the sentence itself. In particular, we'll see that — contrary to what we've assumed until now — S is like every other phrase in that it, too, has a head.

Also, you might have been wondering why in Chapter 5 I never talked about **matrix interrogatives** when I first introduced you to Yes–No and wh-questions. (In that chapter, we only discussed **embedded interrogatives**.) In Section 11.3 you'll see how *do*-support comes into play here, and therefore why I wanted to wait until after Chapter 10 to talk about this.

Then, our foray into matrix questions will lead us to a whole new way of looking at phrase structure in Section 11.4. This new way of looking at phrase structure won't dispense with the concept of PS rules, so much as build on them in such a way as to make them much simpler. This simpler format for PS rules will in turn make it easier to talk about the one lexical category we haven't yet covered, namely, the **adverb**.

11.2 tense as the head of S

Let's revisit our phrase structure rules in order to take stock of an outstanding question which we're now in a position to address. Here are all the PS rules with their latest revisions, in (1):

(1) Phrase Structure Rules:

   a. CP   →   C S

   b. S   →   NP [±tns] (NEG) VP

   c. NP   → $\left\{ \begin{array}{l} \text{(det)} \\ \text{(PossNP)} \end{array} \right\}$ (AP*) N $\left\{ \begin{array}{l} \text{(PP*)} \\ \text{(CP)} \end{array} \right\}$

   d. PossNP   → $\left\{ \begin{array}{l} \text{(det)} \\ \text{(PossNP)} \end{array} \right\}$ (AP*) PossN $\left\{ \begin{array}{l} \text{(PP*)} \\ \text{(CP)} \end{array} \right\}$

   e. VP   →   V (VP) (PP) (NP) $\left\{ \begin{array}{l} \text{(NP)} \\ \text{(S)} \\ \text{(CP)} \end{array} \right\}$ (AP) (PP*)

f. PP   →   (mod) P $\begin{Bmatrix} (NP) \\ (PP) \end{Bmatrix}$

g. AP   →   (deg) A

Side Note 1:

In the PS rules in (1), there are only three terminal nodes in addition to [±tns] (besides the heads C, N, PossN, V, P, and A). However, note that — in contrast with [±tns] — these are all **optional**: (*det*) inside NP & PossNP; (*mod*) inside PP; and (*deg*) inside AP.

As you know very well by now, each **phrase** is named for its **head**: the phrase headed by N is an NP; the phrase headed by V is a VP; and so on. The list in (2) gives an account of the head for each of the phrases in (1), which is the one obligatory **terminal node** (Chapter 2, Term Box 4) in the phrase:

(2)   a.   CP is headed by C

       b.   **S is headed by ?**

       c.   NP is headed by N

       d.   PossNP is headed by PossN

       e.   VP is headed by V

       f.   PP is headed by P

       g.   AP is headed by A

Term Box 1

Important reminder: Every phrase has one **obligatory terminal node**. This is always the phrase's **head**.

Thus, as we already noted in Term Box 6 in Chapter 2, the phrase we call "S" — the sentence itself — is the only phrase in our list of rules in (1) for which we haven't identified a head.

On the one hand, we might just accept it as a fact of nature not to be questioned, that S doesn't have a head. On the other hand, the fact that all the other phrases have heads should make us suspicious: why should S be any different? It is, after all, a phrase. And furthermore, like every other phrase, S contains one terminal node which is obligatory, namely [±tns].

Since the definition of a head is "the one obligatory terminal node inside a phrase" (Term Box 1), then it follows that **the head of S must be [±tns]**:

(2')   a.   CP is headed by C

       b.   **S is headed by [±tns]**

  c. NP is headed by N

  d. PossNP is headed by PossN

  e. VP is headed by V

  f. PP is headed by P

  g. AP is headed by A

This logical conclusion has led researchers in syntax to abandon the short-hand label "S" for the sentence. Instead — to remain consistent with labels like "noun phrase" (NP), "verb phrase" (VP), etc. — syntacticians started to use the label **tense phrase**, and **TP** for short, as the new label for the **sentence**. This is illustrated in the PS rules in (3):

(3) REVISED Phrase Structure Rules:

  a. CP   → C TP

  b. **TP**   → NP [±tns] (NEG) VP

  c. NP   → $\left\{ \begin{array}{l} \text{(det)} \\ \text{(PossNP)} \end{array} \right\}$ (AP*) N $\left\{ \begin{array}{l} \text{(PP*)} \\ \text{(CP)} \end{array} \right\}$

  d. PossNP → $\left\{ \begin{array}{l} \text{(det)} \\ \text{(PossNP)} \end{array} \right\}$ (AP*) PossN $\left\{ \begin{array}{l} \text{(PP*)} \\ \text{(CP)} \end{array} \right\}$

  e. VP   → V (VP) (PP) (NP) $\left\{ \begin{array}{l} \text{(NP)} \\ \text{(TP)} \\ \text{(CP)} \end{array} \right\}$ (AP) (PP*)

  f. PP   → (mod) P $\left\{ \begin{array}{l} \text{(NP)} \\ \text{(PP)} \end{array} \right\}$

  g. AP   → (deg) A

Side Note 2: The development of phrase structure theory

Historically, phrase structure theorists started out in the 1950s using the label "S" for the sentence. Then in the 1980s, syntacticians moved to the label **IP**, for "inflectional phrase." The convention then subsequently shifted from use of the label IP, to use of the label TP. The switch from IP to TP was driven by the idea that **inflection** encompasses not only **tense**, but also **agreement**. This also led to the theory that there is an "agreement phrase" (**AgrP**) inside the sentence. The twists and turns of the history of phrase structure theory involves a fascinating and complex story that you can learn about in an advanced syntax course!

And let's just fix one last detail, so that our TP rule remains completely consistent with our other rules: the head of TP is T, which we know will always be expressed as either [+tns] or [-tns]:

(3b')   TP   →   NP T (NEG) VP

Given this new label, we can now draw the deep structure and surface structure trees of any sentence (such as (71) and (72) in Chapter 10, *John does not like pizza*) as follows:

DEEP STRUCTURE: SURFACE STRUCTURE:

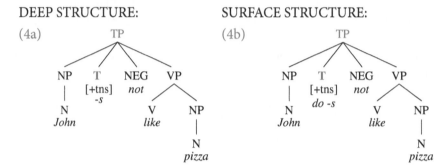

For now, nothing has changed except the label we're using for the sentence, which is now TP instead of S. However, as we'll see in Section 11.4, the phrase structure trees you see in (4a) and (4b) — and in fact everywhere else in this book — will also be revised, in light of yet another new consideration. In order to understand that consideration, let's turn to the question of matrix interrogatives in Section 11.3.

11.3 matrix interrogatives

In Chapter 5 we explored the syntax of **embedded Yes–No questions** and **wh-questions**. As a brief review, consider the examples in (5) and (6). The former contains embedded Yes–No questions, and the latter contains embedded wh-questions (underlined):

(5) a. Mary wonders <u>if Sue is a good surgeon</u>.   word order: *Sue > is*

    b. Mary wonders <u>whether Sue is a good surgeon</u>. word order: *Sue > is*

(6) a. Bill wondered <u>what Sue would fix</u>.   word order: *Sue > would*

    b. Bill wondered <u>when Sue would fix the sink</u>. word order: *Sue > would*

You'll also recall that the embedded Yes–No questions we analyzed didn't involve any movement operations particular to interrogatives. The embedded wh-questions, though, involved movement of the wh-phrase to the C position within CP. In (7) and (8) I provide surface structure trees for (5a) and (6a) as a refresher. Note that these surface structure trees look a bit different from those in Chapter 5 because I'm using all of our newfangled tools from Chapters 9 and 10 (and also those we've added in this chapter), such as **affix lowering**, **verb movement**, the **T position**, and the label **TP** (in place of S). But also note that nothing is different from Chapter 5 in terms of the analysis specific to embedded interrogatives.

SURFACE STRUCTURE FOR (5a) (*Mary wonders if Sue is a good surgeon*):

(7)

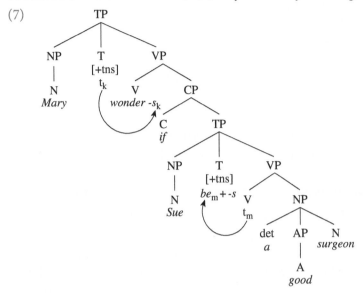

SURFACE STRUCTURE FOR (6a) (*Bill wondered what Sue would fix*):

(8)

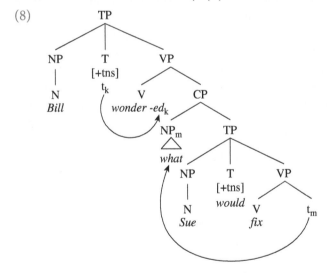

So that's the story for **embedded interrogatives**, for many English speakers. See Side Note 5 for syntactic variation in this regard, though.

But **matrix interrogatives** are a different story for many English speakers. I had held off talking about matrix interrogatives because we first needed to establish some principles about verb forms and verb movement — something which wasn't necessary in order to understand the behavior of embedded interrogatives in Chapter 5. Now that we've covered all of that in Chapters 8 through 10, we're able to fully appreciate the difference between embedded and matrix questions.

To understand the difference, compare the word order you see in the underlined strings in (5) and (6) with the word order you see in the examples in (9) and (10). In particular, pay attention to the position of the subject NP, in relation to the tensed verb:

Yes–No question:

(9) a. **Is Sue** a good surgeon?   word order: *is > Sue*

   b. **Would Sue** fix the sink?   word order: *would > Sue*

Wh-question:

(10) a. What **is Sue** doing?   word order: *is > Sue*

   b. What **would Sue** fix?   word order: *would > Sue*

11.3.1 matrix yes–no questions: the landing site for the tensed aux

Let's start with an examination of Yes–No questions. If you compare the embedded Yes–No questions in (5) and the matrix Yes–No questions in (9), you'll see that while the former involve the expected word order between subject and tensed aux, (*Sue > is*), the latter involves a change in this order (*is > Sue*; *would > Sue*). This switch in word order in matrix questions is sometimes referred to as **subject–auxiliary inversion**, because it's as if these two constituents invert their order.

So what exactly is subject–aux inversion, syntactically speaking? It's an example of a **verb movement operation**. In Chapter 10 we discussed at length the phenomenon of auxiliary verb movement to the [+tns] position. The example in (11) is a refresher; again, note that the tree here looks a bit different from those in Chapter 10 because of our newfangled proposal that S is TP:

SURFACE STRUCTURE:

(11)   *Rick has given the mantel a third coat of paint.*

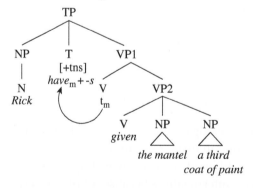

Chapter 10 only talked about the kind of verb movement we see in (11), namely, movement of the leftmost auxiliary *have* or *be* (and also main verb *be*) to the [+tns] position (when there is no modal). But the interrogatives you see in (9) and (10) exemplify another kind of verb movement. In this kind of movement, the auxiliary in the [+tns] position moves further up, to a position to the left of the subject. A first-pass sketch of this second movement is illustrated in (12), where I label this particular brand of movement "movement #2":

FIRST-PASS AT AN ANALYSIS OF THE SURFACE STRUCTURE

(12)   *Is Sue a good surgeon?*

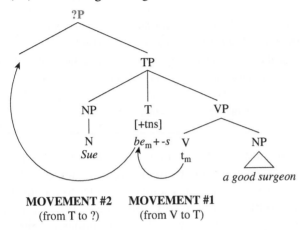

MOVEMENT #2	MOVEMENT #1
(from T to ?)	(from V to T)

Side Note 3

Recall from Chapter 10 that main verb *be* has the syntactic behavior of an auxiliary. So from now on, when I say "auxiliary verb," keep in mind that I mean "auxiliary verbs and main verb *be*."

But what is this position to the left of the subject to which the verb moves? Given that CP is the only phrase that's higher than TP, it makes sense to pursue the idea that ?P in (12) is none other than CP. This is illustrated in (13):

SURFACE STRUCTURE

(13)   *Is Sue a good surgeon?*

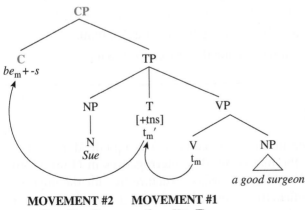

MOVEMENT #2	MOVEMENT #1
(from T to C)	(from V to T)

Term Box 2

You'll notice in (13) that the two movements leave two different traces, the lowest t_m, and the **intermediate trace** t_m'. They have the same index because they are both traces of the moved constituent be_m. To distinguish these two traces, syntacticians use the prime symbol. Thus, we would call the lowest trace in (13) "t-m," and the intermediate trace "t-m-prime." Don't confuse the concept of an intermediate trace with the concept of an **intermediate bar-level**, which I talk about in Section 11.3.2.1.

Thus, subject–auxiliary inversion, which is exhibited in matrix Yes–No questions, is simply a kind of verb movement. To distinguish movement #1 from movement #2 seen in (13), syntacticians sometimes refer to the former as **V-to-T movement**, and to the latter as **T-to-C movement**. When you do Exercise [1] below, you'll be reminded that modals do not undergo a movement #1 (because they're born in the T position).

It doesn't matter how many auxiliary verbs there are in a string: it will always be the tensed aux (i.e. the leftmost one) that moves to C. You can verify this with the examples in (14) through (17) (where in the interrogative, the underscore __ indicates the T position from which the leftmost aux moved):

(14)   a.   John **has** left.
         b.   **Has** John __ left?

(15)   a.   John **could** have left.
         b.   **Could** John __ have left?
         c.   *Have John **could** left?

(16)   a.   John **could** have been leaving by now.
         b.   **Could** John __ have been leaving by now?
         c.   *Have John **could** been leaving by now?
         d.   *Been John **could** have leaving by now?

(17)   a.   John **has** been leaving the office at 7:00 p.m. for years.
         b.   **Has** John __ been leaving the office at 7:00 p.m.?
         c.   *Been John **has** leaving the office at 7:00 p.m.?

EXERCISE [1]

Using the discussion in this section and (13) as a guide, draw surface structure trees for the matrix Yes–No interrogatives in (14b), (15b), (16b), and (17b). Also, draw a surface structure tree for the ungrammatical (17c) to confirm that untensed auxiliaries (i.e. auxiliaries not in the [+tns] position) do not move to C.

11.3.1.1 *Do*-support in T-to-C movement

It's time to get back to *do*-support, which we discussed in Section 10.3.2 in the context of **negated declaratives** like those in (18):

(18)   a.   John **does** not like pizza.

       b.   John **does**n't like pizza.

Compare (18a,b) with the corresponding non-negated version of these sentences in (18c):

(18)   c.   John likes pizza.

As you'll recall, **dummy** *do* is inserted in the presence of a negative marker (*not* or *n't*) because in NEG's presence, the inflectional marker is prevented from joining up with the main verb below via affix lowering. (And as we know, the main verb never raises to the [+tns] position.) Thus, in order for the inflectional marker to have something to attach itself to, the [+tns] position is filled by the auxiliary verb *do*, which comes to the inflectional suffix's rescue. This "dummy" is just a semantically empty aux which serves the function of verbal material that the suffixes -*s*, -Ø, and -*ed* can attach to.

As in fact we saw in Chapter 5, English also exhibits *do*-support in matrix interrogatives, whenever there's no auxiliary in the sentence (cf. (36) in Chapter 5):

(19)   a.   **Did** Mary devour the pizza?

       b.   What **did** Mary devour?

Compare (19a,b) with the corresponding declarative version of these sentences in (19c):

(19)   c.   Mary devoured the pizza.

Let's go through the different features of our analysis of sentence structure which lead to the logical consequence that T-to-C movement gives rise to *do*-support (as in (19a) and (19b)), when there is no other auxiliary verb in the sentence. We'll focus just on Yes–No questions for now.

First, as we just saw in (13) through (17), T-to-C movement entails that some aux inside the [+tns] position moves to the C position. Thus, when an aux is present in a structure, T-to-C movement operates on a <u>surface structure</u> which already has an aux in the [+tns] position — whether that aux got into that position by being born there (like a modal) or via V-to-T movement (as happens with aux *have* and *be*).

However, in the case of a declarative like that in (19c), which corresponds to the interrogatives in (19a) and (19b), there is no aux in the [+tns] position. Instead, recall from Chapter 10 that in the deep structure of a declarative sentence like (19c), the affix in the [+tns] position (be it -*s* or -Ø or -*ed*) lowers to the verb. I recap this in (20) and (21):

DEEP STRUCTURE (for (19c) *Mary devoured the pizza*, but also for (19a) *Did Mary devour the pizza?*)

(20)

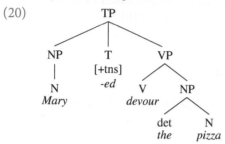

SURFACE STRUCTURE (cf. (19c) *Mary devoured the pizza*)

(21)

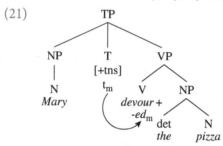

But if T-to-C movement in interrogatives entails movement of some aux inside the [+tns] position to the C position, then the surface structure in (21) (which reflects the declarative in (19c)) could not possibly be the starting point for T-to-C movement. This is because affix lowering as in (21) permanently evacuates the tensed material in the [+tns] position (i.e. *-s* or *-ed* or *-ø*). As a result, T-to-C movement could not take place, as there would be nothing in the [+tns] position that can move to C.

This is the reason we get *do*-support in matrix interrogatives. Since T-to-C movement entails that some aux inside [+tns] must move to C, there has to be an aux inside the [+tns] position, in order for this to happen. If there is no aux in the sentence (as in the deep structure in (20)), then for T-to-C movement to take place, one has to be inserted. Thus, while the tree in (20) is the deep structure for both the declarative in (19c) and the matrix question in (19a), in the formation of an interrogative, the affix doesn't lower, as in (21). Instead, in the formation of an interrogative, *do* is inserted, as in (22):

TRANSITIONAL STRUCTURE ((19a) *Did Mary devour the pizza?*)

(22)

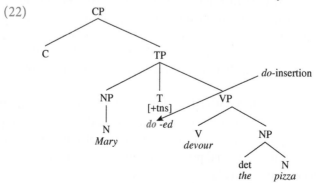

Side Note 4

Note that *do*-support takes place before affix lowering has a chance to. This also explains why in T-to-C movement structures, the main verb is a bare infinitive as in (19a,b) (*devour*), as opposed to tensed, as in (19c) (*devoured*).

Once *do* is inserted into the [+tns] position, then T-to-C movement can take place, because we now have an aux in T that can move up to C. This is depicted in (23):

SURFACE STRUCTURE ((19a) *Did Mary devour the pizza?*)

(23)

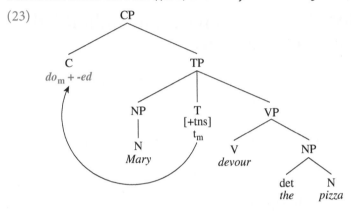

EXERCISE [2]

Using the preceding discussion and the structures in (20), (22), and (23) as a guide, draw **deep**, **transitional**, and **surface** structure trees for the following matrix Yes–No interrogatives (that's three trees each):

{1} Does Sue like her Mustang?
{2} Do they want to finish the job?

11.3.2 matrix wh-questions and the landing site for the wh-phrase

Let's get back to the verb movement (T-to-C) analysis in (13). This works fine for Yes–No questions, but what about wh-questions, such as in (10)? Clearly, wh-questions also exhibit subject–aux inversion (*is > Sue*; *would > Sue*), which means that they also involve T-to-C movement, as in (13). The problem with wh-questions is this: they involve movement <u>also</u> of the wh-phrase to the left of the subject NP:

(10') **What would** Sue fix?   (*what > would > Sue*)

But if the C head is occupied by the tensed auxiliary in matrix questions (as in (13)), then what position does the wh-phrase move to? In our analysis of embedded wh-questions, as in (8) above (… *what Sue would fix*), this was not an issue, because our embedded questions did not involve subject–aux inversion (*Sue > would*). As such, we were able to use the C head position as the **landing site** for movement of the wh-phrase. But what would the landing site for the wh-phrase be in the matrix interrogative in (10) if it's occupied by the tensed aux?

Term Box 3

The position to which a constituent moves is the **landing site**.

Side Note 5: T-to-C movement: embedded versus matrix questions

The one notable difference between **matrix** and **embedded questions**, for many English speakers, is the following:

The grammar of many English speakers:
[A] Embedded questions do not exhibit T-to-C movement (as in the structures in (5) through (8))
[B] Matrix questions exhibit T-to-C movement (as in the structures in (9) and (10))

However: as you may already have guessed, there is variation in this regard! Many English speakers <u>allow</u> T-to-C movement in **embedded questions**, without any difference in meaning. You'll get a chance to work with this concept in Exercise [5]. For now, consider {1}, which for many speakers is equivalent in meaning to (5a) and (6a):

{1}   a. Bill wondered what would Sue fix.   (embedded Q: *would > Sue*)
      b. Mary wonders is Sue a good surgeon.   (embedded Q: *is > Sue*)

Furthermore, there are also English speakers who <u>avoid</u> T-to-C movement in **matrix questions**, again, without any difference in meaning. So, consider {2}, which for many speakers is equivalent in meaning to (10b):

{2}   What Sue would fix?   (matrix Q: *Sue > would*)

What kind of speaker are <u>you</u>?

Note that a movement operation can't simply create — out of thin air — a new position to serve as the landing site for the moved wh-phrase. In fact, no movement operation we've seen thus far involves the creation of a position that didn't already exist as a result of the PS rules. For example, **passivization** involves movement of an object NP to an <u>already existing</u> "subject position" (i.e. the left branch immediately dominated by TP). V-to-T movement involves movement of the leftmost aux to an <u>already existing</u> [+tns] position. T-to-C movement involves movement of the aux in the [+tns] position to an <u>already existing</u> C position. Landing sites for movement are thus syntactic positions that exist at deep structure; they are created by phrase structure rules.

In order to follow this principle, we have to assume that there's an already existing position to the left of C which can serve as the wh-phrase's landing site in matrix wh-questions. But what is this position? In (24) I provide a first-pass sketch:

FIRST-PASS AT AN ANALYSIS OF THE SURFACE STRUCTURE

(24)   *What would Sue fix?*

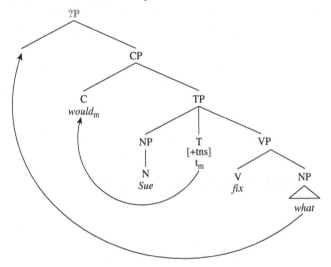

11.3.2.1 Intermediate levels of a phrase

Let's assume that our proposal in Chapter 5, namely, that the wh-phrase moves to CP, was correct. This means that there must be two positions within CP: one to which the wh-phrase moves, and one to which the tensed aux moves. Our mystery phrase (i.e. ?P in (24)) is thus also a CP. Before we refine this proposal even further, I'll provide a second-pass sketch of this idea, in (25):

SECOND-PASS AT AN ANALYSIS OF THE SURFACE STRUCTURE

(25)   *What would Sue fix?*

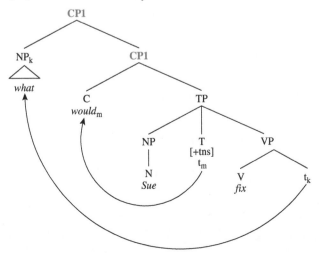

The two positions within CP in (25) entail that one and the same CP has "two layers," so to speak. We must be very careful to understand that the two CP layers in (25) are not two different CPs but, rather, two layers of the same CP. This is a very different situation from what we saw in Chapter 10, in examples like (40), where we had multiple VPs (VP1, VP2, VP3). Each one of these VPs was an independent phrase, headed by completely distinct verbs. VP1 in (40) is headed by *have*; VP2 in (40) is headed by *been*; VP3 in (40) is headed by *given*. In contrast, the CP in (25) here is one single phrase, headed only by one C (which is occupied by the moved auxiliary *would*).

Current theories of phrase structure differentiate between the two layers of CP1 in examples like (25), which are called **projections** of C. You can think of it like this: the head of the phrase **projects** layers of the phrase. The highest layer is the **maximal projection**, and the lower layer is an **intermediate projection**. The maximal projection is the layer that gets the label with a "P" in it (e.g., "CP"). The intermediate projection is termed a **bar-level**, where the "bar" is notated with the symbol ′. The surface structure tree in (26) illustrates this. So compare the final analysis in (26) with our second-pass try in (25):

Term Box 4: Head movement vs. phrase movement

If you continue your studies in syntax, you'll learn that the two movements in (25)/(26) are considered to be of two very different types. Notice how verb movement (either V-to-T movement, or T-to-C movement) involves movement of a head from one head position to another head position. This is known as **head-to-head movement**. In contrast, wh-movement involves movement of a phrase. Current theories of phrase structure and movement operations adopt the hypothesis that — much in the way heads can only move to head positions — that phrases can only move to phrasal positions. This means that the left branch position immediately dominated by CP in (26)/(27) must be a position reserved for phrases. Such positions reserved for phrases are referred to as **specifier positions**.

FINAL ANALYSIS OF THE SURFACE STRUCTURE

(26)

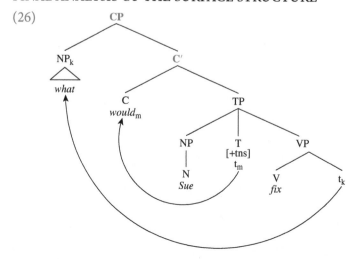

Thus, we call the intermediate projection "C-bar." The maximal projection is CP. Again: both C′ and CP are projections of C.

EXERCISE [3]

Using the foregoing discussion and the structure in (26) as a guide, draw surface structure trees for the following matrix wh-interrogatives. Keep in mind that our analysis of *do*-support in Section 11.3.1.1 applies to any cases of *do*-support in wh-questions.

{1} When will Bill finish the job?
{2} What did Sue fix?
{3} What time do they start their work?
{4} What can Bill fix for us today?

Now, using the **specifier position** of CP (i.e. the position to which the wh-phrase moves in (26)), see if you can figure out where the **adjunct clauses** move to in the sentences in (62) in Chapter 5. Draw (62a) as a deep structure, and (62a′) as its corresponding surface structure.

11.3.2.1.1 Revisiting embedded wh-questions

The analysis in (26) causes us to revisit our analysis of wh-movement in embedded questions from Chapter 5, an example of which we saw above in (8). Given our revised understanding of the landing site for wh-phrases, we have to reanalyze (8) as in (27), with the wh-phrase moving not to C but rather to the position above it:

SURFACE STRUCTURE FOR (6a) (*Bill wondered what Sue would fix*); compare with the now defunct analysis in (8):

(27)

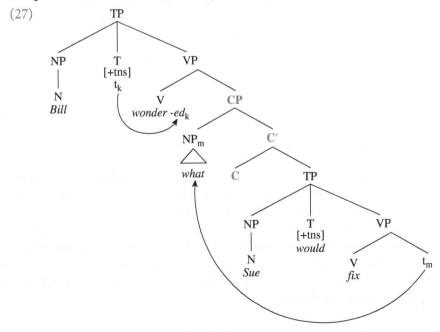

EXERCISE [4]: Embedded CPs

Redo Exercise [8] from Chapter 5 following our new analysis of wh-movement captured in (27).

EXERCISE [5]: More embedded CPs

Draw surface structure trees for the sentences in {1} in Side Note 5, and for the sentence in {2} in Side Note 6.

Side Note 6: Doubly-filled embedded CPs

Note that our new analysis of CP in (27), which involves two positions inside the embedded CP, leaves open one position, namely C, for something to fill it. This is actually a good thing because it allows us to describe syntactic variation in English embedded interrogatives. As we saw in Side Note 5, many English speakers allow T-to-C movement in embedded interrogatives:

{1}   Bill wondered **what would** Sue fix.

Alternatively, in many dialects of English (including Middle English, i.e. the English of Chaucer's time), speakers allow the presence of the complementizer *that* in embedded interrogatives, as in {2}:

{2}   Bill wondered **[which sink] that** Sue fixed.   (adapted from Henry 1995)

Again, our new theory of CP depicted in (27) actually allows us to explain such syntactic variation. Without the two positions inside CP, we'd have no way of accommodating both *what + would* and *which sink + that* in these examples. You can learn about English varieties with such doubly-filled CPs in Henry (1995) and Wolfram & Christian (1976).

11.4 x-bar and binary branching

To recap: the behavior of matrix wh-questions led us to discover that there are actually two positions inside CP, namely, the C head plus a higher position to its left (i.e. the **specifier** of CP). Our revision of phrase structure theory thus involves an analysis in which a phrase such as CP has an **intermediate projection**, as you see in (26) and (27). This is not a rejection of the theory of phrase structure rules, so much as it is a refinement of the theory. The question which now arises, of course, is whether phrases other than CP should also be analyzed in this way.

11.4.1 X-bar schema

If you choose to continue in your study of syntax, you'll find that the answer to the question posed immediately above is "Yes." The structure we see for CP in (26)/(27) also applies to TP, NP, VP, PP, and AP. In fact, because every phrase is analyzed as having the structure we see for CP in (26)/(27), phrase structure theory is currently understood not in terms of the PS rules we see in (3) but, rather, in terms of a phrase structure schema known as the **X-bar schema** or the **X-bar format**. The X-bar schema is sketched in (28). Compare (28) with the CP in (26)/(27):

X-bar schema:

(28)

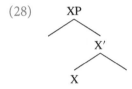

The structure in (28) is identical to that which you see for the CP in (26)/(27). In (28), the "X" is simply a **variable** standing in for any head you like. The X-bar schema thus summarizes the structure for all phrases in one simple format. So NP also has this structure, as in (29):

(29)

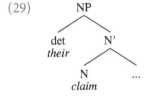

(e.g., (6) in Chapter 6, *their claim that Sue read the newspaper*)

Likewise, TP (i.e. the sentence itself) has this structure, as in (30):

(30)

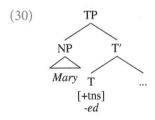

(e.g., (20) above, *Mary devoured the pizza*)

Likewise, PP also has this structure, as in (31):

(31)

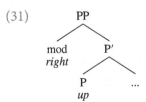

(e.g., (42a) in Chapter 4, *right up the hill*)

And likewise, AP also has this structure, as in (32) (see Side Note 8):

(32)

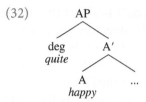

(e.g., *quite happy with their work*)

Side Note 7:

You may be wondering why I haven't given an example of VP under the new X-bar schema. The fact is, current theories do also assume this structure for VP:

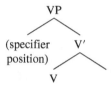

The question of what resides in the left branch position immediately dominated by VP (i.e. the **specifier position**) is a complicated one. If you want to know more, I encourage you to continue your study of syntactic theory!

Side Note 8:

Although we haven't seen this until now, as I'm sure you can easily digest at this point, an AP can embed a phrase like a PP (*happy **with their work***) or a CP (*happy **that they did the work***). This requires a revision of the AP PS rule in (3), to include PP and CP:

$$AP \rightarrow (deg)\, A \begin{Bmatrix} (PP) \\ (CP) \end{Bmatrix}$$

11.4.2 binary branching

The structures in (29), (30), (31), and (32) — all of which follow the X-bar schema in (28) — contrast with what we previously saw for these examples, which were structures involving **ternary branching**, that is, structures with three branches:

Old ternary-branching versions of the structures in (29), (30), (31), and (32):

(33)

NP	TP	PP	AP
det N ...	NP T VP	mod P ...	deg A ...

We motivated the X-bar schema in Section 11.3.2, based on the need for this kind of structure for CP. As you can see, the X-bar format can be extended to all phrases, and naturally gives rise to **binary branching** structures for all of them (see Term Box 1 in Chapter 2). This contrasts with the **ternary branching** structures in (33), or even the **multiple branching** (or, **n-ary branching**) structures we've seen through Chapters 2 through 10. If our new theory of phrase structure is on the right track, then it suggests that all of phrase structure is binary branching.

It's possible you've already seen this strictly binary-branching approach to phrase structure in other introductory books. I hope, though, that it's clear why I waited until this final chapter to introduce X-bar phrase structure (and binary branching) to you. For students who are completely new to the study of syntactic structure, it's important to first motivate the most basic issues revolving around phrase structure, as we did in Chapters 1–10, before we can understand the motivation for the more advanced theoretical concepts.

In more advanced reading on the topic, you'll also see that the X-bar format allows for **multiple bar-levels**, to accommodate modifiers. In the examples in (28) through (32), we see only one bar-level. Multiple bar-levels refers to situations in which there is more than one bar-level. The examples in (34) illustrate the X-bar schema with two and three bar-levels:

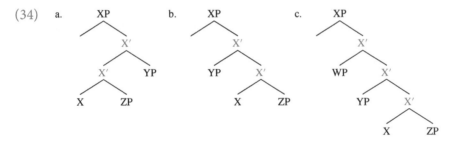

The structures in (34a) and (34b) illustrate structures with two bar-levels. The difference between the two is that the constituent I've called "YP" is **adjoined to the right** in (34a), and to the left in (34b). The structure in (34c) has three bar-levels, with the YP and WP constituents both **adjoined to the left** (see Side Note 10). These are a few arbitrarily chosen abstractions.

In order to deeply understand this aspect of X-bar phrase structure in relation to real English examples, we would need to engage in extensive discussion of its empirical and theoretical motivation, something for which this book is not suited. So I encourage you to continue your studies with a more advanced book on syntax. But just as a preview: consider an NP like one we would have seen in Chapter 2, such as *the happy professor of linguistics with brown hair*. Under our previous theory of PS rules, the structure of this NP would have contained five branches:

(35)

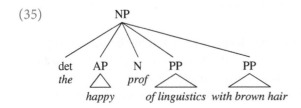

The multiple branching structure for NP in (35) is sometimes referred to as a **flat structure**. Under the binary-branching X-bar schema introduced in this chapter, coupled with the view that a single phrase can have multiple bar-levels, this NP would have the structure in (36):

(36)

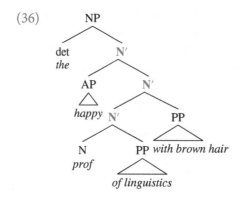

Side Note 9: Nonbranching structures

The idea that phrase structures do not go beyond binary branches doesn't mean we can't have a structure with a single branch, such as the following X-bar structure for the NP *a book*:

In this structure, there are no constituents to the right of the N *book*, so there's no second branch dominated by N'.

EXERCISE [6]

Using the X-bar format, draw deep structure trees for the following XPs:

{1} AP: very sad about his departure
{2} PP: right from the freezer
{3} NP: her crazy belief that the world is flat

The structure in (36) has three bar-levels dominated by the **maximal projection** NP. The structure in (36) follows the X-bar schema, with the addition of the theory that a head can project any number of levels up to the maximal projection, each bar-level providing another **node** to which a modifier can adjoin. But there are many other aspects to the structure in (36) which need to be motivated. For example, why is the PP *of linguistics* depicted as a sister to the N *prof*, but the PP *with brown hair* is not? Why can't this latter PP also be sister to N, giving rise to a ternary-branching structure for the lowest N'? Again, your future studies in syntactic theory will provide you with answers to these questions, and many others raised in this chapter (and indeed, in this book).

11.5 adverbs

In this book, we've barely talked about adverbs. The topic of English adverbs itself can take up an entire book — in fact multiple books, as the linguistics literature on adverbs attests! In this final section of this final chapter, we'll limit ourselves to a preliminary sketch of how this lexical category fits into syntactic structure, now that we have our new X-bar theory of phrase structure in place. One of the numerous interesting consequences of this particular theory of phrase structure is that we can analyze the syntax of adverbs fairly straightforwardly.

Let's start with the negative marker *not*, which thus far is the one example we've seen of an adverb. In our previous theory of phrase structure, we incorporated *not* into the PS rule for TP (the sentence). I'll repeat that PS rule here:

(37)   TP   →   NP T (NEG) VP

The rule in (37) correctly captures the fact that T (which houses the [±tns] feature) is the head of TP, and that the negative marker is an optional element within TP (in contrast with NP and VP, which are obligatory). However the rule is problematic, in that — even without the negative marker — it results in a multiple branching structure. As we saw in Sections 11.3 and 11.4, current phrase structure theory eliminates multiple branching structures in favor of binary branching. In the deep structure in (30), we saw what the binary-branching analysis of TP looks like under X-bar theory; let's take another look here, with the entire deep structure fleshed out, for the sentence *Mary devoured the pizza*:

DEEP STRUCTURE FOR *Mary devoured the pizza*

(38)

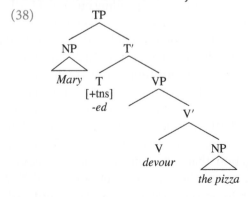

The structures for TP and VP in (38) respect X-bar format. But now what if we wanted to add the negative marker *not*? How would that fit into this structure?

If we're rejecting the concept of ternary branching, we can no longer assume that *not* is immediately dominated by the node which also immediately dominates T. In other words, the ternary-branching structure seen in (39) is not possible:

INCORRECT TREE:

(39)

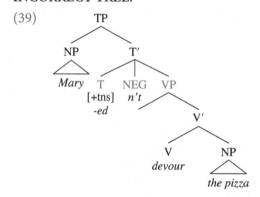

One possible way to accommodate the adverb *not* — without violating the binary-branching requirement — would be to plug it into the specifier position of VP:

FIRST PASS SKETCH:

(40)

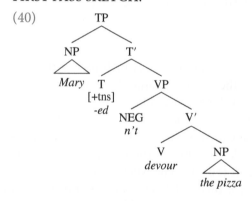

The hypothesis that an adverb can occupy the specifier position of the VP as in (40) is actually something which isn't unheard of in the history of the literature on phrase structure theory. But let's count on your impending pursuit of further study in syntax to reveal that there are numerous factors which call for other hypotheses. One of the problems with the hypothesis in (40) has to do with the meaning of sentential negation. As we discussed in Section 10.2.2, the sentential negative marker modifies the entire **proposition**. So the sentence *Mary didn't devour the pizza* (with a neutral intonation) means something like *It is not the case that Mary devoured the pizza*. So any analysis of the syntactic position of the negative marker should take this into account. The analysis in (40) has the unfortunate feature of depicting the negative marker as a modifier of VP.

One theory of sentential negation that takes into account the issue of semantics holds that the negative marker heads its own phrase, called **NegP** (for "negative phrase"). In order to account for the observed word order between the tensed aux, the negative marker, and the following verb, we can preliminarily propose that NegP occurs between TP and VP, as follows:

SECOND PASS SKETCH:

(41)

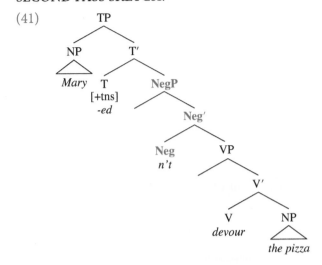

Let's take the hypothesis in (41) regarding NegP to suggest that, generally speaking, this is how adverbs are incorporated into sentence structure.

Under this view, let's consider the following example, which involves the addition of the adverb *always*:

(42)   Mary did**n't always** devour her meals.

The sentence in (42) contains the two adverbs *not* and *always*, both of which occur to the left of the main verb *devour*. So how do we fit <u>two</u> adverbs into the structure in (40)? Well, if each adverb heads its own **AdvP** (for "adverb phrase"), then we can propose the following structure for (42):

(43)

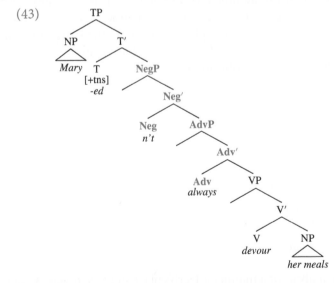

If this approach is the right way to go, then this means that every time we use an adverb, we incorporate it into the structure this way, no matter how many adverbs in the sentence. So if we add the adverb *voraciously* to the sentence in (42)/(43), we end up with the following structure:

(44)   Mary did**n't always voraciously** devour her meals. (cf. (42)/(43))

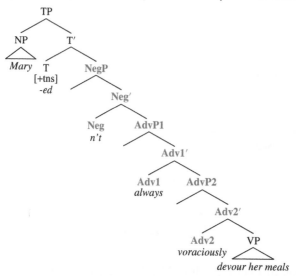

However, our analysis of adverb syntax becomes more complicated (and therefore, this book leaves the question open) once we consider the fact that some adverbs, like *voraciously, quickly, concentratedly*, etc. (i.e. **manner adverbs**) have some freedom regarding their place in the overall order of words in the sentence. So compare the example in (44) with (45):

(45)   Mary did**n't always** devour her meals **voraciously**.

The syntactic placement of the adverb *voraciously* in (45) suggests that this kind of adverb might actually be adjoined within the VP, at least in some cases. Note that in contrast with the negative marker *not*, a manner adverb like *voraciously* modifies the verb itself. The example in (46) shows the structure with the manner adverb within VP (to the right of the NP object), modifying the V *devour*, as per the observed **word order** in (45):

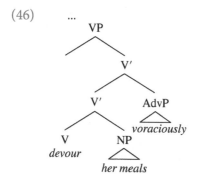

If this is the correct analysis of a manner adverb's place in the syntactic structure, then even when such a manner adverb precedes the V, the question arises as to whether it isn't simply adjoined within VP. So compare the hypothesis in (47) with that in (44):

(47)

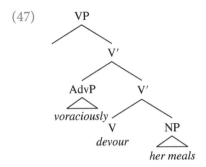

Side Note 10: Right adjunction vs. left adjunction

Note that the structures in (46) and (47) correspond to the X-bar schemas in (34a) and (34b). Specifically, the AdvP in (46) corresponds to the YP in (34b), and the AdvP in (47) corresponds to the YP in (34a).

The issue becomes more complicated still when we consider the fact that there are many different classes of adverbs, where each class shows itself to have a distinct behavior, and distinct requirements for their placement in the word order of the sentence. In addition to manner adverbs, we also have **aspectual adverbs** (e.g., *just, already, still, yet, anymore*); **evidential adverbs** (e.g., *evidently, apparently*); **time adverbs** (e.g., *yesterday, today, tomorrow, this morning, Tuesday, at 10:00, on Tuesdays*); **modal adverbs** (e.g., *probably, possibly*); and speaker oriented adverbs (e.g., *frankly, honestly, hopefully*). The following example is just one illustration of how we use these adverbs simultaneously, in a single sentence:

(48)   **Apparently** Mary **probably already happily** gave her book to John **this morning**.

EXERCISE [7]

Using the X-bar format and the preceding discussion, try to come up with a deep structure tree for the sentence in (48).

> ## Side Note 11: Adverbial PPs
>
> In previous chapters we saw examples of "adverbial PPs" or "adjunct PPs," such as the those in the sentence in {1}:
>
> {1} *John ate the pizza <u>in the kitchen</u> <u>at 10:00</u>.*
>
> In terms of our understanding of **modification**, nothing has changed: these PPs are constituents within VP. Because they're not selected by the verb (see Chapter 5 for **selection**), they're considered **adjuncts** or **adverbials**. Using the structure in (46) as a guide, see if you can draw a deep structure tree for {1}.

Note that *apparently* appears to the left of the subject *Mary*, raising the question of whether this AdvP is higher than TP, or higher than CP. I leave this question to your future studies in syntactic theory!

11.6 conclusions

Let's conclude first with a summary of our revised phrase structure rules, pre-X-bar style:

(49)
$$CP \rightarrow C \quad TP$$

$$TP \rightarrow NP \ T \ (NEG) \ VP$$

$$NP \rightarrow \begin{Bmatrix} (det) \\ (PossNP) \end{Bmatrix} (AP^*) \ N \begin{Bmatrix} (PP^*) \\ (CP) \end{Bmatrix}$$

$$PossNP \rightarrow \begin{Bmatrix} (det) \\ (PossNP) \end{Bmatrix} (AP^*) \ PossN \begin{Bmatrix} (PP^*) \\ (CP) \end{Bmatrix}$$

$$VP \rightarrow V \ (VP) \ (PP) \ (NP) \begin{Bmatrix} (NP) \\ (TP) \\ (CP) \end{Bmatrix} (AP) \ (PP^*)$$

$$PP \rightarrow (mod) \ P \begin{Bmatrix} (NP) \\ (PP) \end{Bmatrix}$$

$$AP \rightarrow (deg) \ A \begin{Bmatrix} (PP) \\ (CP) \end{Bmatrix}$$

$$NegP \rightarrow Neg \begin{Bmatrix} (AdvP) \\ (VP) \end{Bmatrix}$$

$$AdvP \rightarrow Adv \begin{Bmatrix} (AdvP) \\ (VP) \end{Bmatrix}$$

Our biggest revision to the old PS rules in this chapter was to the **sentence**. The fact that we no longer conceptualize the sentence as a headless phrase is a huge accomplishment. We discovered that like all other phrases, S has a head and this head is T. Hence our switch to the nomenclature **TP**.

In Section 11.3, though, we started to see reasons for changing the structure of CP, such that the rule for CP in (49) is no longer sufficient. Specifically, we saw that **matrix wh-questions** involve movement of the wh-phrase to CP (much as we saw for **embedded wh-questions**). However, in addition, many English speakers also exhibit **T-to-C movement** in matrix wh-questions, raising the issue of how to accommodate <u>both</u> the moved wh-phrase <u>and</u> the moved verb, both inside the CP. This caused us to propose the idea of multiple positions within CP, as in (26).

This in turn pushed us towards a new **binary branching** conceptualization of phrase structure which generalizes across categories, namely, the X-bar format. I laid out the basic format in (28), but as the possibilities in (34) show, a phrase can have multiple **bar-levels** to accommodate adjoined phrases to the left and/or to the right of the head. In addition, as we saw in Side Note 9, a head does not have to take a **complement**; as such, a head can be **immediately dominated** by a nonbranching bar-level (as in Side Note 9). Furthermore, a phrase may not have a specifier, in which case, it isn't necessary to draw the left branch immediately dominated by the **maximal projection**. Thus, the VP in (46), for example, would more accurately be drawn with a nonbranching VP, as in (46'):

(46')

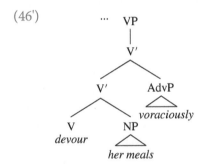

In order to take all of these variations on the X-bar format into account, we can write a general phrase structure rule which captures these aspects of the X-bar schema as follows:

Summary of X-bar PS rules:

(50) XP → (spec) X′

X′ → X′ (YP) or (YP) X′

X′ → X (ZP)

As we said in Section 11.4.1, the "X" is simply a **variable** standing in for any head. The rules in (50) thus summarize the rules for all phrases: CP, TP, NP, PossNP, VP, PP, AP, NegP, AdvP.

This approach to phrase structure makes it more straightforward to conceptualize how the **adverb phrase** fits into the overall structure of the sentence. For more on the syntax of adverbs, you can take a look at Cinque (1999), whose highly developed theory involves structures like what you see in (44).

But what of the differences between the different phrases that we see in the old-style PS rules in (49)? How can the X-bar format account for the fact that while TP can directly contain a VP, NP does not (for example)? And likewise, how does it account for the fact that N can be immediately followed by a PP, but T cannot be? This is information (captured in the old-style PS rules) that the new X-bar theoretic rules do not encode. So where are these differences between categories encoded in the grammar?

Answers to these questions can be found in Chomsky (1981; 1986), Haegeman (1994), and Carnie (2012). If you pursue your studies in this area, you'll learn that the crux of the matter is to do with the distinct semantic properties of T and N (... and V and P and A...). The distinct semantic properties of the various **lexical** (V, N, A, P, Adv) and **functional** (C, T, P) **categories** are already known to the language user, independent of syntax, simply by virtue of knowledge of the **lexicon** (see Sections 5.2.1 and 5.2.3). As such, the information about what kinds of elements can be contained in the phrases projected by each head does not need to be encoded in PS rules. Since knowledge of the semantics of lexical and functional categories entails knowledge of what will go with V, what will go with N, what will go with T, what will go with V (etc.), there's no need to encode this information in the PS rules. Thus, if we think of our old-style PS rules as a model of an English speaker's knowledge, then we have to admit that it's not a perfect model, as it contains a lot of redundant information.

You might then wonder at this point why I started this book with these old-style PS rules. Here, I'd like you to think back to where you started in Chapter 1, and back to the skills you developed in Chapters 2 through 10. While the old-style PS rules might not be the most elegant model of a speaker's knowledge of phrase structure, it's also easy to appreciate how they still stand as a tool well-suited for training the beginning syntax student to analyze sentences.

list of terms/concepts

adjunct clause
adjunction (adjunct; adjoin;
   adverbial; right adjunction vs.
   left adjunction)
adverb (manner adverb; evidential
   adverb; aspectual adverb; time
   adverb; modal adverb)
adverb phrase (AdvP)
affix lowering
agreement
agreement phrase (AgrP)
bar-levels (projections; intermediate
   projections)
binary branching (vs. ternary
   branching /multiple branching /
   n-ary branching /nonbranching)
complement

deep structure
dominance (immediate dominance)
do-support in questions (subject–
   auxiliary inversion)
doubly-filled CP
dummy *do*
embedded interrogative (embedded
   question)
flat structure (vs. hierarchical
   structure)
functional category
head (vs. phrase)
head position
head-to-head movement (vs. phrasal
   movement)
inflection
inflectional phrase (IP)

intermediate bar-level
intermediate projection
intermediate trace
landing site
lexical category
lexicon
matrix interrogative (matrix question;
   vs. embedded question)
maximal projection
mental lexicon
modification
multiple bar-levels
negated declaratives
negation
negative phrase (NegP)
node
paradigm levelling in the presence
   of *n't*
passivization
phrase (vs. head)
projections (project)
proposition
selection

specifier position
subject–auxiliary inversion (T-to-C
   movement)
surface structure
tense
tense head
tense phrase (TP)
terminal node (obligatory terminal
   node vs. optional terminal node)
ternary branching
T position
transitional structure
T-to-C movement
variable
verb movement (verb raising; V-to-T
   movement; T-to-C movement)
V-to-T movement
wh-questions
word order
X-bar theory (X-bar schema; X-bar
   format)
Yes-No questions

references

Carnie, Andrew (2012). *Syntax: A Generative Introduction*. Third edition. Wiley Blackwell.

Chomsky, Noam (1981). *Lectures on Government and Binding: The Pisa Lectures*. Berlin: Mouton de Gruyter.

Chomsky, Noam (1986). *Barriers*. Cambridge, MA: MIT Press.

Cinque, Guglielmo (1999). *Adverbs and Functional Heads: A Cross-linguistic Perspective*. Oxford: Oxford University Press.

Haegeman, Liliane (1994). *Introduction to Government and Binding Theory*. Second edition. Wiley Blackwell.

Henry, Alison (1995). *Belfast English and Standard English: Dialect Variation and Parameter Setting*. Oxford: Oxford University Press.

Wolfram, Walt & Donna Christian (1976). *Appalachian Speech*. Arlington, VA: Center for Applied Linguistics.

Index

Understanding Sentence Structure: An Introduction to English Syntax, First Edition.
Christina Tortora.
© 2018 John Wiley & Sons, Inc. Published 2018 by John Wiley & Sons, Inc.